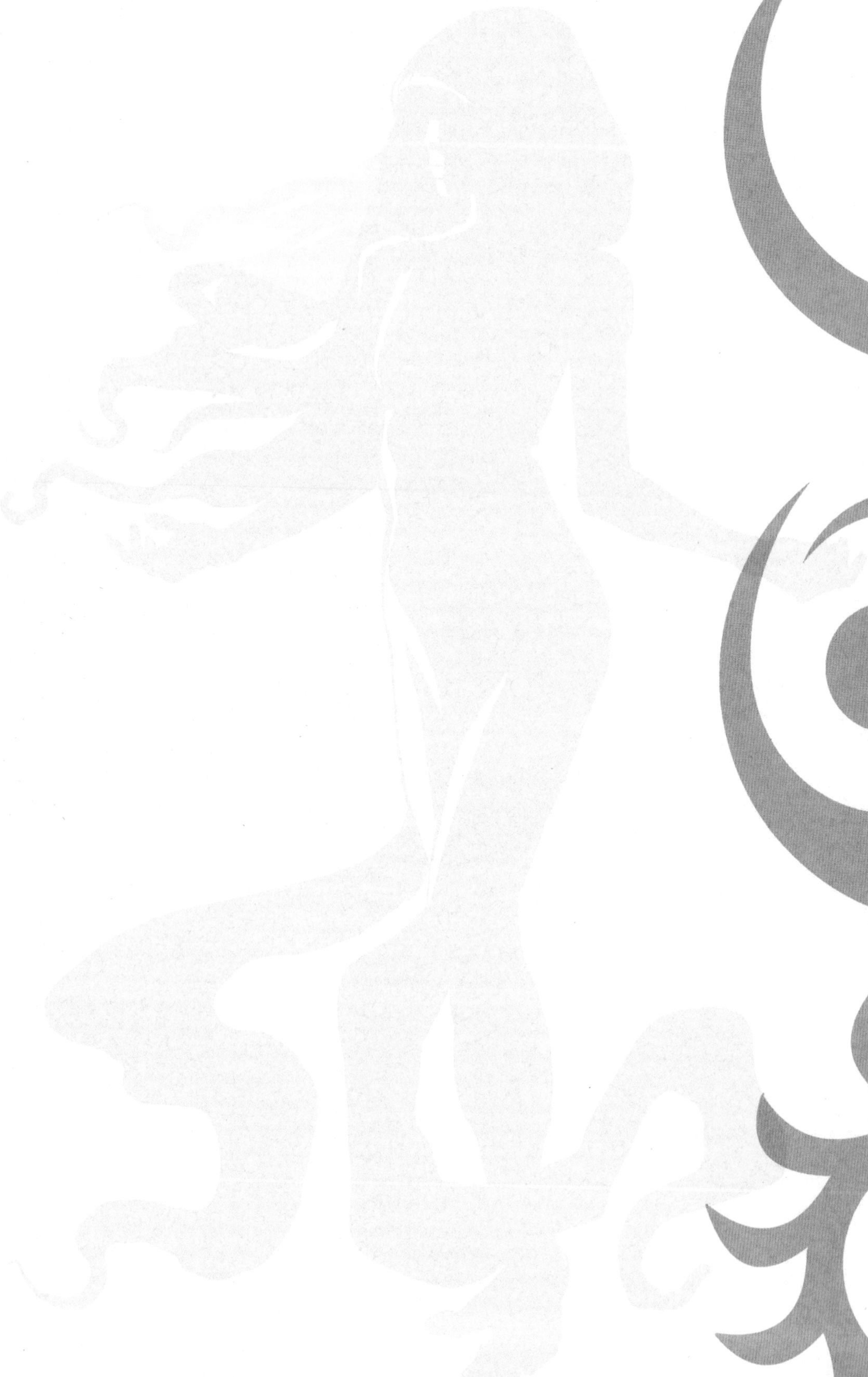

SKIN&EARTH™

VOLUME ONE

STORY, ART and LETTERING by LIGHTS

EXECUTIVE PROJECT COORDINATORS:
ASHLEY POITEVIN and CHRIS TAYLOR
for LAST GANG (AN ENTERTAINMENT ONE COMPANY)
FRANKI CHAN
for IHEARTCOMIX
www.iamlights.com / @lights

Nick Barrucci, CEO / Publisher
Juan Collado, President / COO
Joe Rybandt, Executive Editor
Matt Idelson, Senior Editor
Anthony Marques, Associate Editor
Kevin Ketner, Assistant Editor
Jason Ullmeyer, Art Director
Geoff Harkins, Senior Graphic Designer
Cathleen Heard, Graphic Designer
Alexis Persson, Graphic Designer
Chris Caniano, Digital Associate
Rachel Kilbury, Digital Multimedia Associate
Brandon Dante Primavera, V.P. of IT and Operations
Rich Young, Director of Business Development
Alan Payne, V.P. of Sales and Marketing
Pat O'Connell, Sales Manager

Online at www.DYNAMITE.com
On Facebook /Dynamitecomics
On Instagram /Dynamitecomics
On Twitter @dynamitecomics

PEFC Certified
Printed on paper from
sustainably managed
forests and controlled
sources
PEFC
PEFC/01-31-106   www.pefc.org

Softcover ISBN13: 978-1-5241-0603-4
Hardcover ISBN13: 978-1-5241-0626-3

First Printing 10 9 8 7 6 5 4 3 2 1

SKIN & EARTH™, VOLUME 1. First printing. Contains materials originally published in magazine form as
SKIN & EARTH™, VOLUME 1: Issues 1-6. Published by Dynamite Entertainment, 113 Gaither Dr., STE 205, Mt. Laurel, NJ 08054.

For information regarding press, media rights, foreign rights,
licensing, promotions, and advertising e-mail: marketing@dynamite.com

OH WOW HI:

I'm sitting here in my tour bus in Chicago on the 'We Were Here' Tour reflecting on the past nine months since I announced Skin&Earth as a project. The journey I've been on - creating it all - and the acceptance and love I've received while taking on an entirely new art form, has literally changed me as a person.

Every night, I see Ens and Mitsukis, even Priests in the crowd; show-goers dressed as their favourite characters from Skin&Earth. It throws me right back to two years ago deliberating how each character would look and feel, how they would walk and talk, and putting a little bit of myself into each one of them. You see, En is me, through and through. Her reactions, her self deprecation, her insecurities and her desire to always see the good in things. But Mitsuki is also me, she's my ideals, who I maybe wish I was. Writing these two very different beings came so fluidly because this was a story I needed to tell for a long time.

At its very core, Skin&Earth is a story about coming to understand the familiar darkness that finds you at your lowest and emerging on the other side stronger for it. That darkness comes in many forms, sometimes it's very beautiful and sometimes it tears us apart from the inside. Sometimes we hold it so close that we have a hard time letting go of it. It can become a lover and a friend, our darkest secret, or our bolt of confidence. But regardless of how the story unfolds, it's just that: it's our story. I wanted to show, in the form of a fantastical tale, that the path to our end game is never pretty, but there is beauty in just that. Those flaws and those moments of weakness are what it takes to get to our strengths. Those bad decisions have to happen so we can learn how to make better ones. Those things we regret only teach us how to do something we're proud of. It's all part of our origin story. After all, and to quote one of my favourite pages of the book, "the only way to the light is through the darkness."

I learned a lot about myself while writing and drawing this book. First and foremost, I learned that you'd be amazed at what you can accomplish when you put a shit ton of time into something. Making a comic-album crossover has always been a dream of mine, but I always brushed that idea away telling myself I just didn't know how.

Though I can't recall the exact moment, it was around the summer of 2015 that I made the decision in my heart of hearts and mind of minds (all the things of things, because that's what it was gonna take) to really just do it. I think that week I went into a book store and bought up like six books on how to "do" comics. In the end I really just learned that there is no single way to do it. It's fucking art! There are no rules. And that was a very freeing discovery because when I dove into this it was like running around without a head or hands or legs. I tapped almost everyone I had a line to in the industry for advice (special shout outs to BKV and McKelvie). I practiced drawing every day. I read comics every day. I attended panels (shoutout Gail Simone, G. Willow Wilson, Babs Tarr and Sana Takeda for answering a lot of my awkward questions in panels. I know you don't know me and probably will never read this but I love you). I watched webinars, tutorials. Endless YouTube university.

All the while I was writing songs set to this story I wanted to tell. Going into song writing sessions with a mood and concept right out of the gate was a complete dream, and a break from the norm. Typically the first few hours of a session is spent figuring out what the hell to write about, then you have to get all TMI with a perfect stranger about your current emotional baggage in order to get to the good stuff. This time around I got to blame everything on En (even though every song is secretly about my experiences, surprise surprise). "Okayyyyy, so this is the part in the story where En, at her lowest point, meets Mitsuki, who rides in like a goddess to protect and guard En in her darkest hour." *Proceeds to write a song about being traumatized by horrible visions that occur the minute you become a parent to better equip you to protect your child from harm*. Enter "New Fears".

I should note that the names of the characters were different for the first year of the writing process. I knew they weren't right, but I just stuck with that until the right ones came. That was another big discovery I made during this creative experience–there's no such thing as good writing, just good re-writing. The first character sketches sucked pretty bad, and some of the original dialogue and story movements were really awful. But I knew deep down that with work, they'd get better. I worked on perfecting this story every single day, into the wee hours of the morning (even developed insomnia, which is what "Moonshine" is about!) and right up until the night before the final issue went to print. I was fixing dialogue and finalizing the art, getting the faces right, and putting every bit of what I had into Skin&Earth as you see it now.
I had absolutely zero sense of what people would think. Every now and then throughout the process I would stop and see other art or read other stories or books that were just so incredible and would look at my fledgling baby comic and get down on myself. And that was another discovery along the way, don't compare art to art. Just do your fucking best with the skill set that you have, pour your heart into it, and someone might like it. And if that someone is just you, that's goddamn good enough!

I'm so proud of what I accomplished, it was blood, sweat, wine and a lot of love that went into making this book. You can see the progression of my art from the beginning to the end, and at the very least, I hope you enjoy the journey. Someone came up to me the other day and said "I always thought I had to pick either music or art to pursue, and you reminded me I could just do both." And I guess I will turn that around and say the same to every single person who has picked up this book. I love you, enjoy!

- LOVE, LIGHTS

WELCOME TO
SKIN&EARTH

This project is more than just a record and more than just a comic. Each chapter has a corresponding song, and when you experience them together you might notice things you never did before, you may even feel the color palettes or the emotion in the pages more vividly than taking in one without the other.

On each chapter's title page throughout this book you will find a QR code. Scan it and you will be taken to the music tied to that part of the story, corresponding music videos that bring the story to life and other rad content.

Experience this project however you like, but I recommend you pour your ass a glass of wine, take your time, and ENJOY!

IPHONE INSTRUCTIONS

OPEN CAMERA   **SCAN** SHARECODE   **CLICK** POP-UP

ANDROID INSTRUCTIONS

DOWNLOAD QR READER   **OPEN** QR READER   **SCAN** SHARECODE

LOOK FOR THIS CODE THROUGHOUT THE BOOK
AND SCAN IT FOR MUSIC, VIDEOS AND MORE.
(THIS ONE HAS SPECIAL BONUS CONTENT)
GO AHEAD...TRY IT.

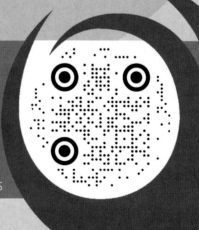

And if all else fails, there will be a link for each code: http://mxt.pe/LTBONUS

INDEX

THE COMIC		THE ALBUM
ISSUE 1:	CHAPTER/TRACK 1&2	1. INTRO 2. SKYDIVING
ISSUE 2:	CHAPTER/TRACK 3&4	3. UNTIL THE LIGHT 4. SAVAGE
ISSUE 3:	CHAPTER/TRACK 5&6	5. NEW FEARS 6. MORPHINE
ISSUE 4:	CHAPTER/TRACK 7&8	7. WE WERE HERE 8. KICKS
ISSUE 5:	CHAPTER/TRACK 9,10,11	9. GIANTS 10. MOONSHINE 11. INTERLUDE
ISSUE 6:	CHAPTER/TRACK 12,13,14	12. MAGNETIC FIELD 13. FIGHT CLUB 14. ALMOST HAD ME

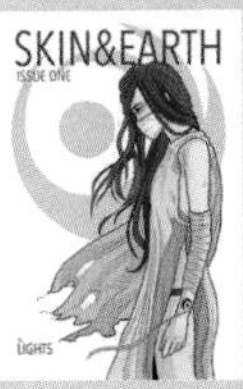
SKIN&EARTH
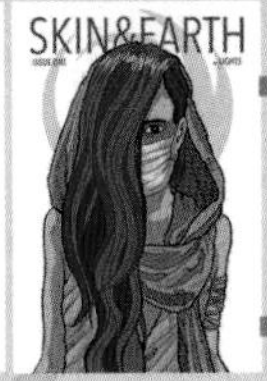
SKIN&EARTH
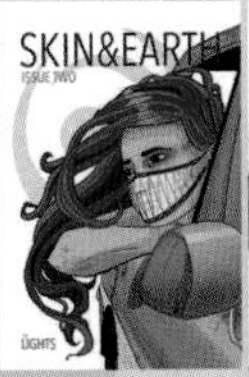
SKIN&EARTH
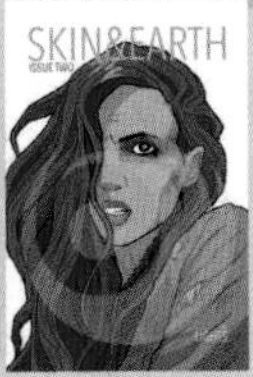
SKIN&EARTH
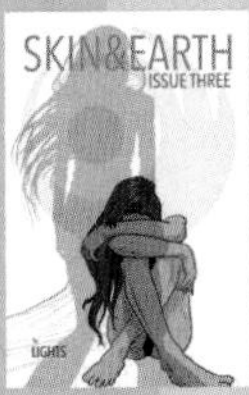
SKIN&EARTH
ISSUE THREE
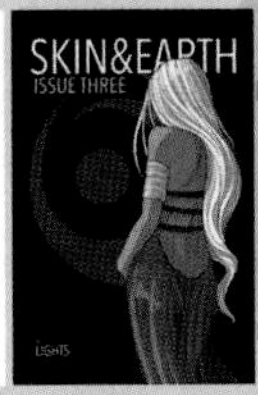
SKIN&EARTH
ISSUE THREE
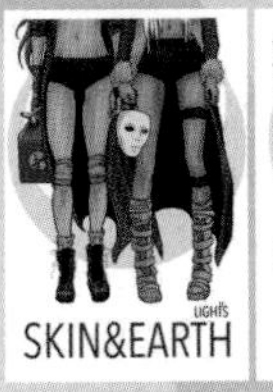
SKIN&EARTH
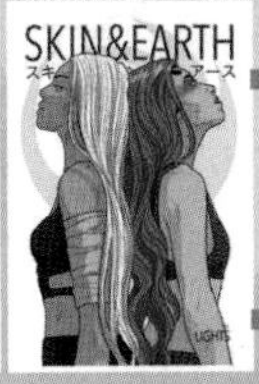
SKIN&EARTH
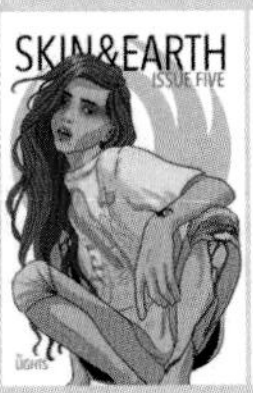
SKIN&EARTH
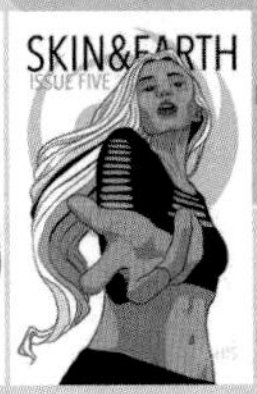
SKIN&EARTH
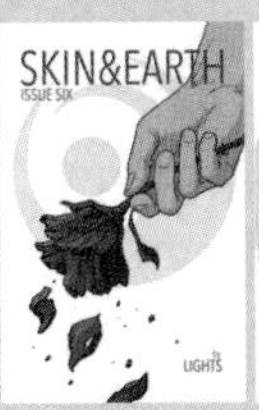
SKIN&EARTH
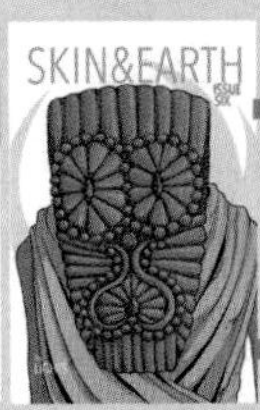
SKIN&EARTH

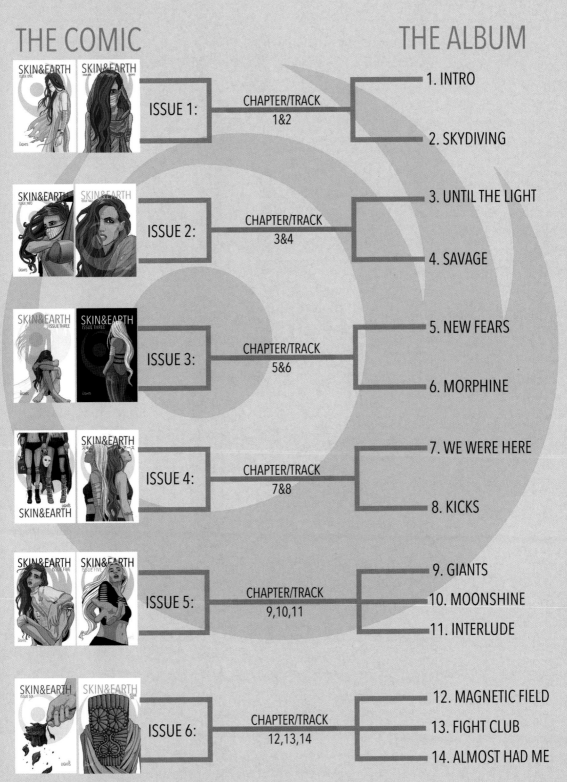

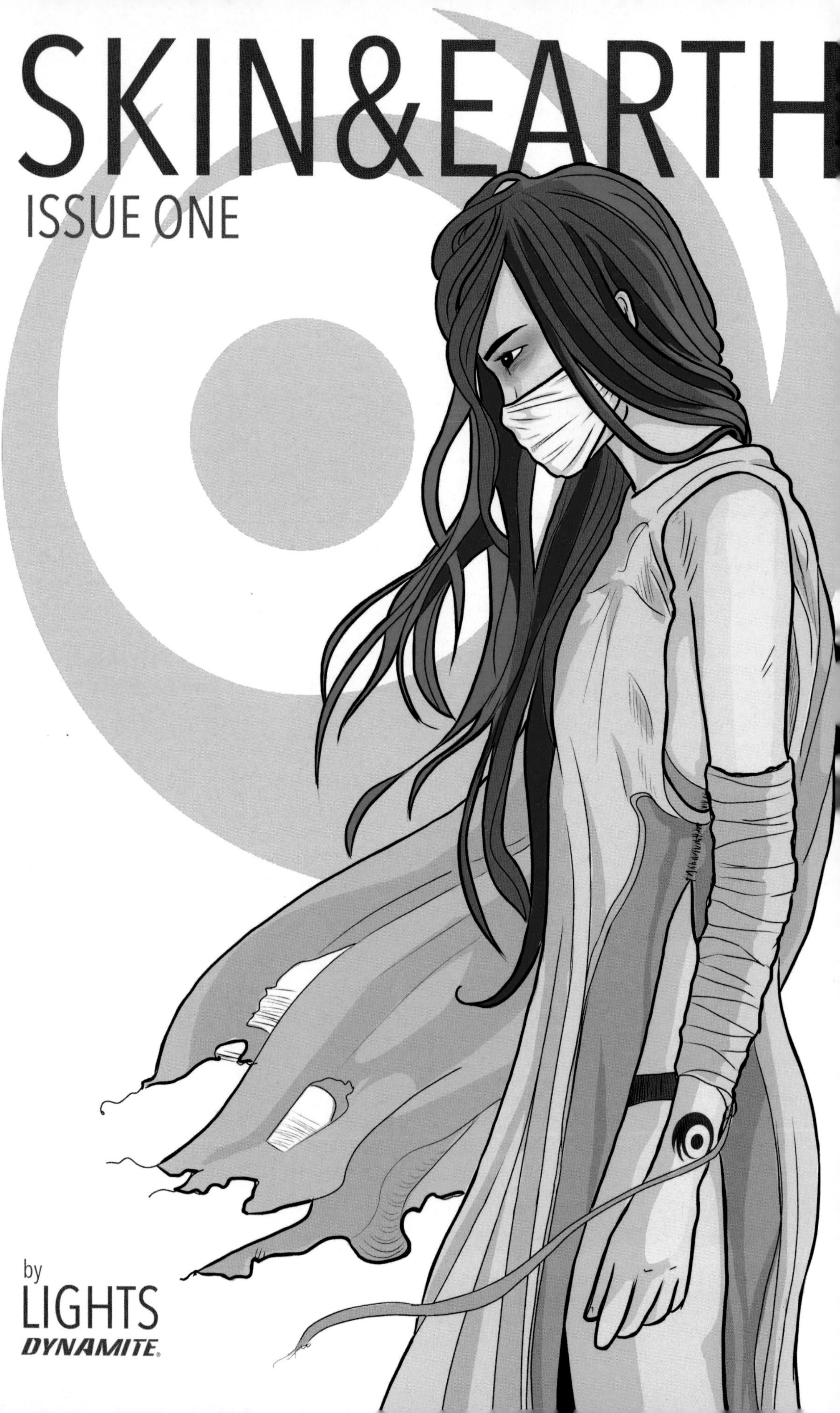
SKIN&EARTH
ISSUE ONE
by
LIGHTS
DYNAMITE

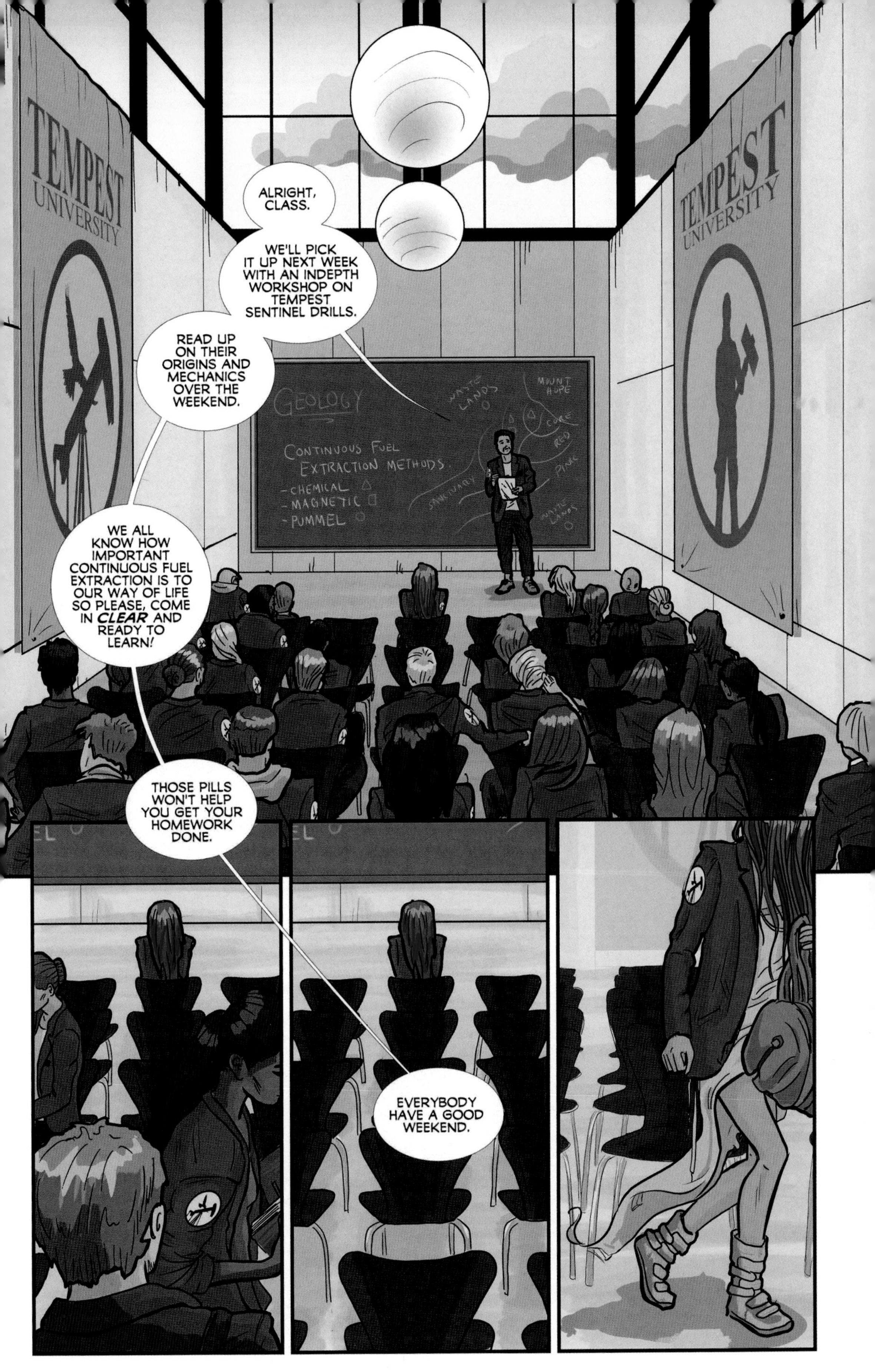
TEMPEST UNIVERSITY
TEMPEST UNIVERSITY
GEOLOGY
CONTINUOUS FUEL EXTRACTION METHODS
-CHEMICAL
-MAGNETIC
-PUMMEL
MOUNT HOPE
CORE
RED
PINK
SANCTUARY
ALRIGHT, CLASS.
WE'LL PICK IT UP NEXT WEEK WITH AN INDEPTH WORKSHOP ON TEMPEST SENTINEL DRILLS.
READ UP ON THEIR ORIGINS AND MECHANICS OVER THE WEEKEND.
WE ALL KNOW HOW IMPORTANT CONTINUOUS FUEL EXTRACTION IS TO OUR WAY OF LIFE SO PLEASE, COME IN CLEAR AND READY TO LEARN!
THOSE PILLS WON'T HELP YOU GET YOUR HOMEWORK DONE.
EVERYBODY HAVE A GOOD WEEKEND.

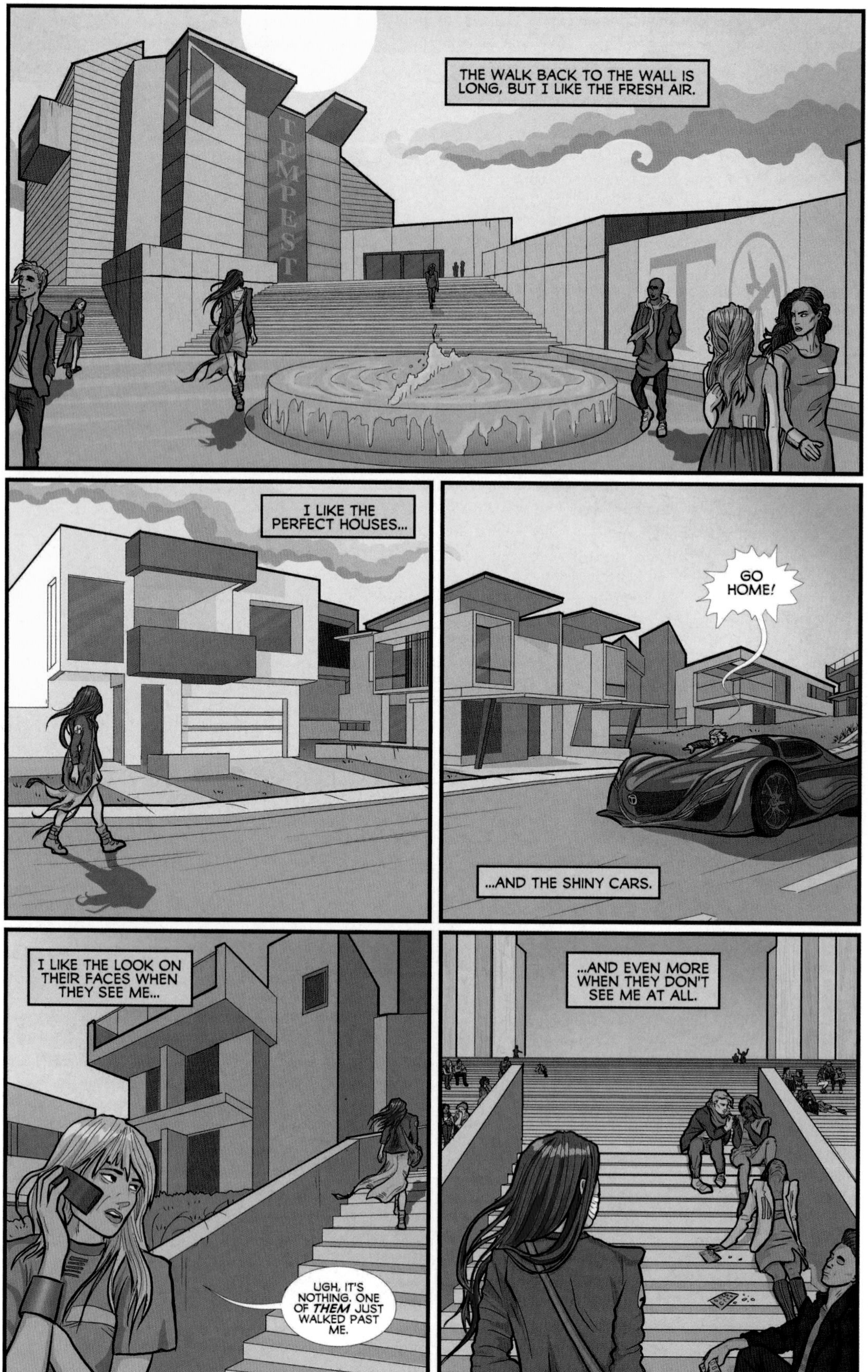
THE WALK BACK TO THE WALL IS LONG, BUT I LIKE THE FRESH AIR.
TEMPEST
I LIKE THE PERFECT HOUSES...
GO HOME!
...AND THE SHINY CARS.
I LIKE THE LOOK ON THEIR FACES WHEN THEY SEE ME...
UGH, IT'S NOTHING. ONE OF *THEM* JUST WALKED PAST ME.
...AND EVEN MORE WHEN THEY DON'T SEE ME AT ALL.

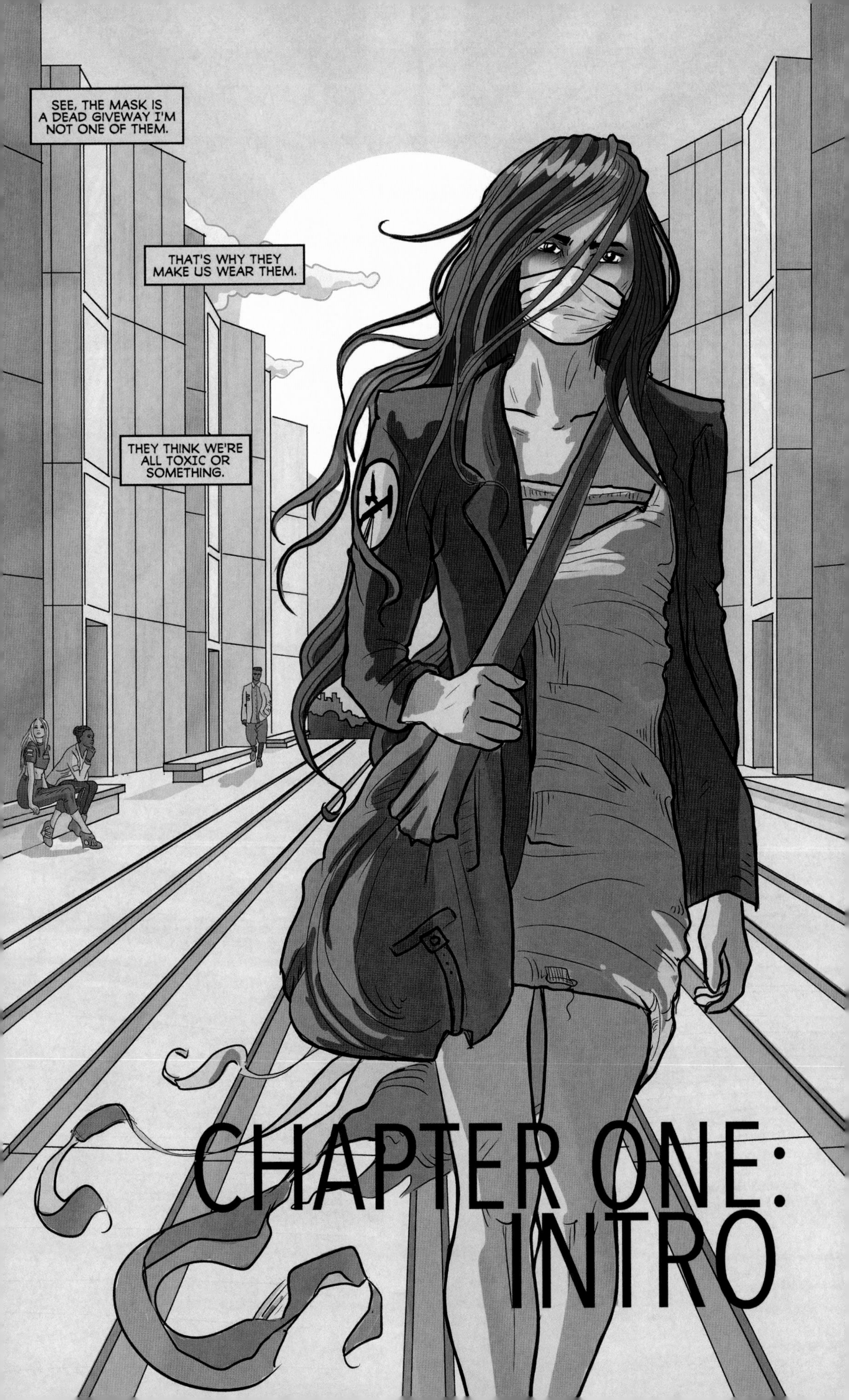
SEE, THE MASK IS A DEAD GIVEWAY I'M NOT ONE OF THEM.
THAT'S WHY THEY MAKE US WEAR THEM.
THEY THINK WE'RE ALL TOXIC OR SOMETHING.
CHAPTER ONE: INTRO

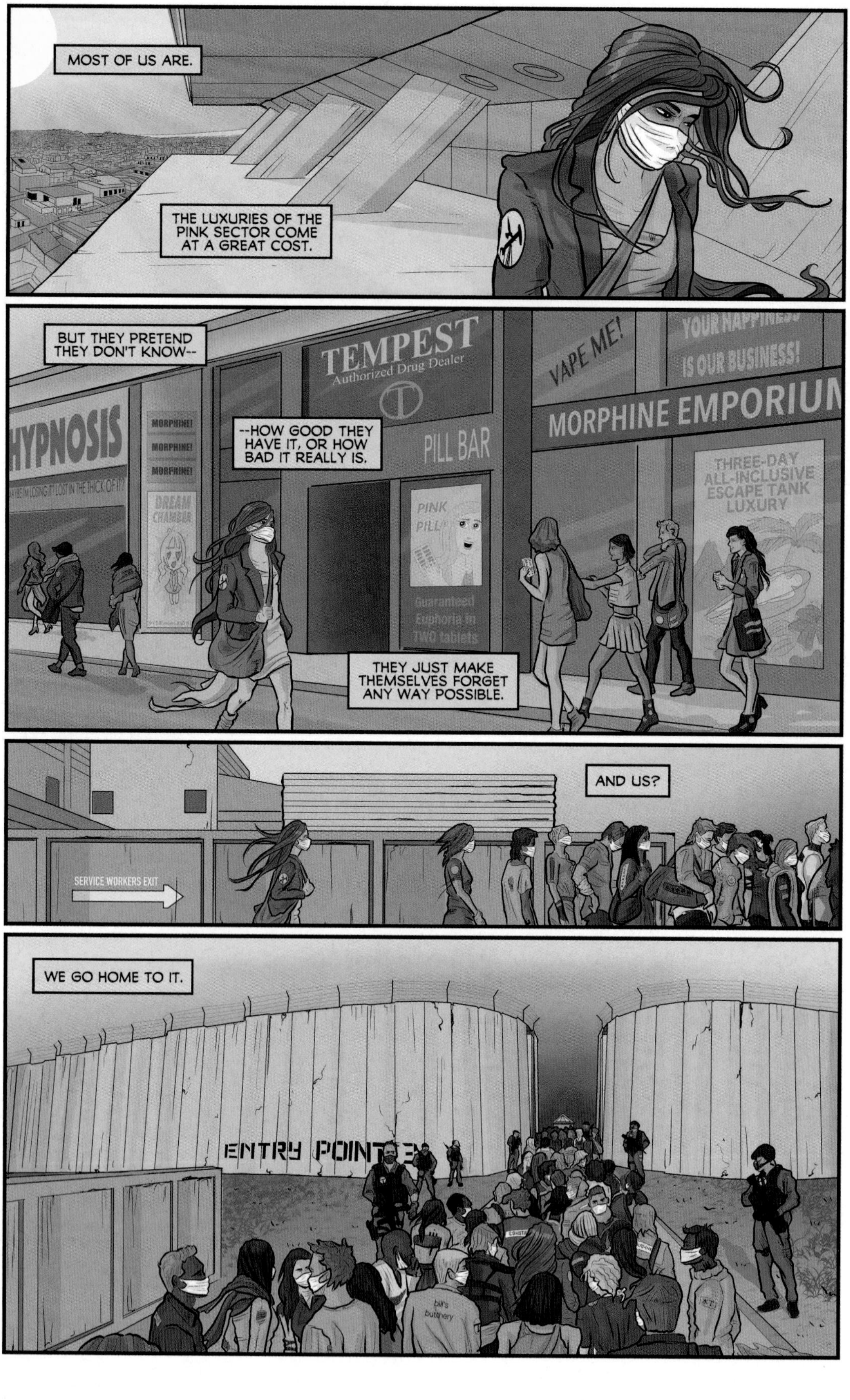

MOST OF US ARE.
THE LUXURIES OF THE PINK SECTOR COME AT A GREAT COST.
BUT THEY PRETEND THEY DON'T KNOW--
HYPNOSIS
MORPHINE!
MORPHINE!
MORPHINE!
DREAM CHAMBER
TEMPEST
Authorized Drug Dealer
PILL BAR
VAPE ME!
IS OUR BUSINESS!
MORPHINE EMPORIU
--HOW GOOD THEY HAVE IT, OR HOW BAD IT REALLY IS.
PINK PILL®
Guaranteed Euphoria in TWO tablets
THREE-DAY ALL-INCLUSIVE ESCAPE TANK LUXURY
THEY JUST MAKE THEMSELVES FORGET ANY WAY POSSIBLE.
AND US?
SERVICE WORKERS EXIT
WE GO HOME TO IT.
ENTRY POINT
bill's butchery

DAMN.

PRIEST

Woke up alone by the fire...

Where the hell did you go?

Sent two weeks ago

OPTIONS

STILL NOTHING.

NEXT!

WHAT'S THIS?

STUDENT VISA.

HOLD UP...FOR REAL?

YOUR NAME IS EN JIN?

LIKE... *ENGINE?*

GOD, YOUR PARENTS DO NOT GIVE A *FUCK!*

HELL, I'D REV THAT...

STUDENT VISA
TEMPEST UNIVERSITY

#5849254

ENAIA JIN

Class: RED
Restrictions:
EXIT CURFEW
Wt: 50kg
Ht: 163cm
Sex: F
Eyes: BRN
Hair: RED

MADISON OASIS

WELL, THEY'RE DEAD, SO...

CUTE, YOU THINK I CARE IF ONE OF YOU PEOPLE KICKS THE DAMN BUCKET?

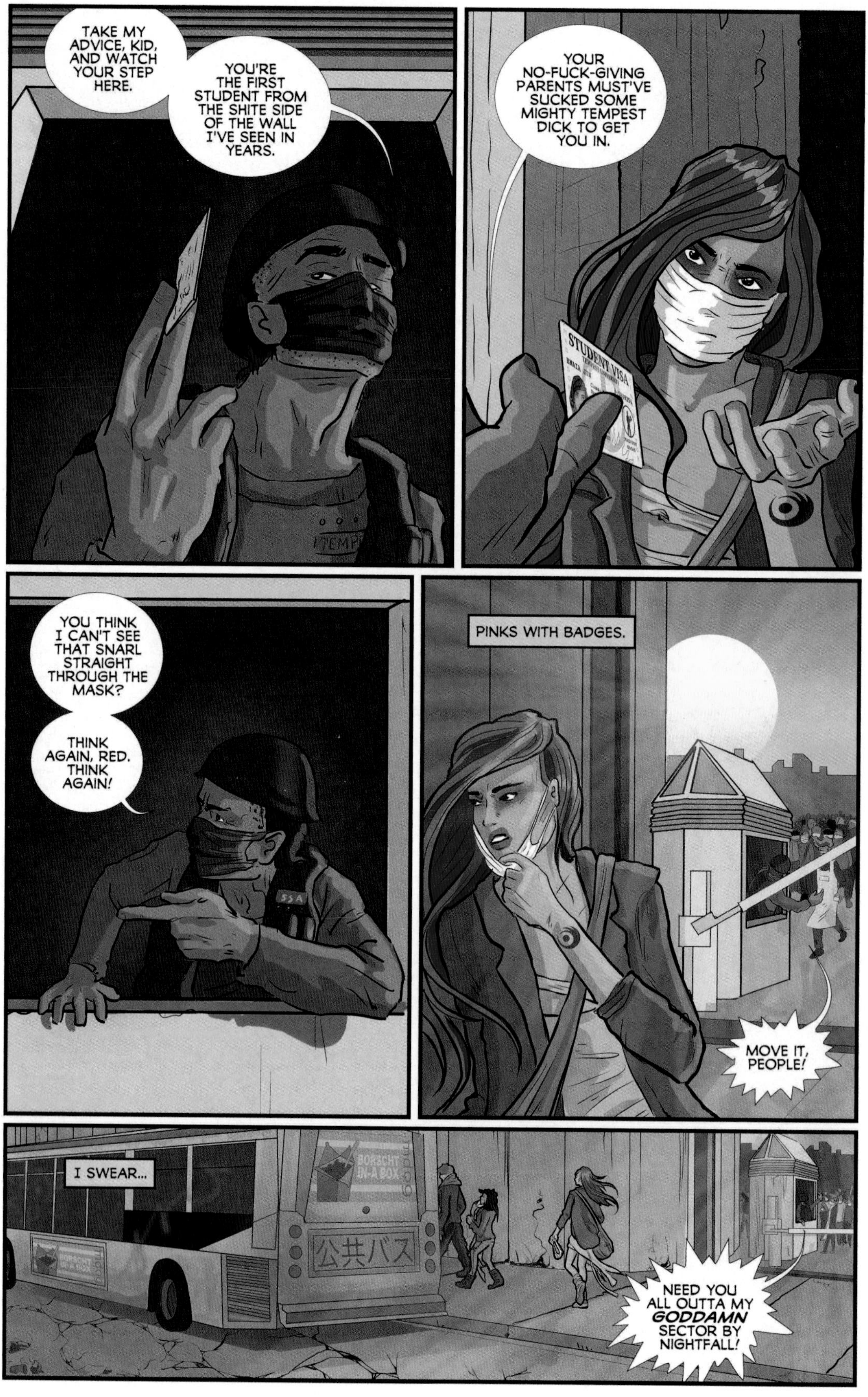
TAKE MY ADVICE, KID, AND WATCH YOUR STEP HERE.
YOU'RE THE FIRST STUDENT FROM THE SHITE SIDE OF THE WALL I'VE SEEN IN YEARS.
YOUR NO-FUCK-GIVING PARENTS MUST'VE SUCKED SOME MIGHTY TEMPEST DICK TO GET YOU IN.
STUDENT VISA
YOU THINK I CAN'T SEE THAT SNARL STRAIGHT THROUGH THE MASK?
THINK AGAIN, RED. THINK AGAIN!
PINKS WITH BADGES.
MOVE IT, PEOPLE!
I SWEAR...
BORSCHT IN-A BOX
公共バス
NEED YOU ALL OUTTA MY *GODDAMN* SECTOR BY NIGHTFALL!

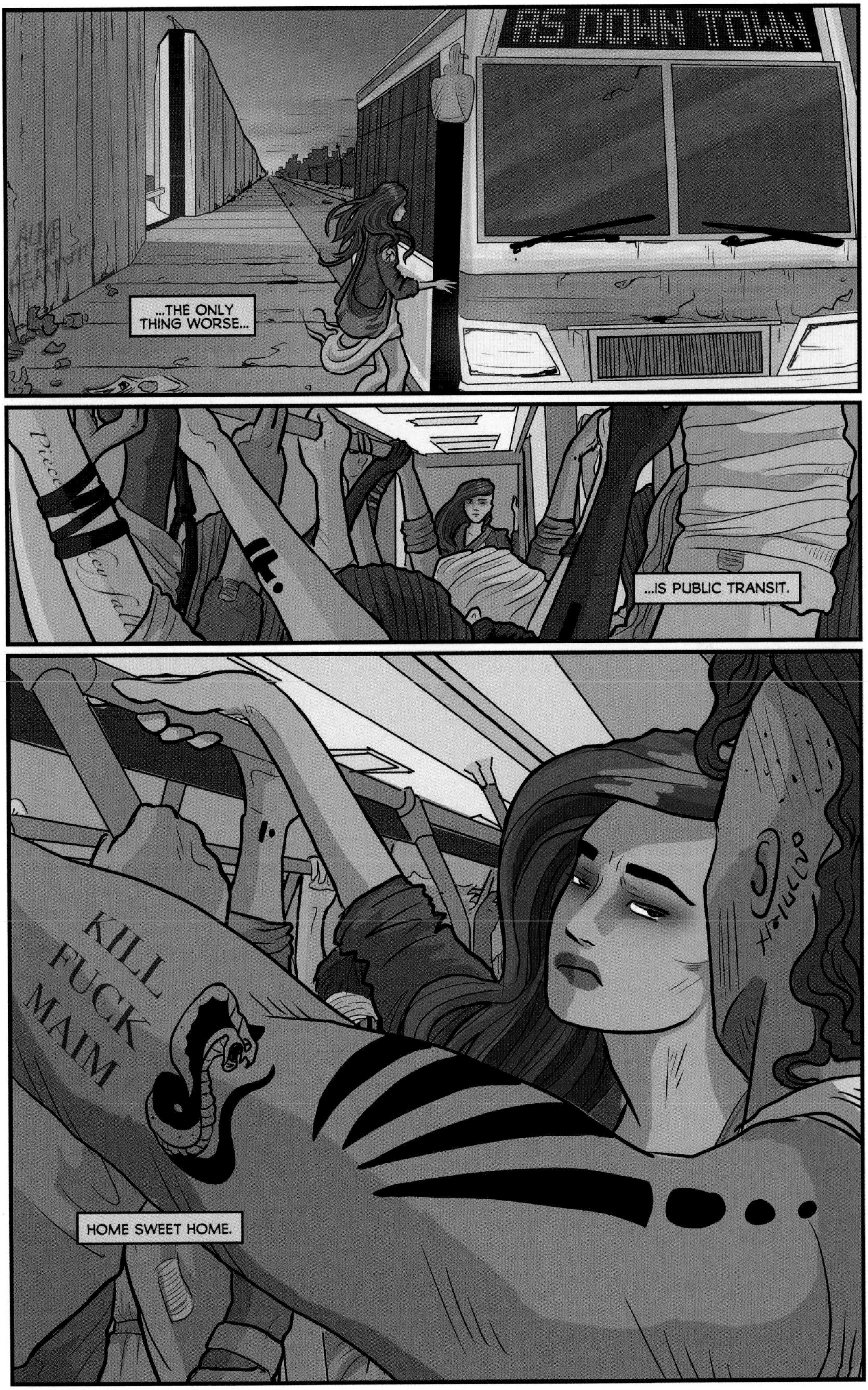
AS DOWN TOWN
...THE ONLY THING WORSE...
...IS PUBLIC TRANSIT.
KILL
FUCK
MAIM
HOME SWEET HOME.

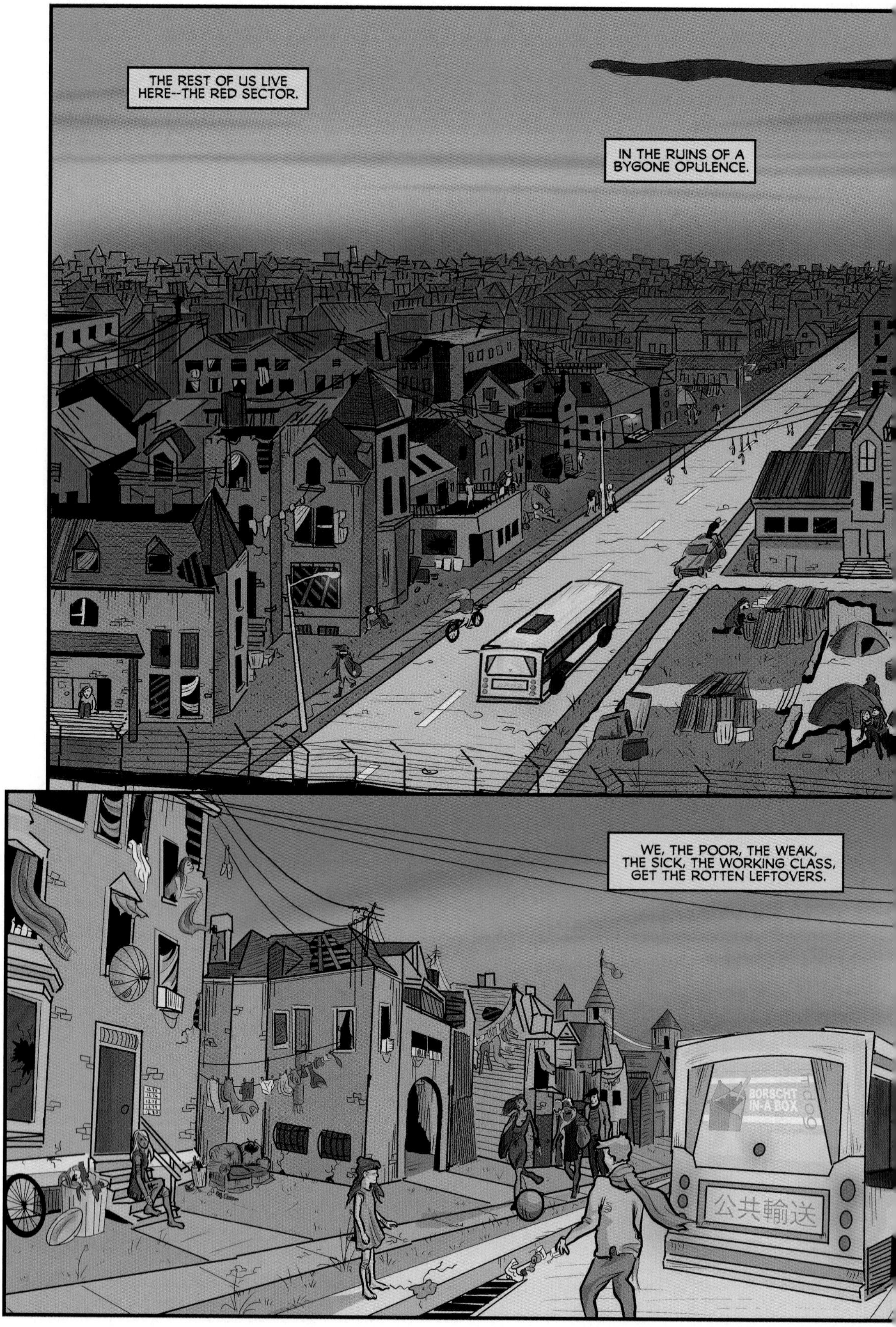
THE REST OF US LIVE HERE--THE RED SECTOR.
IN THE RUINS OF A BYGONE OPULENCE.
WE, THE POOR, THE WEAK, THE SICK, THE WORKING CLASS, GET THE ROTTEN LEFTOVERS.
BORSCHT IN-A BOX
公共輸送

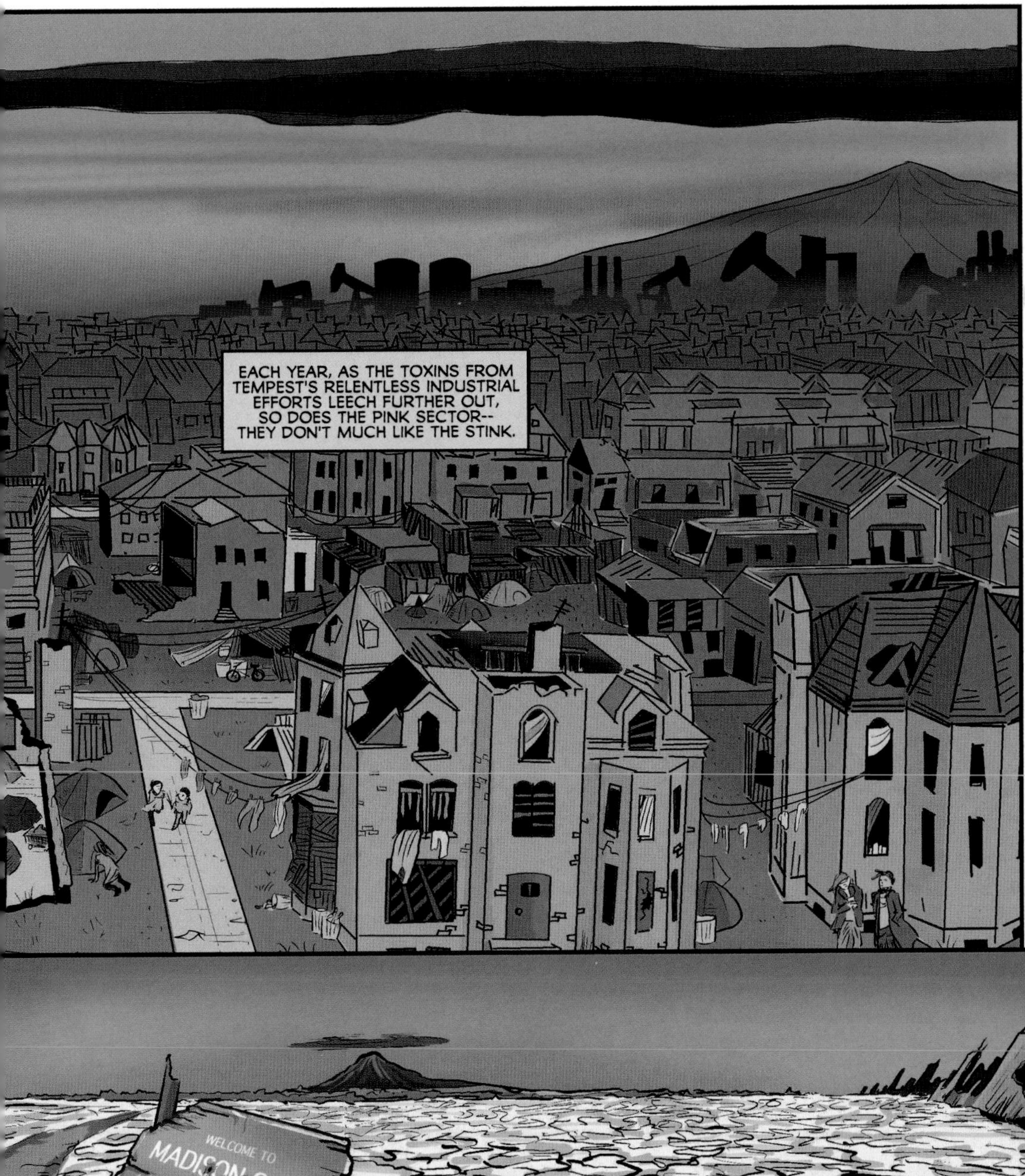
EACH YEAR, AS THE TOXINS FROM TEMPEST'S RELENTLESS INDUSTRIAL EFFORTS LEECH FURTHER OUT, SO DOES THE PINK SECTOR-- THEY DON'T MUCH LIKE THE STINK.

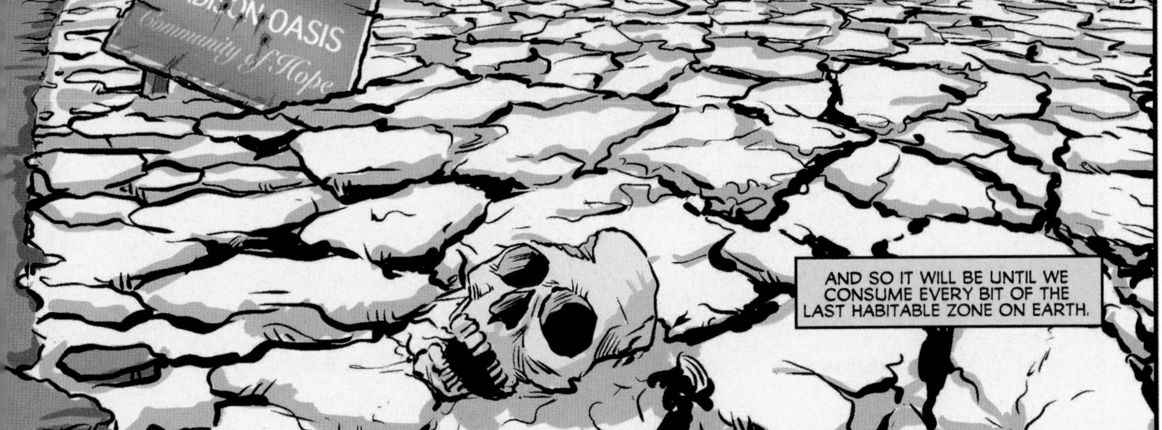
WELCOME TO
MADISON OASIS
Community of Hope
AND SO IT WILL BE UNTIL WE CONSUME EVERY BIT OF THE LAST HABITABLE ZONE ON EARTH.

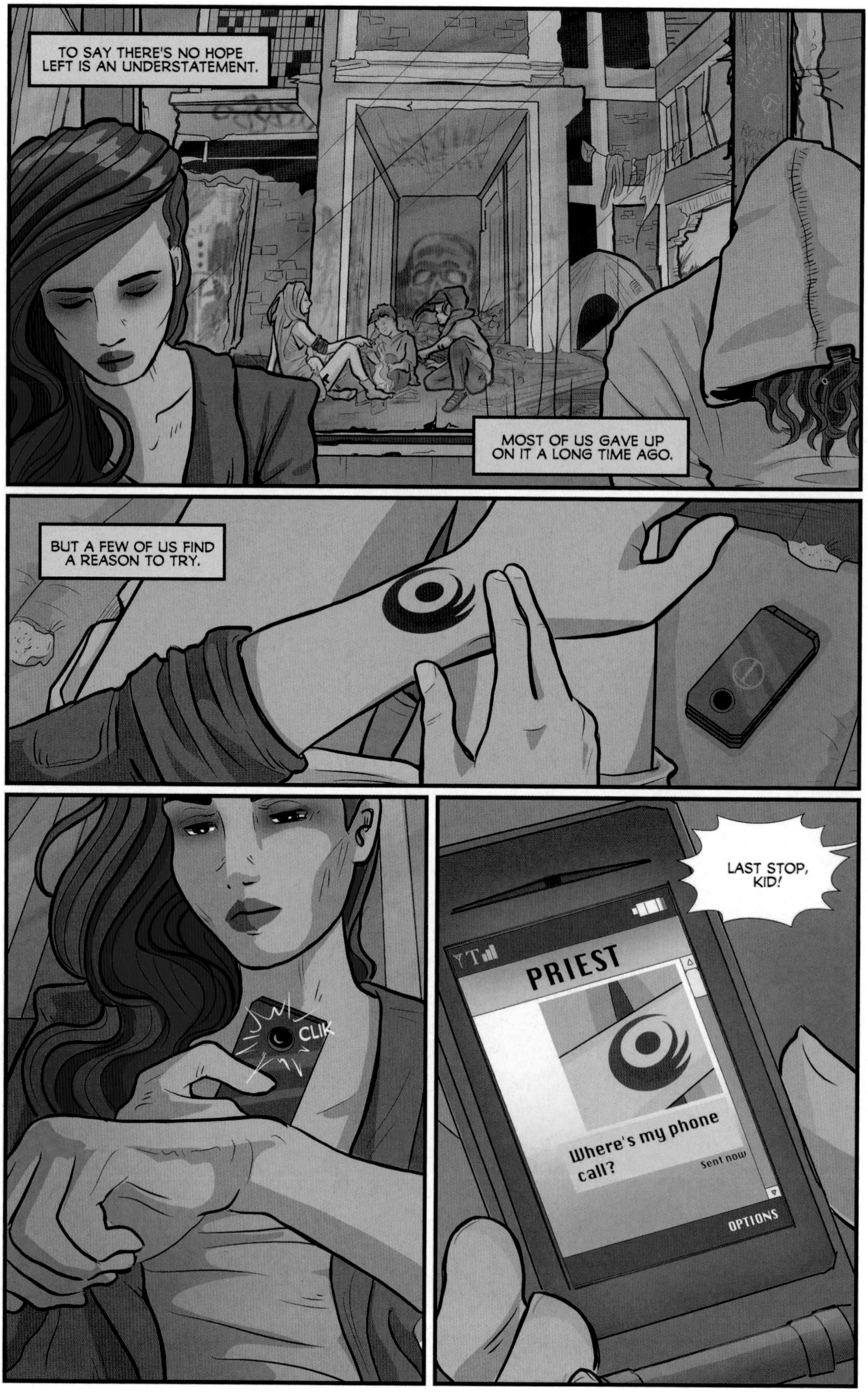

TO SAY THERE'S NO HOPE LEFT IS AN UNDERSTATEMENT.
MOST OF US GAVE UP ON IT A LONG TIME AGO.
BUT A FEW OF US FIND A REASON TO TRY.
CLIK
LAST STOP, KID!
PRIEST
Where's my phone call?
Sent now
OPTIONS

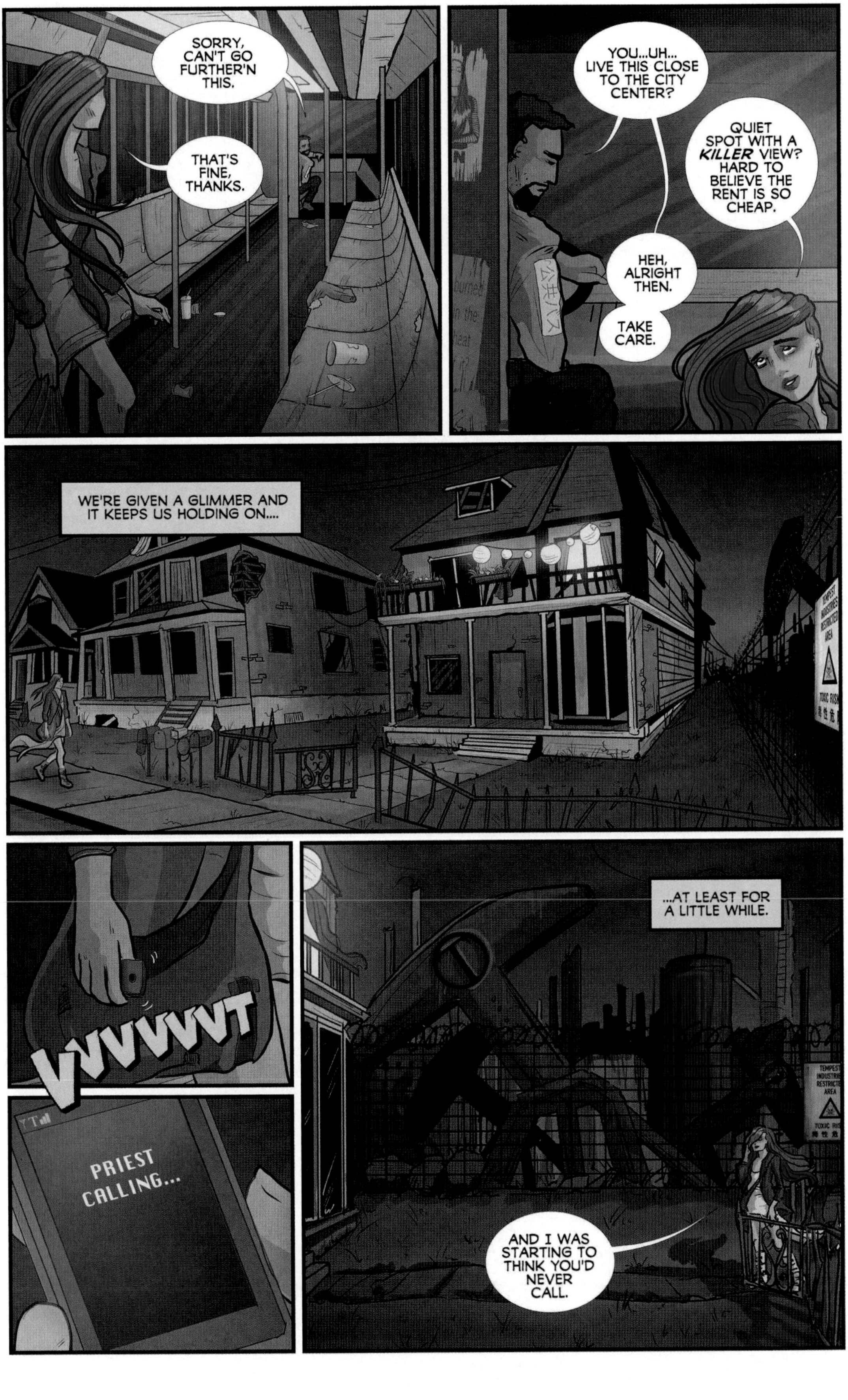
SORRY, CAN'T GO FURTHER'N THIS.
THAT'S FINE, THANKS.
YOU...UH... LIVE THIS CLOSE TO THE CITY CENTER?
QUIET SPOT WITH A KILLER VIEW? HARD TO BELIEVE THE RENT IS SO CHEAP.
HEH, ALRIGHT THEN.
TAKE CARE.
WE'RE GIVEN A GLIMMER AND IT KEEPS US HOLDING ON....
TEMPEST INDUSTRIES RESTRICTED AREA
TOXIC RISK
VVVVVVT
PRIEST CALLING...
...AT LEAST FOR A LITTLE WHILE.
AND I WAS STARTING TO THINK YOU'D NEVER CALL.

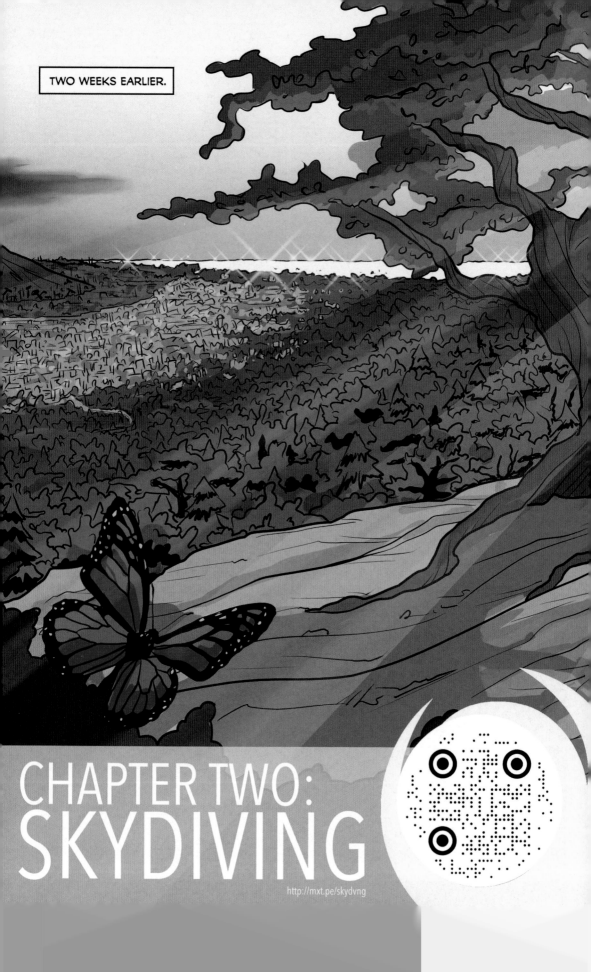

TWO WEEKS EARLIER.

CHAPTER TWO:
SKYDIVING

http://mxt.pe/skydvng

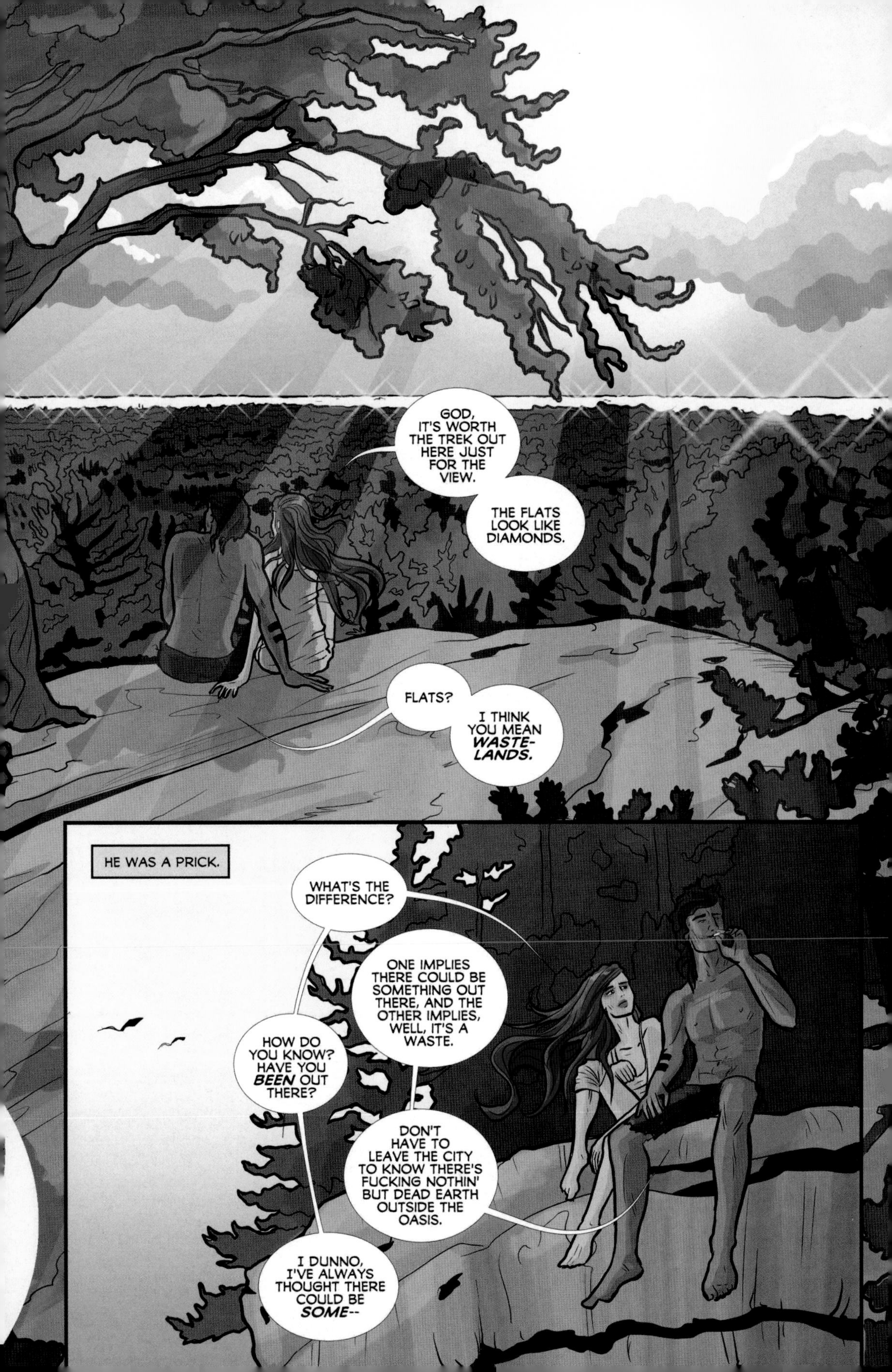
GOD, IT'S WORTH THE TREK OUT HERE JUST FOR THE VIEW.
THE FLATS LOOK LIKE DIAMONDS.
FLATS?
I THINK YOU MEAN *WASTE-LANDS.*
HE WAS A PRICK.
WHAT'S THE DIFFERENCE?
ONE IMPLIES THERE COULD BE SOMETHING OUT THERE, AND THE OTHER IMPLIES, WELL, IT'S A WASTE.
HOW DO YOU KNOW? HAVE YOU *BEEN* OUT THERE?
DON'T HAVE TO LEAVE THE CITY TO KNOW THERE'S FUCKING NOTHIN' BUT DEAD EARTH OUTSIDE THE OASIS.
I DUNNO, I'VE ALWAYS THOUGHT THERE COULD BE *SOME*--

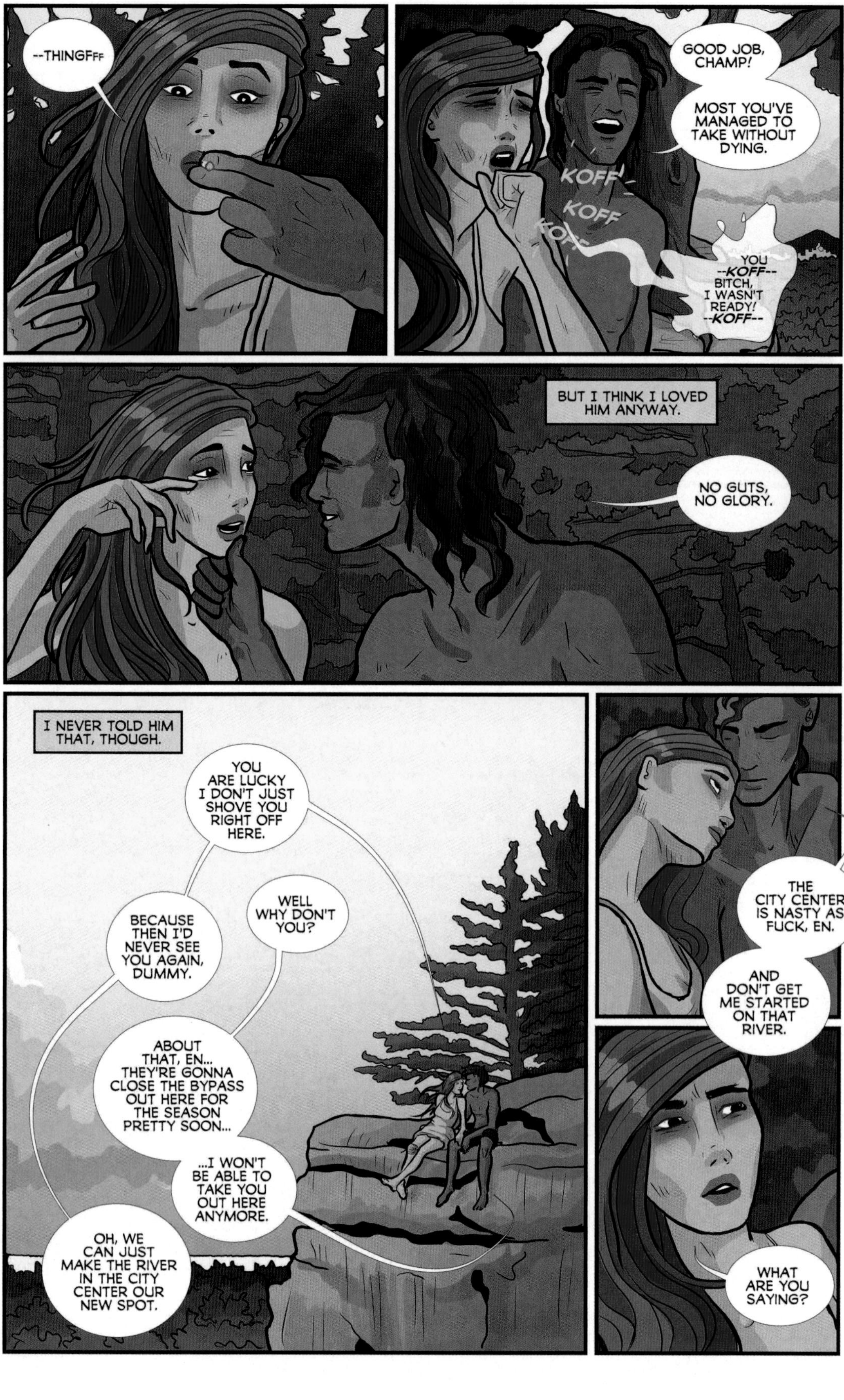
--THINGFFF
GOOD JOB, CHAMP!
MOST YOU'VE MANAGED TO TAKE WITHOUT DYING.
KOFF
KOFF
KOFF
YOU --KOFF-- BITCH, I WASN'T READY! --KOFF--
BUT I THINK I LOVED HIM ANYWAY.
NO GUTS, NO GLORY.
I NEVER TOLD HIM THAT, THOUGH.
YOU ARE LUCKY I DON'T JUST SHOVE YOU RIGHT OFF HERE.
BECAUSE THEN I'D NEVER SEE YOU AGAIN, DUMMY.
WELL WHY DON'T YOU?
ABOUT THAT, EN... THEY'RE GONNA CLOSE THE BYPASS OUT HERE FOR THE SEASON PRETTY SOON...
...I WON'T BE ABLE TO TAKE YOU OUT HERE ANYMORE.
OH, WE CAN JUST MAKE THE RIVER IN THE CITY CENTER OUR NEW SPOT.
THE CITY CENTER IS NASTY AS FUCK, EN.
AND DON'T GET ME STARTED ON THAT RIVER.
WHAT ARE YOU SAYING?

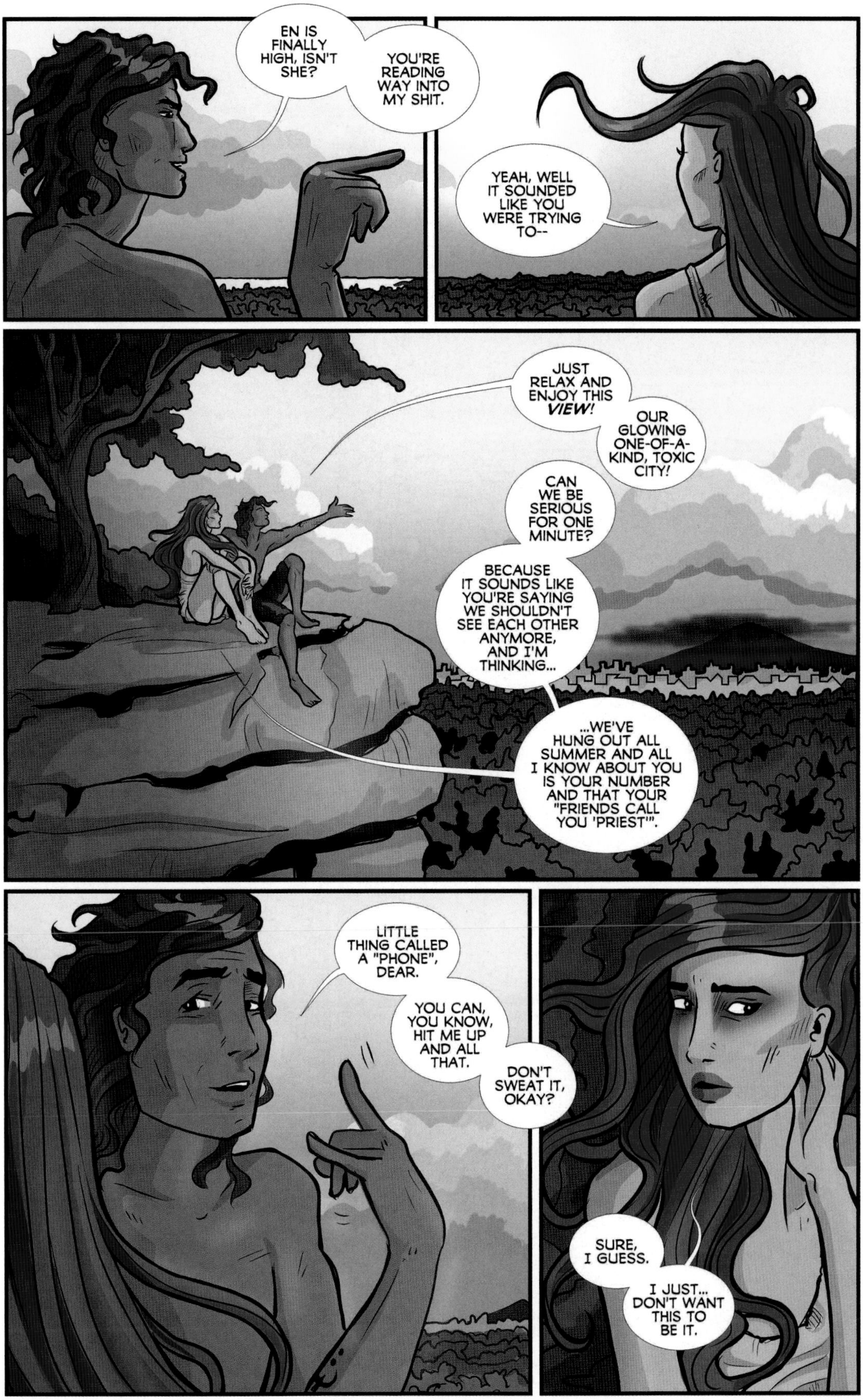
EN IS FINALLY HIGH, ISN'T SHE?
YOU'RE READING WAY INTO MY SHIT.
YEAH, WELL IT SOUNDED LIKE YOU WERE TRYING TO--
JUST RELAX AND ENJOY THIS *VIEW*!
OUR GLOWING ONE-OF-A-KIND, TOXIC CITY!
CAN WE BE SERIOUS FOR ONE MINUTE?
BECAUSE IT SOUNDS LIKE YOU'RE SAYING WE SHOULDN'T SEE EACH OTHER ANYMORE, AND I'M THINKING...
...WE'VE HUNG OUT ALL SUMMER AND ALL I KNOW ABOUT YOU IS YOUR NUMBER AND THAT YOUR "FRIENDS CALL YOU 'PRIEST'".
LITTLE THING CALLED A "PHONE", DEAR.
YOU CAN, YOU KNOW, HIT ME UP AND ALL THAT.
DON'T SWEAT IT, OKAY?
SURE, I GUESS.
I JUST... DON'T WANT THIS TO BE IT.

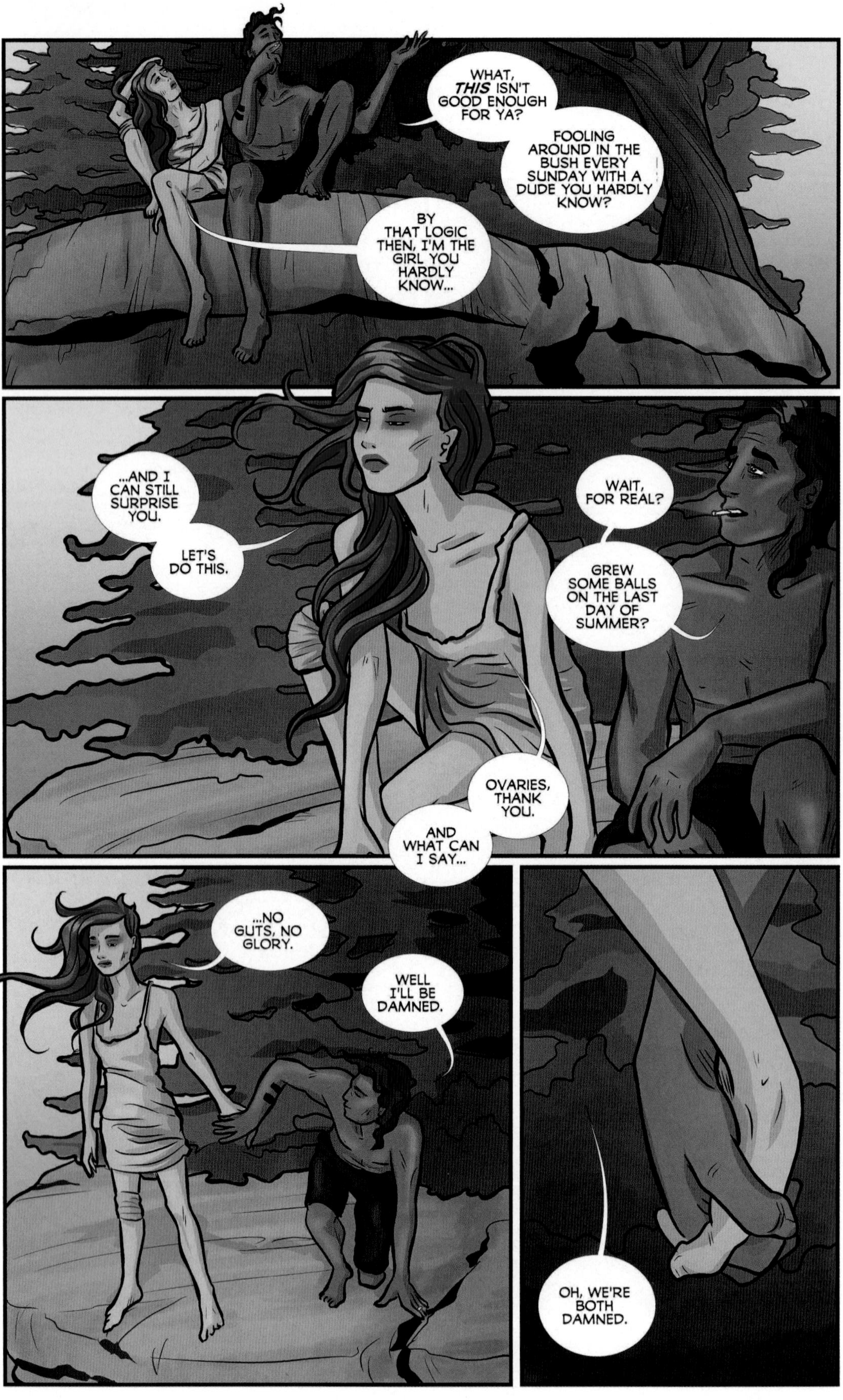
WHAT, *THIS* ISN'T GOOD ENOUGH FOR YA?
FOOLING AROUND IN THE BUSH EVERY SUNDAY WITH A DUDE YOU HARDLY KNOW?
BY THAT LOGIC THEN, I'M THE GIRL YOU HARDLY KNOW...
...AND I CAN STILL SURPRISE YOU.
LET'S DO THIS.
WAIT, FOR REAL?
GREW SOME BALLS ON THE LAST DAY OF SUMMER?
OVARIES, THANK YOU.
AND WHAT CAN I SAY...
...NO GUTS, NO GLORY.
WELL I'LL BE DAMNED.
OH, WE'RE BOTH DAMNED.

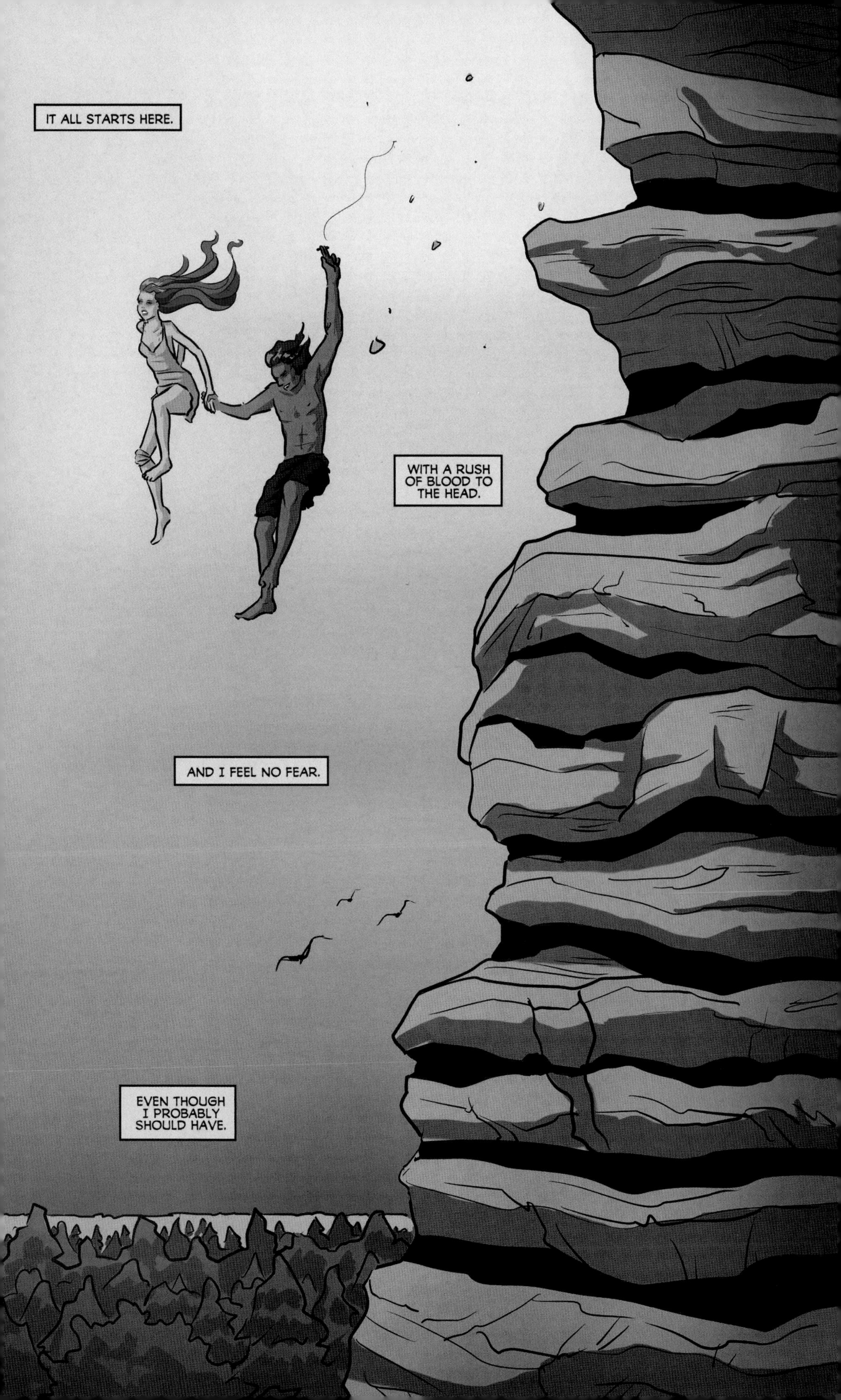
IT ALL STARTS HERE.
WITH A RUSH OF BLOOD TO THE HEAD.
AND I FEEL NO FEAR.
EVEN THOUGH I PROBABLY SHOULD HAVE.

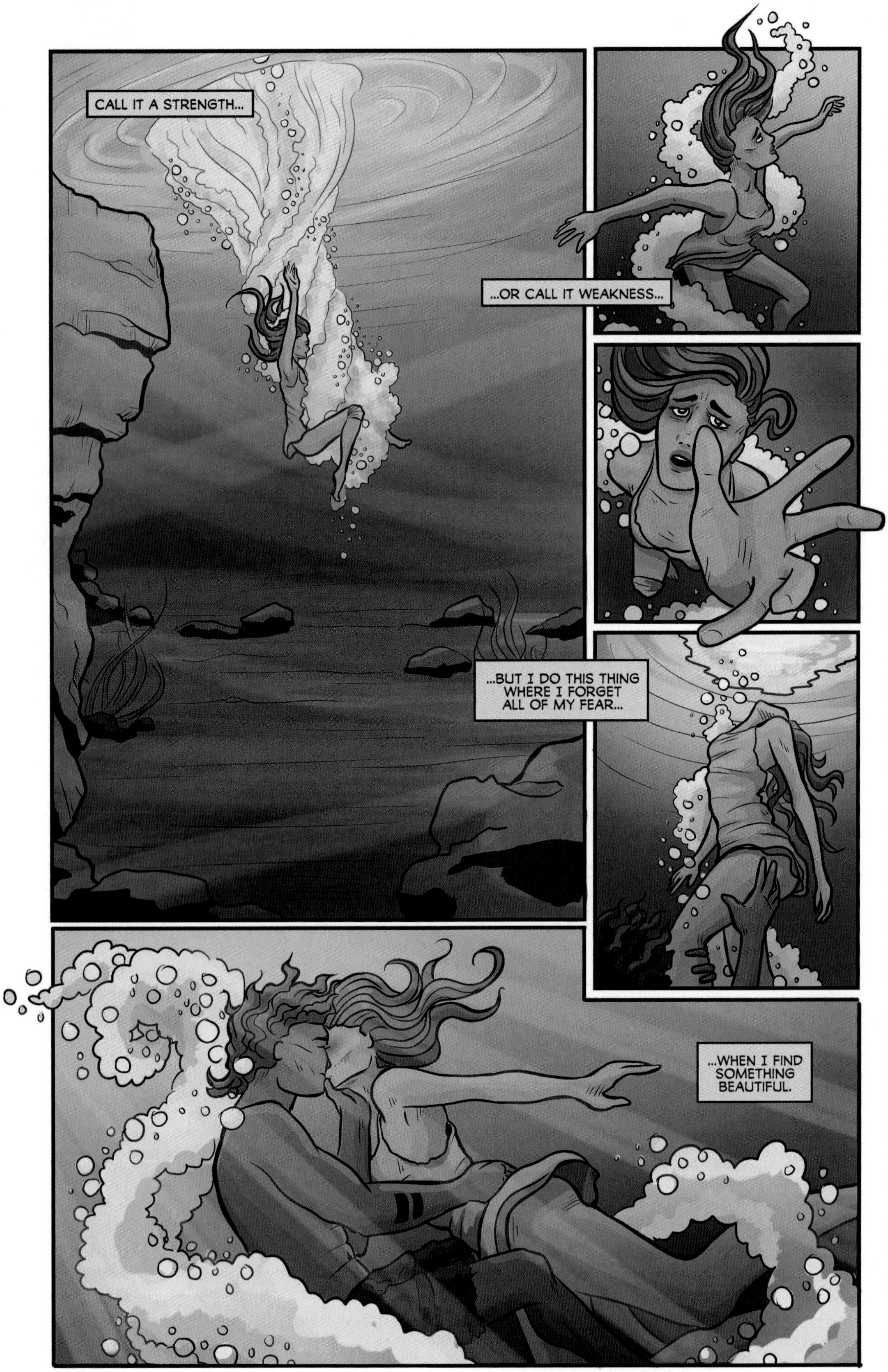
CALL IT A STRENGTH...
...OR CALL IT WEAKNESS...
...BUT I DO THIS THING WHERE I FORGET ALL OF MY FEAR...
...WHEN I FIND SOMETHING BEAUTIFUL.

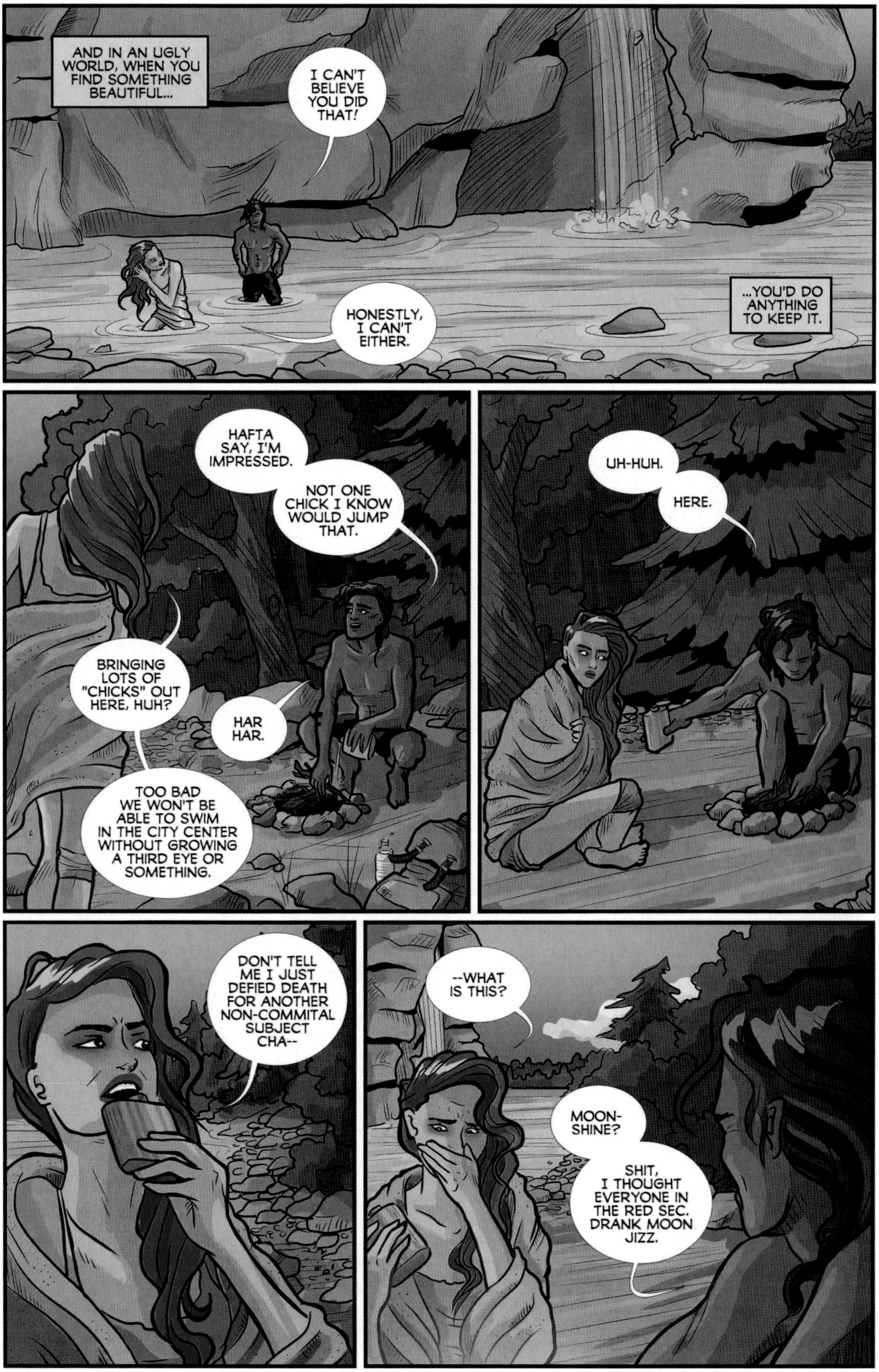
AND IN AN UGLY WORLD, WHEN YOU FIND SOMETHING BEAUTIFUL...
I CAN'T BELIEVE YOU DID THAT!
HONESTLY, I CAN'T EITHER.
...YOU'D DO ANYTHING TO KEEP IT.
HAFTA SAY, I'M IMPRESSED.
NOT ONE CHICK I KNOW WOULD JUMP THAT.
BRINGING LOTS OF "CHICKS" OUT HERE, HUH?
HAR HAR.
TOO BAD WE WON'T BE ABLE TO SWIM IN THE CITY CENTER WITHOUT GROWING A THIRD EYE OR SOMETHING.
UH-HUH.
HERE.
DON'T TELL ME I JUST DEFIED DEATH FOR ANOTHER NON-COMMITAL SUBJECT CHA--
--WHAT IS THIS?
MOON-SHINE?
SHIT, I THOUGHT EVERYONE IN THE RED SEC. DRANK MOON JIZZ.

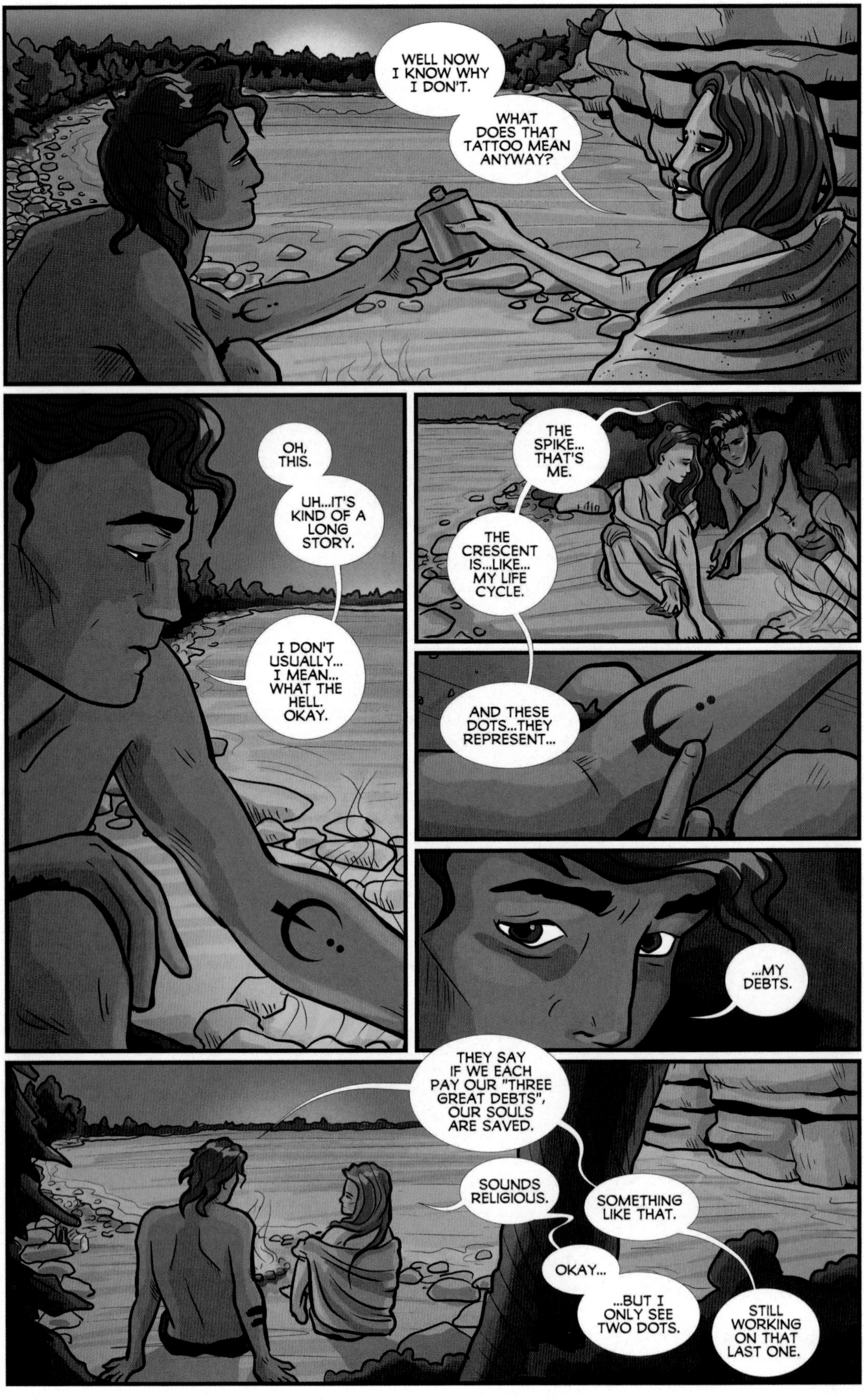
WELL NOW I KNOW WHY I DON'T.
WHAT DOES THAT TATTOO MEAN ANYWAY?
OH, THIS.
UH...IT'S KIND OF A LONG STORY.
I DON'T USUALLY... I MEAN... WHAT THE HELL. OKAY.
THE SPIKE... THAT'S ME.
THE CRESCENT IS...LIKE... MY LIFE CYCLE.
AND THESE DOTS...THEY REPRESENT...
...MY DEBTS.
THEY SAY IF WE EACH PAY OUR "THREE GREAT DEBTS", OUR SOULS ARE SAVED.
SOUNDS RELIGIOUS.
SOMETHING LIKE THAT.
OKAY...
...BUT I ONLY SEE TWO DOTS.
STILL WORKING ON THAT LAST ONE.

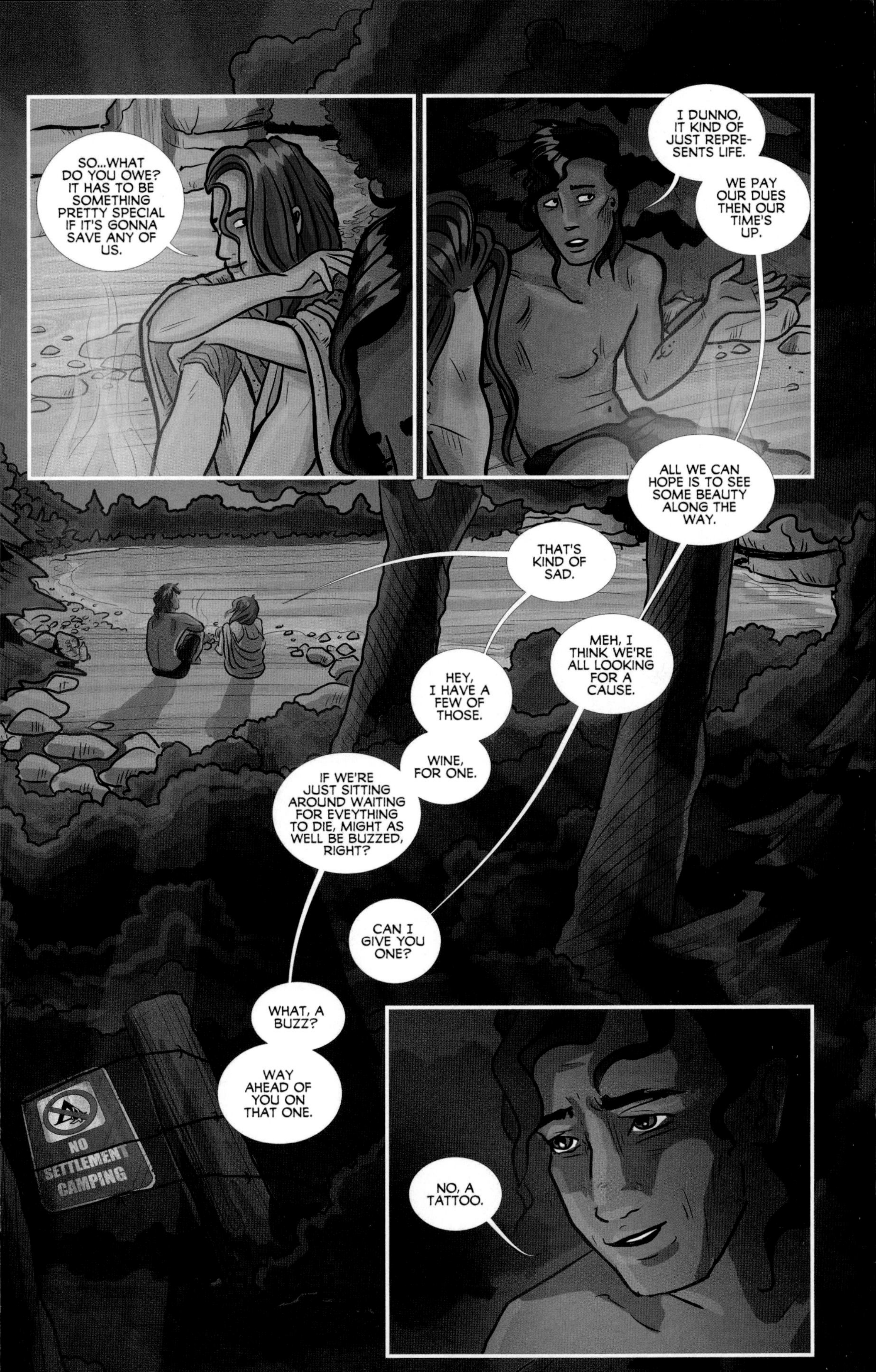
SO...WHAT DO YOU OWE? IT HAS TO BE SOMETHING PRETTY SPECIAL IF IT'S GONNA SAVE ANY OF US.
I DUNNO, IT KIND OF JUST REPRE-SENTS LIFE.
WE PAY OUR DUES THEN OUR TIME'S UP.
ALL WE CAN HOPE IS TO SEE SOME BEAUTY ALONG THE WAY.
THAT'S KIND OF SAD.
MEH, I THINK WE'RE ALL LOOKING FOR A CAUSE.
HEY, I HAVE A FEW OF THOSE.
WINE, FOR ONE.
IF WE'RE JUST SITTING AROUND WAITING FOR EVEYTHING TO DIE, MIGHT AS WELL BE BUZZED, RIGHT?
CAN I GIVE YOU ONE?
WHAT, A BUZZ?
WAY AHEAD OF YOU ON THAT ONE.
NO SETTLEMENT CAMPING
NO, A TATTOO.

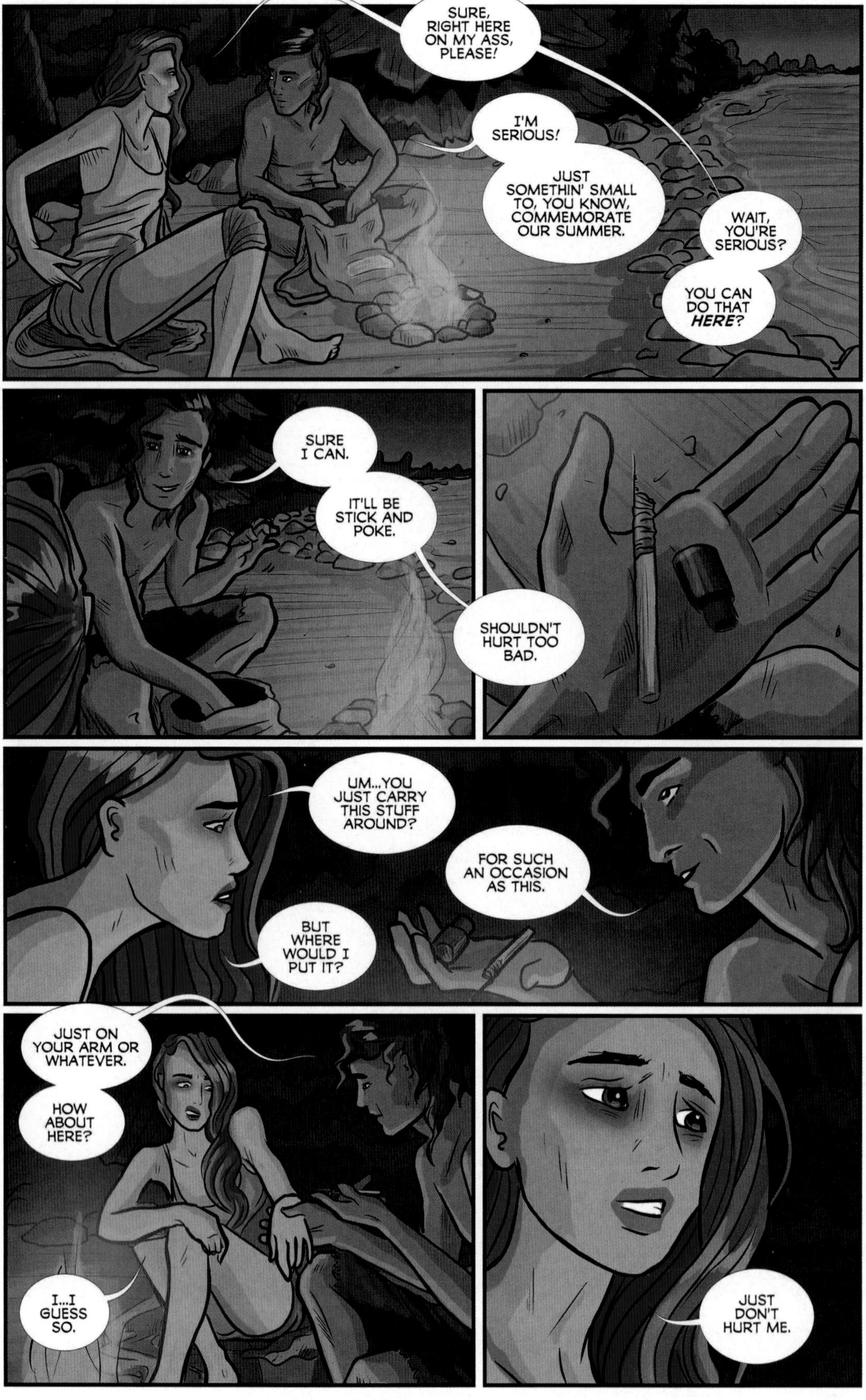
SURE, RIGHT HERE ON MY ASS, PLEASE!
I'M SERIOUS!
JUST SOMETHIN' SMALL TO, YOU KNOW, COMMEMORATE OUR SUMMER.
WAIT, YOU'RE SERIOUS?
YOU CAN DO THAT *HERE*?
SURE I CAN.
IT'LL BE STICK AND POKE.
SHOULDN'T HURT TOO BAD.
UM...YOU JUST CARRY THIS STUFF AROUND?
FOR SUCH AN OCCASION AS THIS.
BUT WHERE WOULD I PUT IT?
JUST ON YOUR ARM OR WHATEVER.
HOW ABOUT HERE?
I...I GUESS SO.
JUST DON'T HURT ME.

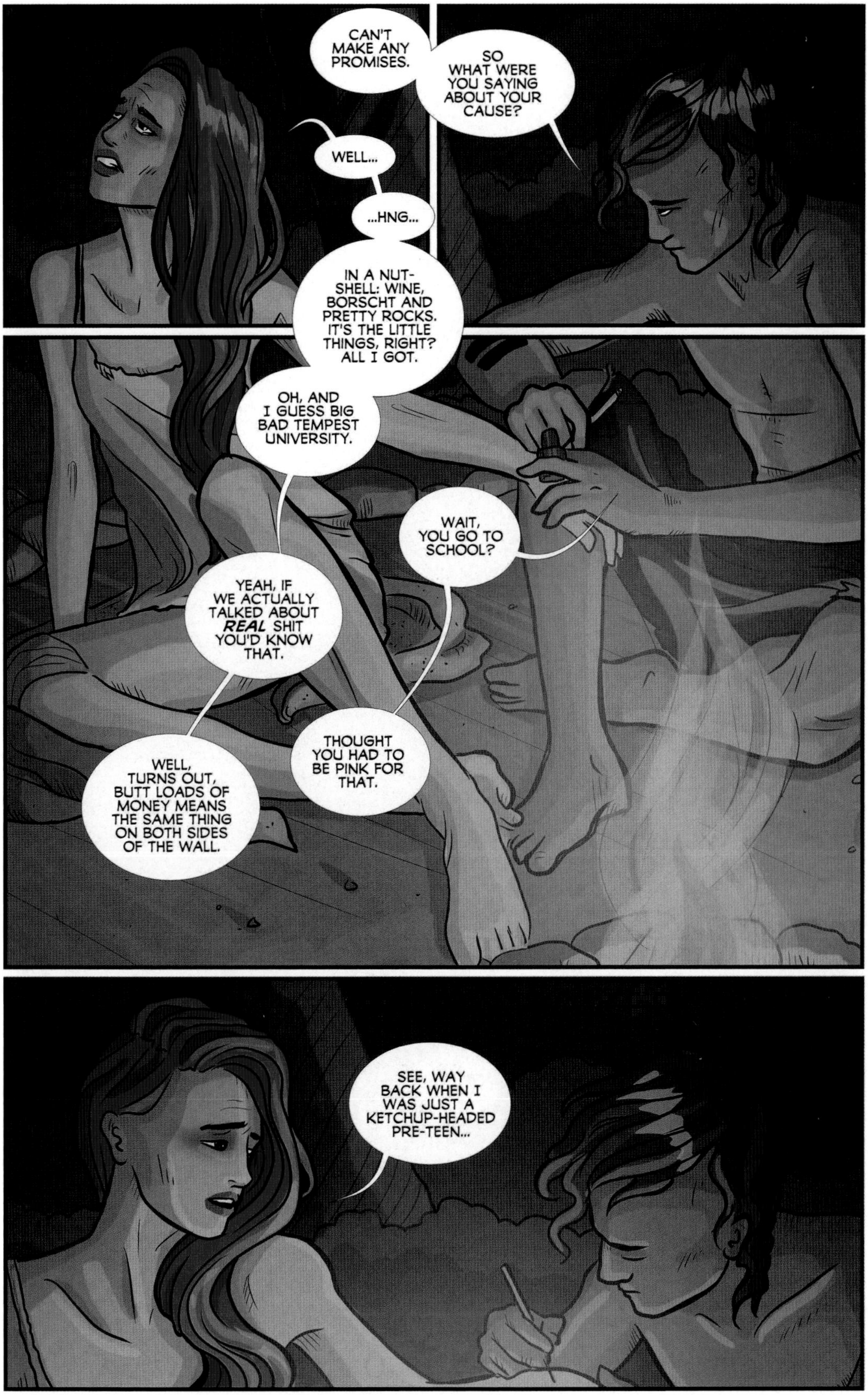
CAN'T MAKE ANY PROMISES.
SO WHAT WERE YOU SAYING ABOUT YOUR CAUSE?
WELL...
...HNG...
IN A NUT-SHELL: WINE, BORSCHT AND PRETTY ROCKS. IT'S THE LITTLE THINGS, RIGHT? ALL I GOT.
OH, AND I GUESS BIG BAD TEMPEST UNIVERSITY.
WAIT, YOU GO TO SCHOOL?
YEAH, IF WE ACTUALLY TALKED ABOUT *REAL* SHIT YOU'D KNOW THAT.
THOUGHT YOU HAD TO BE PINK FOR THAT.
WELL, TURNS OUT, BUTT LOADS OF MONEY MEANS THE SAME THING ON BOTH SIDES OF THE WALL.
SEE, WAY BACK WHEN I WAS JUST A KETCHUP-HEADED PRE-TEEN...

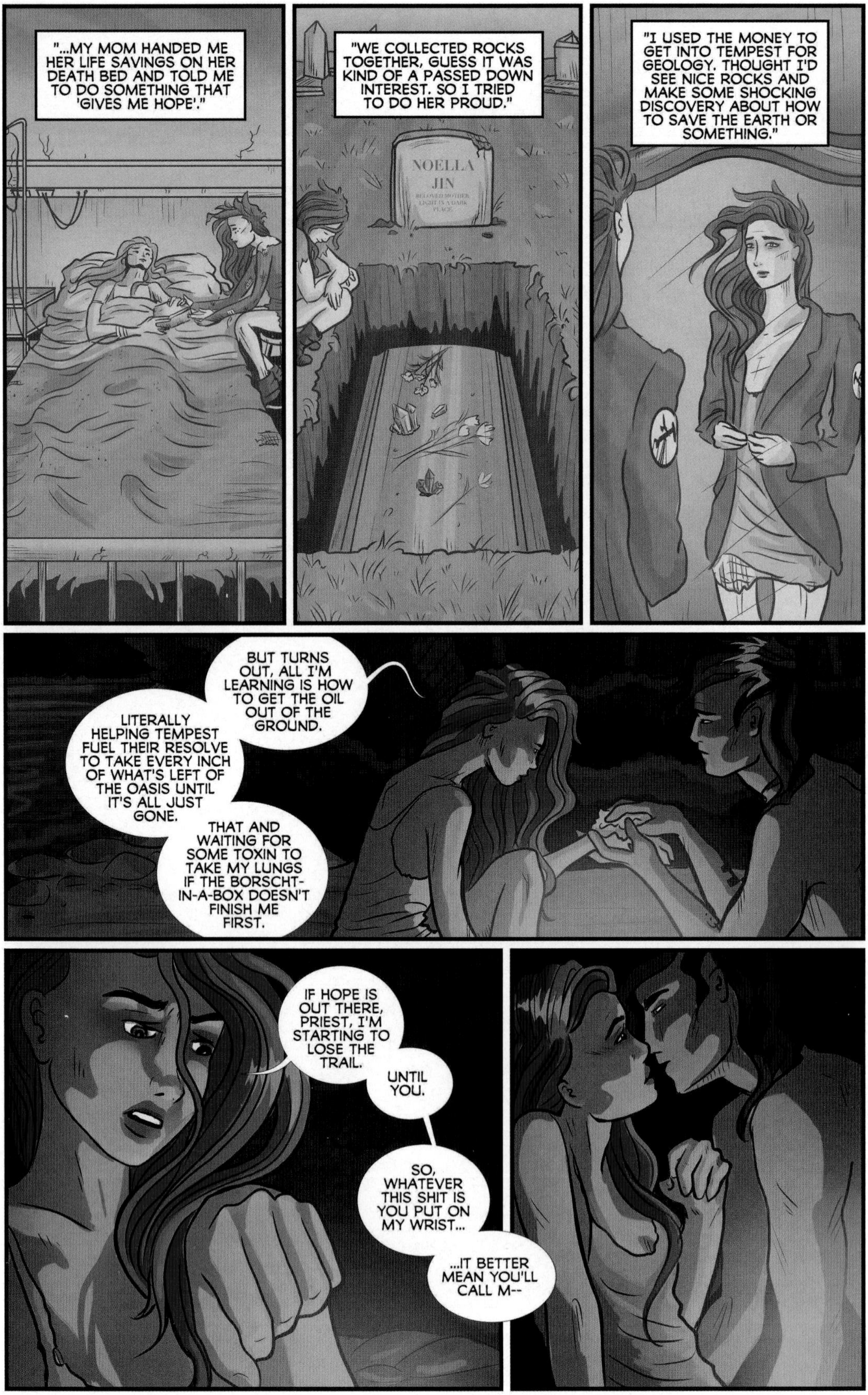
"...MY MOM HANDED ME HER LIFE SAVINGS ON HER DEATH BED AND TOLD ME TO DO SOMETHING THAT 'GIVES ME HOPE'."
"WE COLLECTED ROCKS TOGETHER, GUESS IT WAS KIND OF A PASSED DOWN INTEREST. SO I TRIED TO DO HER PROUD."
NOELLA JIN
"I USED THE MONEY TO GET INTO TEMPEST FOR GEOLOGY. THOUGHT I'D SEE NICE ROCKS AND MAKE SOME SHOCKING DISCOVERY ABOUT HOW TO SAVE THE EARTH OR SOMETHING."
BUT TURNS OUT, ALL I'M LEARNING IS HOW TO GET THE OIL OUT OF THE GROUND.
LITERALLY HELPING TEMPEST FUEL THEIR RESOLVE TO TAKE EVERY INCH OF WHAT'S LEFT OF THE OASIS UNTIL IT'S ALL JUST GONE.
THAT AND WAITING FOR SOME TOXIN TO TAKE MY LUNGS IF THE BORSCHT-IN-A-BOX DOESN'T FINISH ME FIRST.
IF HOPE IS OUT THERE, PRIEST, I'M STARTING TO LOSE THE TRAIL.
UNTIL YOU.
SO, WHATEVER THIS SHIT IS YOU PUT ON MY WRIST...
...IT BETTER MEAN YOU'LL CALL M--

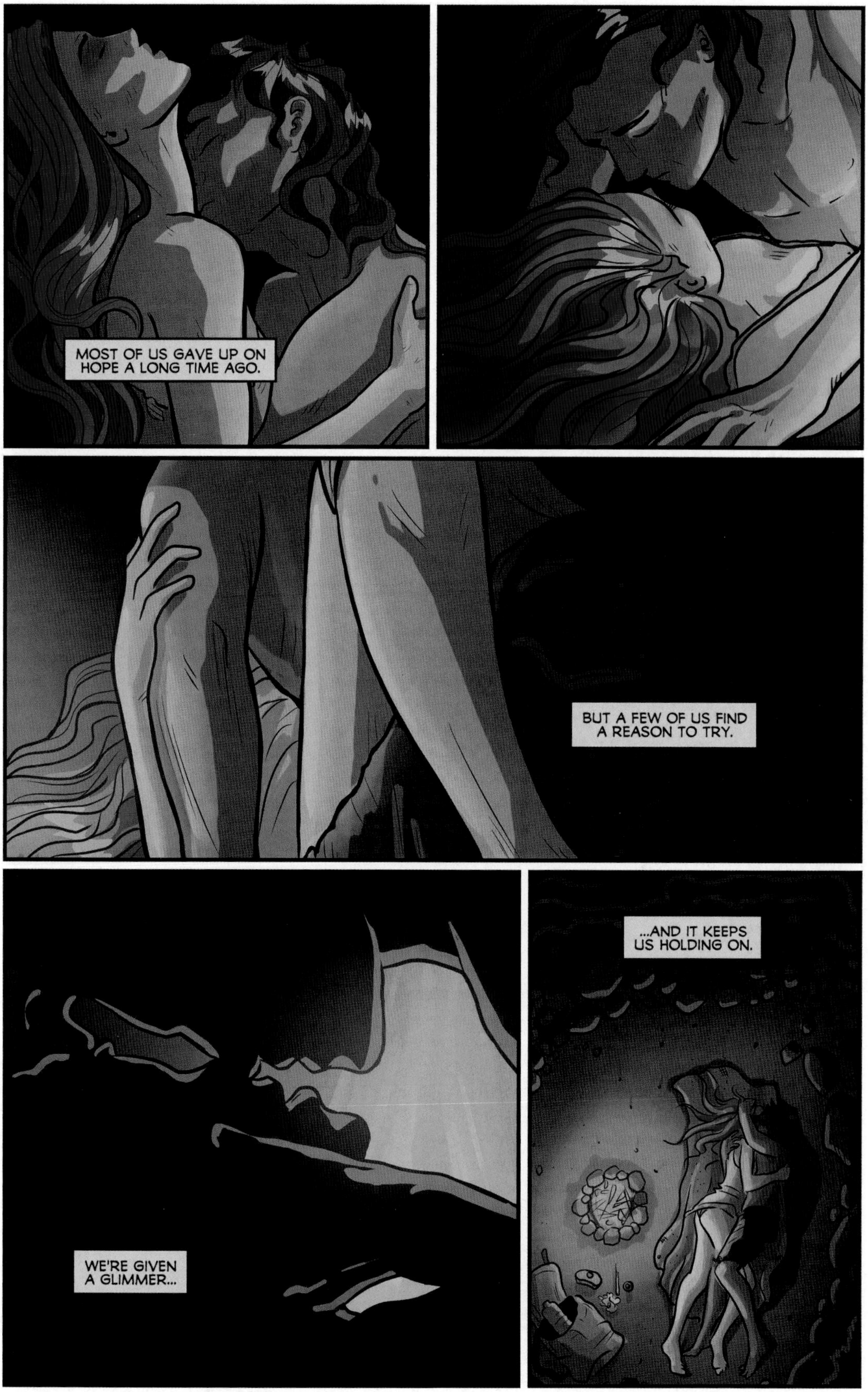
MOST OF US GAVE UP ON HOPE A LONG TIME AGO.
BUT A FEW OF US FIND A REASON TO TRY.
WE'RE GIVEN A GLIMMER...
...AND IT KEEPS US HOLDING ON.

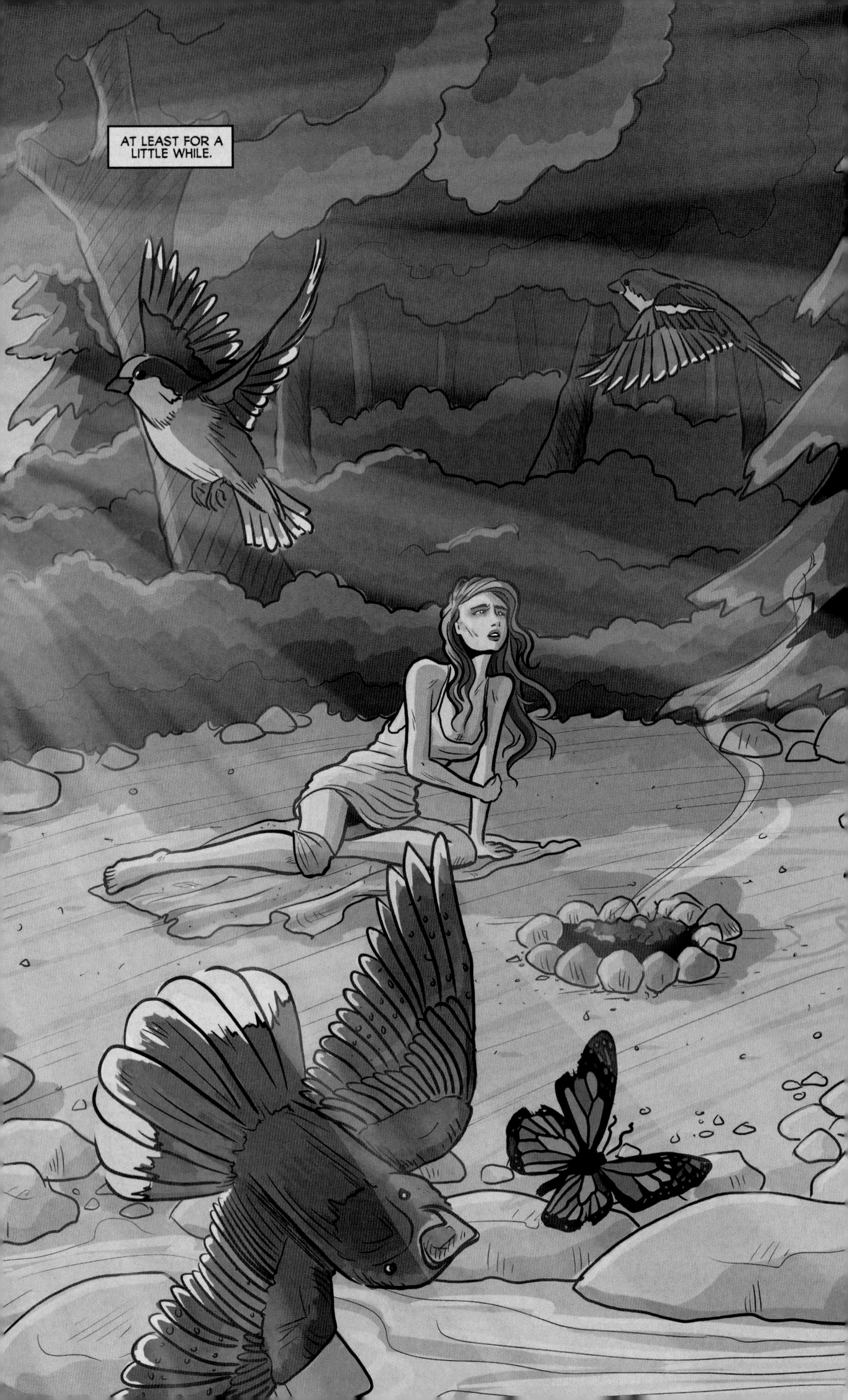
AT LEAST FOR A LITTLE WHILE.

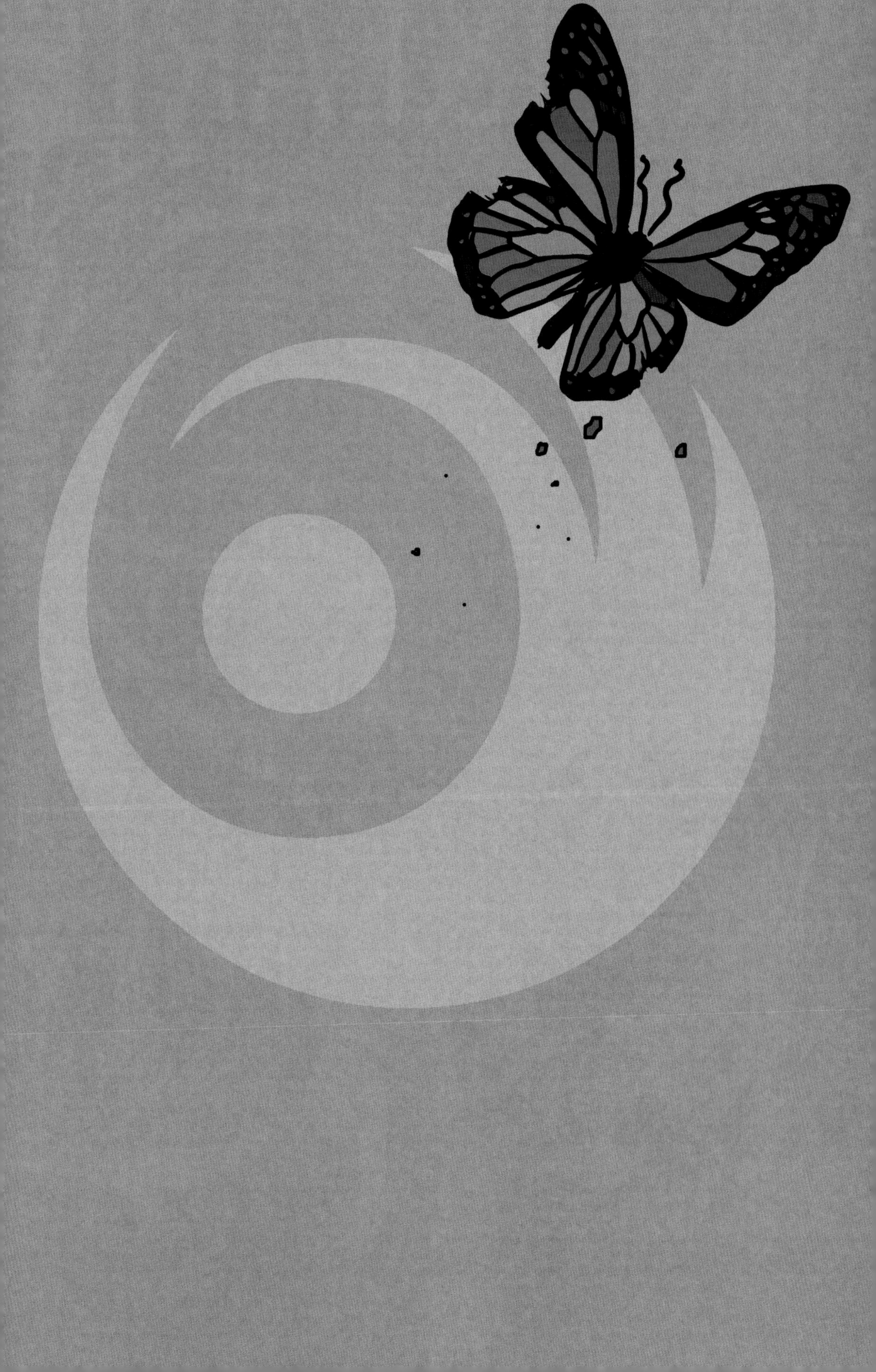

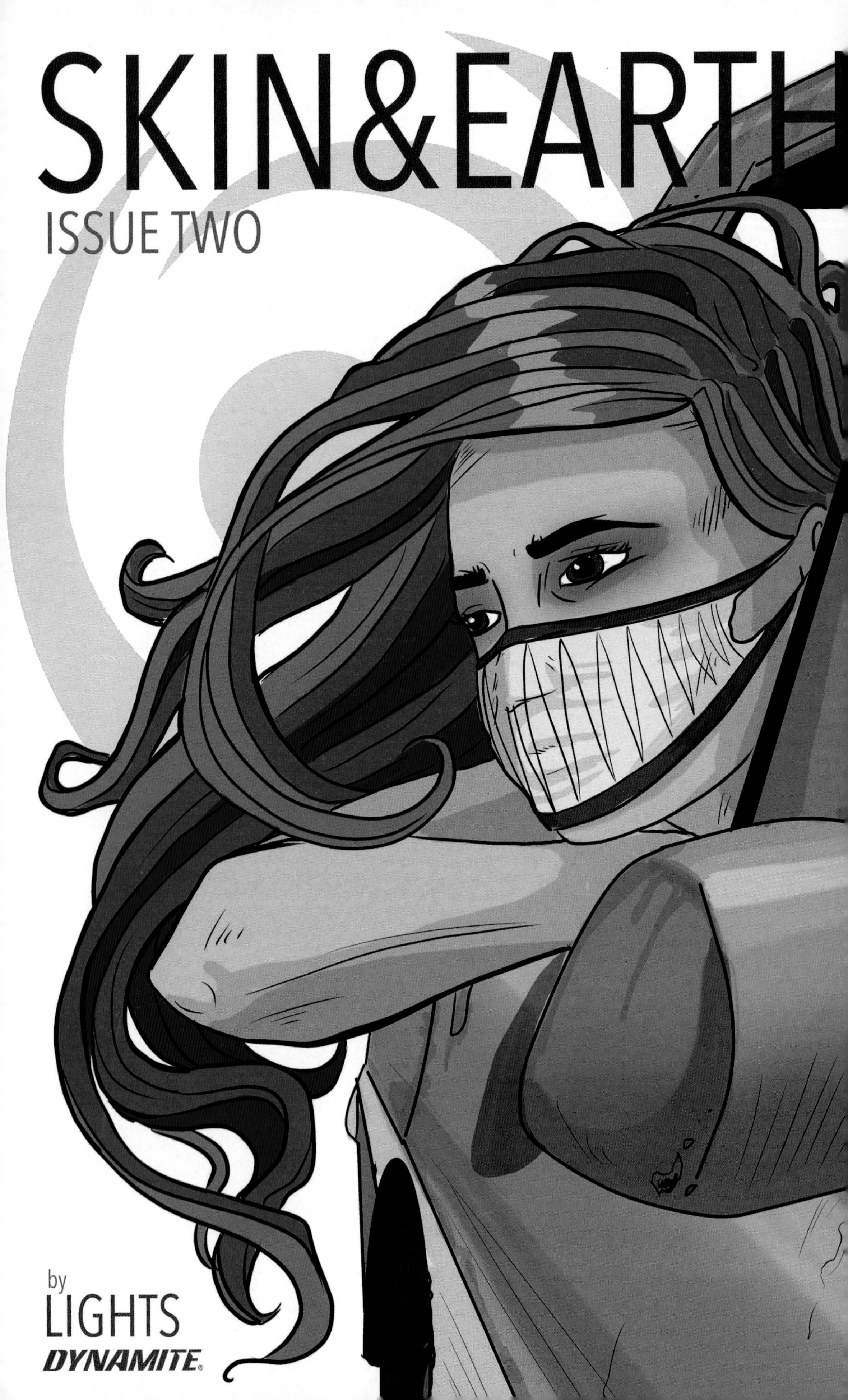
SKIN&EARTH
ISSUE TWO
by
LIGHTS
DYNAMITE

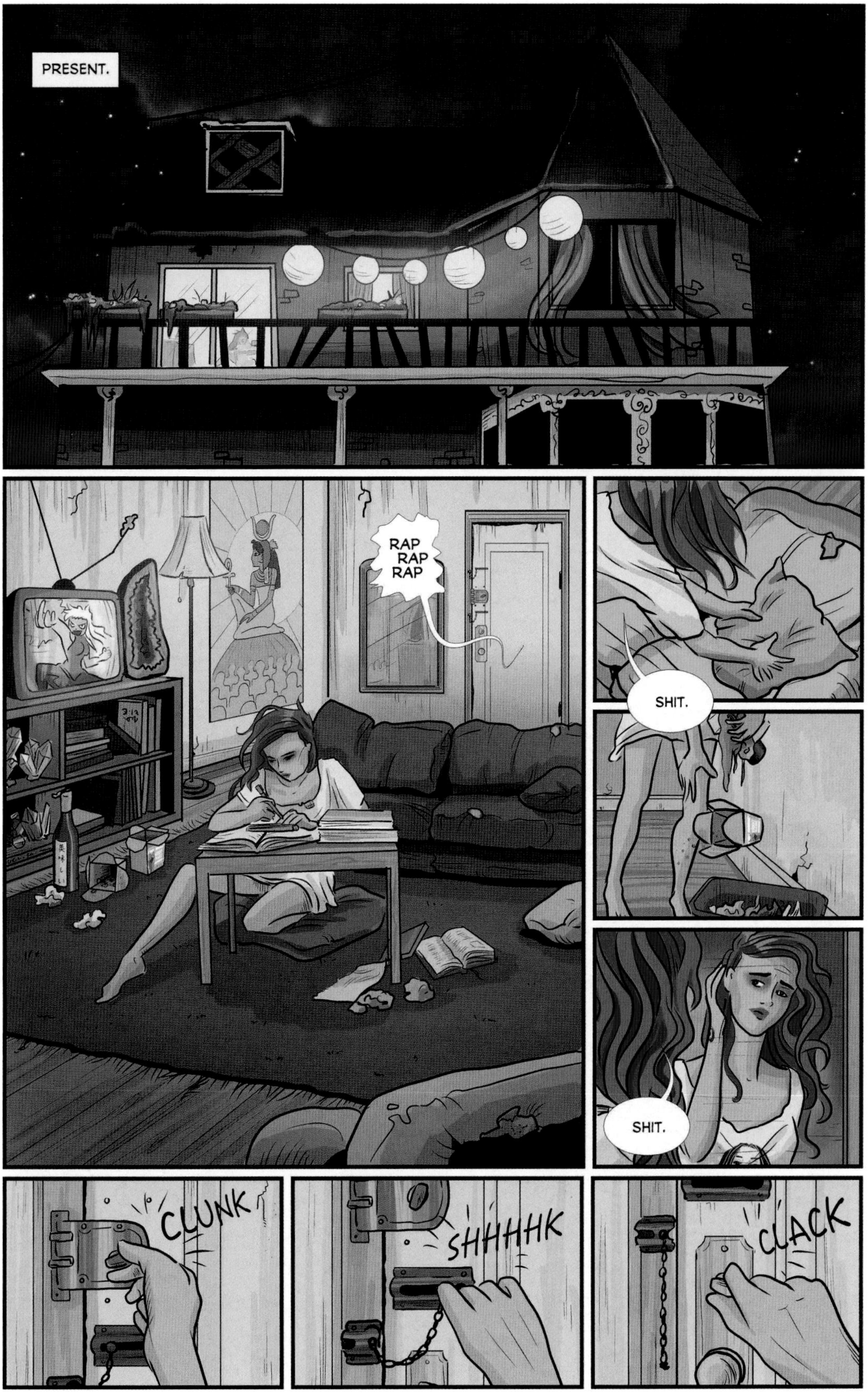
PRESENT.
RAP RAP RAP
SHIT.
SHIT.
CLUNK
SHHHHK
CLACK

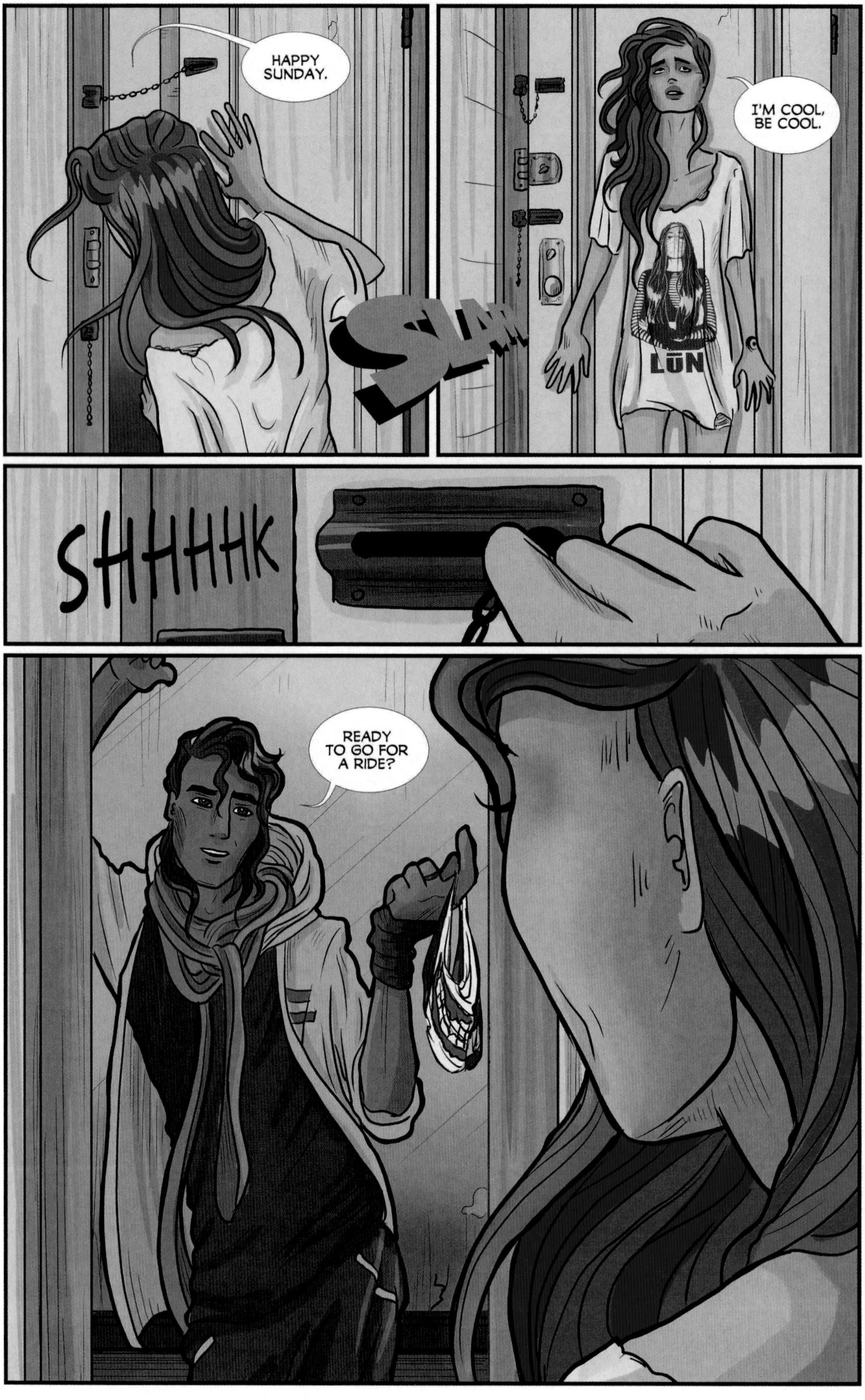
HAPPY SUNDAY.
SLAM
I'M COOL, BE COOL.
LŪN
SHHHHK
READY TO GO FOR A RIDE?

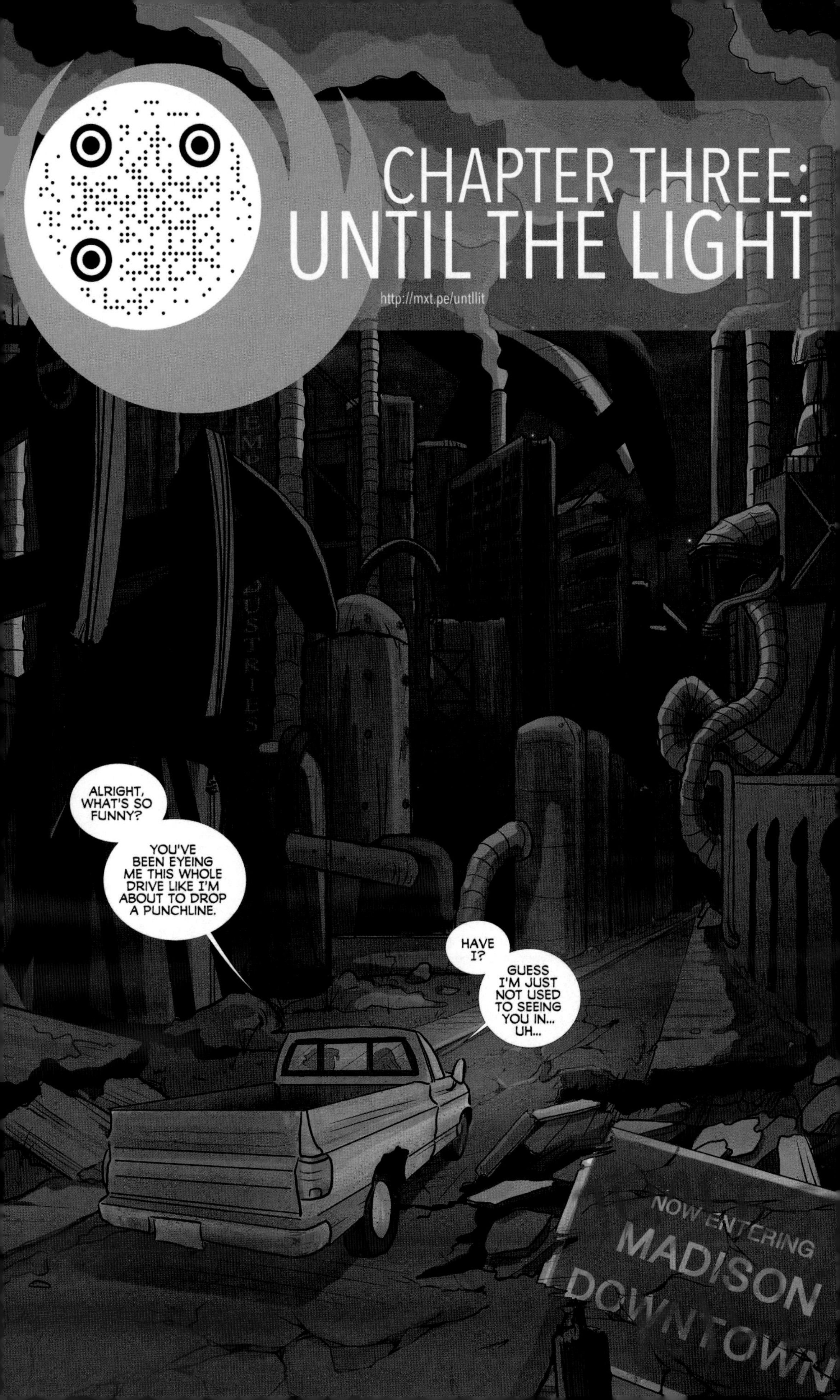
CHAPTER THREE:
UNTIL THE LIGHT
http://mxt.pe/untllit
ALRIGHT, WHAT'S SO FUNNY?
YOU'VE BEEN EYEING ME THIS WHOLE DRIVE LIKE I'M ABOUT TO DROP A PUNCHLINE.
HAVE I?
GUESS I'M JUST NOT USED TO SEEING YOU IN... UH...
NOW ENTERING
MADISON
DOWNTOWN

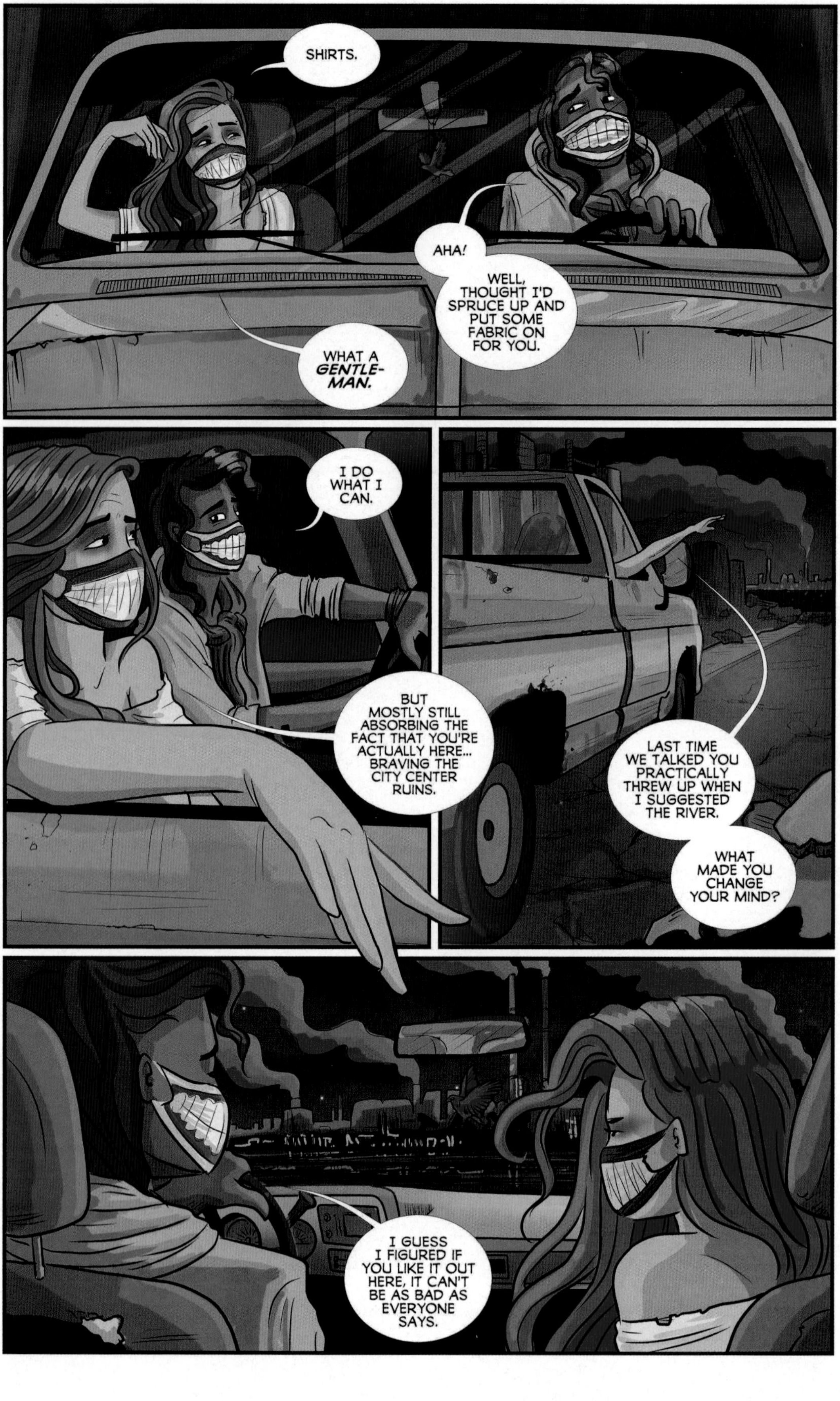
SHIRTS.
AHA!
WELL, THOUGHT I'D SPRUCE UP AND PUT SOME FABRIC ON FOR YOU.
WHAT A *GENTLEMAN.*
I DO WHAT I CAN.
BUT MOSTLY STILL ABSORBING THE FACT THAT YOU'RE ACTUALLY HERE... BRAVING THE CITY CENTER RUINS.
LAST TIME WE TALKED YOU PRACTICALLY THREW UP WHEN I SUGGESTED THE RIVER.
WHAT MADE YOU CHANGE YOUR MIND?
I GUESS I FIGURED IF YOU LIKE IT OUT HERE, IT CAN'T BE AS BAD AS EVERYONE SAYS.

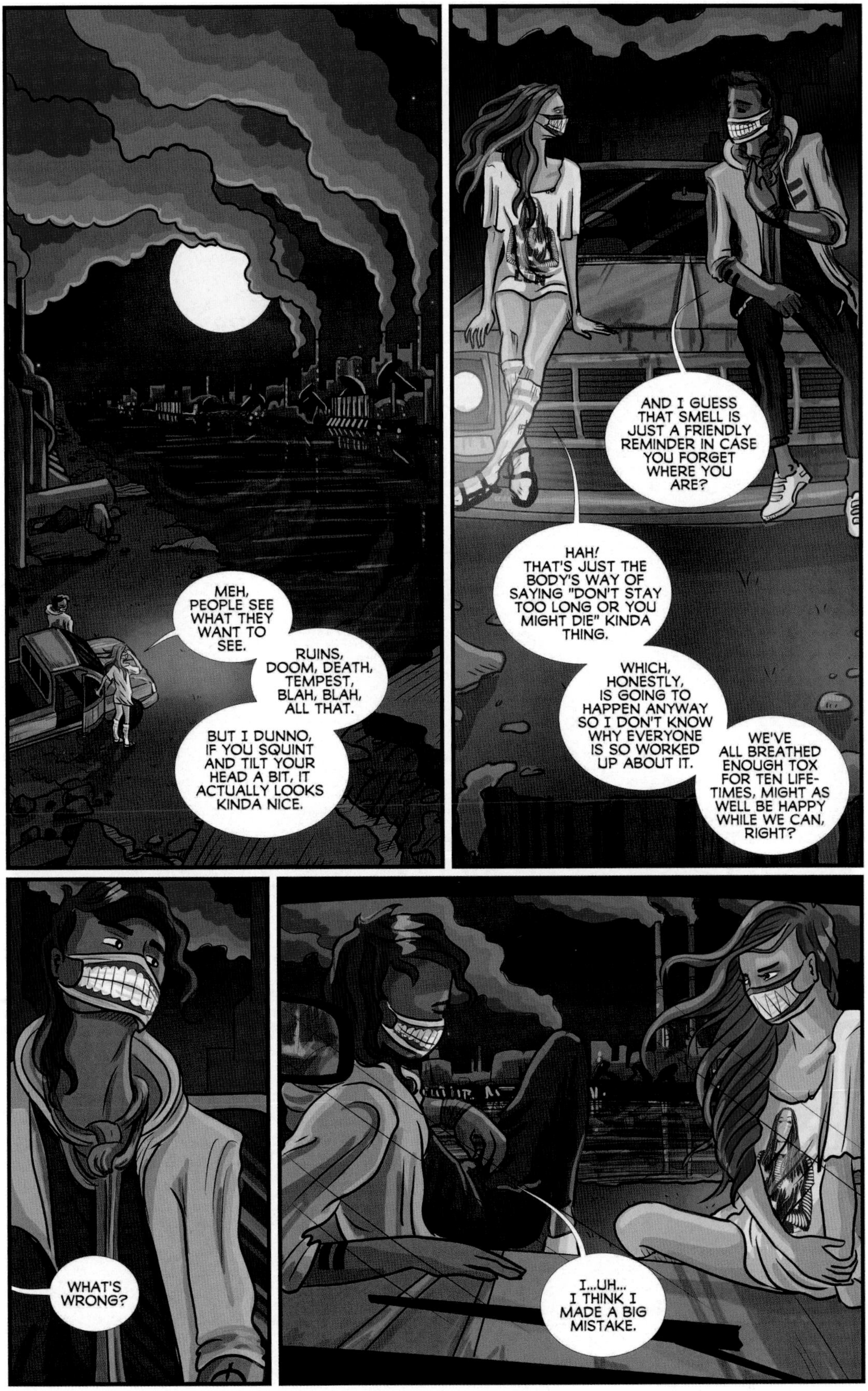
MEH, PEOPLE SEE WHAT THEY WANT TO SEE.
RUINS, DOOM, DEATH, TEMPEST, BLAH, BLAH, ALL THAT.
BUT I DUNNO, IF YOU SQUINT AND TILT YOUR HEAD A BIT, IT ACTUALLY LOOKS KINDA NICE.
AND I GUESS THAT SMELL IS JUST A FRIENDLY REMINDER IN CASE YOU FORGET WHERE YOU ARE?
HAH! THAT'S JUST THE BODY'S WAY OF SAYING "DON'T STAY TOO LONG OR YOU MIGHT DIE" KINDA THING.
WHICH, HONESTLY, IS GOING TO HAPPEN ANYWAY SO I DON'T KNOW WHY EVERYONE IS SO WORKED UP ABOUT IT.
WE'VE ALL BREATHED ENOUGH TOX FOR TEN LIFE-TIMES, MIGHT AS WELL BE HAPPY WHILE WE CAN, RIGHT?
WHAT'S WRONG?
I...UH... I THINK I MADE A BIG MISTAKE.

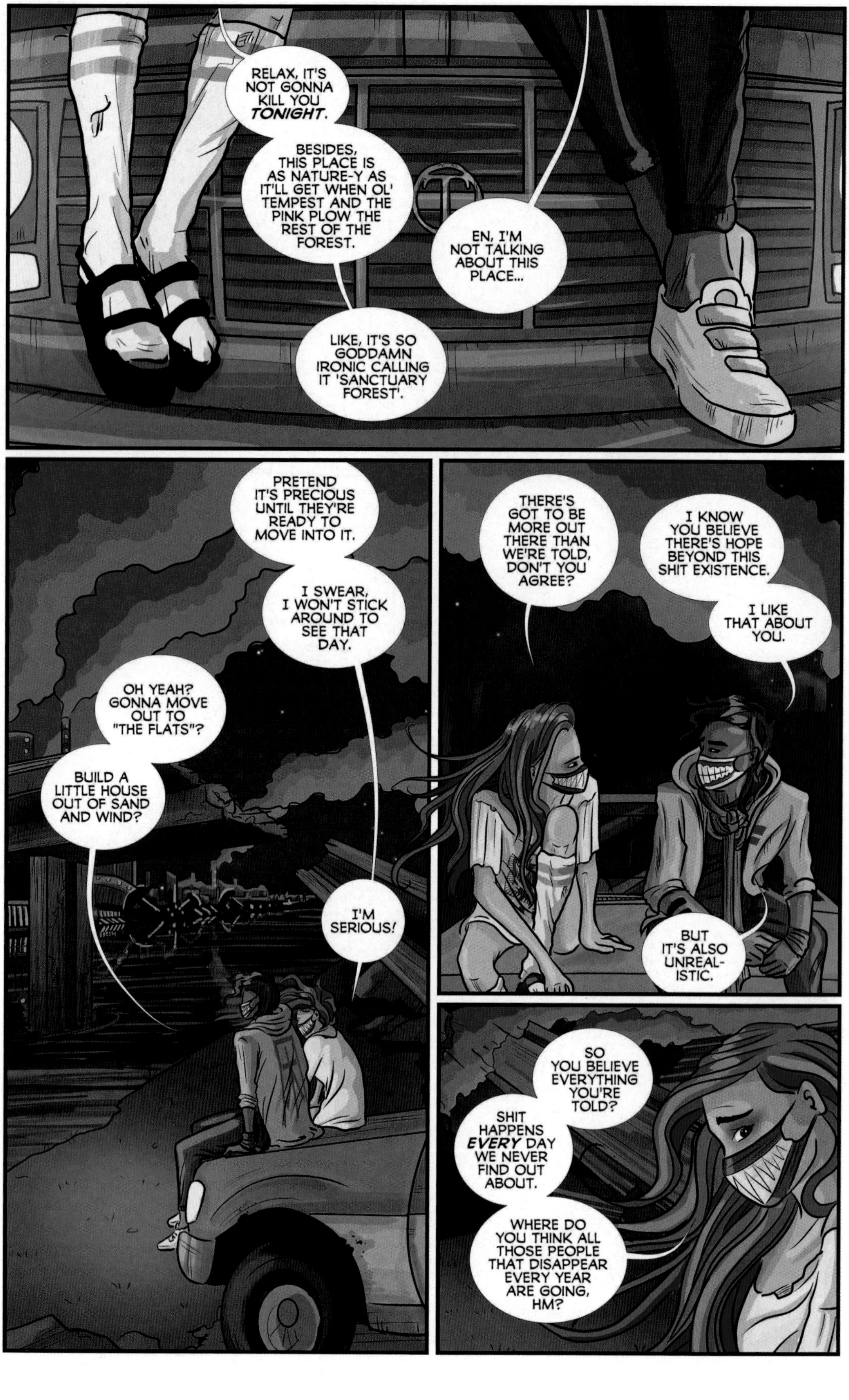
RELAX, IT'S NOT GONNA KILL YOU *TONIGHT*.
BESIDES, THIS PLACE IS AS NATURE-Y AS IT'LL GET WHEN OL' TEMPEST AND THE PINK PLOW THE REST OF THE FOREST.
EN, I'M NOT TALKING ABOUT THIS PLACE...
LIKE, IT'S SO GODDAMN IRONIC CALLING IT 'SANCTUARY FOREST'.
PRETEND IT'S PRECIOUS UNTIL THEY'RE READY TO MOVE INTO IT.
I SWEAR, I WON'T STICK AROUND TO SEE THAT DAY.
OH YEAH? GONNA MOVE OUT TO "THE FLATS"?
BUILD A LITTLE HOUSE OUT OF SAND AND WIND?
I'M SERIOUS!
THERE'S GOT TO BE MORE OUT THERE THAN WE'RE TOLD, DON'T YOU AGREE?
I KNOW YOU BELIEVE THERE'S HOPE BEYOND THIS SHIT EXISTENCE.
I LIKE THAT ABOUT YOU.
BUT IT'S ALSO UNREAL-ISTIC.
SO YOU BELIEVE EVERYTHING YOU'RE TOLD?
SHIT HAPPENS *EVERY* DAY WE NEVER FIND OUT ABOUT.
WHERE DO YOU THINK ALL THOSE PEOPLE THAT DISAPPEAR EVERY YEAR ARE GOING, HM?

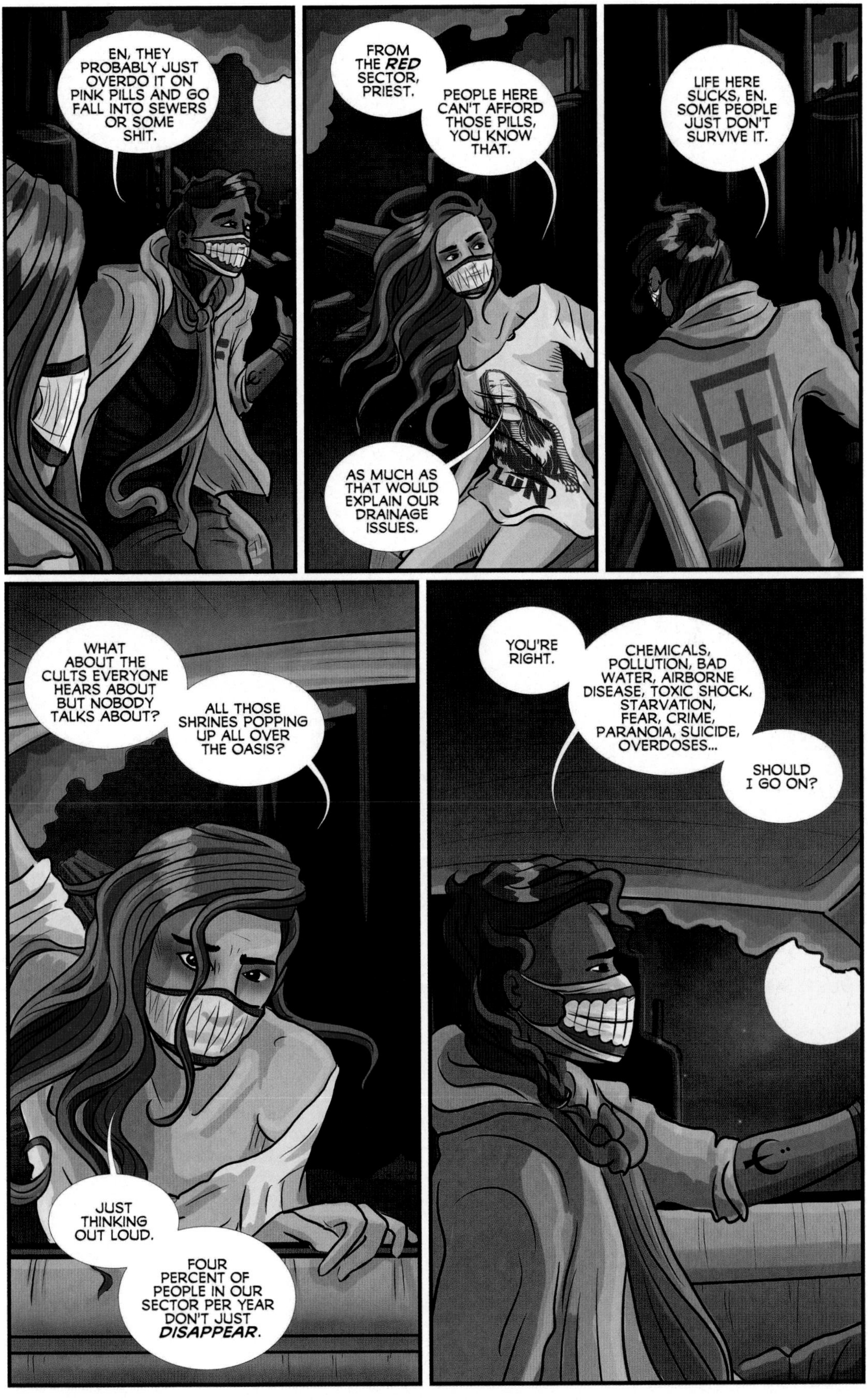

EN, THEY PROBABLY JUST OVERDO IT ON PINK PILLS AND GO FALL INTO SEWERS OR SOME SHIT.
FROM THE ***RED*** SECTOR, PRIEST.
PEOPLE HERE CAN'T AFFORD THOSE PILLS, YOU KNOW THAT.
AS MUCH AS THAT WOULD EXPLAIN OUR DRAINAGE ISSUES.
LIFE HERE SUCKS, EN. SOME PEOPLE JUST DON'T SURVIVE IT.
WHAT ABOUT THE CULTS EVERYONE HEARS ABOUT BUT NOBODY TALKS ABOUT?
ALL THOSE SHRINES POPPING UP ALL OVER THE OASIS?
JUST THINKING OUT LOUD.
FOUR PERCENT OF PEOPLE IN OUR SECTOR PER YEAR DON'T JUST ***DISAPPEAR***.
YOU'RE RIGHT.
CHEMICALS, POLLUTION, BAD WATER, AIRBORNE DISEASE, TOXIC SHOCK, STARVATION, FEAR, CRIME, PARANOIA, SUICIDE, OVERDOSES...
SHOULD I GO ON?

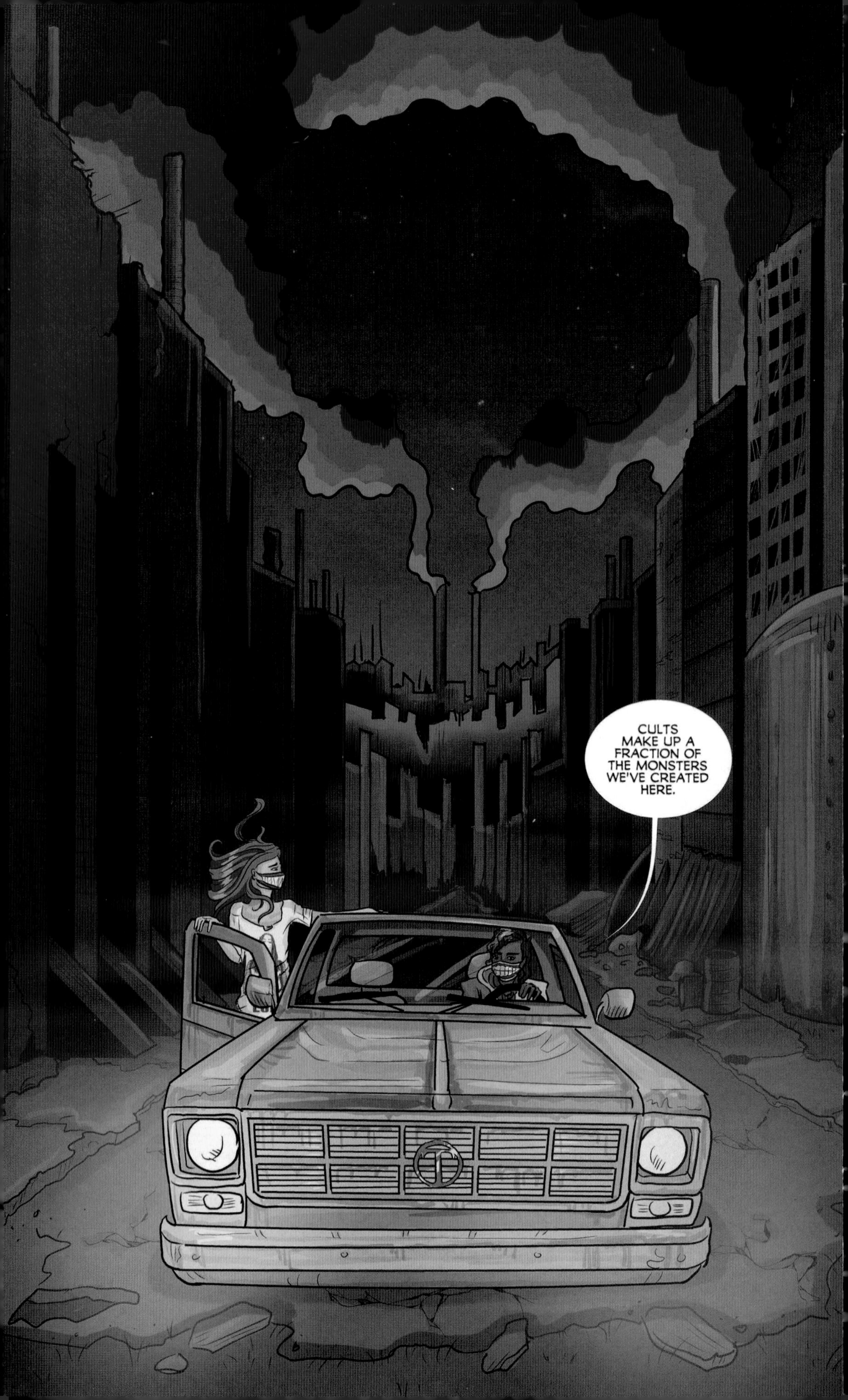
CULTS MAKE UP A FRACTION OF THE MONSTERS WE'VE CREATED HERE.

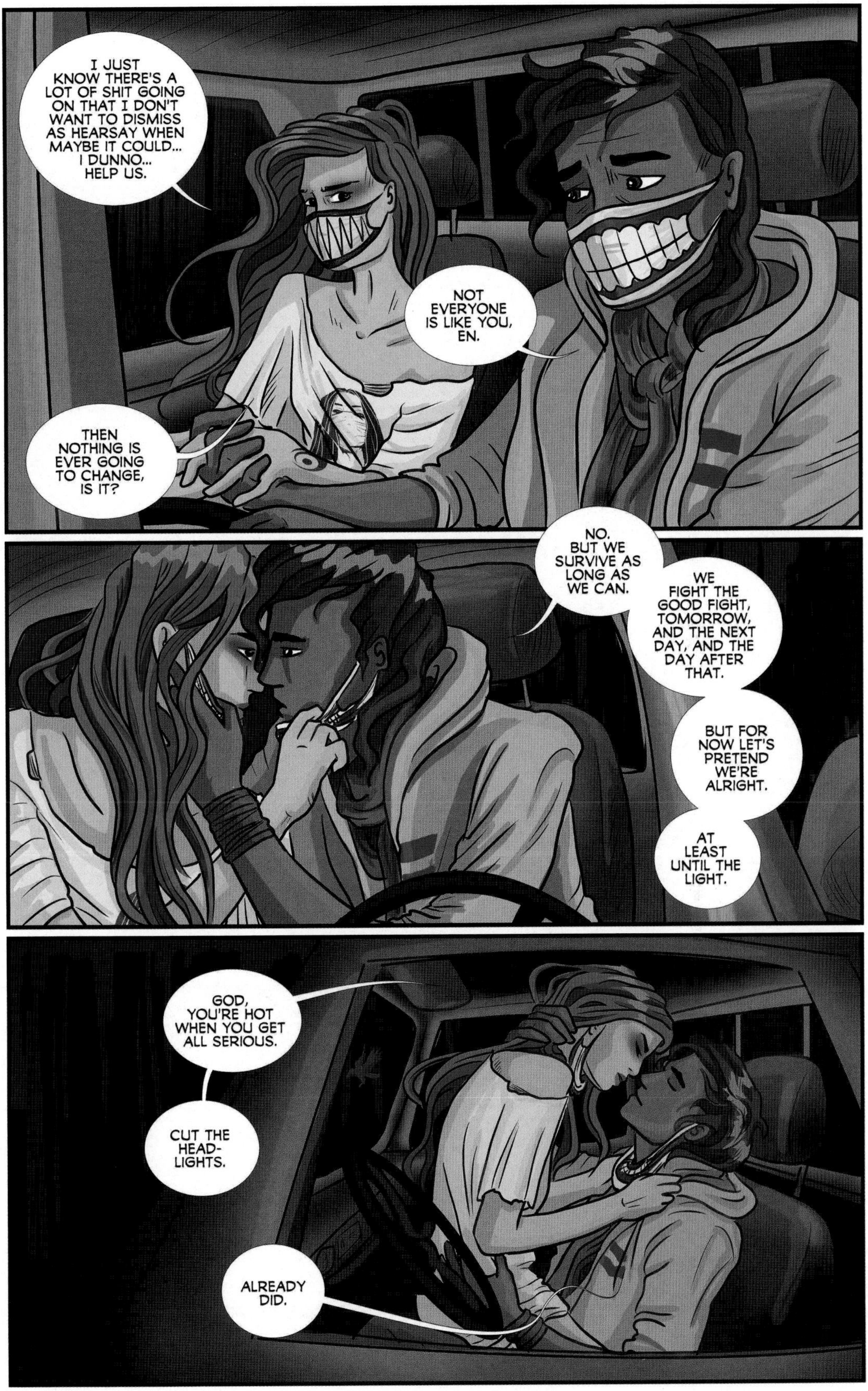
I JUST KNOW THERE'S A LOT OF SHIT GOING ON THAT I DON'T WANT TO DISMISS AS HEARSAY WHEN MAYBE IT COULD... I DUNNO... HELP US.
NOT EVERYONE IS LIKE YOU, EN.
THEN NOTHING IS EVER GOING TO CHANGE, IS IT?
NO. BUT WE SURVIVE AS LONG AS WE CAN.
WE FIGHT THE GOOD FIGHT, TOMORROW, AND THE NEXT DAY, AND THE DAY AFTER THAT.
BUT FOR NOW LET'S PRETEND WE'RE ALRIGHT.
AT LEAST UNTIL THE LIGHT.
GOD, YOU'RE HOT WHEN YOU GET ALL SERIOUS.
CUT THE HEAD-LIGHTS.
ALREADY DID.

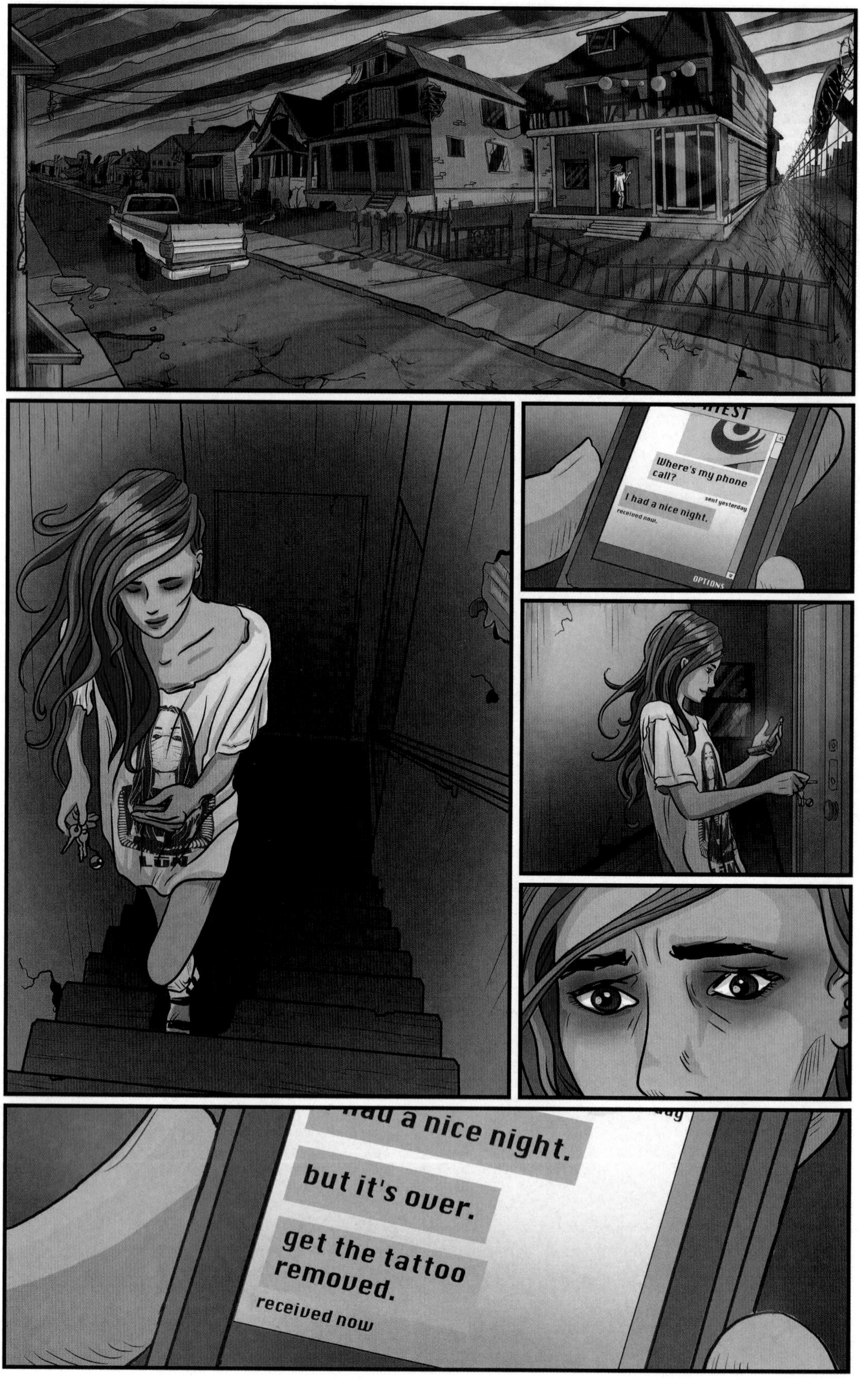
Where's my phone call?
sent yesterday
I had a nice night.
received now.
OPTIONS
had a nice night.
but it's over.
get the tattoo removed.
received now

CHAPTER FOUR: SAVAGE

http://mxt.pe/savages

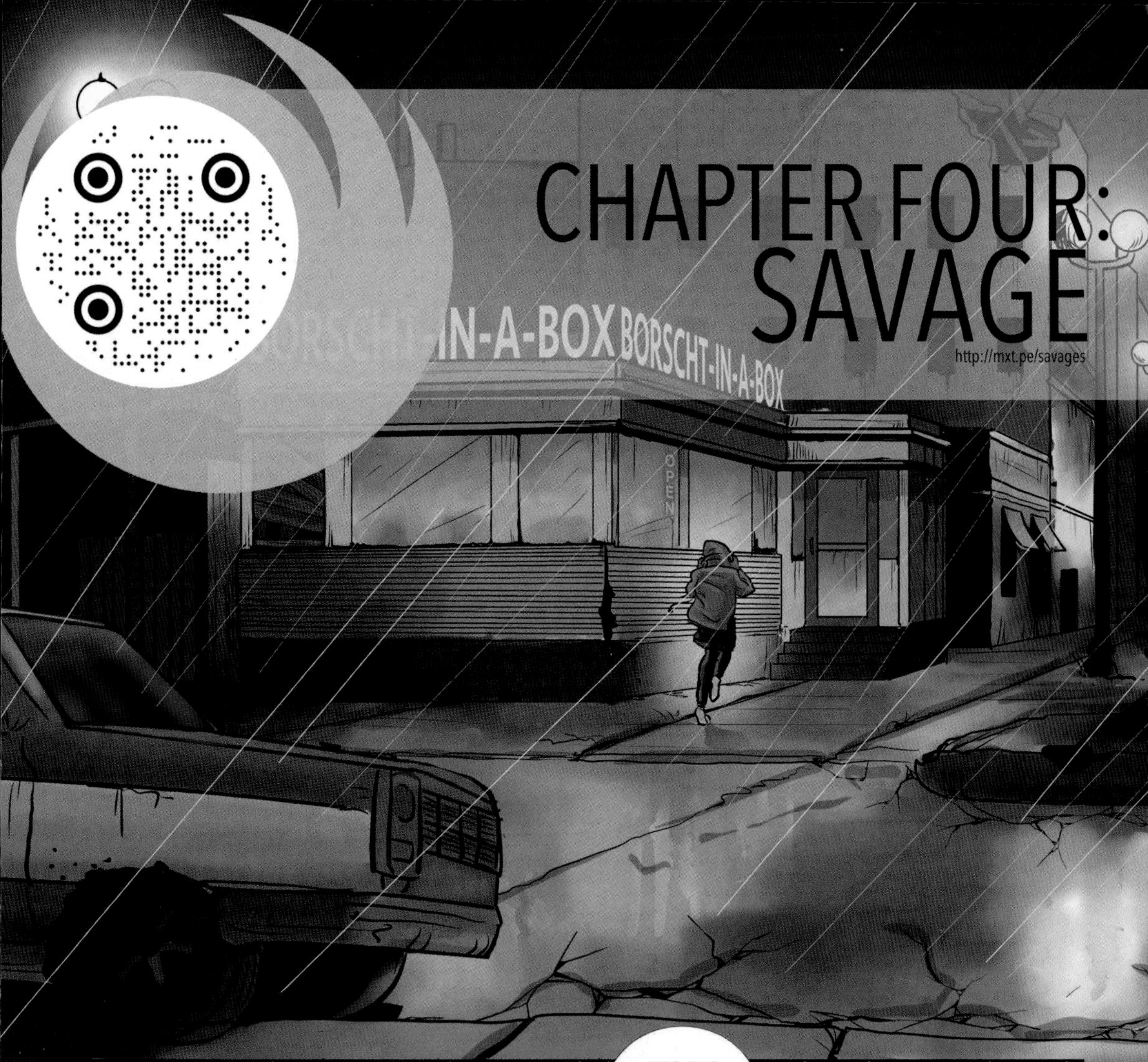
BORSCHT-IN-A-BOX
BORSCHT-IN-A-BOX
OPEN

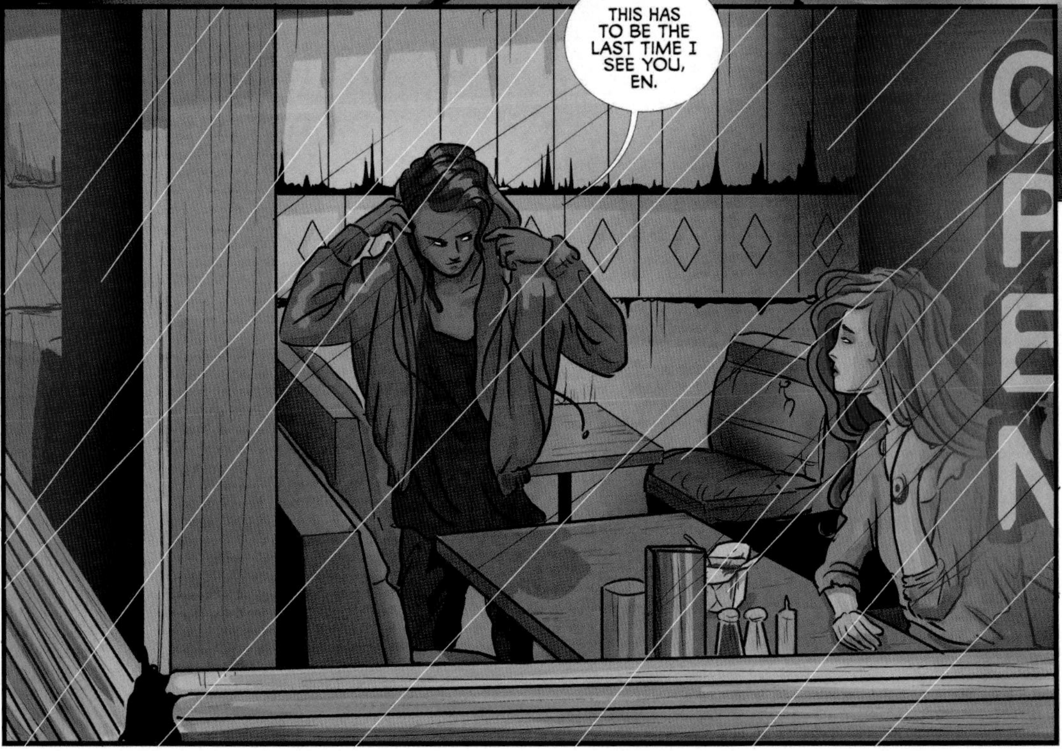
THIS HAS TO BE THE LAST TIME I SEE YOU, EN.
OPEN

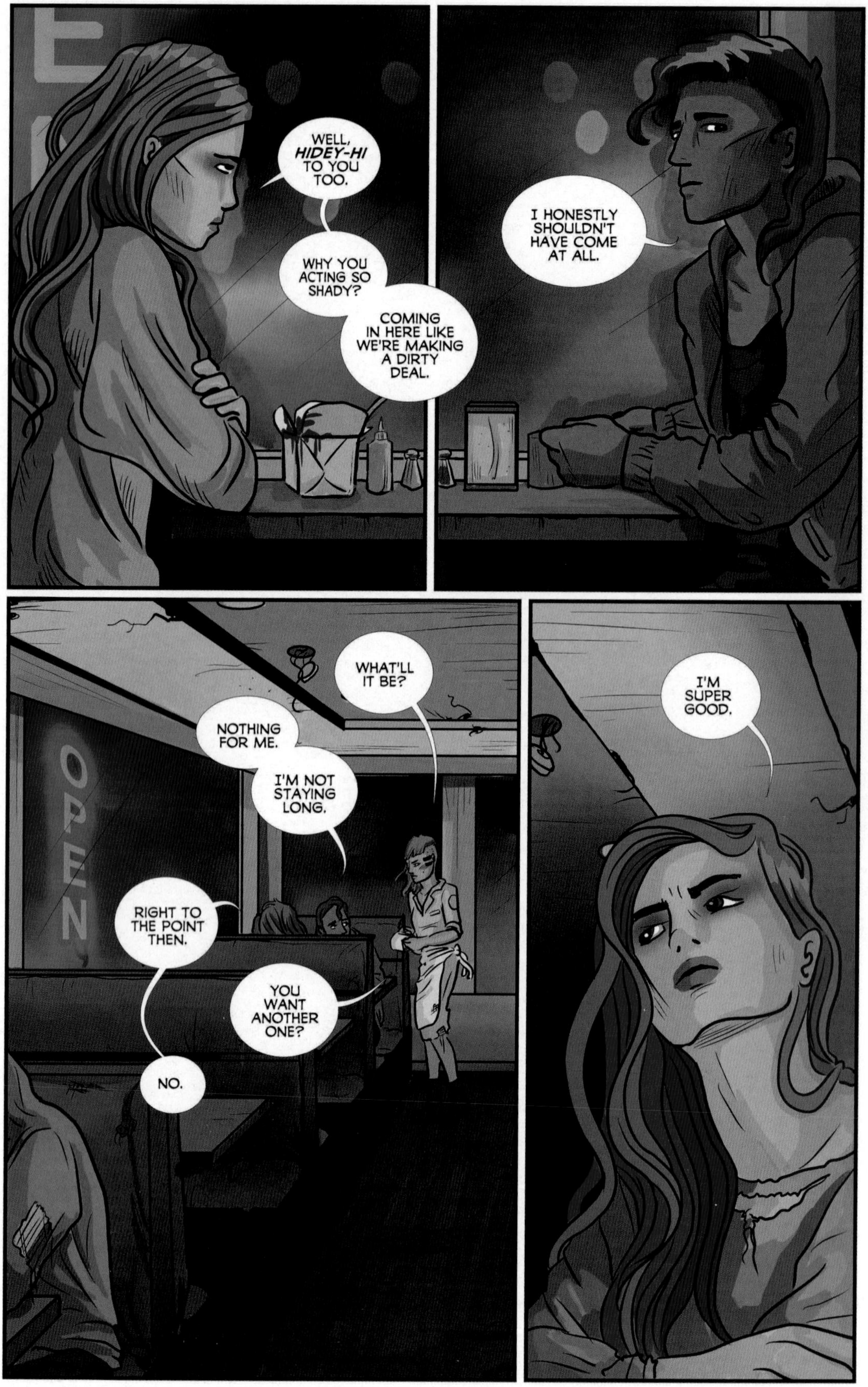
WELL, ***HIDEY-HI*** TO YOU TOO.
WHY YOU ACTING SO SHADY?
COMING IN HERE LIKE WE'RE MAKING A DIRTY DEAL.
I HONESTLY SHOULDN'T HAVE COME AT ALL.
OPEN
WHAT'LL IT BE?
NOTHING FOR ME.
I'M NOT STAYING LONG.
RIGHT TO THE POINT THEN.
YOU WANT ANOTHER ONE?
NO.
I'M SUPER GOOD.

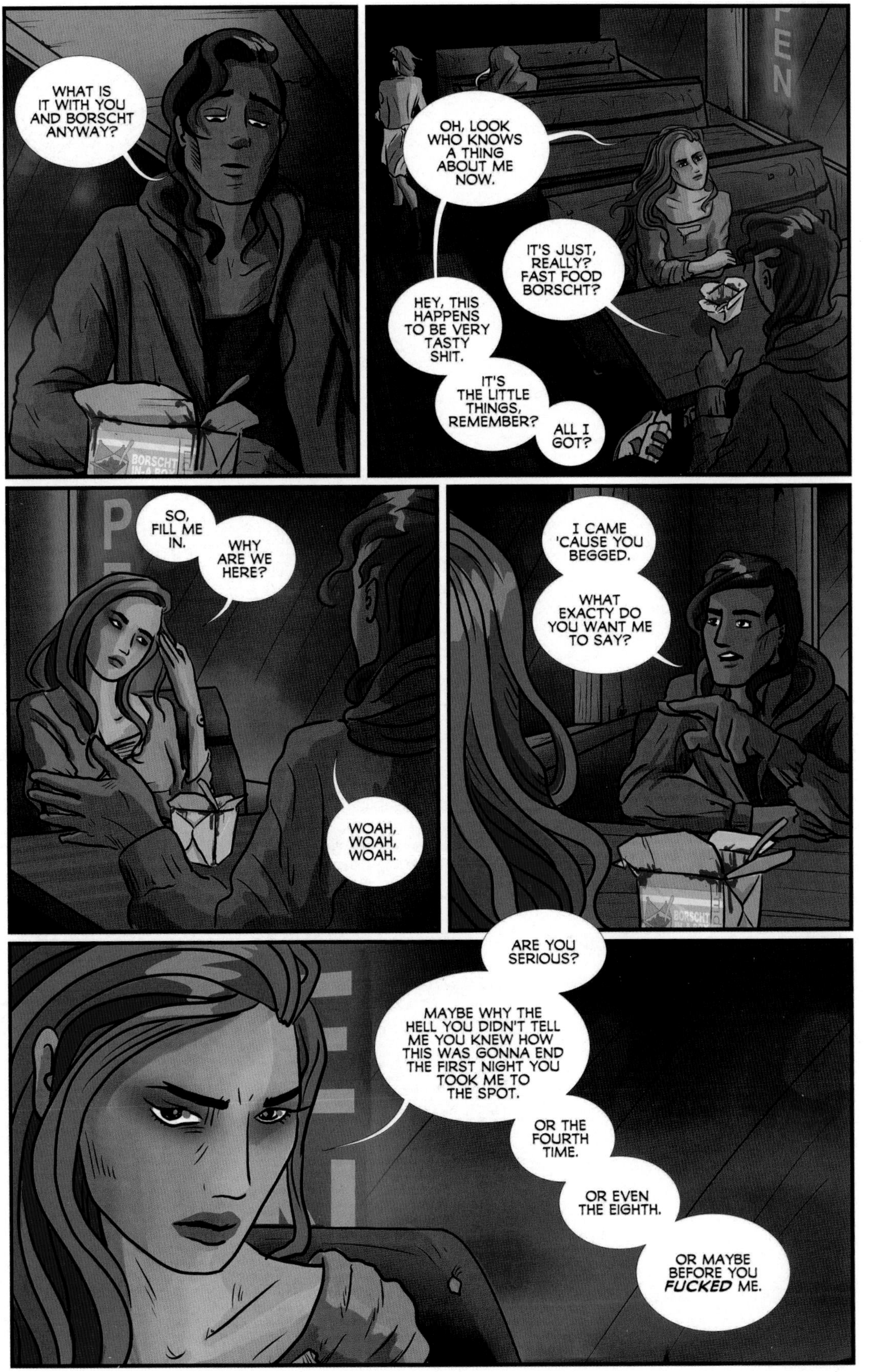
WHAT IS IT WITH YOU AND BORSCHT ANYWAY?
BORSCHT IN-A-BOX
OH, LOOK WHO KNOWS A THING ABOUT ME NOW.
IT'S JUST, REALLY? FAST FOOD BORSCHT?
HEY, THIS HAPPENS TO BE VERY TASTY SHIT.
IT'S THE LITTLE THINGS, REMEMBER?
ALL I GOT?
SO, FILL ME IN.
WHY ARE WE HERE?
WOAH, WOAH, WOAH.
I CAME 'CAUSE YOU BEGGED.
WHAT EXACTY DO YOU WANT ME TO SAY?
ARE YOU SERIOUS?
MAYBE WHY THE HELL YOU DIDN'T TELL ME YOU KNEW HOW THIS WAS GONNA END THE FIRST NIGHT YOU TOOK ME TO THE SPOT.
OR THE FOURTH TIME.
OR EVEN THE EIGHTH.
OR MAYBE BEFORE YOU *FUCKED* ME.

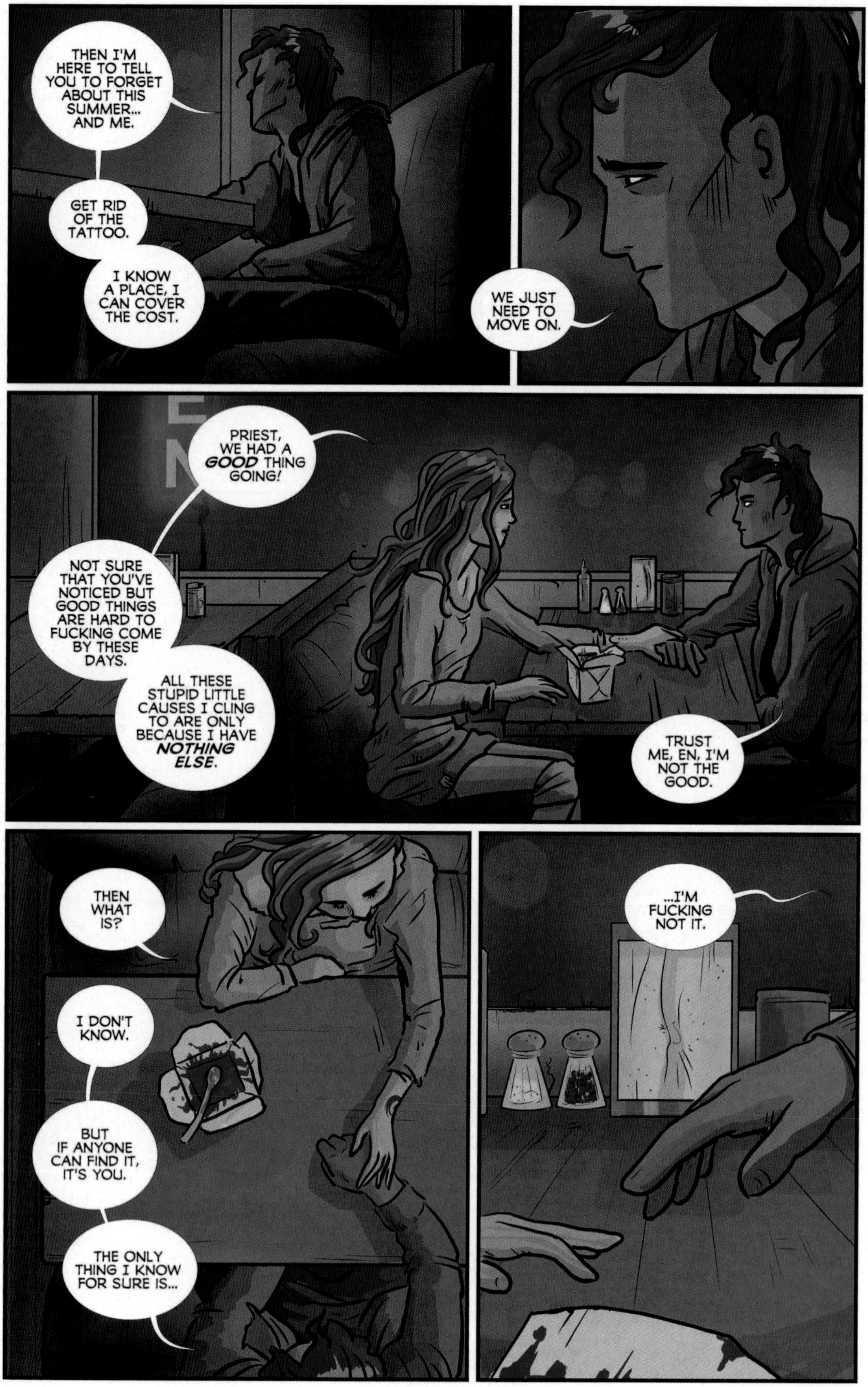
THEN I'M HERE TO TELL YOU TO FORGET ABOUT THIS SUMMER... AND ME.
GET RID OF THE TATTOO.
I KNOW A PLACE, I CAN COVER THE COST.
WE JUST NEED TO MOVE ON.
PRIEST, WE HAD A *GOOD* THING GOING!
NOT SURE THAT YOU'VE NOTICED BUT GOOD THINGS ARE HARD TO FUCKING COME BY THESE DAYS.
ALL THESE STUPID LITTLE CAUSES I CLING TO ARE ONLY BECAUSE I HAVE ***NOTHING ELSE***.
TRUST ME, EN, I'M NOT THE GOOD.
THEN WHAT IS?
I DON'T KNOW.
BUT IF ANYONE CAN FIND IT, IT'S YOU.
THE ONLY THING I KNOW FOR SURE IS...
...I'M FUCKING NOT IT.

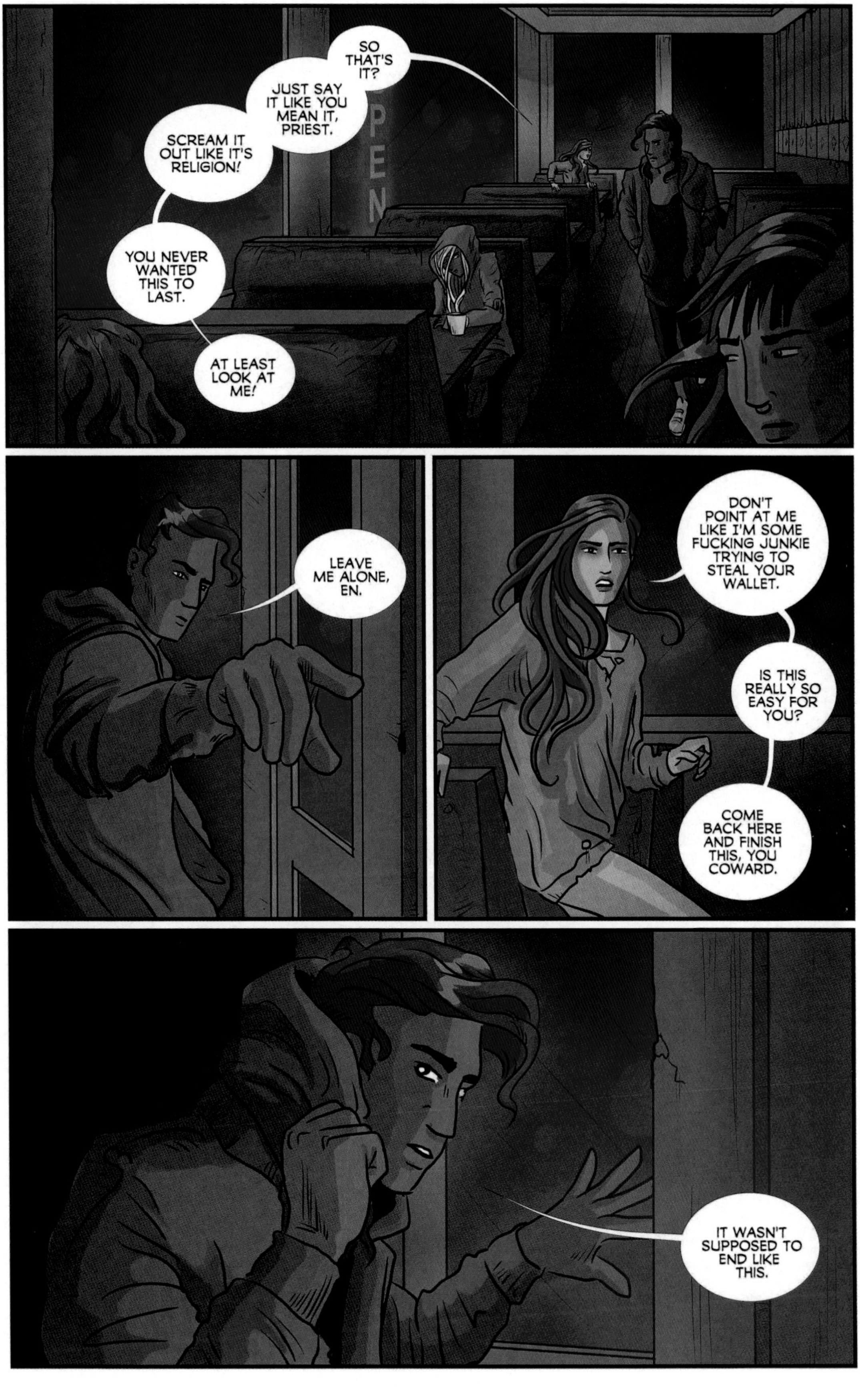
SO THAT'S IT?
JUST SAY IT LIKE YOU MEAN IT, PRIEST.
SCREAM IT OUT LIKE IT'S RELIGION!
YOU NEVER WANTED THIS TO LAST.
AT LEAST LOOK AT ME!
LEAVE ME ALONE, EN.
DON'T POINT AT ME LIKE I'M SOME FUCKING JUNKIE TRYING TO STEAL YOUR WALLET.
IS THIS REALLY SO EASY FOR YOU?
COME BACK HERE AND FINISH THIS, YOU COWARD.
IT WASN'T SUPPOSED TO END LIKE THIS.

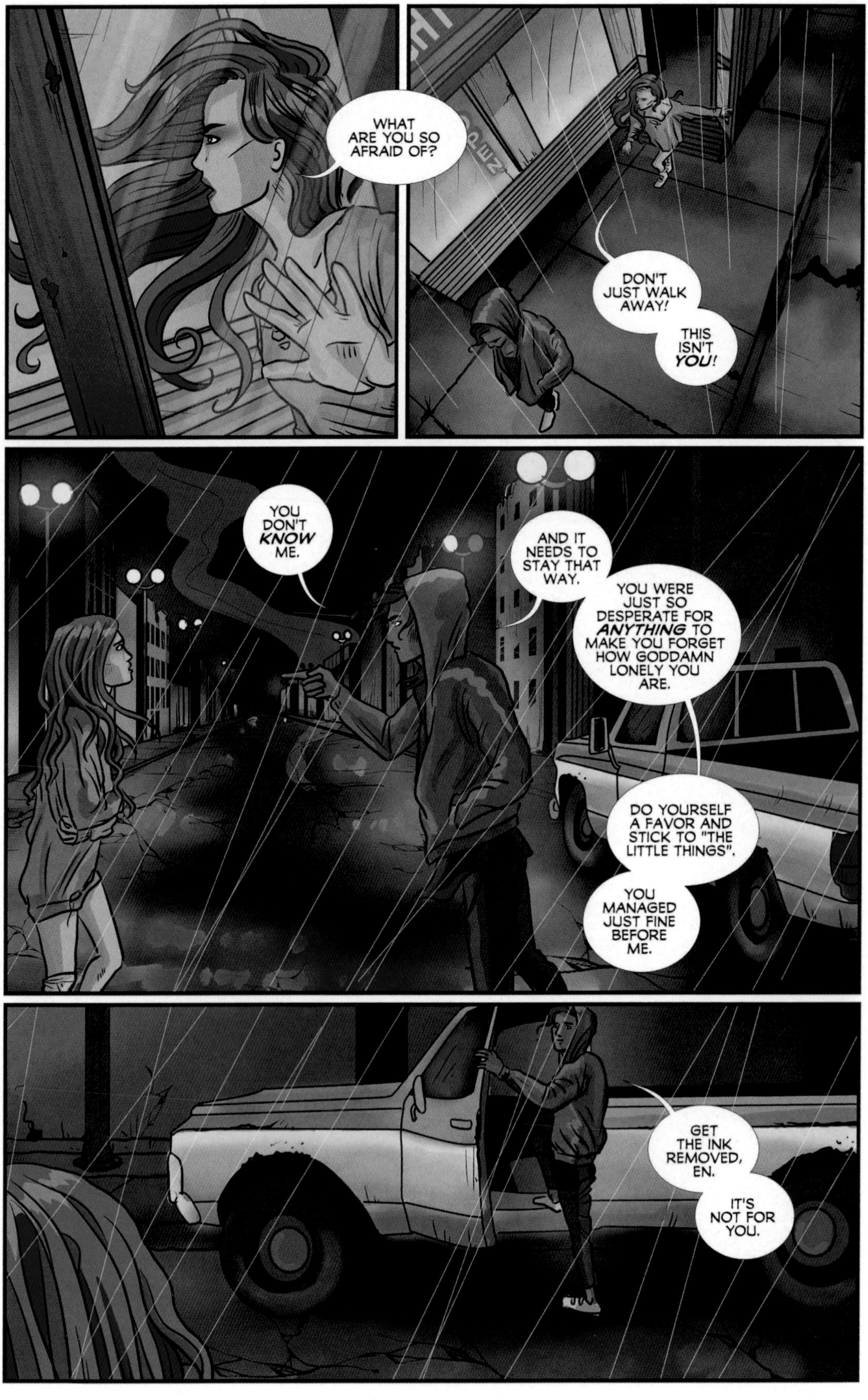
WHAT ARE YOU SO AFRAID OF?
DON'T JUST WALK AWAY!
THIS ISN'T *YOU*!
YOU DON'T *KNOW* ME.
AND IT NEEDS TO STAY THAT WAY.
YOU WERE JUST SO DESPERATE FOR *ANYTHING* TO MAKE YOU FORGET HOW GODDAMN LONELY YOU ARE.
DO YOURSELF A FAVOR AND STICK TO "THE LITTLE THINGS".
YOU MANAGED JUST FINE BEFORE ME.
GET THE INK REMOVED, EN.
IT'S NOT FOR YOU.

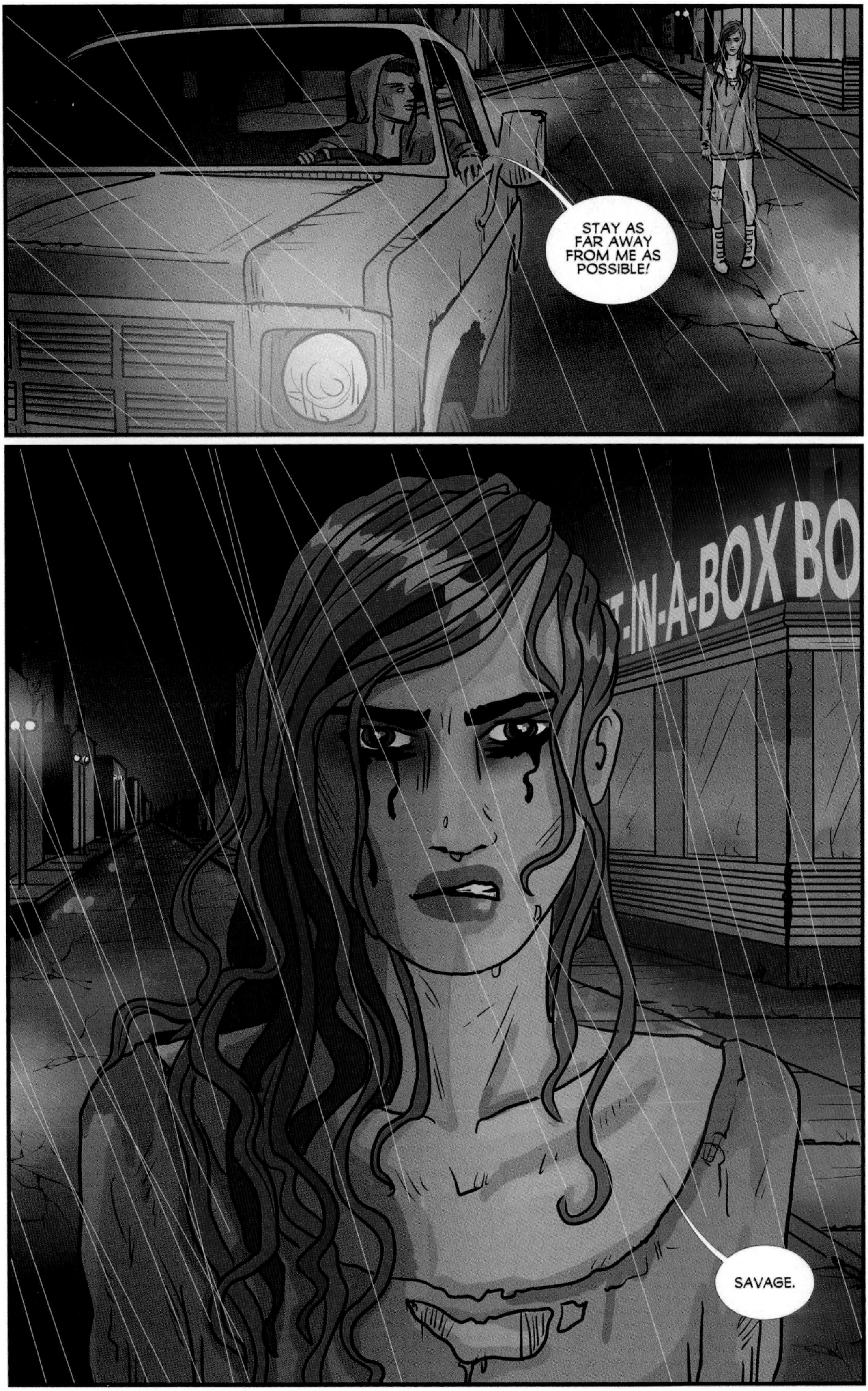
STAY AS FAR AWAY FROM ME AS POSSIBLE!
SAVAGE.

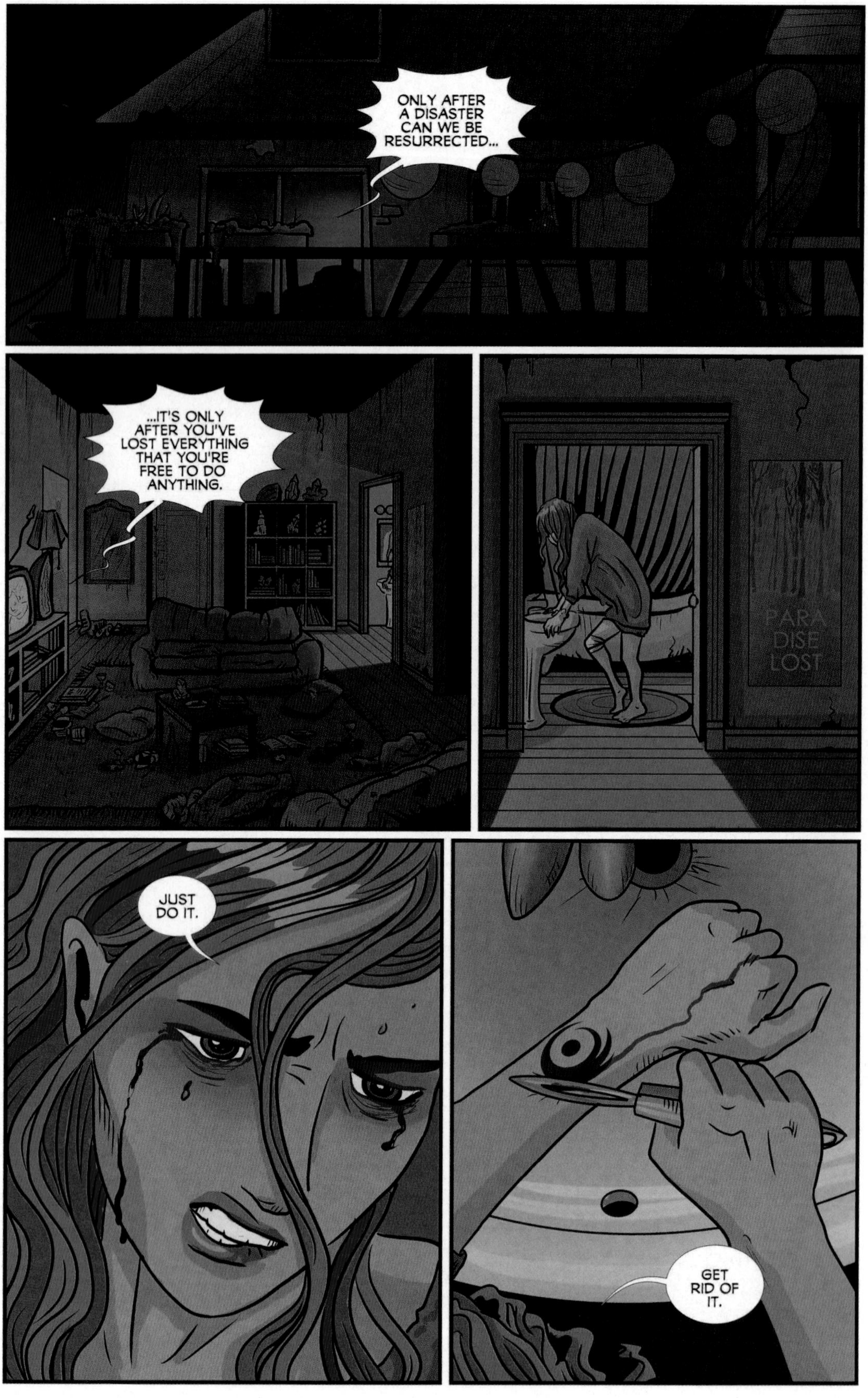
ONLY AFTER A DISASTER CAN WE BE RESURRECTED...
...IT'S ONLY AFTER YOU'VE LOST EVERYTHING THAT YOU'RE FREE TO DO ANYTHING.
PARA DISE LOST
JUST DO IT.
GET RID OF IT.

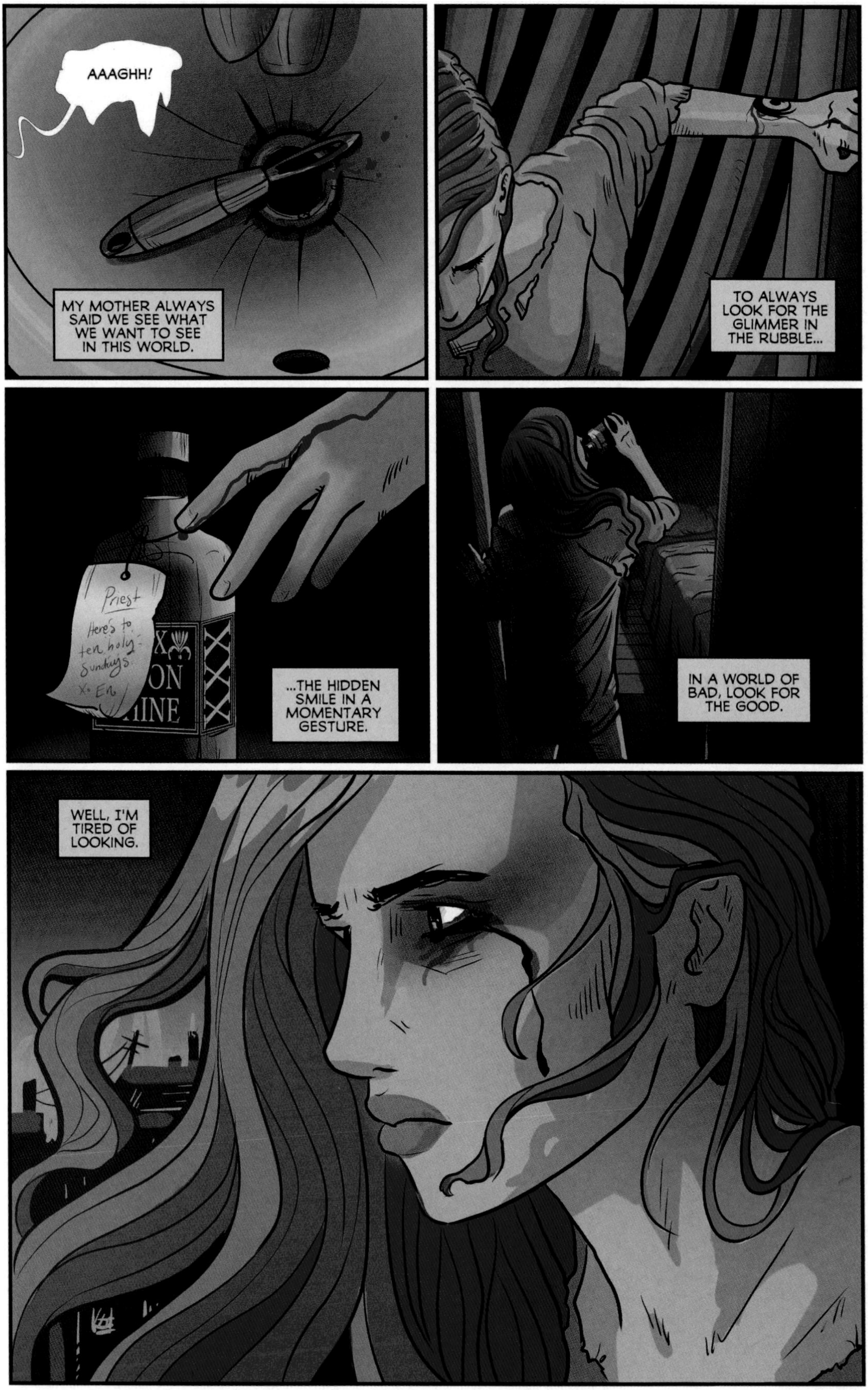
AAAGHH!
MY MOTHER ALWAYS SAID WE SEE WHAT WE WANT TO SEE IN THIS WORLD.
TO ALWAYS LOOK FOR THE GLIMMER IN THE RUBBLE...
Priest
Here's to ten holy Sundays. X. Em
...THE HIDDEN SMILE IN A MOMENTARY GESTURE.
IN A WORLD OF BAD, LOOK FOR THE GOOD.
WELL, I'M TIRED OF LOOKING.

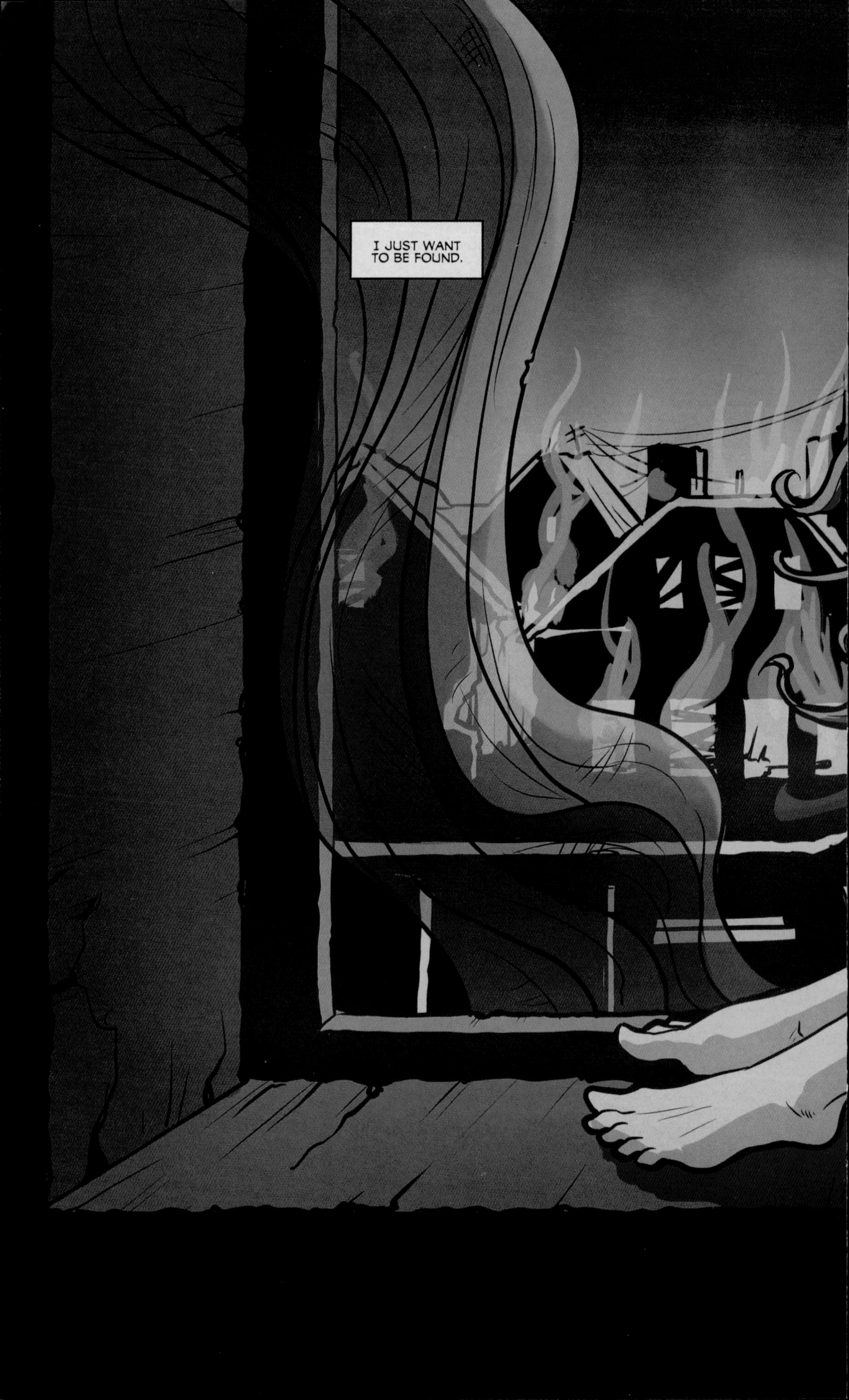
I JUST WANT TO BE FOUND.

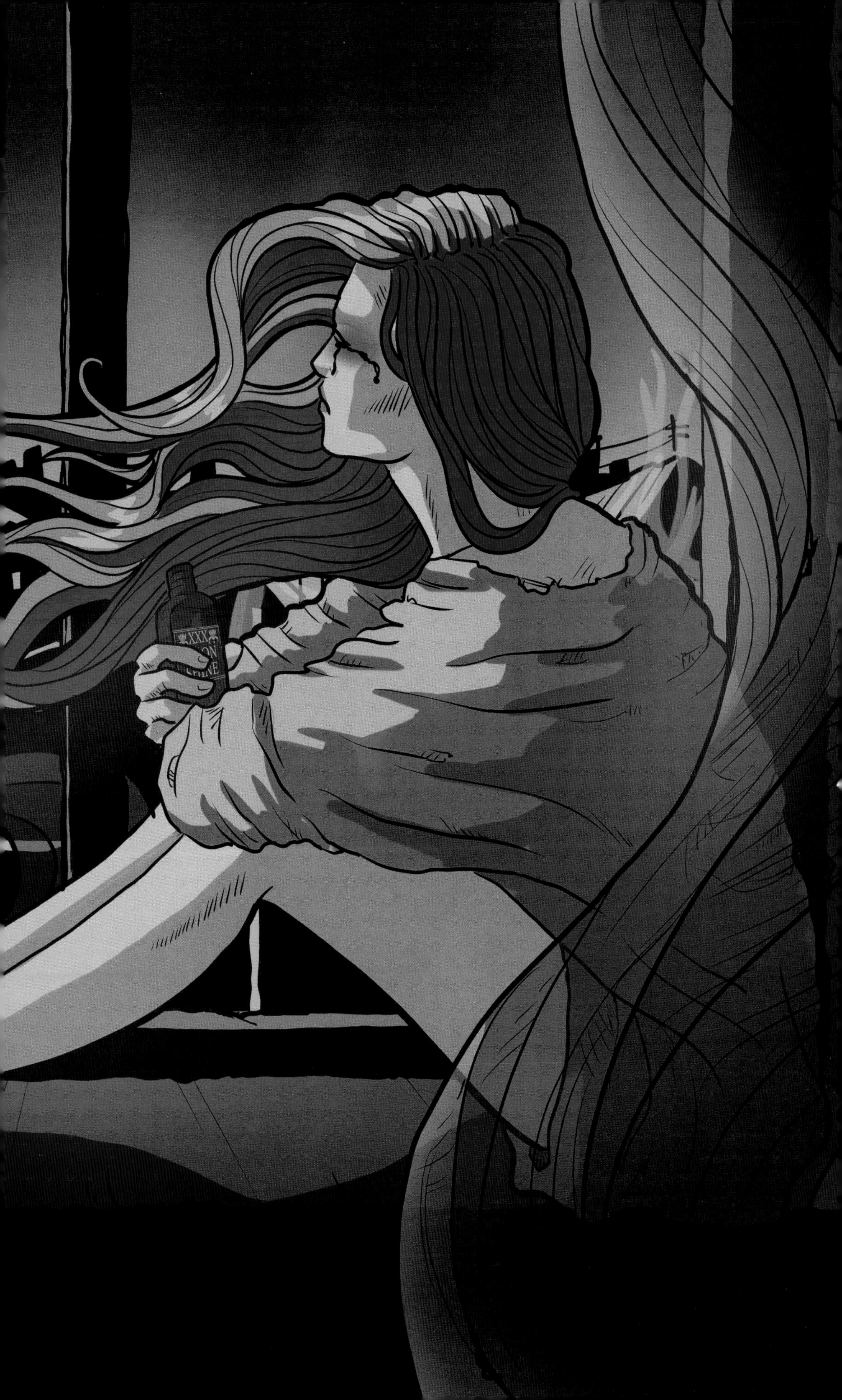
XXX

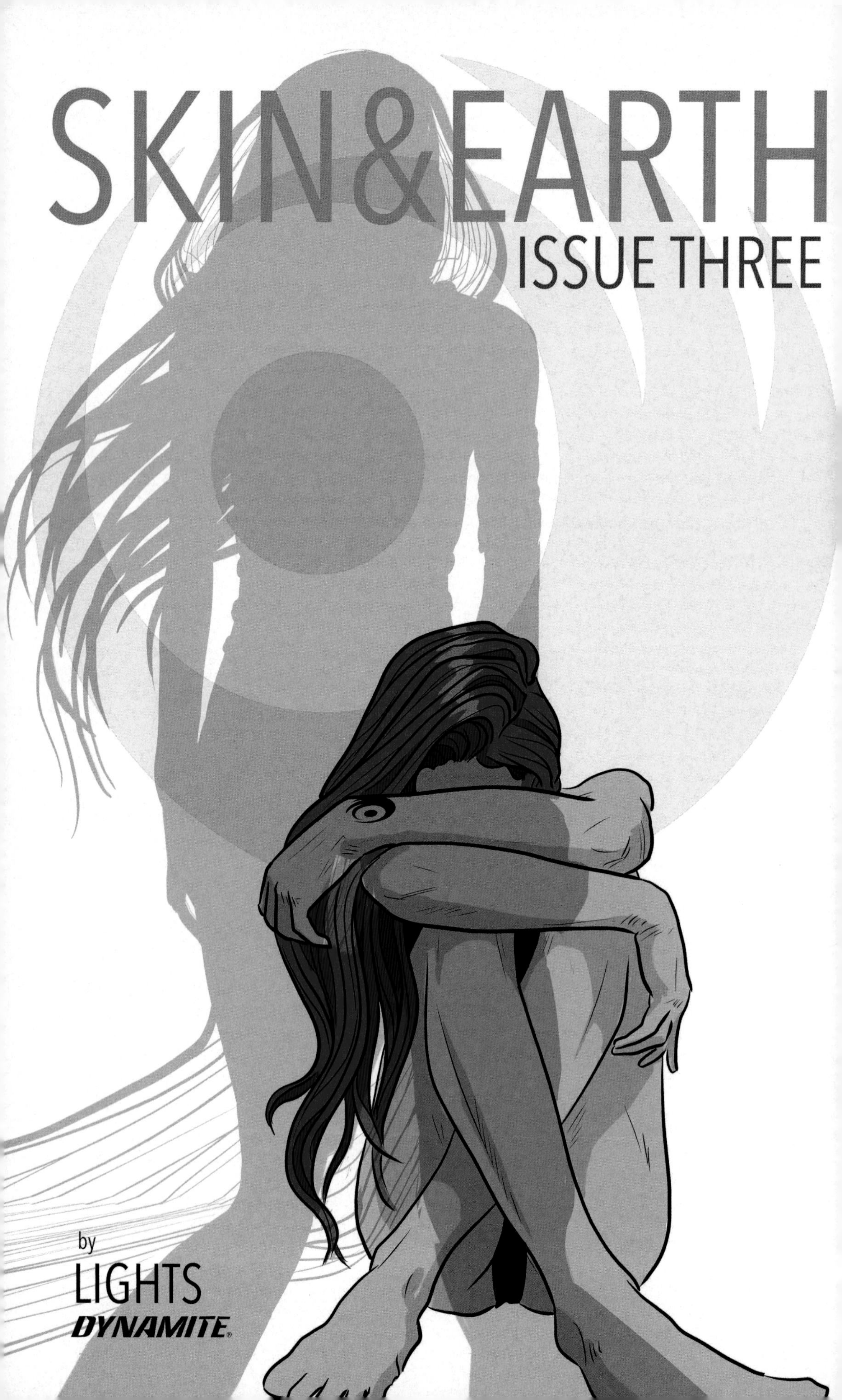
SKIN&EARTH
ISSUE THREE
by
LIGHTS
DYNAMITE

CHAPTER FIVE: NEW FEARS

http://mxt.pe/newfear

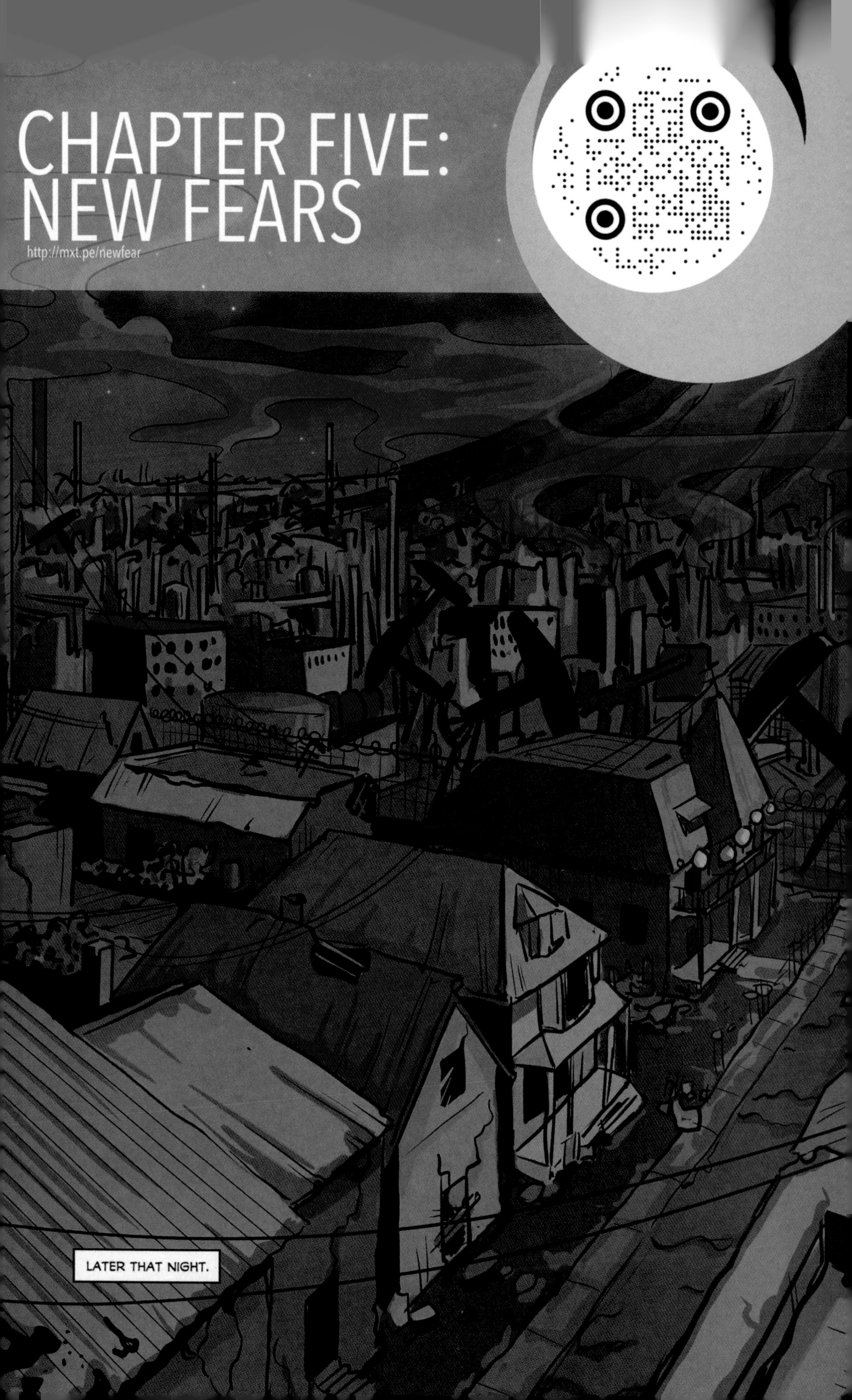
LATER THAT NIGHT.

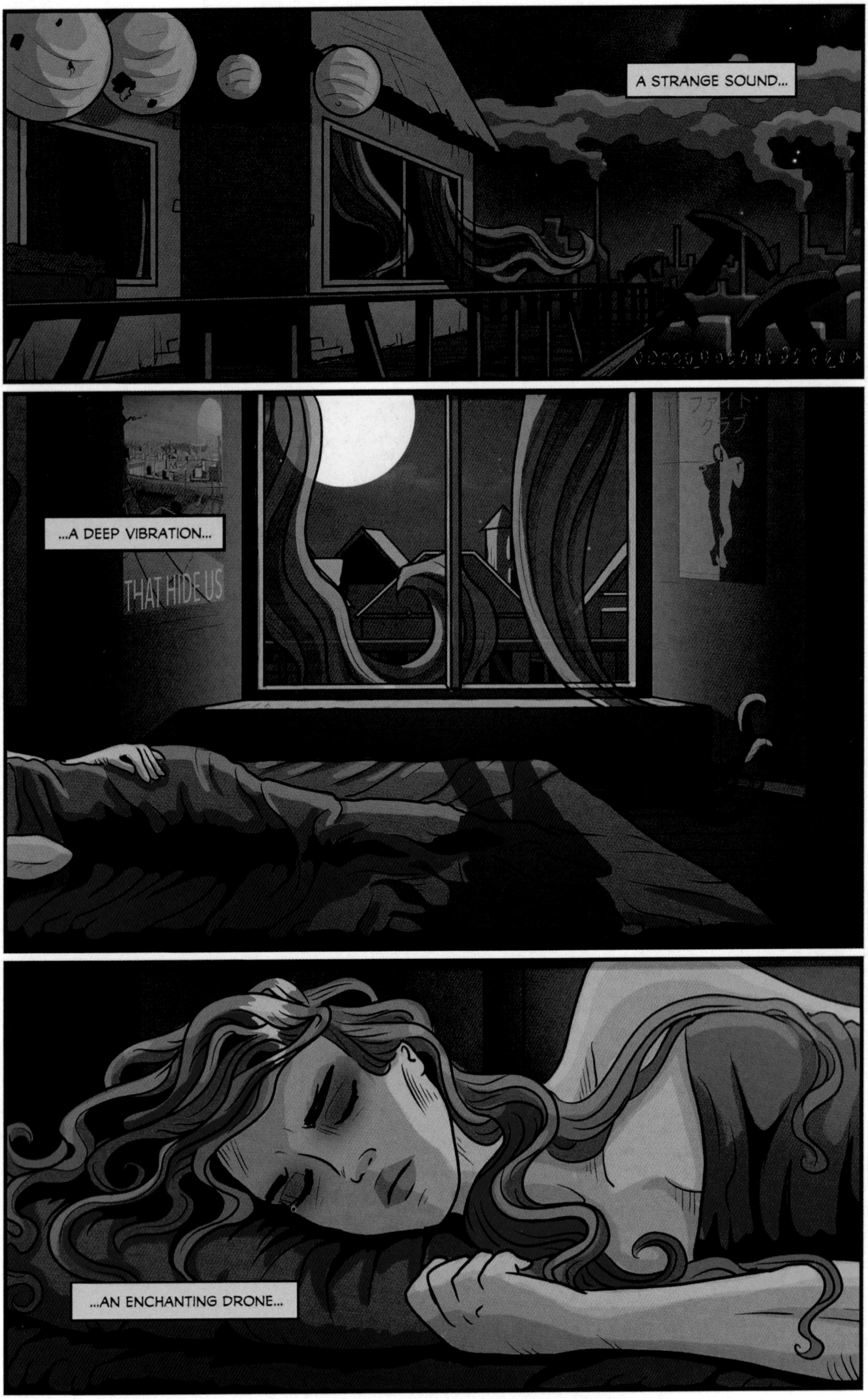
A STRANGE SOUND...
...A DEEP VIBRATION...
THAT HIDE US
ファイト
クラブ
...AN ENCHANTING DRONE...

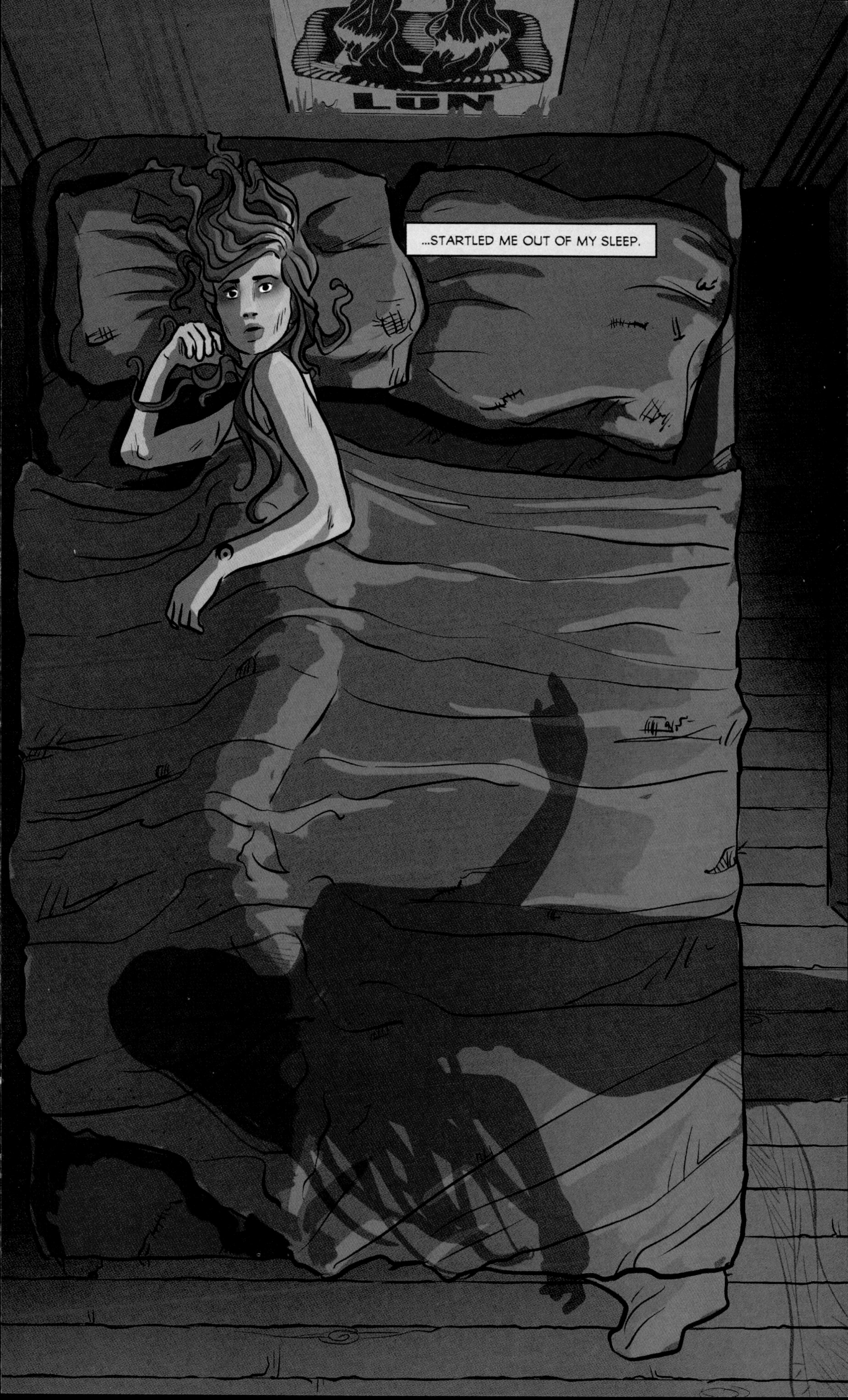
LŪN
...STARTLED ME OUT OF MY SLEEP.

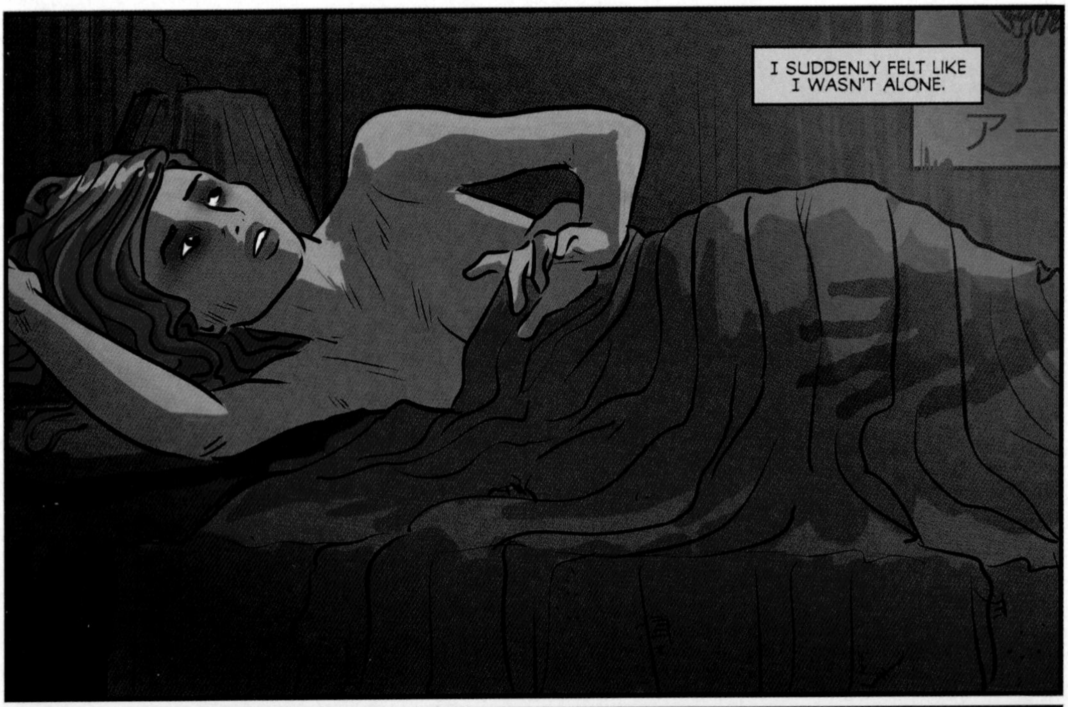
I SUDDENLY FELT LIKE I WASN'T ALONE.

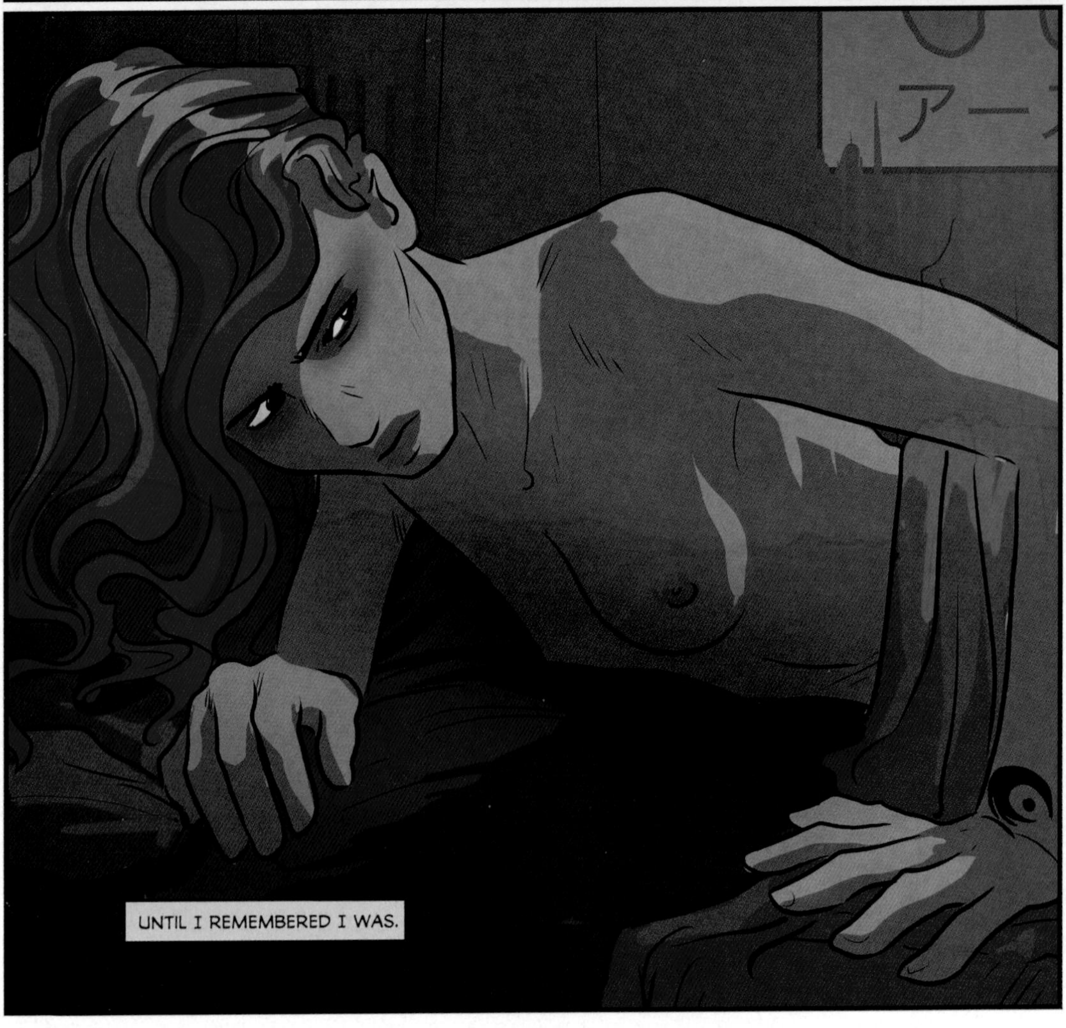
UNTIL I REMEMBERED I WAS.

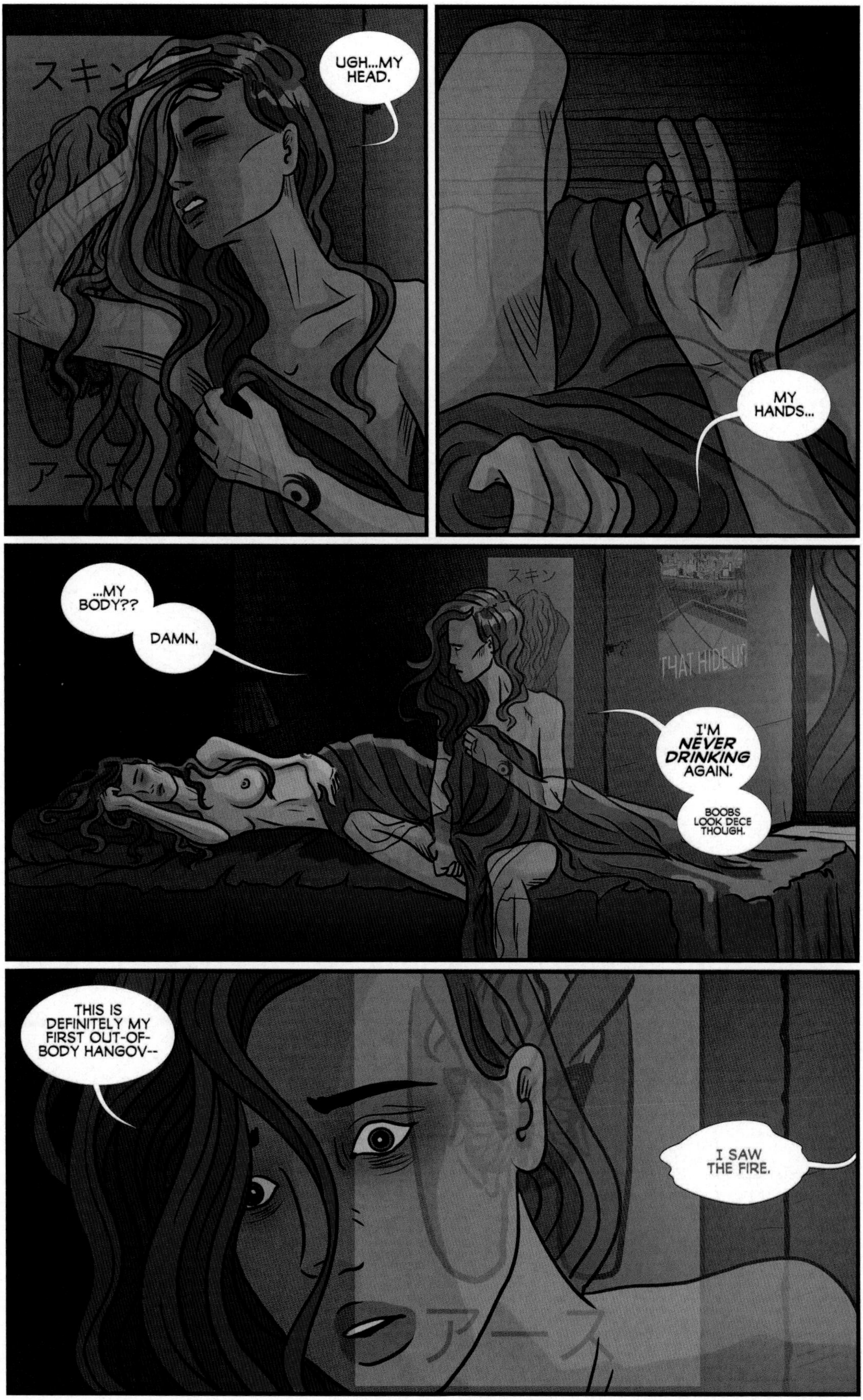

スキン
UGH...MY HEAD.
アース
MY HANDS...
...MY BODY??
DAMN.
スキン
I'M *NEVER DRINKING* AGAIN.
BOOBS LOOK DECE THOUGH.
THIS IS DEFINITELY MY FIRST OUT-OF-BODY HANGOV--
I SAW THE FIRE.
アース

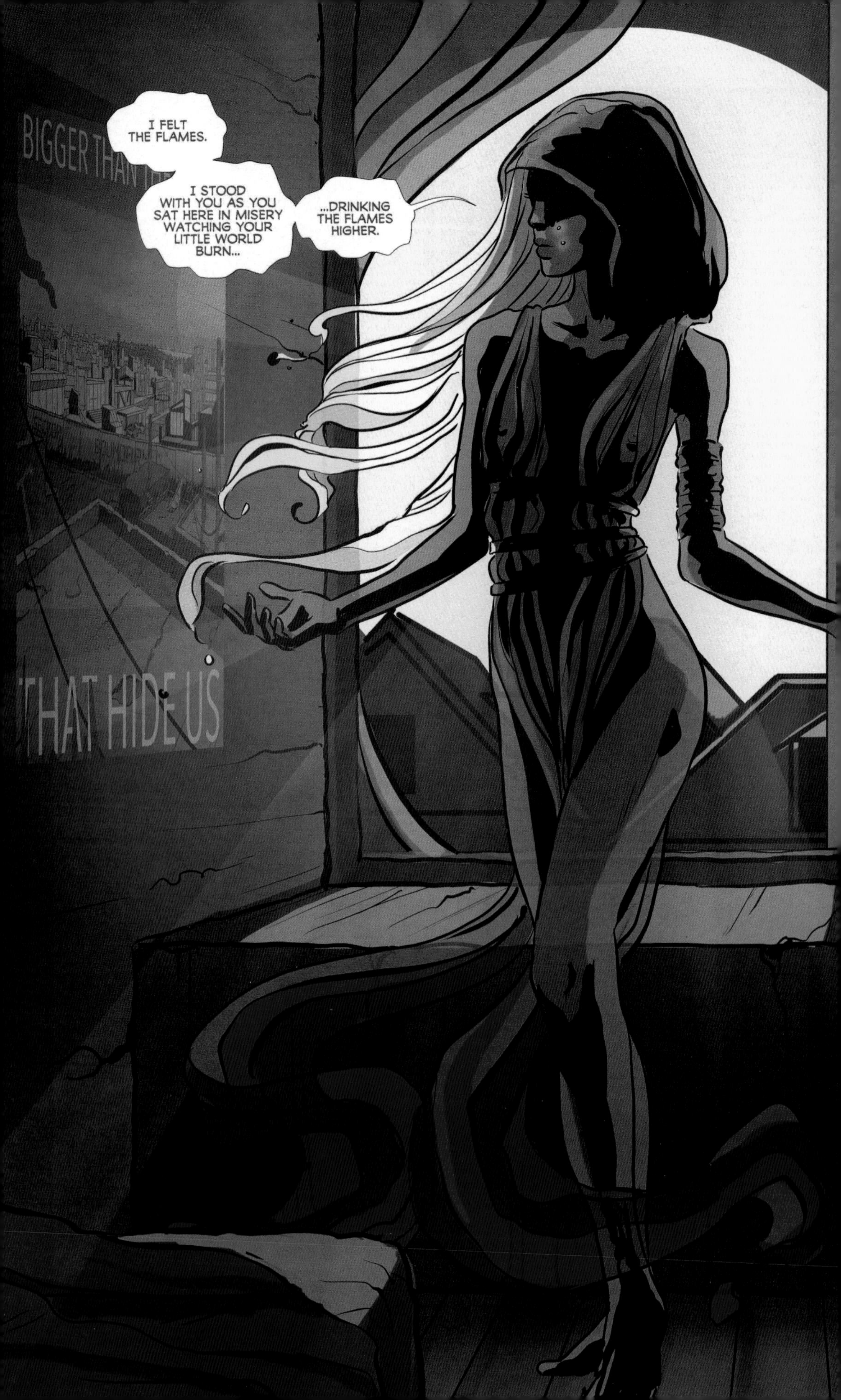
BIGGER THAN
I FELT THE FLAMES.
I STOOD WITH YOU AS YOU SAT HERE IN MISERY WATCHING YOUR LITTLE WORLD BURN...
...DRINKING THE FLAMES HIGHER.
THAT HIDE US

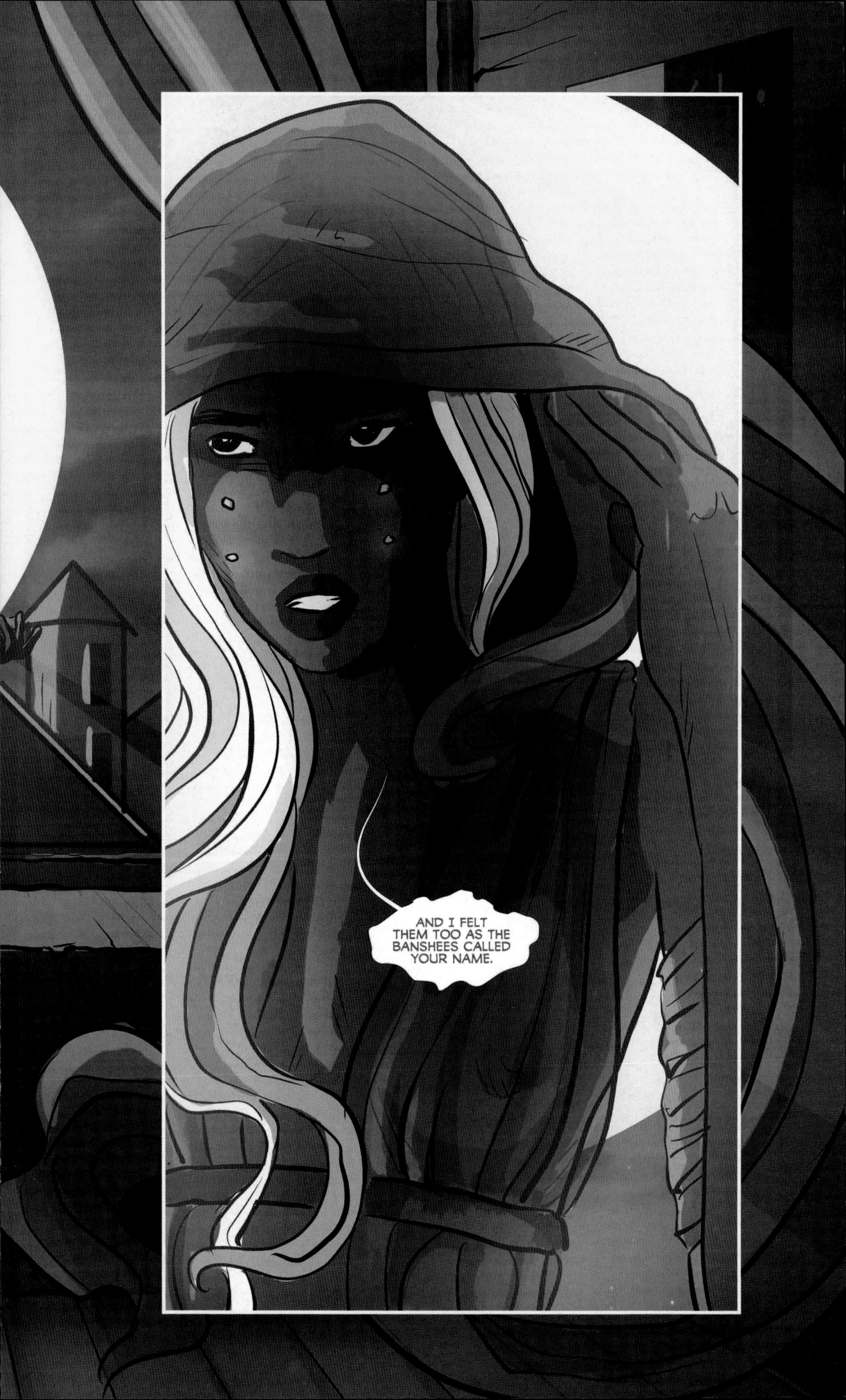
AND I FELT THEM TOO AS THE BANSHEES CALLED YOUR NAME.

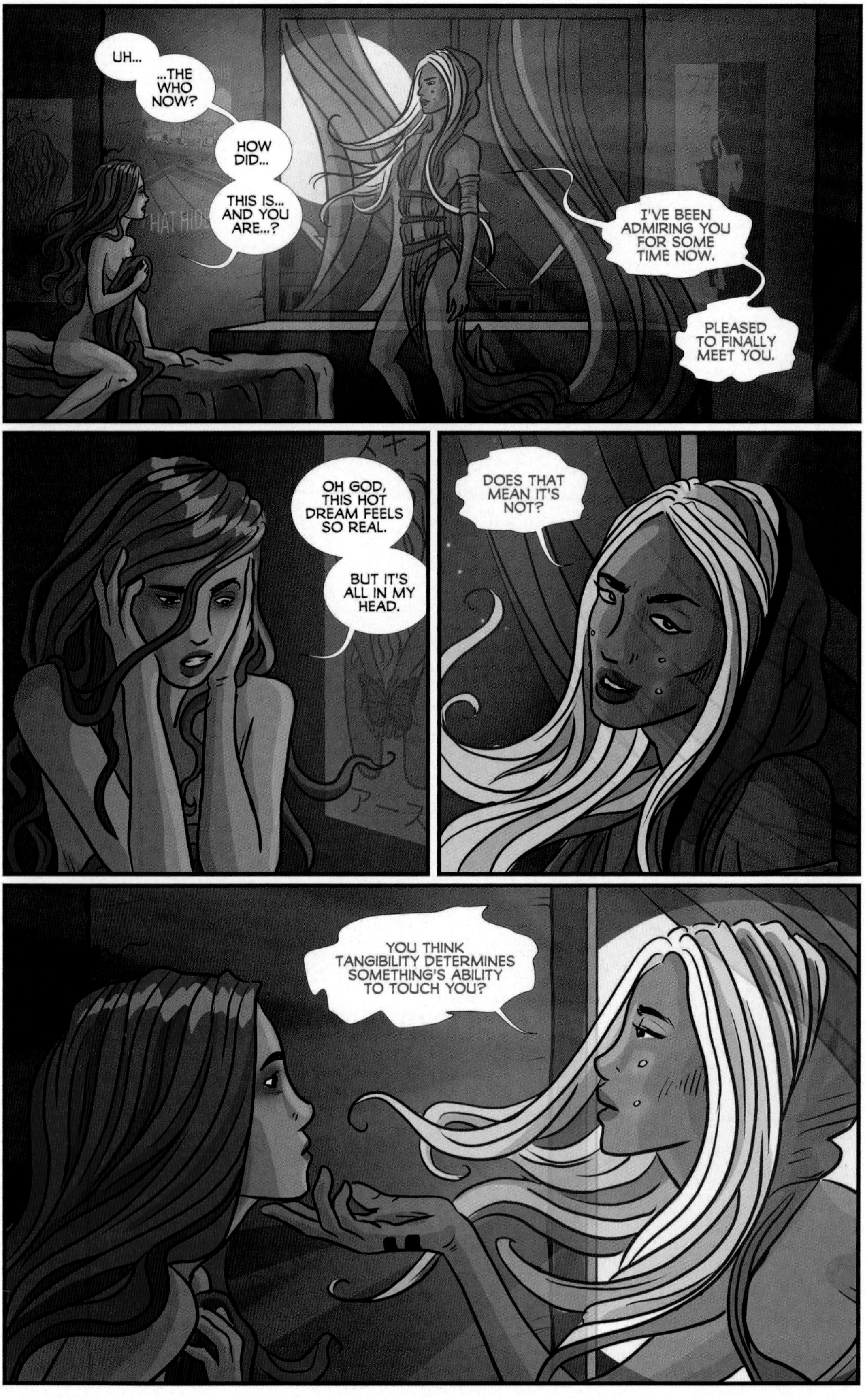
UH...
...THE WHO NOW?
HOW DID...
THIS IS... AND YOU ARE...?
I'VE BEEN ADMIRING YOU FOR SOME TIME NOW.
PLEASED TO FINALLY MEET YOU.
OH GOD, THIS HOT DREAM FEELS SO REAL.
BUT IT'S ALL IN MY HEAD.
DOES THAT MEAN IT'S NOT?
YOU THINK TANGIBILITY DETERMINES SOMETHING'S ABILITY TO TOUCH YOU?

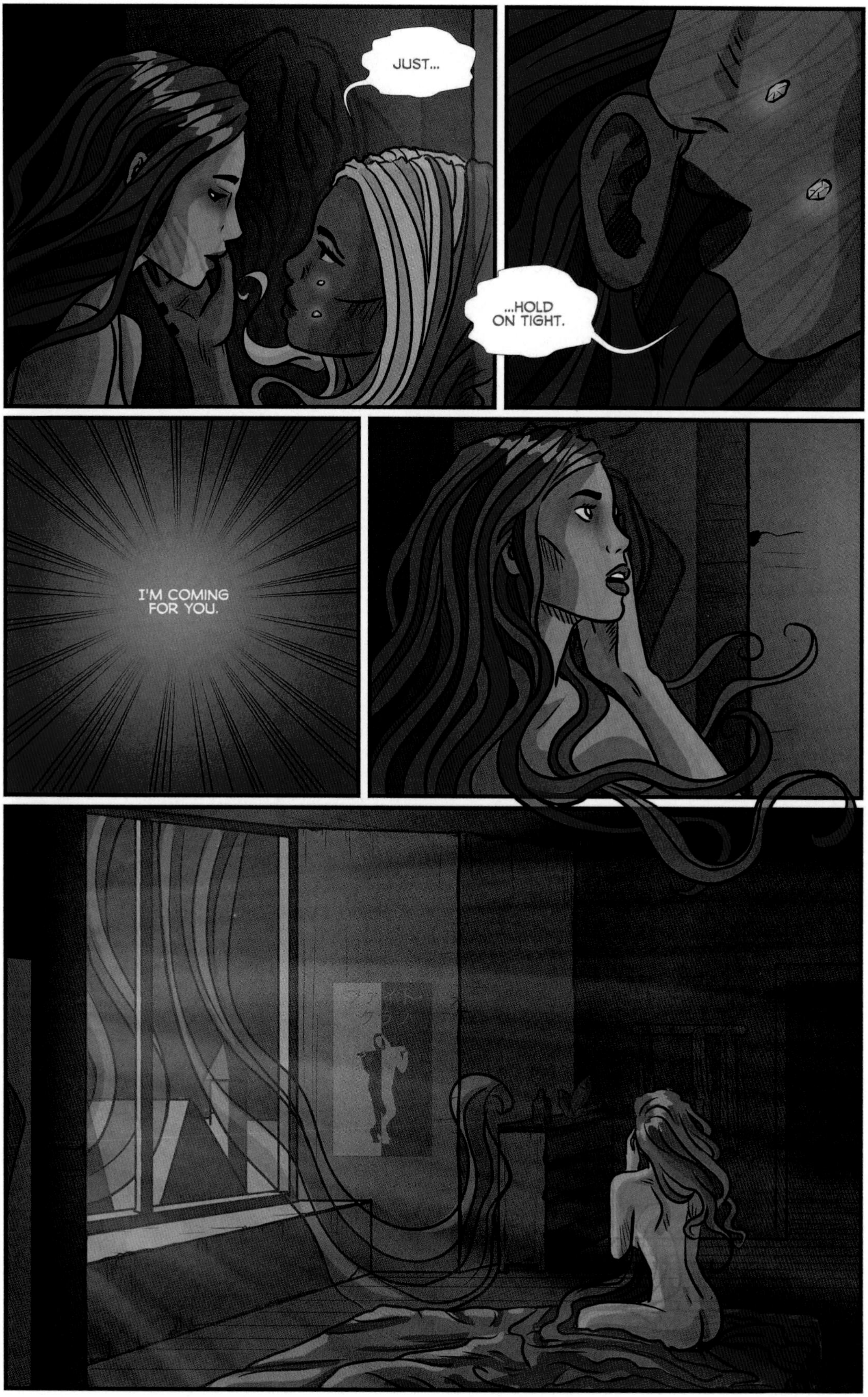
JUST...
...HOLD ON TIGHT.
I'M COMING FOR YOU.

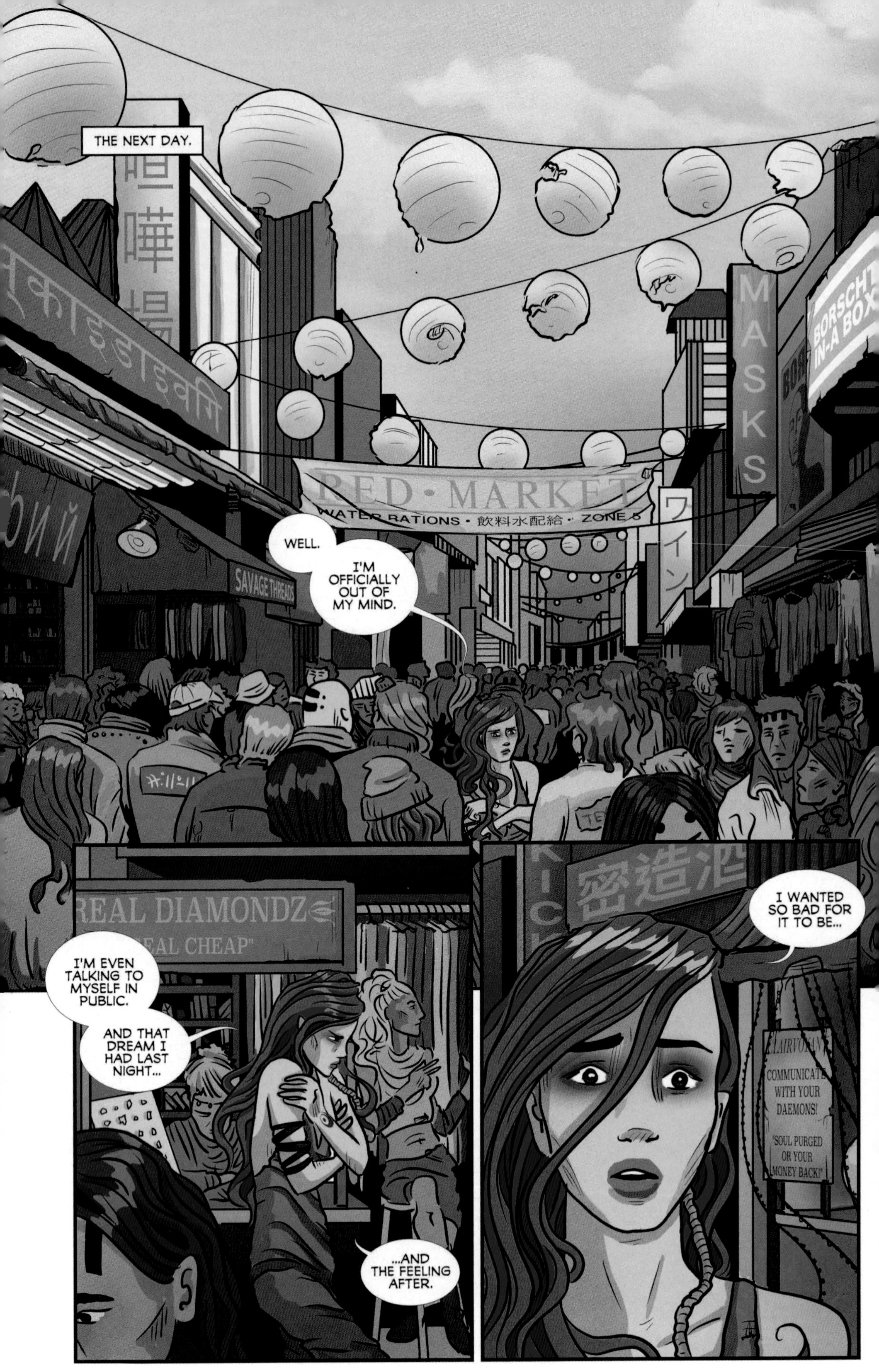
THE NEXT DAY.
WELL.
I'M OFFICIALLY OUT OF MY MIND.
RED • MARKET
WATER RATIONS • 飲料水配給 • ZONE 5
MASKS
BORSCHT IN-A BOX
SAVAGE THREADS
REAL DIAMONDZ
"REAL CHEAP"
I'M EVEN TALKING TO MYSELF IN PUBLIC.
AND THAT DREAM I HAD LAST NIGHT...
...AND THE FEELING AFTER.
密造酒
I WANTED SO BAD FOR IT TO BE...
COMMUNICATE WITH YOUR DAEMONS!
"SOUL PURGED OR YOUR MONEY BACK!"

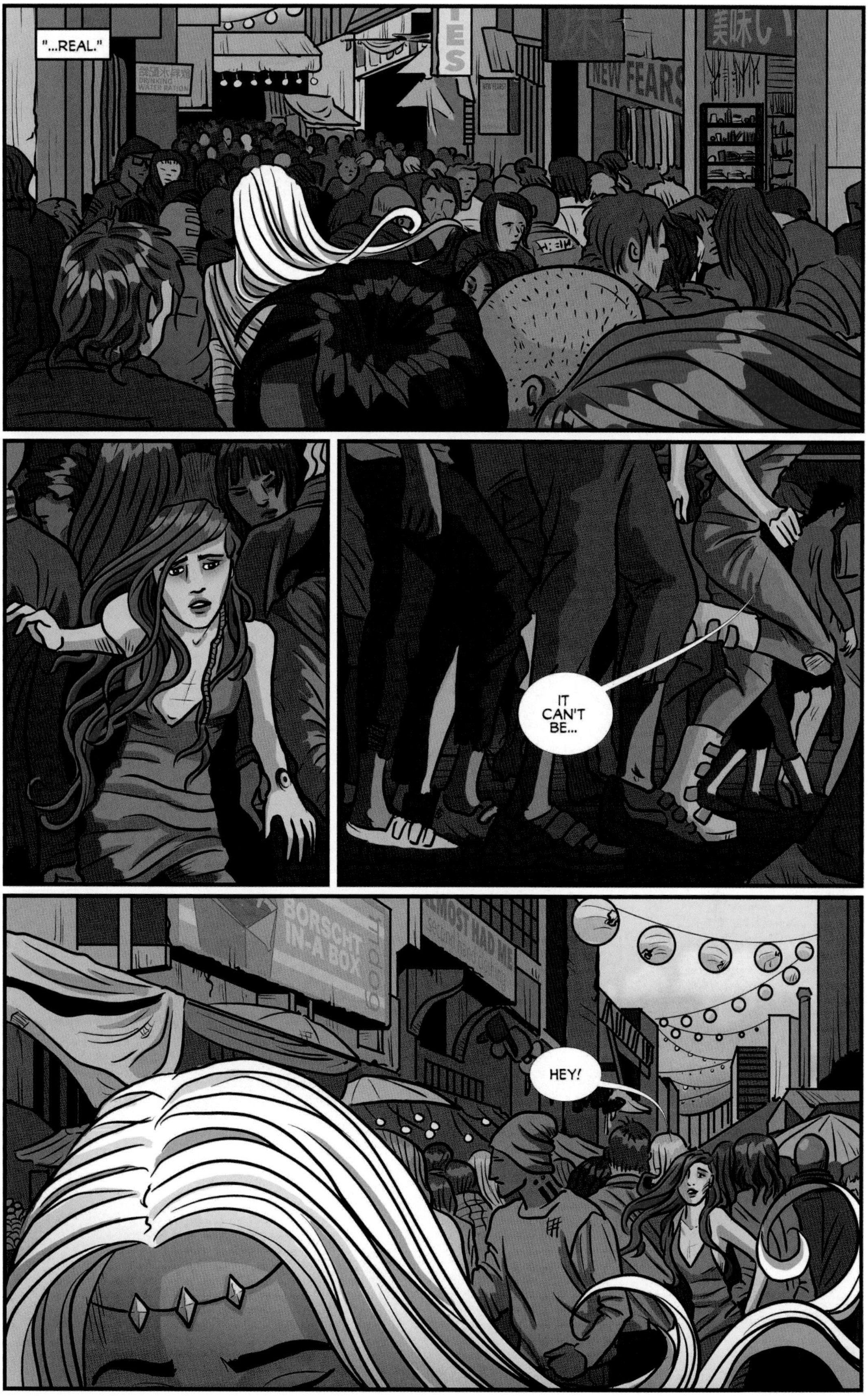
"...REAL."
DRINKING WATER RATION
NEW FEARS
IT CAN'T BE...
BORSCHT IN-A BOX
HEY!

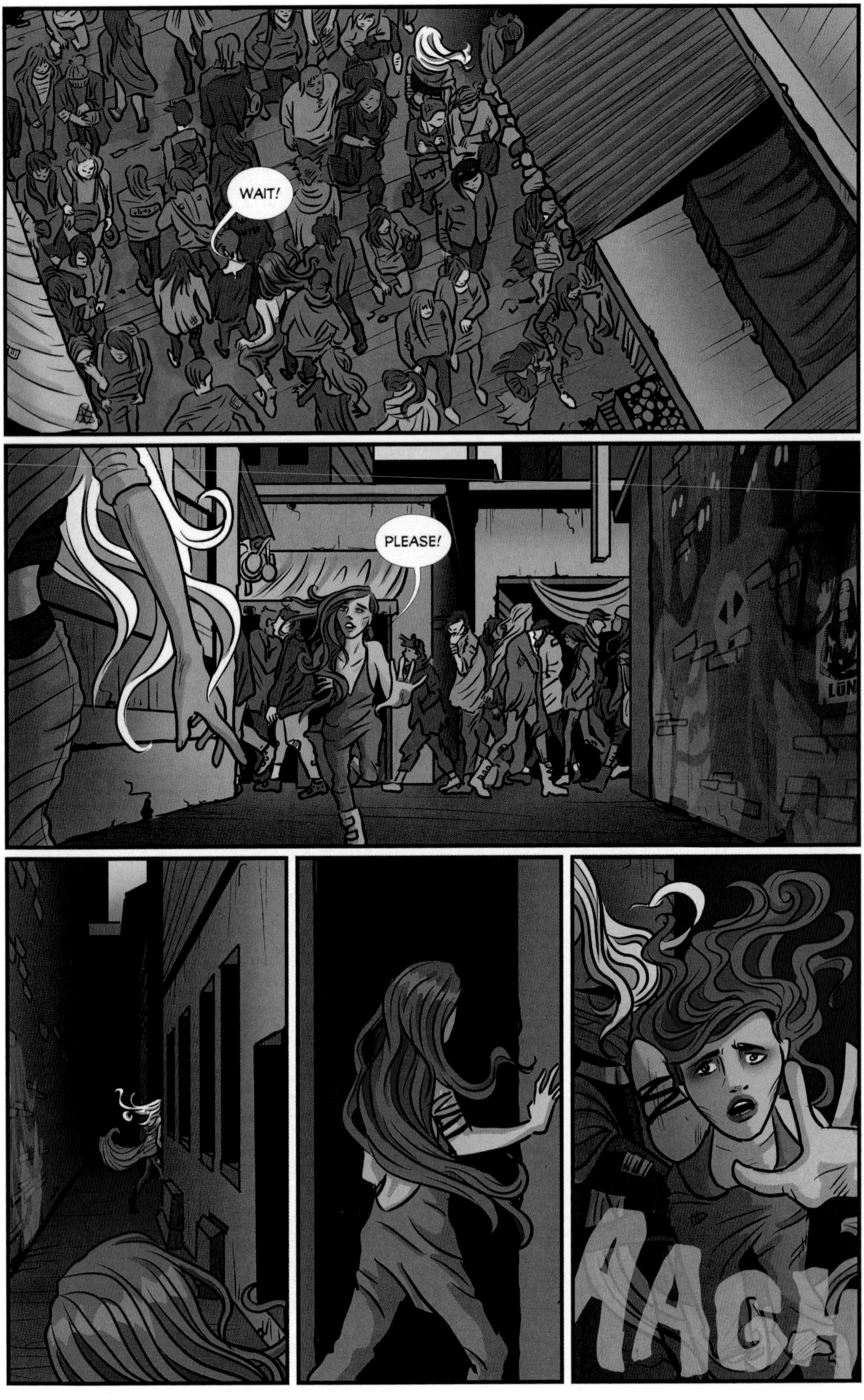
WAIT!
PLEASE!
LÜN
AGH

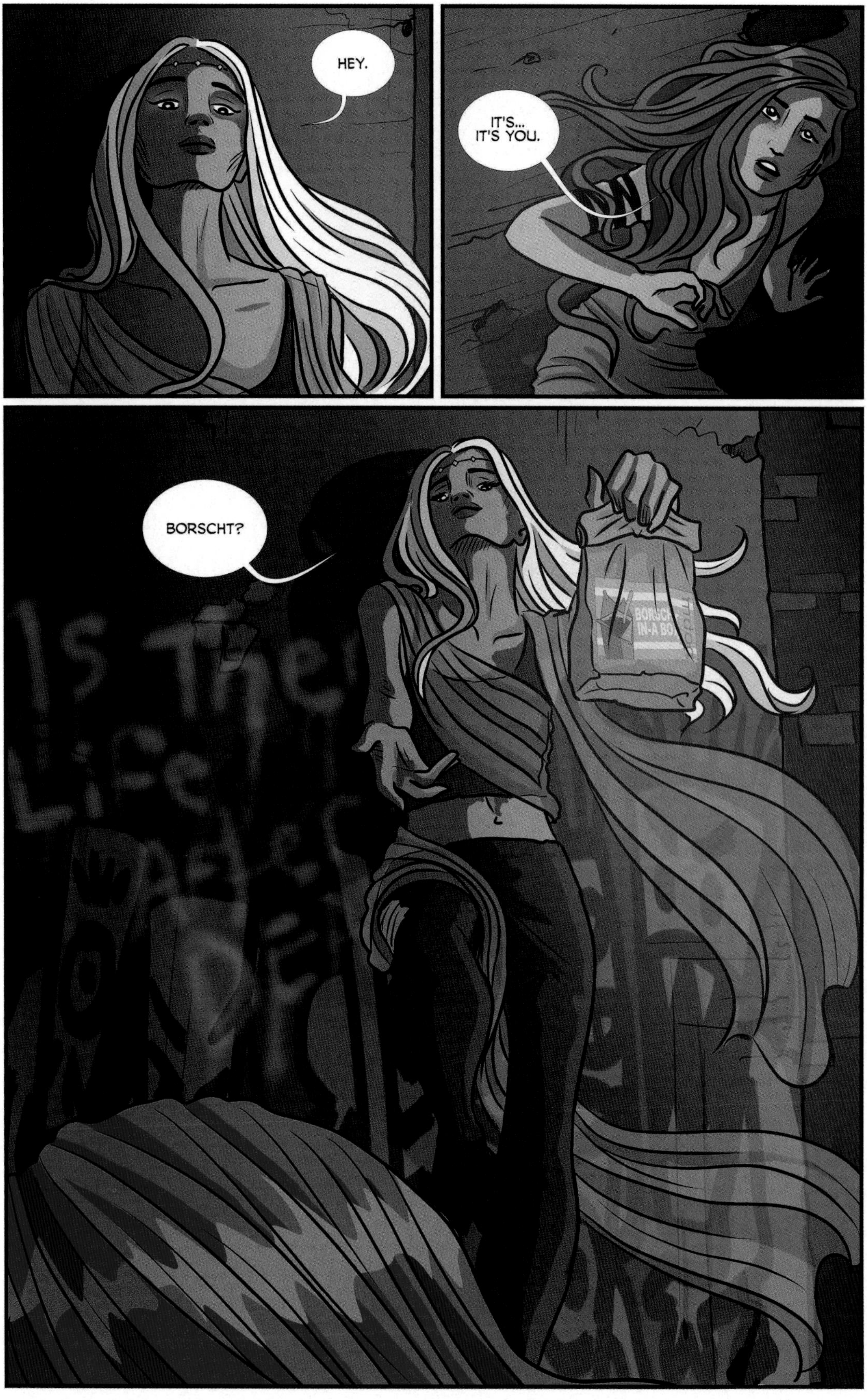
HEY.
IT'S... IT'S YOU.
BORSCHT?

CHAPTER SIX: MORPHINE

http://mxt.pe/morphin

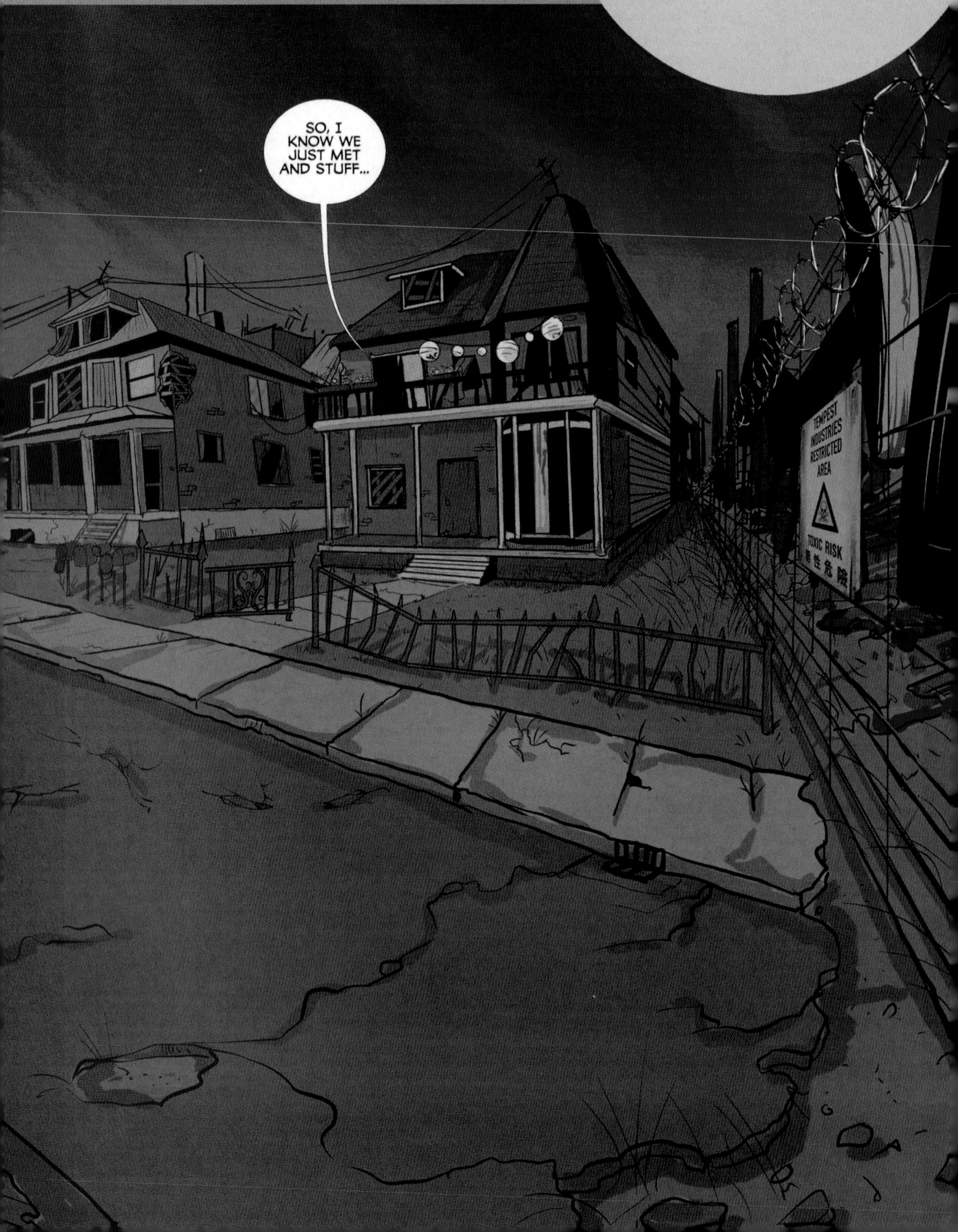
SO, I KNOW WE JUST MET AND STUFF...
TEMPEST INDUSTRIES RESTRICTED AREA
TOXIC RISK
毒性危險

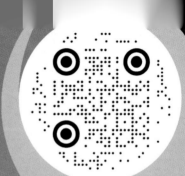

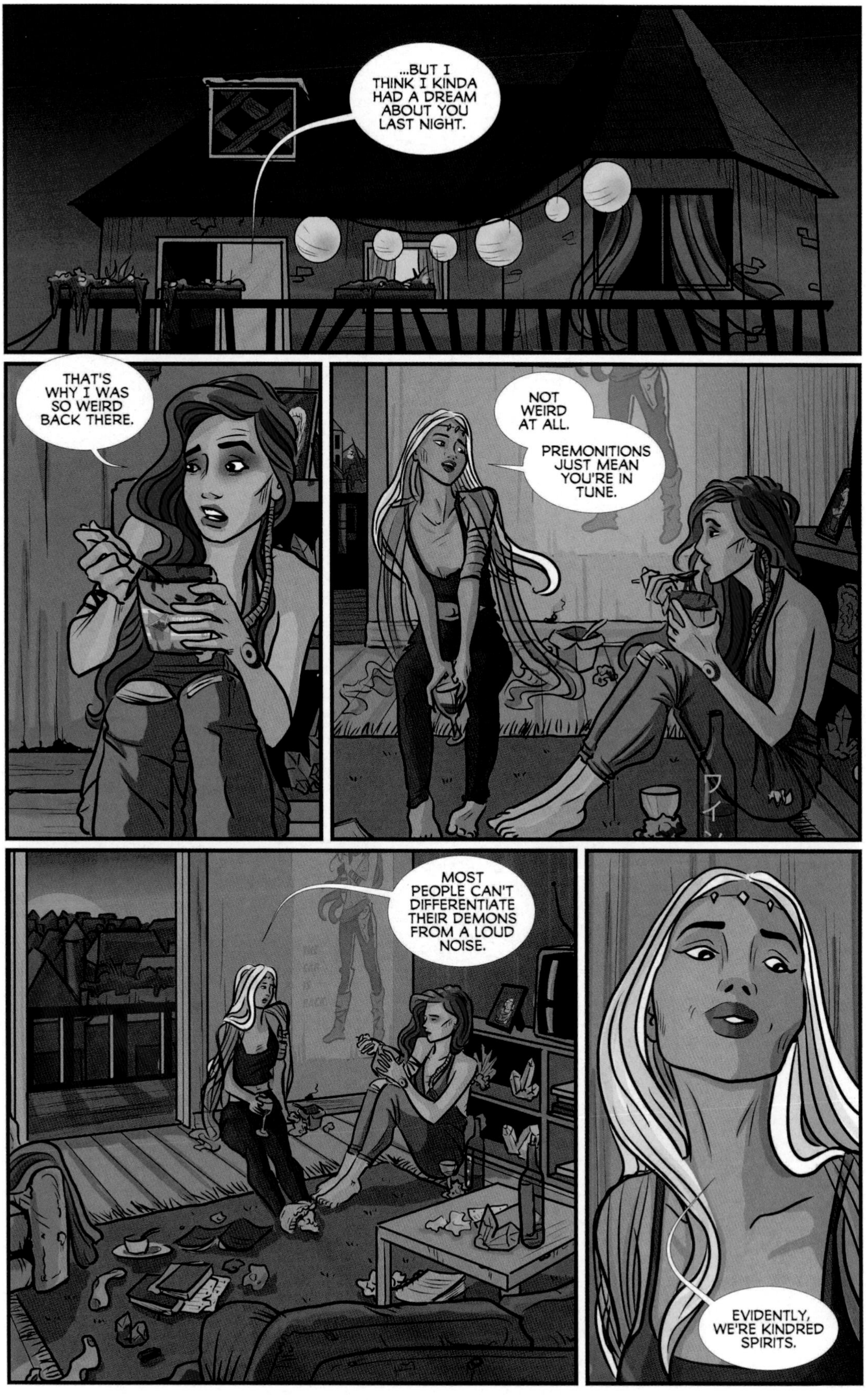
...BUT I THINK I KINDA HAD A DREAM ABOUT YOU LAST NIGHT.
THAT'S WHY I WAS SO WEIRD BACK THERE.
NOT WEIRD AT ALL.
PREMONITIONS JUST MEAN YOU'RE IN TUNE.
MOST PEOPLE CAN'T DIFFERENTIATE THEIR DEMONS FROM A LOUD NOISE.
EVIDENTLY, WE'RE KINDRED SPIRITS.

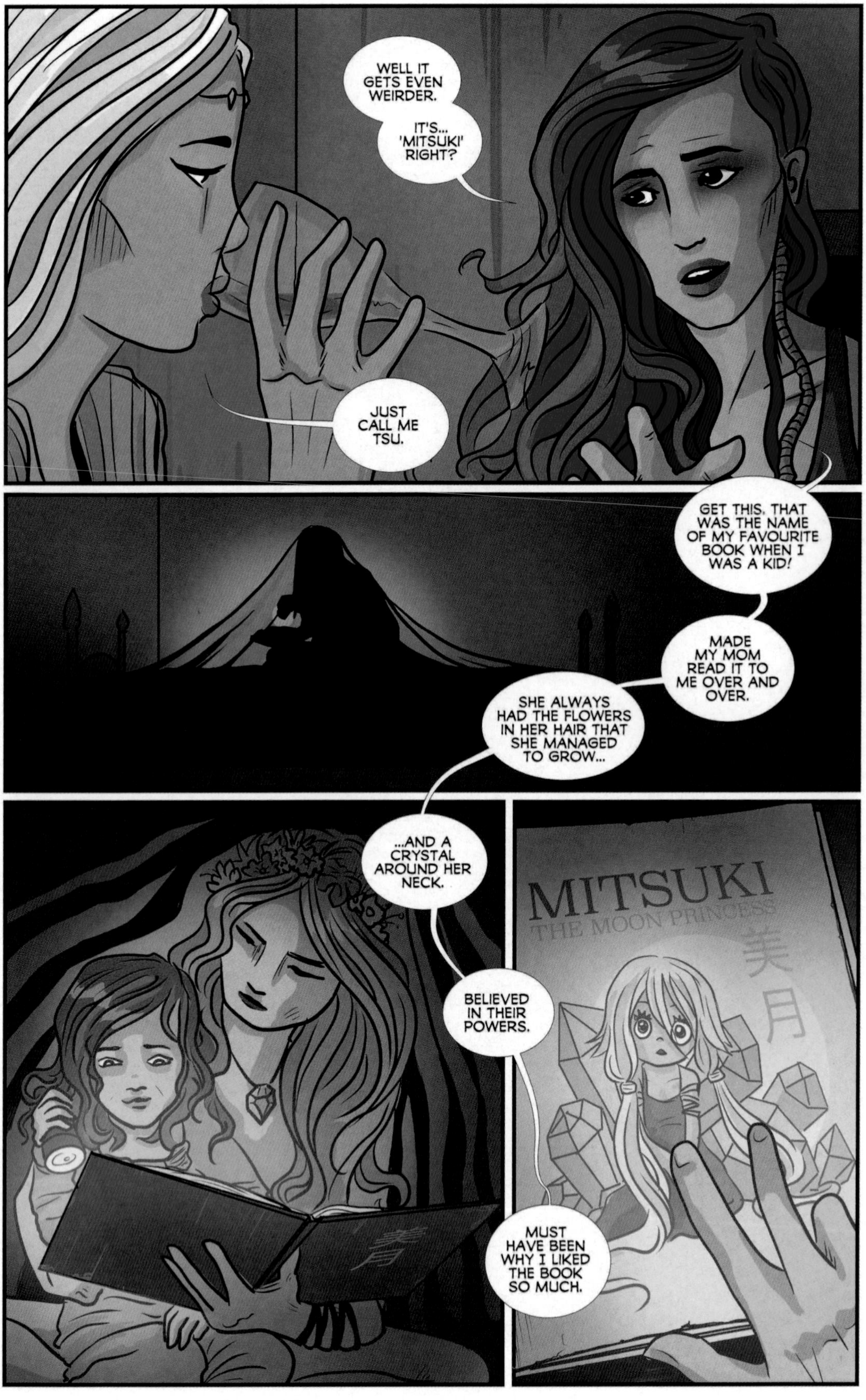
WELL IT GETS EVEN WEIRDER.
IT'S... 'MITSUKI' RIGHT?
JUST CALL ME TSU.
GET THIS. THAT WAS THE NAME OF MY FAVOURITE BOOK WHEN I WAS A KID!
MADE MY MOM READ IT TO ME OVER AND OVER.
SHE ALWAYS HAD THE FLOWERS IN HER HAIR THAT SHE MANAGED TO GROW...
...AND A CRYSTAL AROUND HER NECK.
BELIEVED IN THEIR POWERS.
MUST HAVE BEEN WHY I LIKED THE BOOK SO MUCH.
MITSUKI
THE MOON PRINCESS
美月

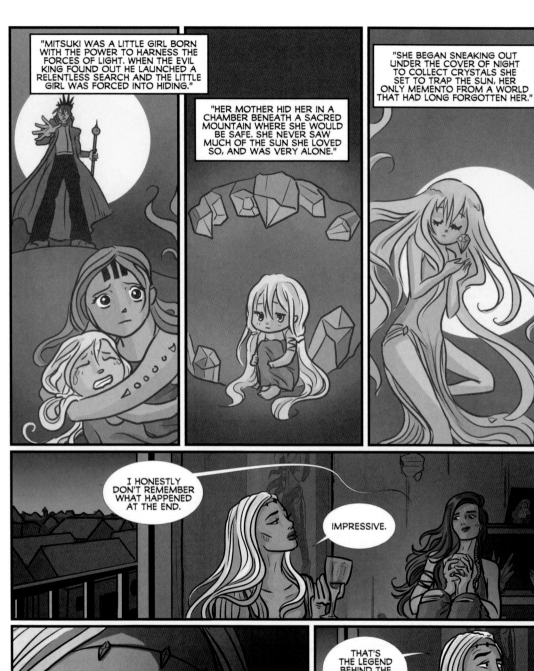

"MITSUKI WAS A LITTLE GIRL BORN WITH THE POWER TO HARNESS THE FORCES OF LIGHT. WHEN THE EVIL KING FOUND OUT HE LAUNCHED A RELENTLESS SEARCH AND THE LITTLE GIRL WAS FORCED INTO HIDING."

"HER MOTHER HID HER IN A CHAMBER BENEATH A SACRED MOUNTAIN WHERE SHE WOULD BE SAFE. SHE NEVER SAW MUCH OF THE SUN SHE LOVED SO, AND WAS VERY ALONE."

"SHE BEGAN SNEAKING OUT UNDER THE COVER OF NIGHT TO COLLECT CRYSTALS SHE SET TO TRAP THE SUN, HER ONLY MEMENTO FROM A WORLD THAT HAD LONG FORGOTTEN HER."

I HONESTLY DON'T REMEMBER WHAT HAPPENED AT THE END.

IMPRESSIVE.

BORN IN DARKNESS, RAISED IN MOONLIGHT.

THAT'S THE LEGEND BEHIND THE NAME, ANWAY.

YOUR MOM SOUNDS NICE.

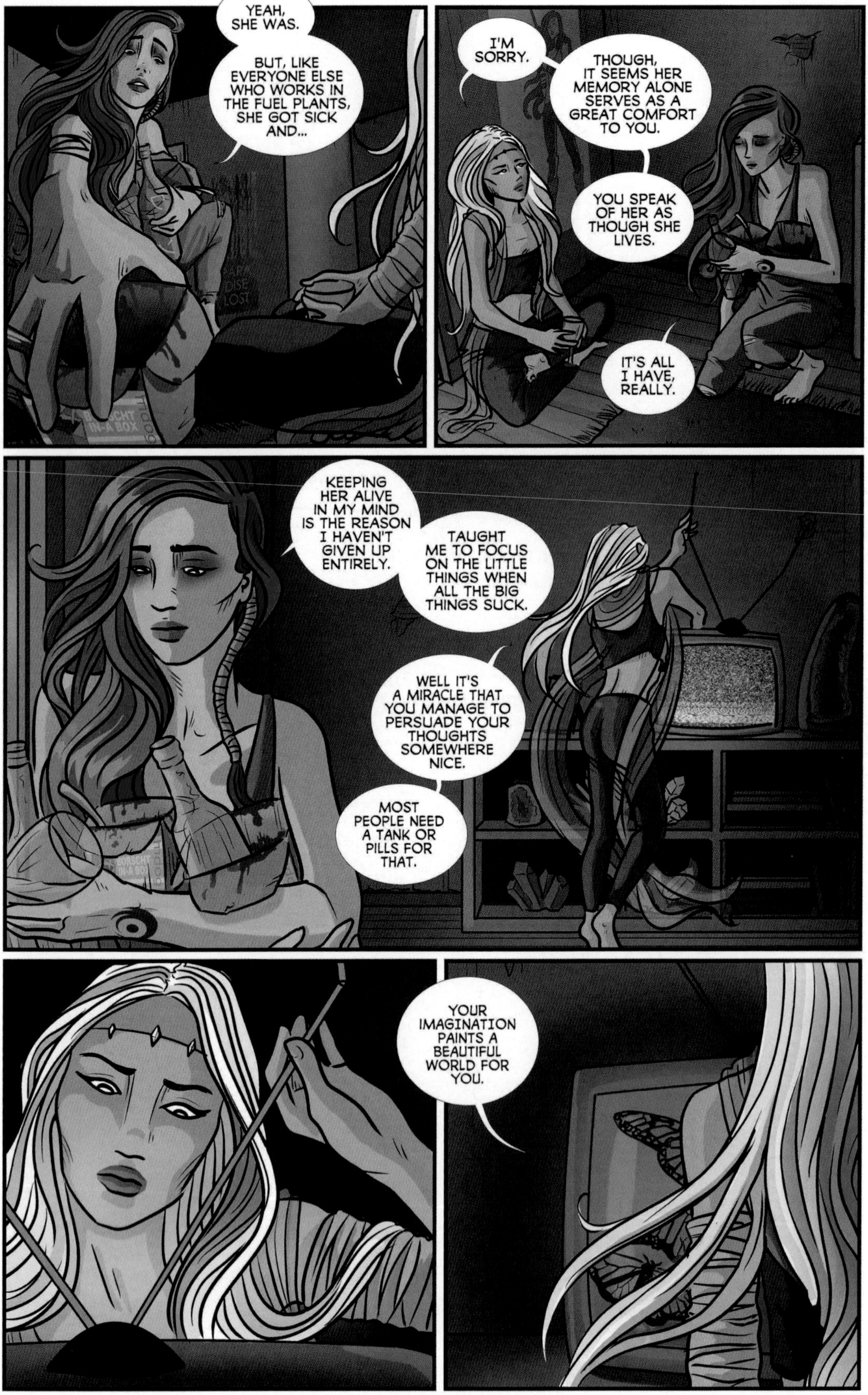
YEAH, SHE WAS.
BUT, LIKE EVERYONE ELSE WHO WORKS IN THE FUEL PLANTS, SHE GOT SICK AND...
BORSCHT IN-A BOX
I'M SORRY.
THOUGH, IT SEEMS HER MEMORY ALONE SERVES AS A GREAT COMFORT TO YOU.
YOU SPEAK OF HER AS THOUGH SHE LIVES.
IT'S ALL I HAVE, REALLY.
KEEPING HER ALIVE IN MY MIND IS THE REASON I HAVEN'T GIVEN UP ENTIRELY.
TAUGHT ME TO FOCUS ON THE LITTLE THINGS WHEN ALL THE BIG THINGS SUCK.
WELL IT'S A MIRACLE THAT YOU MANAGE TO PERSUADE YOUR THOUGHTS SOMEWHERE NICE.
MOST PEOPLE NEED A TANK OR PILLS FOR THAT.
YOUR IMAGINATION PAINTS A BEAUTIFUL WORLD FOR YOU.

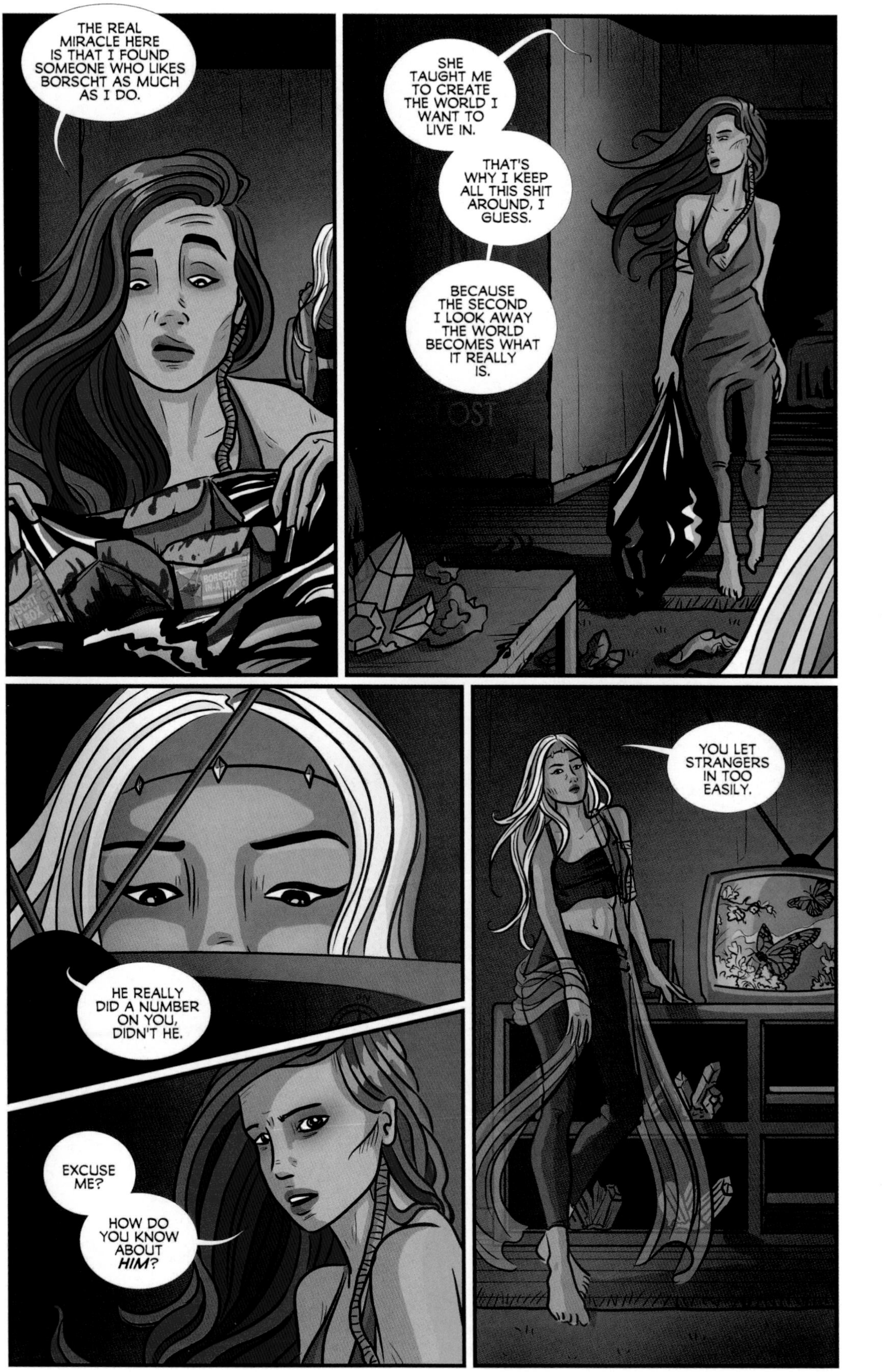
THE REAL MIRACLE HERE IS THAT I FOUND SOMEONE WHO LIKES BORSCHT AS MUCH AS I DO.
BORSCHT IN-A BOX
SHE TAUGHT ME TO CREATE THE WORLD I WANT TO LIVE IN.
THAT'S WHY I KEEP ALL THIS SHIT AROUND, I GUESS.
BECAUSE THE SECOND I LOOK AWAY THE WORLD BECOMES WHAT IT REALLY IS.
LOST
HE REALLY DID A NUMBER ON YOU, DIDN'T HE.
EXCUSE ME?
HOW DO YOU KNOW ABOUT *HIM*?
YOU LET STRANGERS IN TOO EASILY.

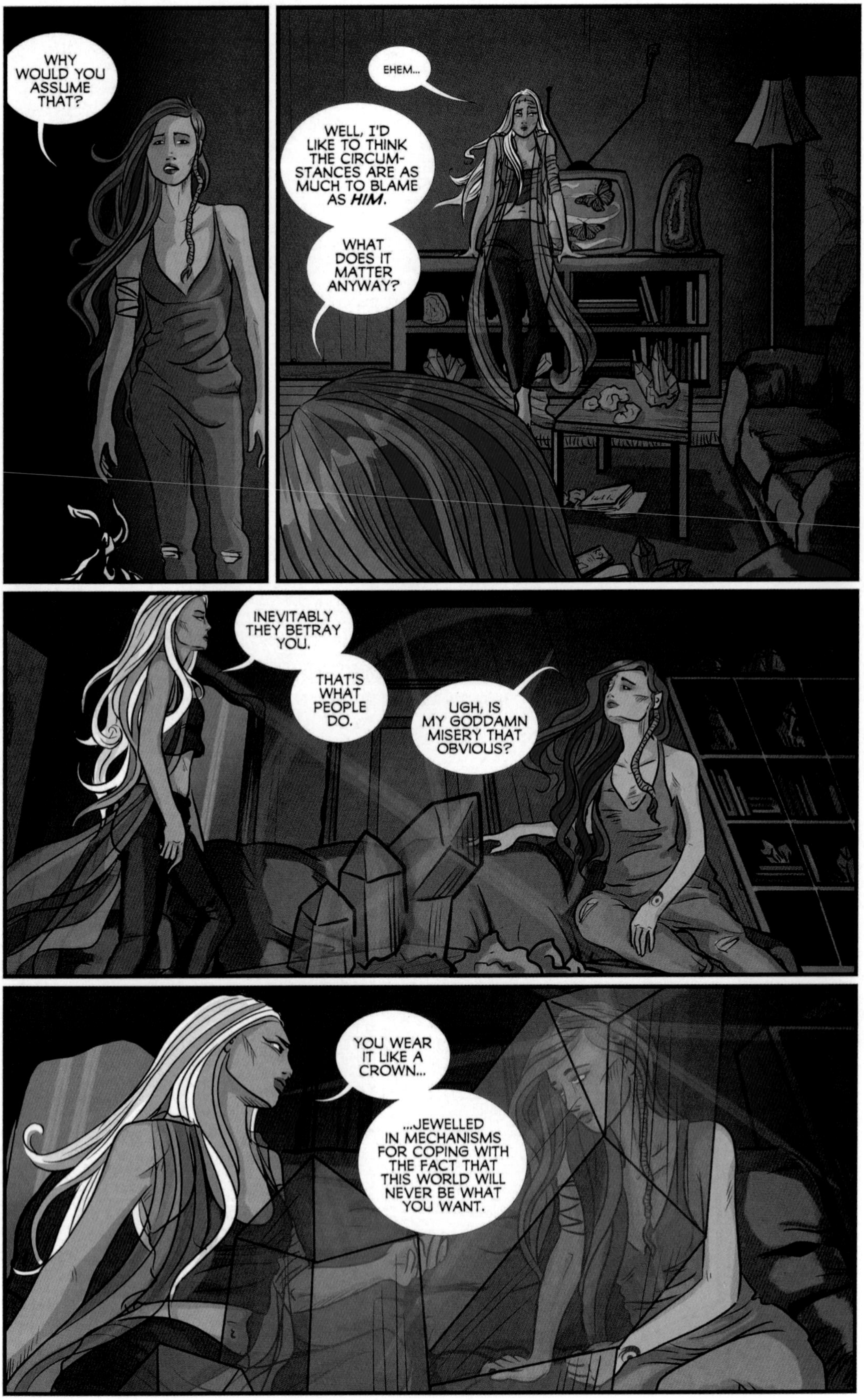
WHY WOULD YOU ASSUME THAT?
EHEM...
WELL, I'D LIKE TO THINK THE CIRCUM-STANCES ARE AS MUCH TO BLAME AS *HIM*.
WHAT DOES IT MATTER ANYWAY?
INEVITABLY THEY BETRAY YOU.
THAT'S WHAT PEOPLE DO.
UGH, IS MY GODDAMN MISERY THAT OBVIOUS?
YOU WEAR IT LIKE A CROWN...
...JEWELLED IN MECHANISMS FOR COPING WITH THE FACT THAT THIS WORLD WILL NEVER BE WHAT YOU WANT.

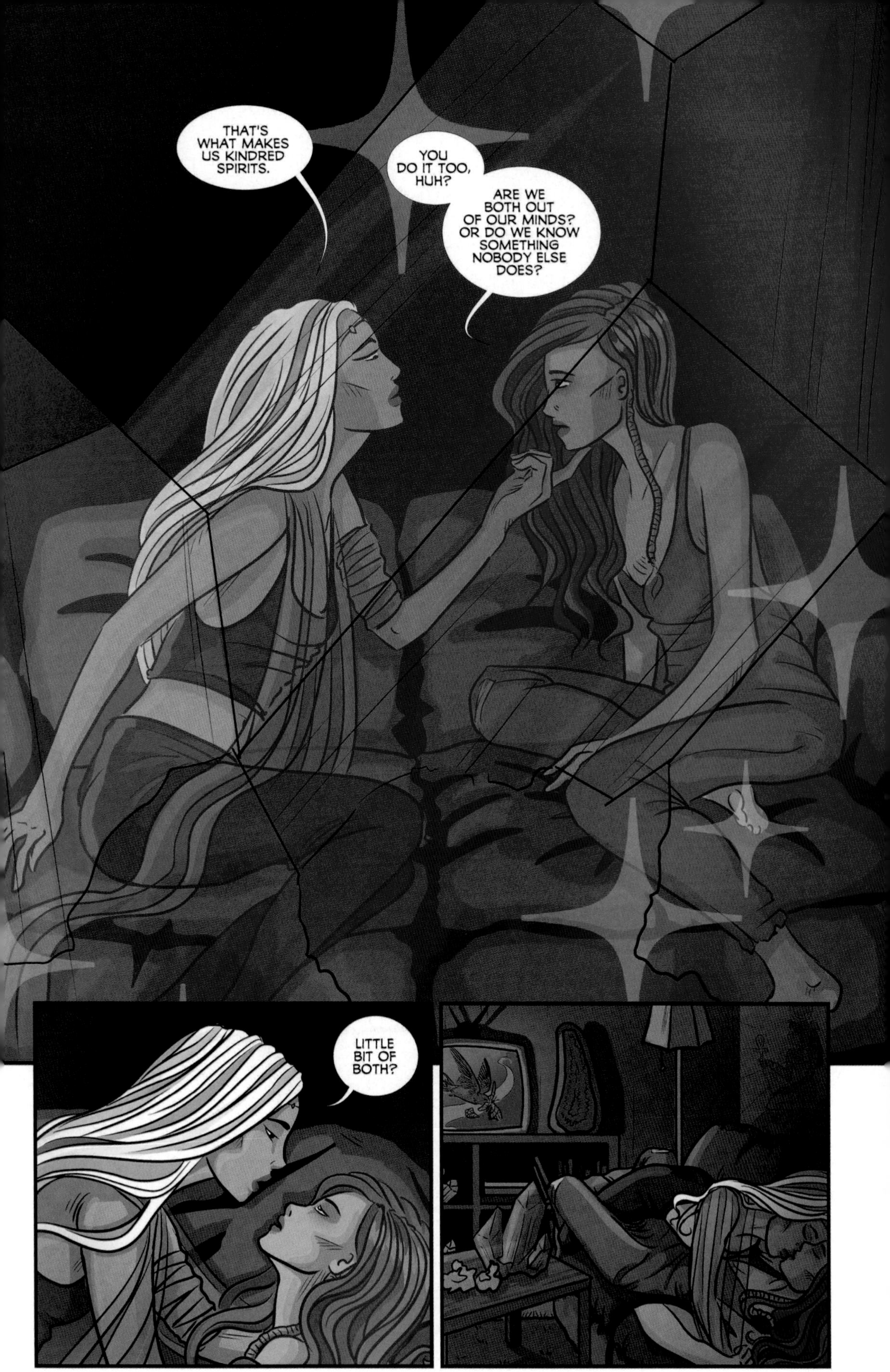
THAT'S WHAT MAKES US KINDRED SPIRITS.
YOU DO IT TOO, HUH?
ARE WE BOTH OUT OF OUR MINDS? OR DO WE KNOW SOMETHING NOBODY ELSE DOES?
LITTLE BIT OF BOTH?

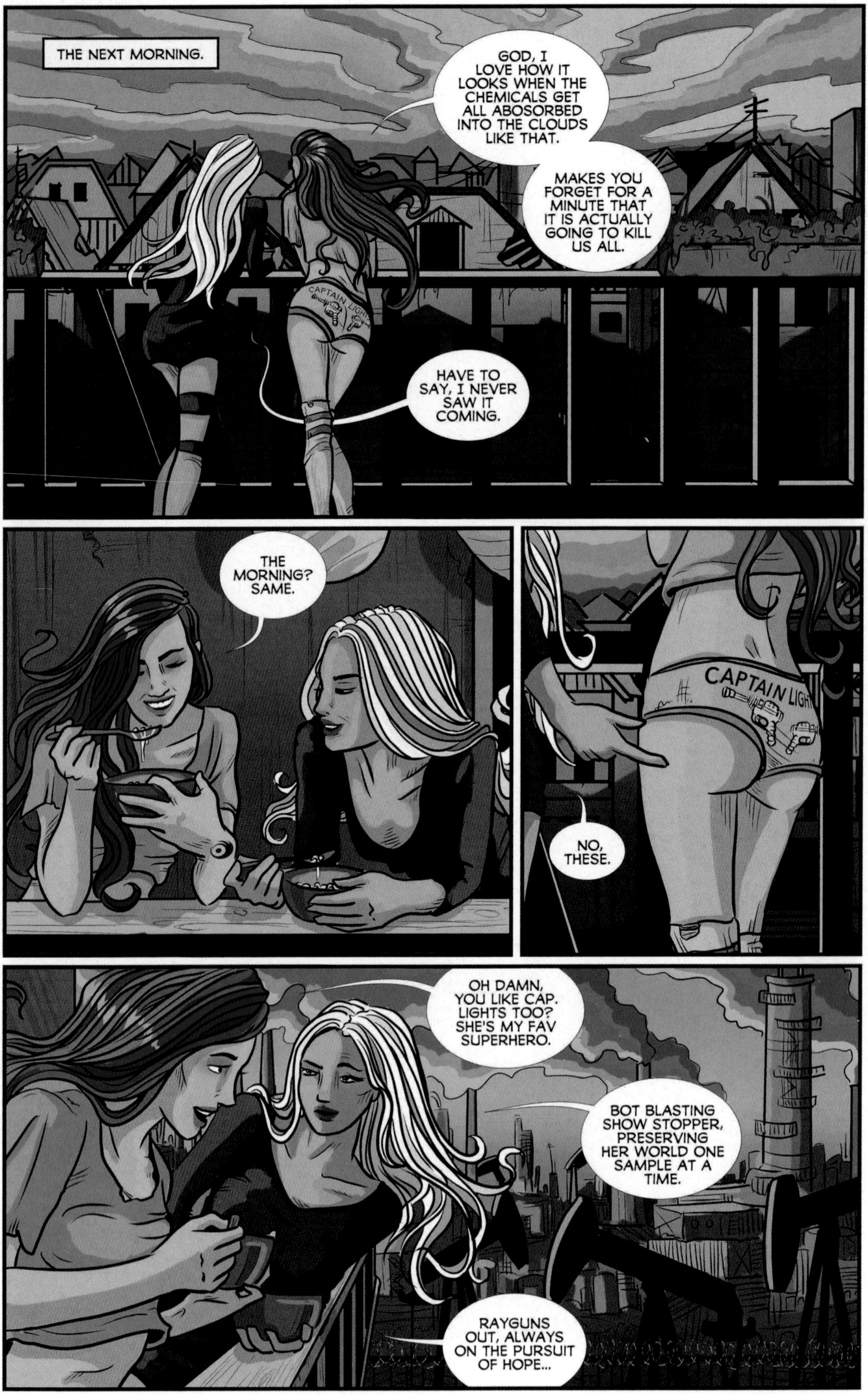
THE NEXT MORNING.
GOD, I LOVE HOW IT LOOKS WHEN THE CHEMICALS GET ALL ABOSORBED INTO THE CLOUDS LIKE THAT.
MAKES YOU FORGET FOR A MINUTE THAT IT IS ACTUALLY GOING TO KILL US ALL.
CAPTAIN LIGHT
HAVE TO SAY, I NEVER SAW IT COMING.
THE MORNING? SAME.
CAPTAIN LIGHT
NO, THESE.
OH DAMN, YOU LIKE CAP. LIGHTS TOO? SHE'S MY FAV SUPERHERO.
BOT BLASTING SHOW STOPPER, PRESERVING HER WORLD ONE SAMPLE AT A TIME.
RAYGUNS OUT, ALWAYS ON THE PURSUIT OF HOPE...

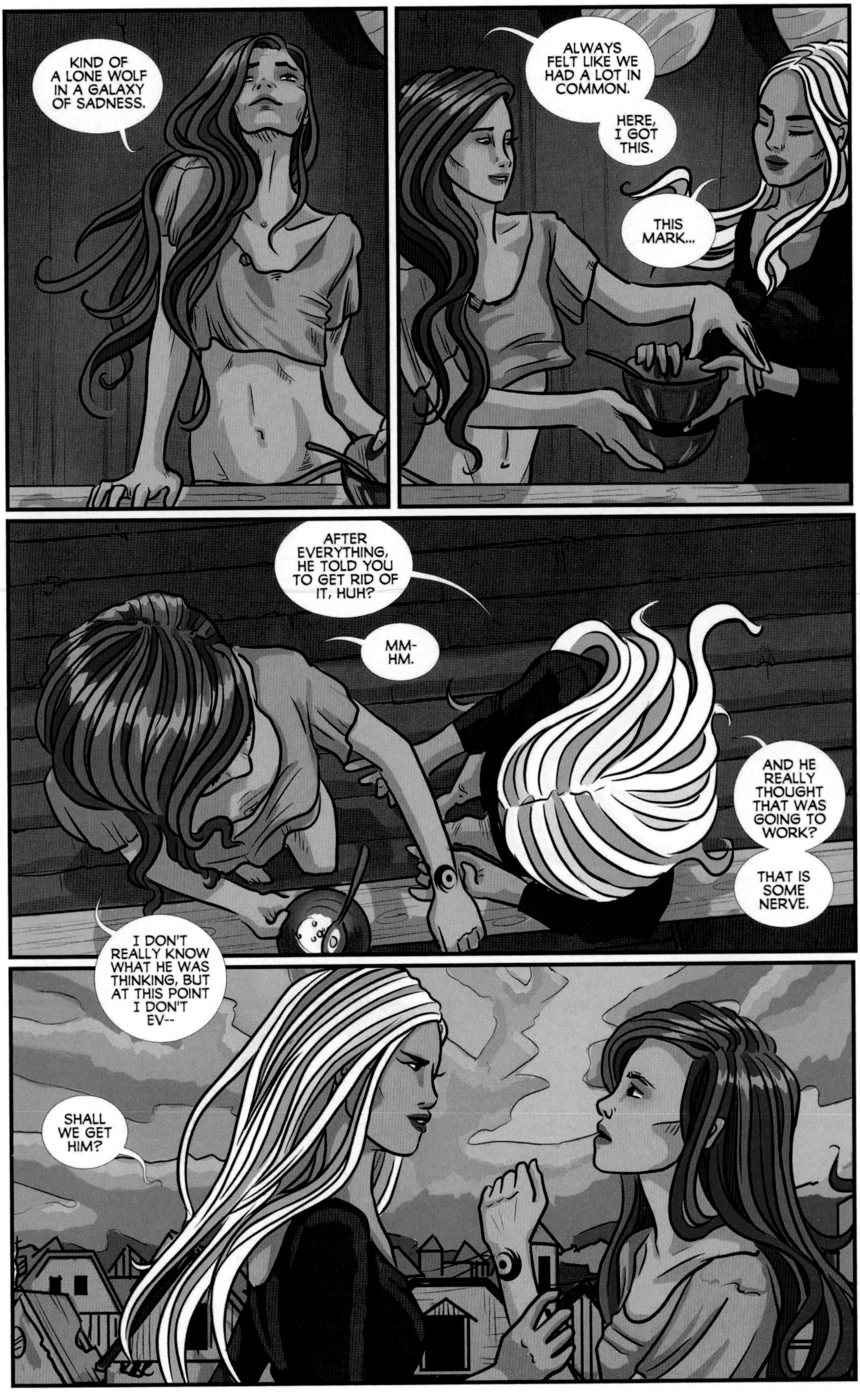
KIND OF A LONE WOLF IN A GALAXY OF SADNESS.
ALWAYS FELT LIKE WE HAD A LOT IN COMMON.
HERE, I GOT THIS.
THIS MARK...
AFTER EVERYTHING, HE TOLD YOU TO GET RID OF IT, HUH?
MM-HM.
AND HE REALLY THOUGHT THAT WAS GOING TO WORK?
THAT IS SOME NERVE.
I DON'T REALLY KNOW WHAT HE WAS THINKING, BUT AT THIS POINT I DON'T EV--
SHALL WE GET HIM?

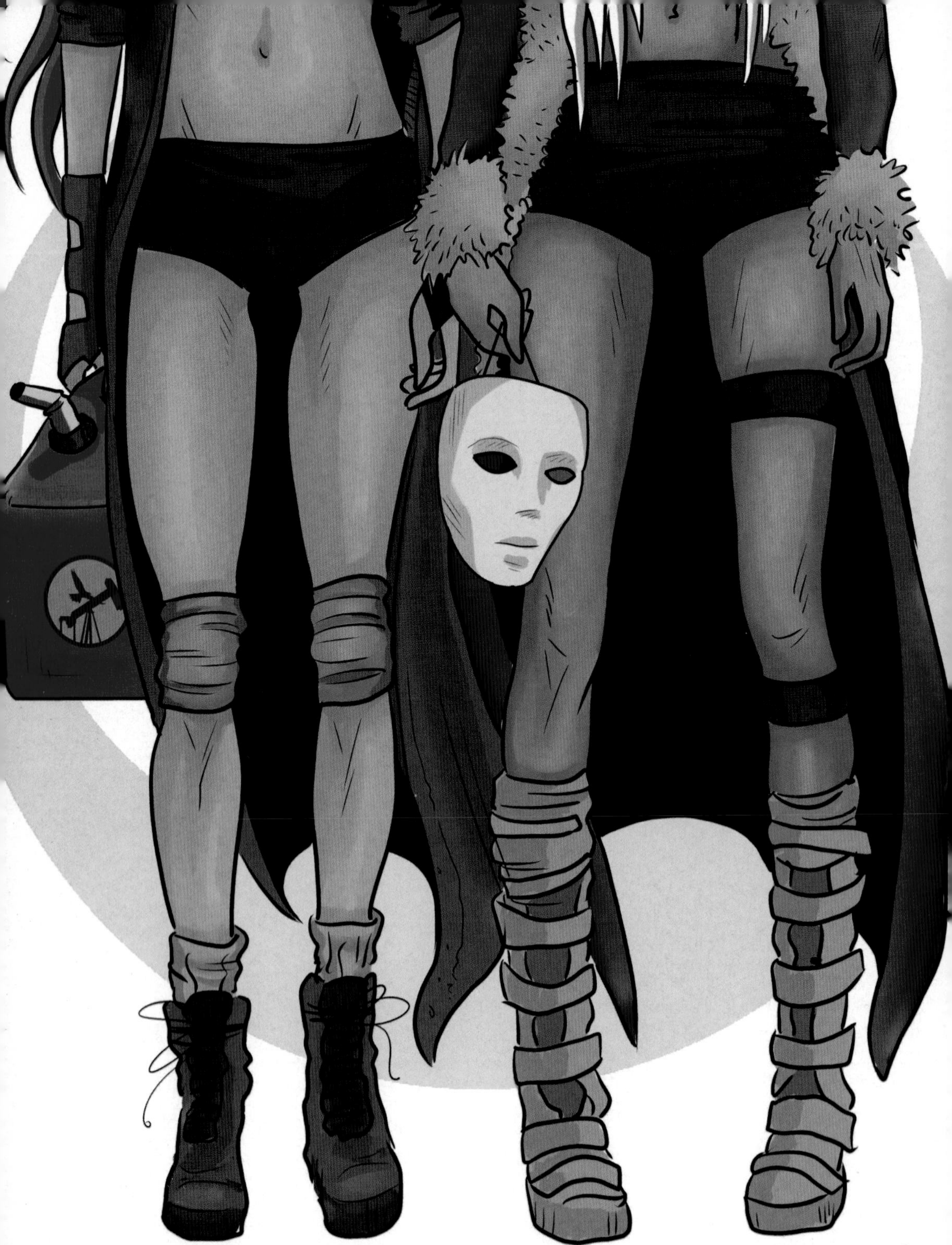

ISSUE FOUR

by LIGHTS

SKIN&EARTH

DYNAMITE

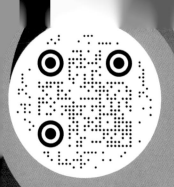

CHAPTER SEVEN: WE WERE HERE

http://mxt.pe/wrehere

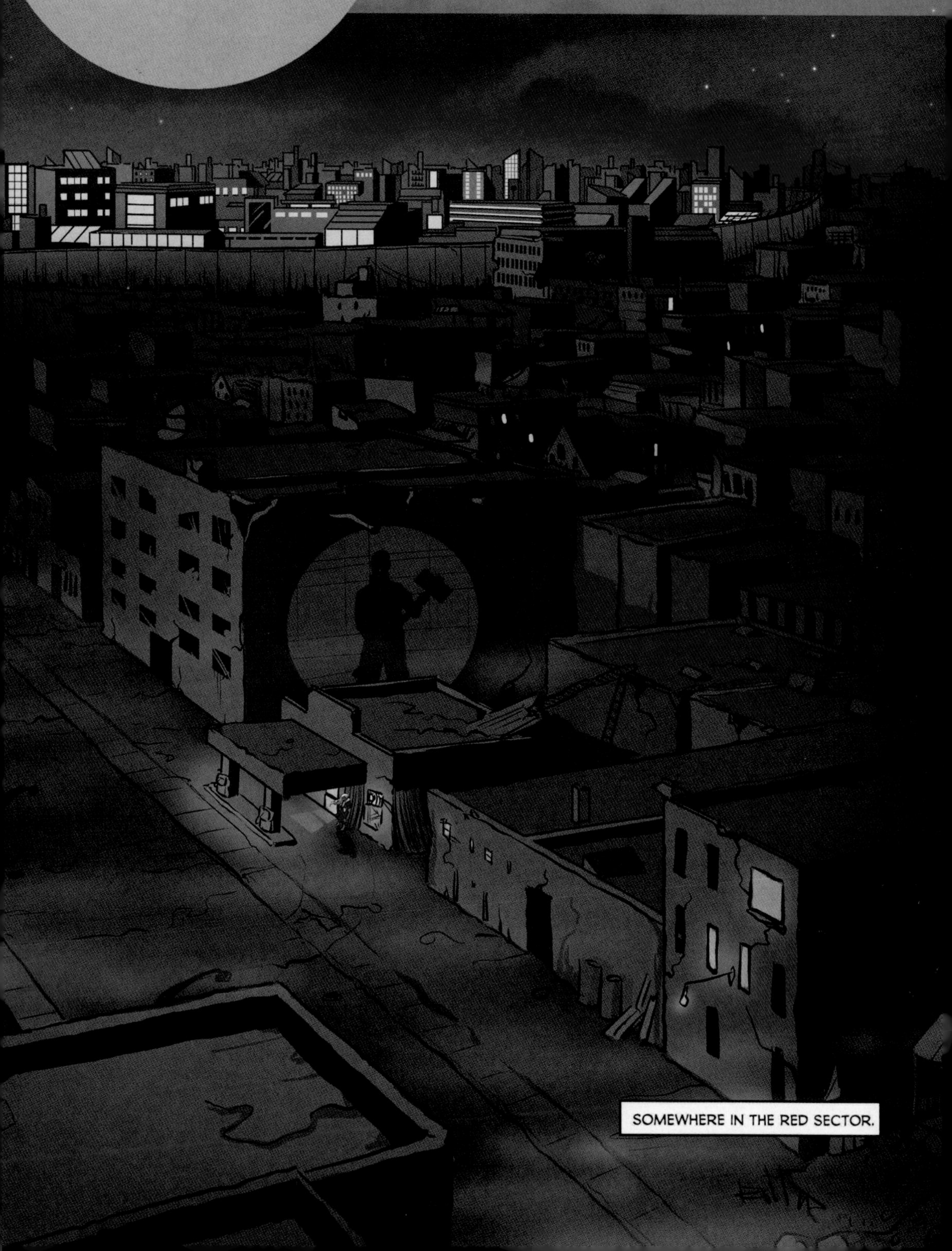
SOMEWHERE IN THE RED SECTOR.

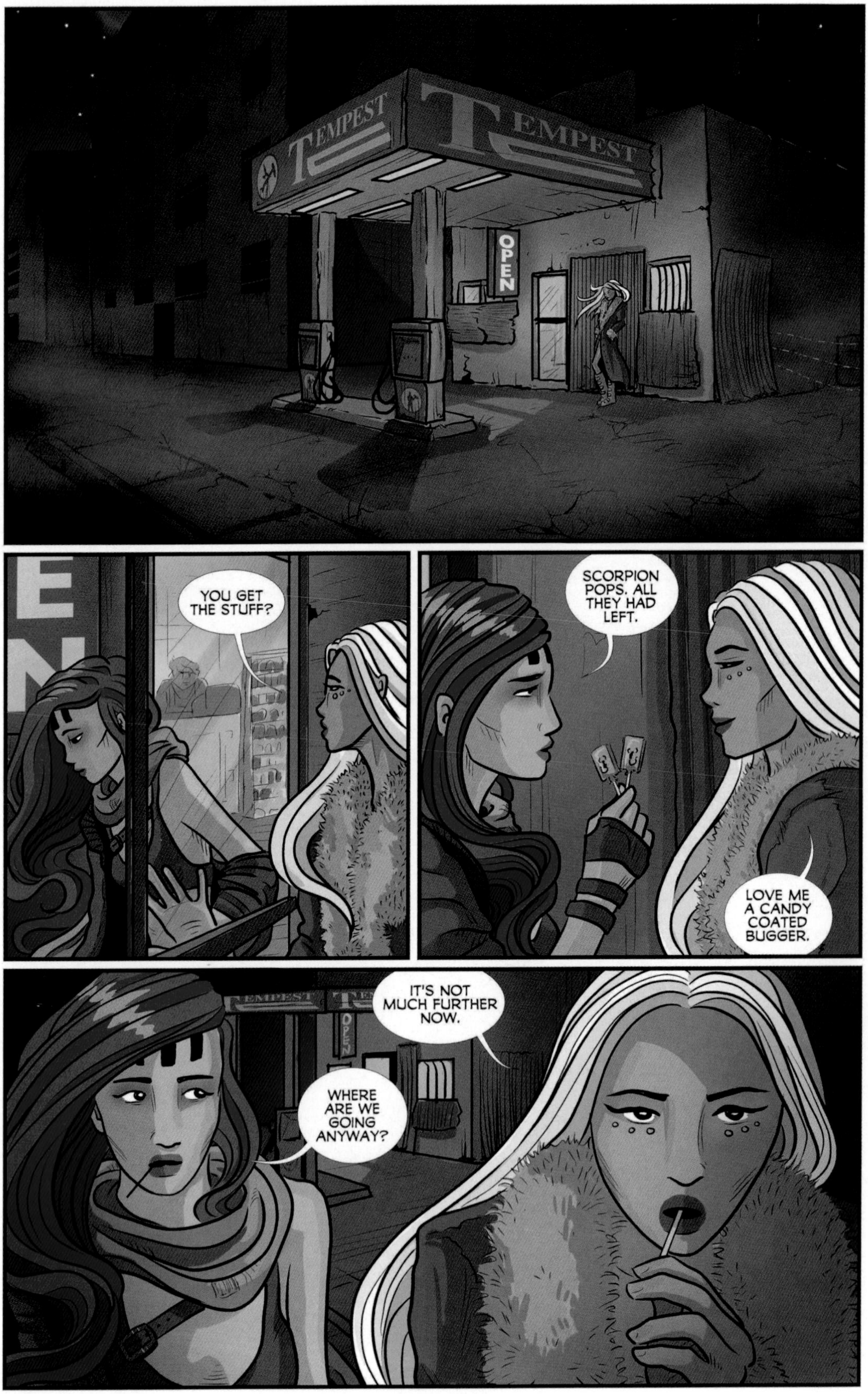
TEMPEST
TEMPEST
OPEN
YOU GET THE STUFF?
SCORPION POPS. ALL THEY HAD LEFT.
LOVE ME A CANDY COATED BUGGER.
IT'S NOT MUCH FURTHER NOW.
WHERE ARE WE GOING ANYWAY?

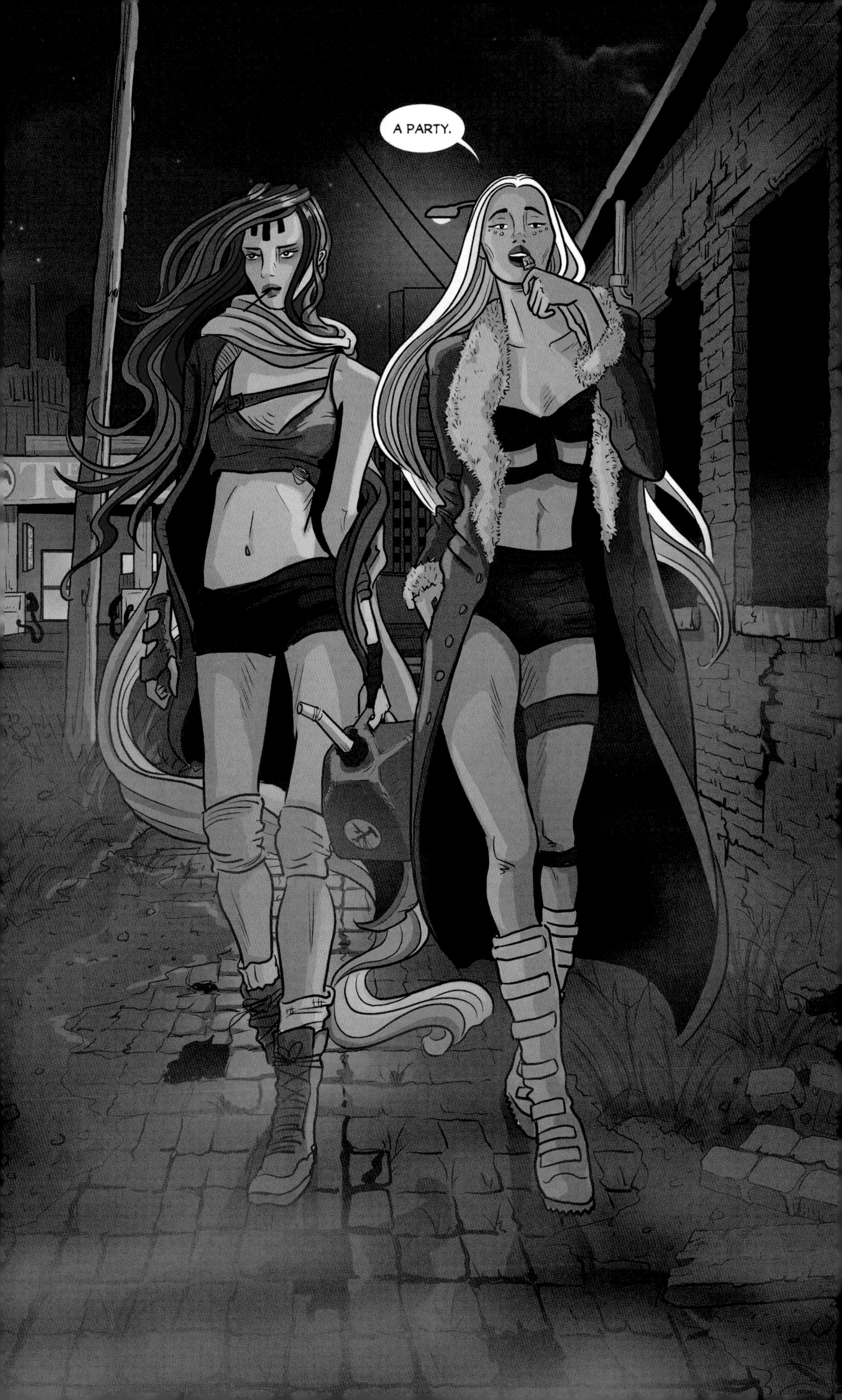
A PARTY.

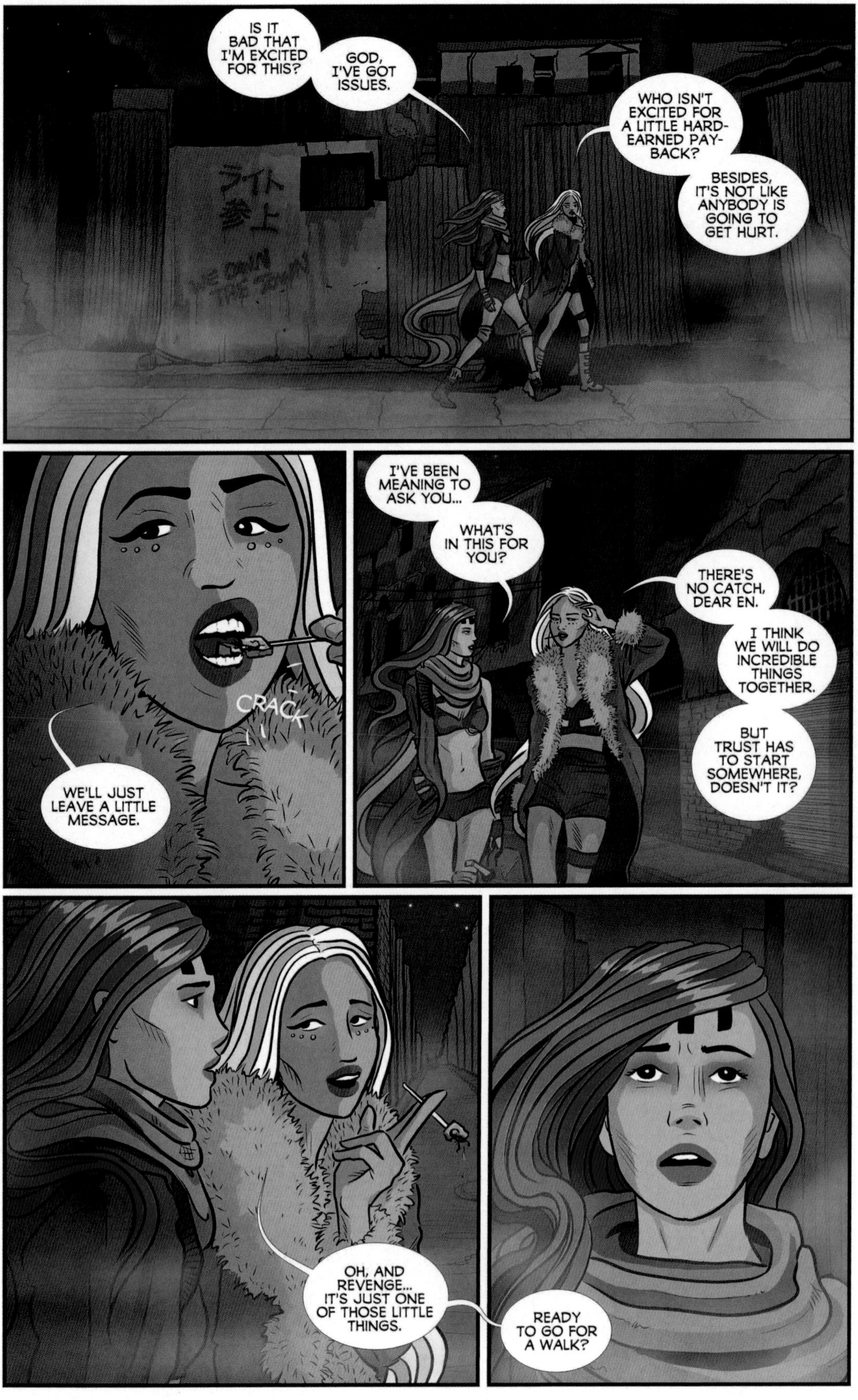
IS IT BAD THAT I'M EXCITED FOR THIS?
GOD, I'VE GOT ISSUES.
WHO ISN'T EXCITED FOR A LITTLE HARD-EARNED PAY-BACK?
BESIDES, IT'S NOT LIKE ANYBODY IS GOING TO GET HURT.
ライト参上
WE OWN THE TOWN
CRACK
WE'LL JUST LEAVE A LITTLE MESSAGE.
I'VE BEEN MEANING TO ASK YOU...
WHAT'S IN THIS FOR YOU?
THERE'S NO CATCH, DEAR EN.
I THINK WE WILL DO INCREDIBLE THINGS TOGETHER.
BUT TRUST HAS TO START SOMEWHERE, DOESN'T IT?
OH, AND REVENGE... IT'S JUST ONE OF THOSE LITTLE THINGS.
READY TO GO FOR A WALK?

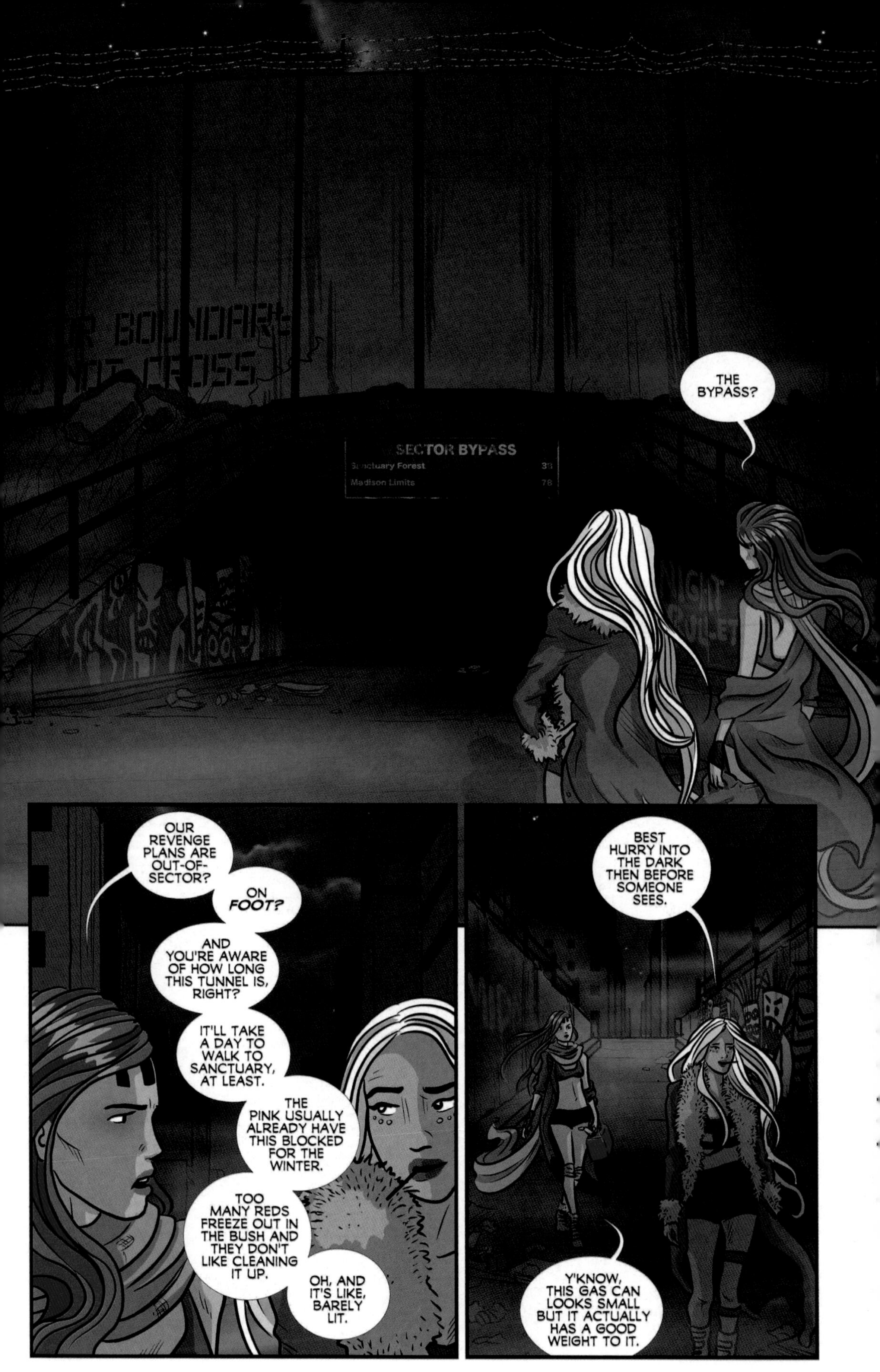
SECTOR BYPASS
Madison Limits 78
THE BYPASS?
OUR REVENGE PLANS ARE OUT-OF-SECTOR?
ON *FOOT?*
AND YOU'RE AWARE OF HOW LONG THIS TUNNEL IS, RIGHT?
IT'LL TAKE A DAY TO WALK TO SANCTUARY, AT LEAST.
THE PINK USUALLY ALREADY HAVE THIS BLOCKED FOR THE WINTER.
TOO MANY REDS FREEZE OUT IN THE BUSH AND THEY DON'T LIKE CLEANING IT UP.
OH, AND IT'S LIKE, BARELY LIT.
BEST HURRY INTO THE DARK THEN BEFORE SOMEONE SEES.
Y'KNOW, THIS GAS CAN LOOKS SMALL BUT IT ACTUALLY HAS A GOOD WEIGHT TO IT.

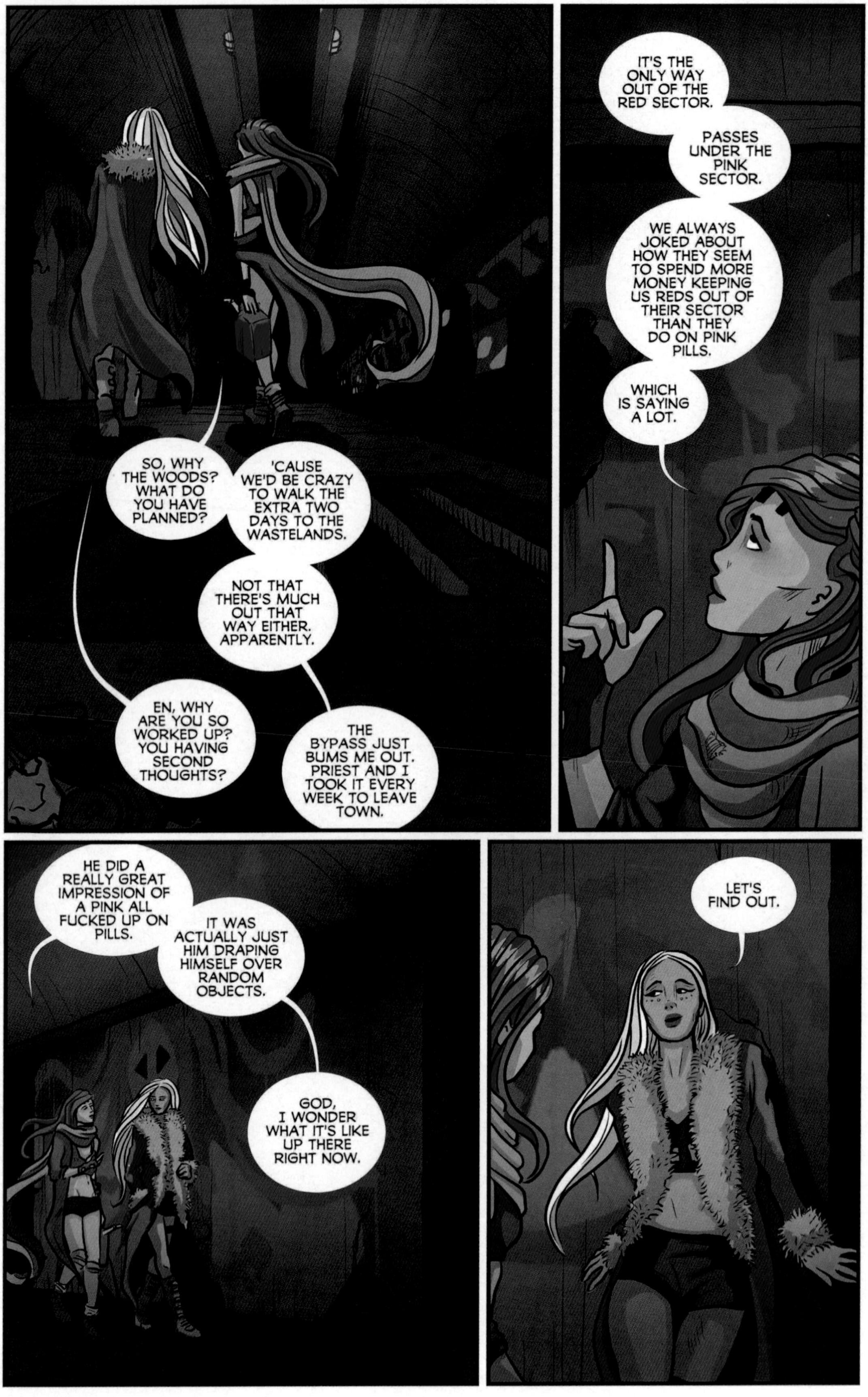
SO, WHY THE WOODS? WHAT DO YOU HAVE PLANNED?
'CAUSE WE'D BE CRAZY TO WALK THE EXTRA TWO DAYS TO THE WASTELANDS.
NOT THAT THERE'S MUCH OUT THAT WAY EITHER. APPARENTLY.
EN, WHY ARE YOU SO WORKED UP? YOU HAVING SECOND THOUGHTS?
THE BYPASS JUST BUMS ME OUT. PRIEST AND I TOOK IT EVERY WEEK TO LEAVE TOWN.
IT'S THE ONLY WAY OUT OF THE RED SECTOR.
PASSES UNDER THE PINK SECTOR.
WE ALWAYS JOKED ABOUT HOW THEY SEEM TO SPEND MORE MONEY KEEPING US REDS OUT OF THEIR SECTOR THAN THEY DO ON PINK PILLS.
WHICH IS SAYING A LOT.
HE DID A REALLY GREAT IMPRESSION OF A PINK ALL FUCKED UP ON PILLS.
IT WAS ACTUALLY JUST HIM DRAPING HIMSELF OVER RANDOM OBJECTS.
GOD, I WONDER WHAT IT'S LIKE UP THERE RIGHT NOW.
LET'S FIND OUT.

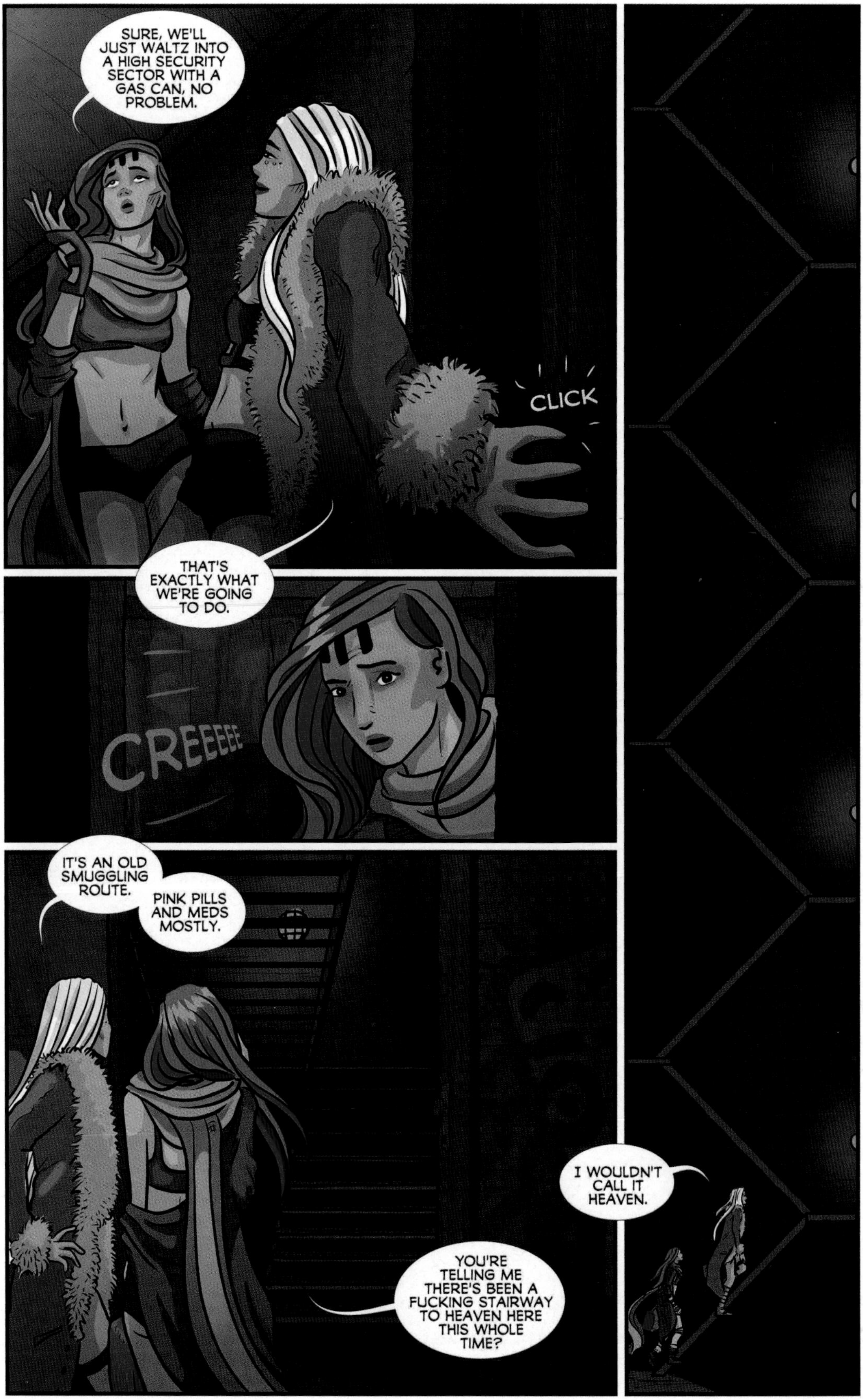
SURE, WE'LL JUST WALTZ INTO A HIGH SECURITY SECTOR WITH A GAS CAN, NO PROBLEM.
CLICK
THAT'S EXACTLY WHAT WE'RE GOING TO DO.
CREEEEE
IT'S AN OLD SMUGGLING ROUTE.
PINK PILLS AND MEDS MOSTLY.
YOU'RE TELLING ME THERE'S BEEN A FUCKING STAIRWAY TO HEAVEN HERE THIS WHOLE TIME?
I WOULDN'T CALL IT HEAVEN.

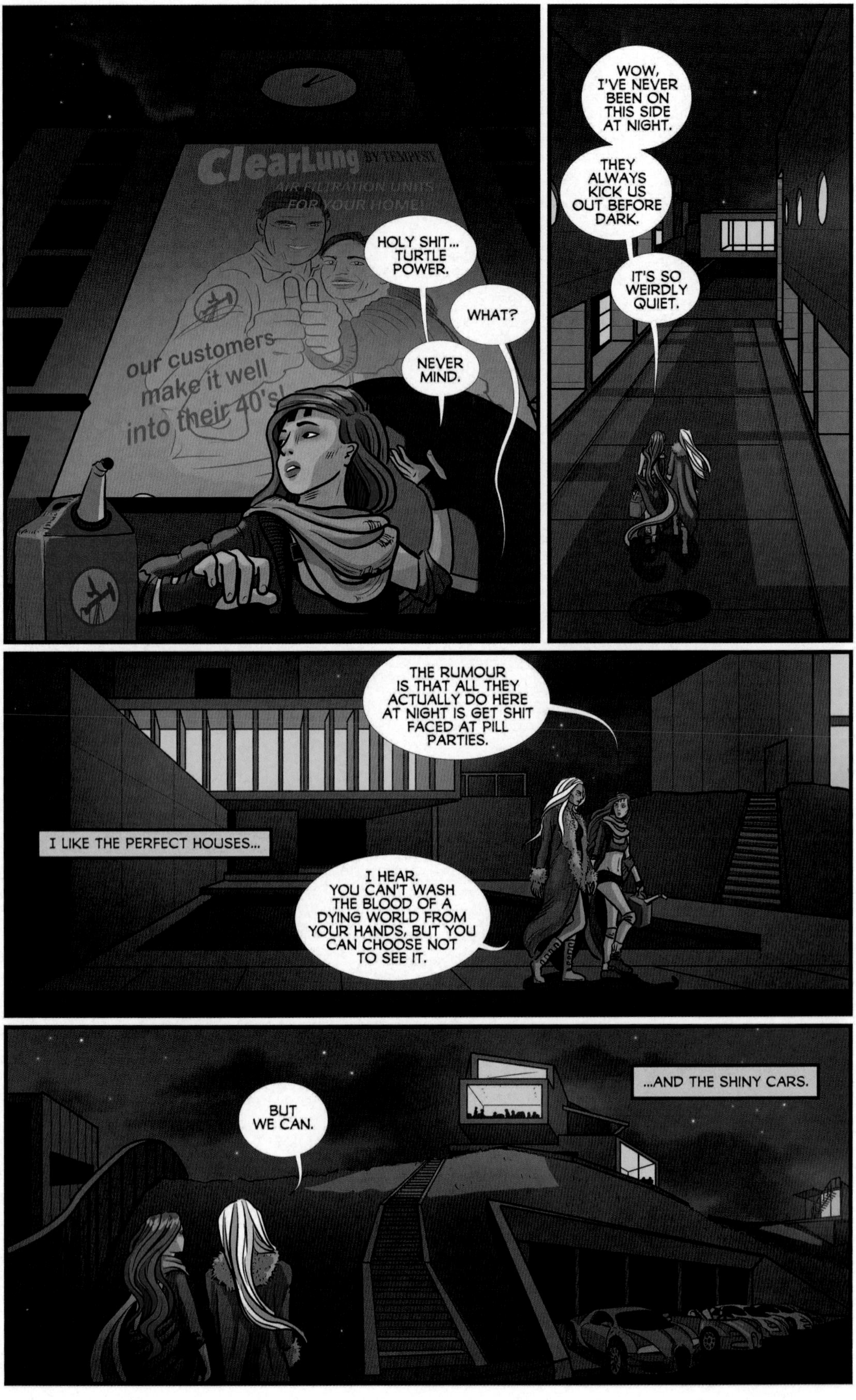
ClearLung BY TEMPEST
AIR FILTRATION UNITS FOR YOUR HOME!
our customers make it well into their 40's!
HOLY SHIT... TURTLE POWER.
WHAT?
NEVER MIND.
WOW, I'VE NEVER BEEN ON THIS SIDE AT NIGHT.
THEY ALWAYS KICK US OUT BEFORE DARK.
IT'S SO WEIRDLY QUIET.
I LIKE THE PERFECT HOUSES...
THE RUMOUR IS THAT ALL THEY ACTUALLY DO HERE AT NIGHT IS GET SHIT FACED AT PILL PARTIES.
I HEAR. YOU CAN'T WASH THE BLOOD OF A DYING WORLD FROM YOUR HANDS, BUT YOU CAN CHOOSE NOT TO SEE IT.
...AND THE SHINY CARS.
BUT WE CAN.

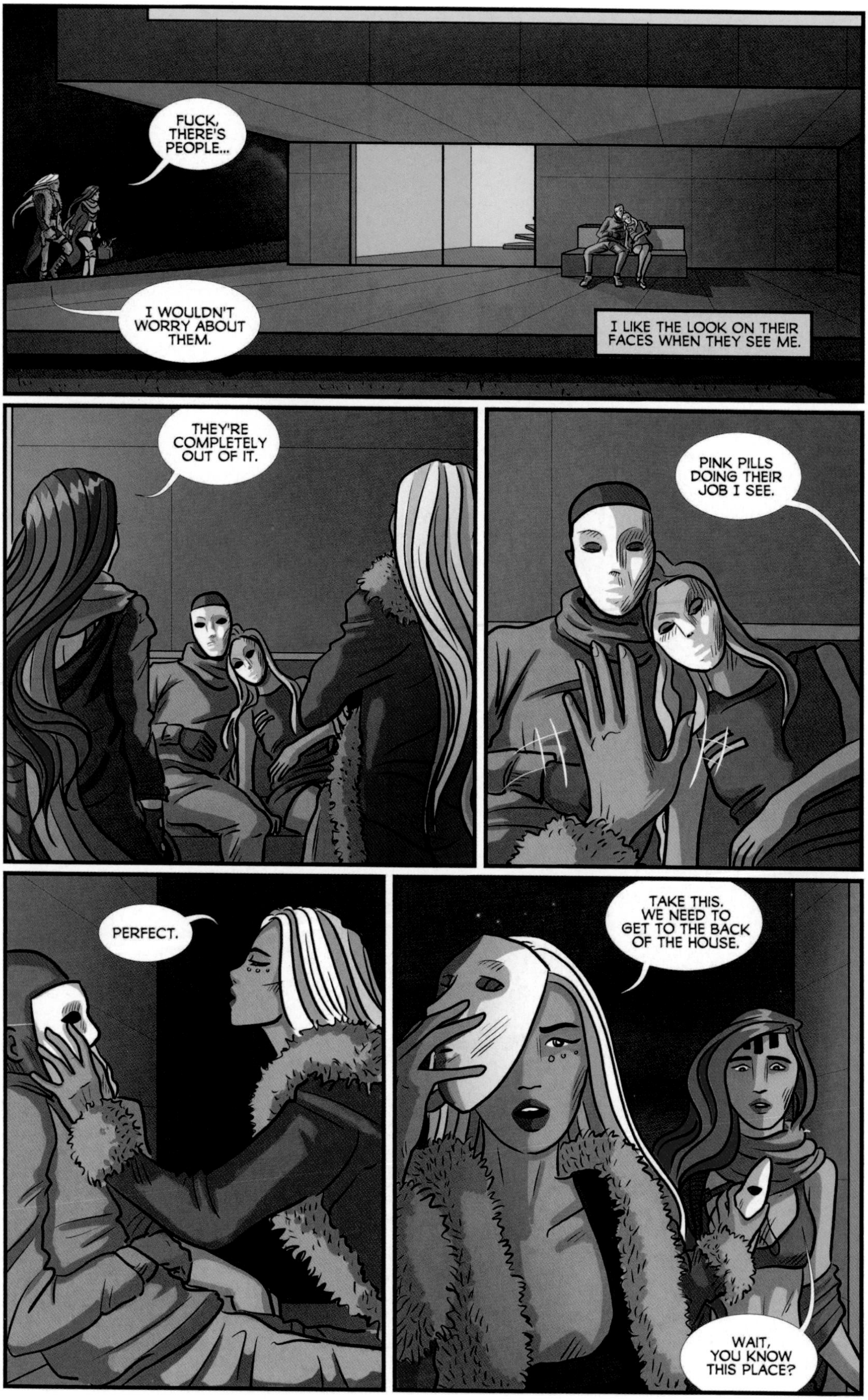
FUCK, THERE'S PEOPLE...
I WOULDN'T WORRY ABOUT THEM.
I LIKE THE LOOK ON THEIR FACES WHEN THEY SEE ME.
THEY'RE COMPLETELY OUT OF IT.
PINK PILLS DOING THEIR JOB I SEE.
PERFECT.
TAKE THIS. WE NEED TO GET TO THE BACK OF THE HOUSE.
WAIT, YOU KNOW THIS PLACE?

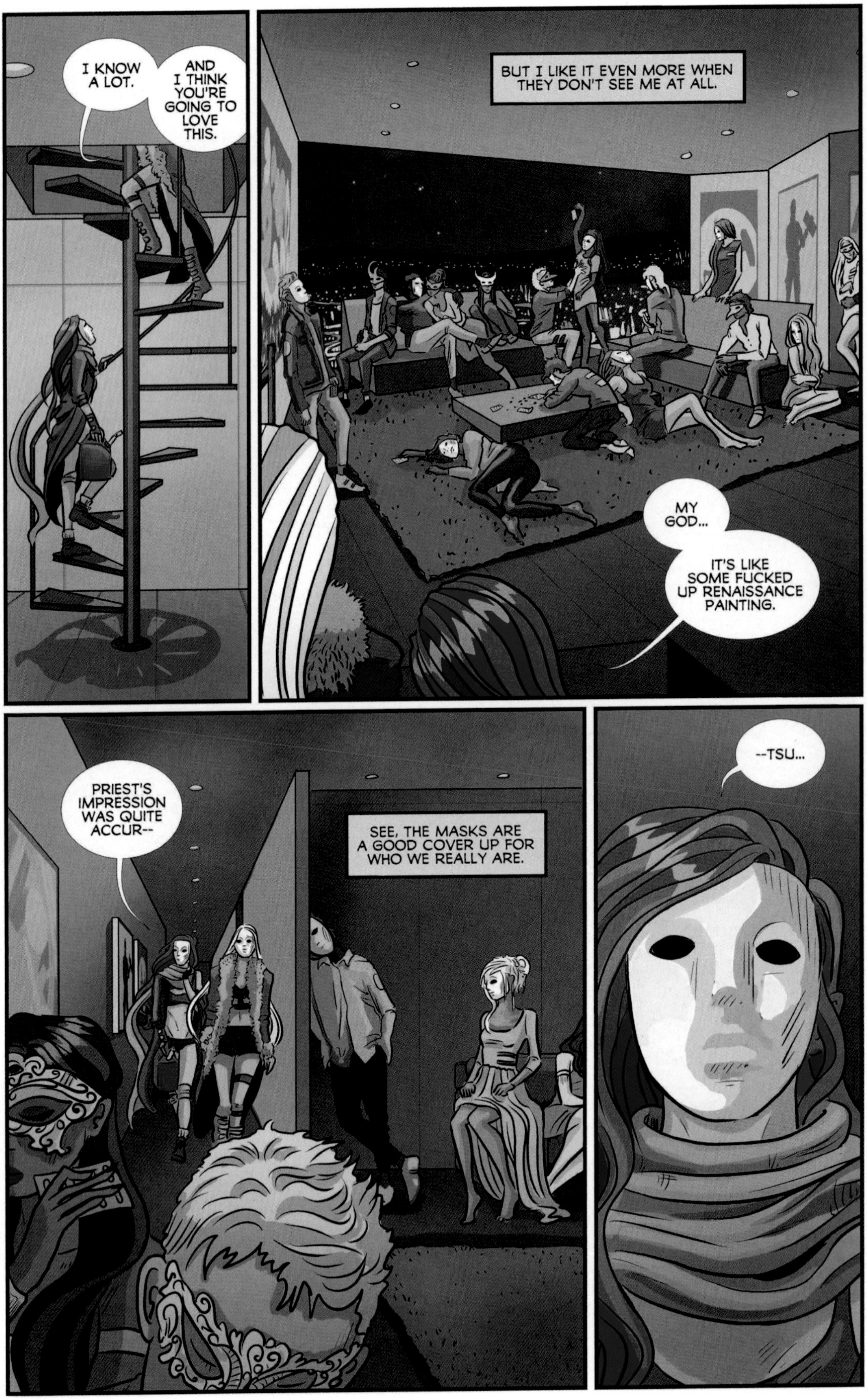
I KNOW A LOT.
AND I THINK YOU'RE GOING TO LOVE THIS.
BUT I LIKE IT EVEN MORE WHEN THEY DON'T SEE ME AT ALL.
MY GOD...
IT'S LIKE SOME FUCKED UP RENAISSANCE PAINTING.
PRIEST'S IMPRESSION WAS QUITE ACCUR--
SEE, THE MASKS ARE A GOOD COVER UP FOR WHO WE REALLY ARE.
--TSU...

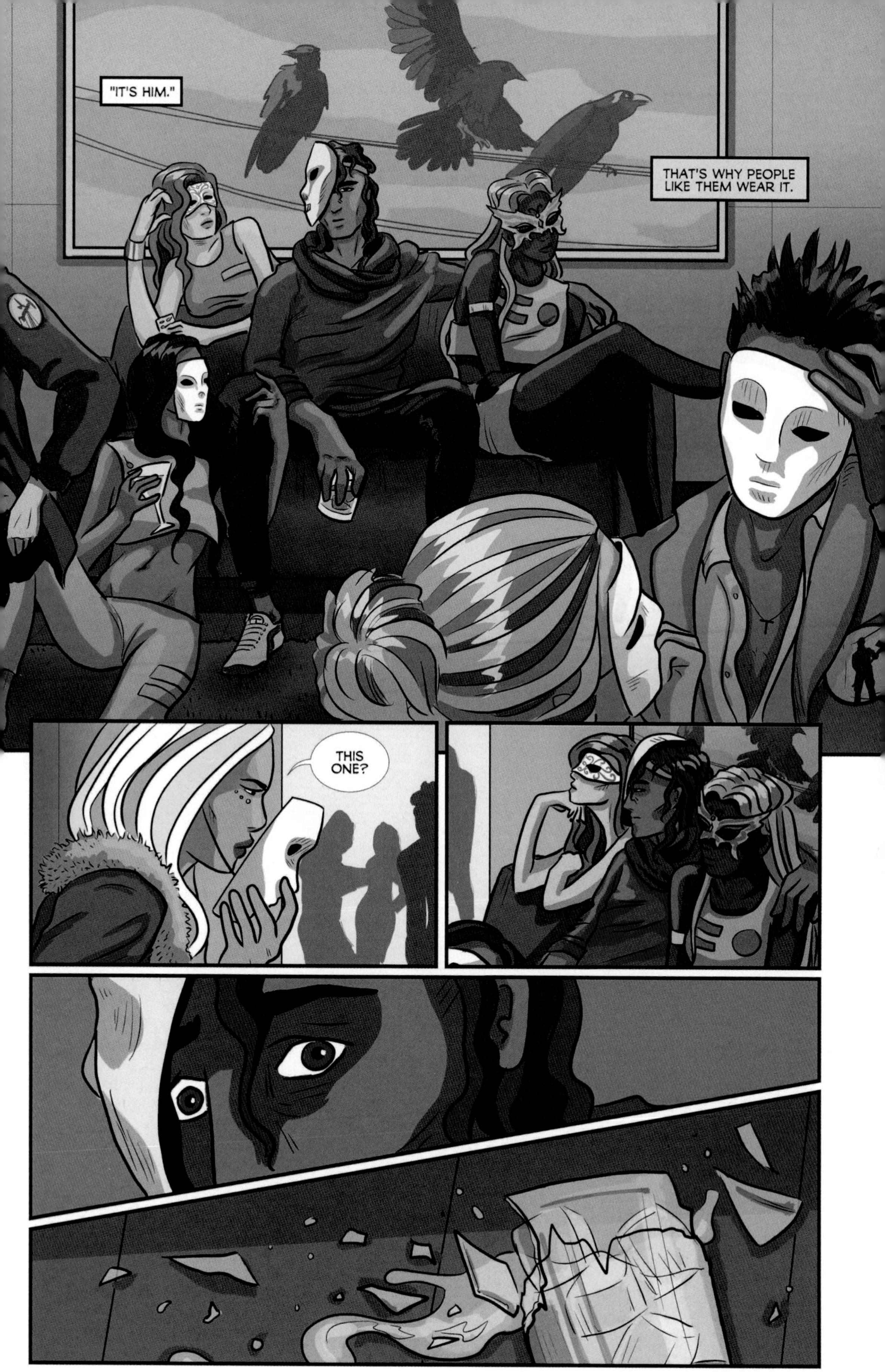
"IT'S HIM."
THAT'S WHY PEOPLE LIKE THEM WEAR IT.
THIS ONE?

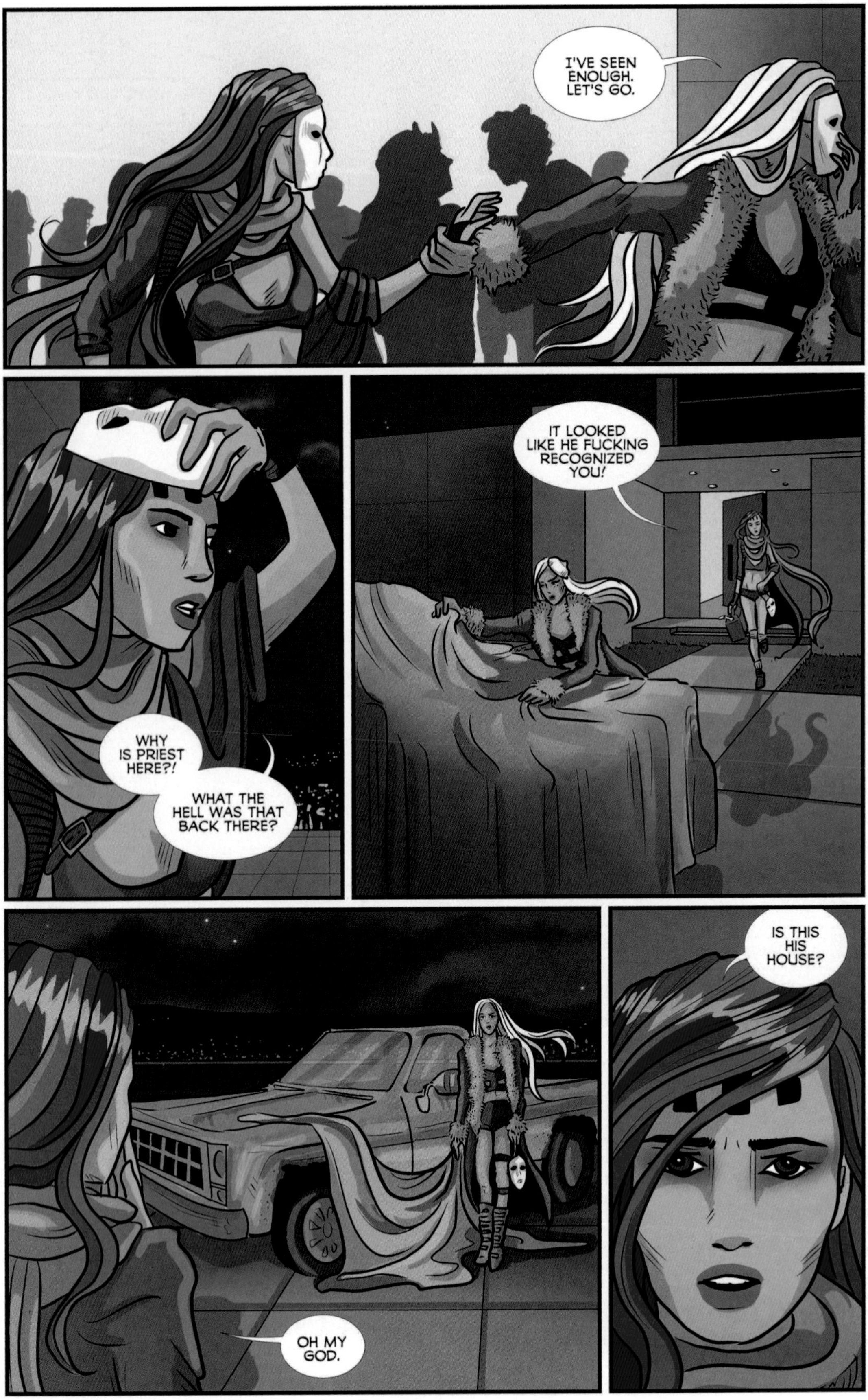
I'VE SEEN ENOUGH. LET'S GO.
WHY IS PRIEST HERE?!
WHAT THE HELL WAS THAT BACK THERE?
IT LOOKED LIKE HE FUCKING RECOGNIZED YOU!
OH MY GOD.
IS THIS HIS HOUSE?

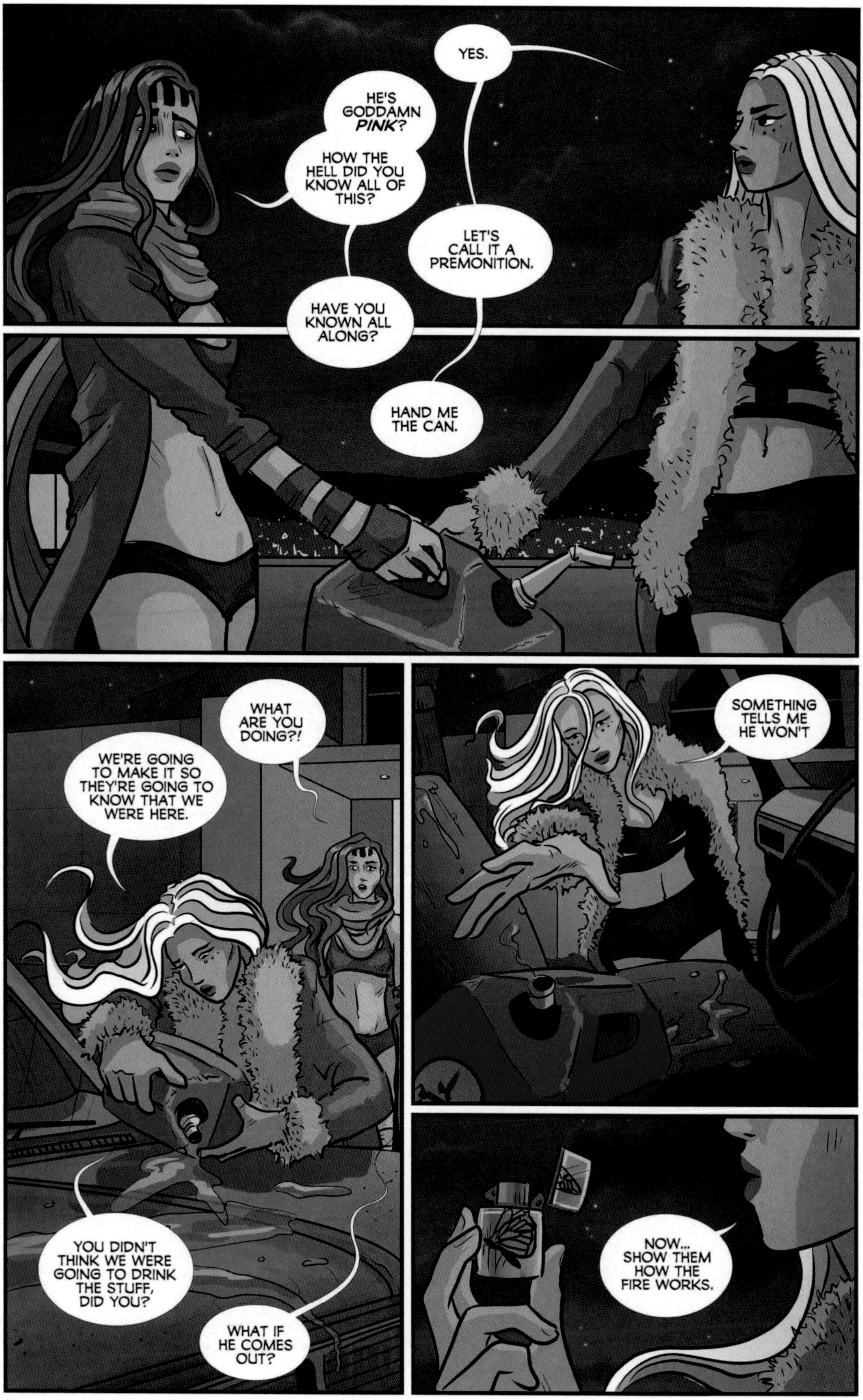

HE'S GODDAMN *PINK*?
HOW THE HELL DID YOU KNOW ALL OF THIS?
YES.
LET'S CALL IT A PREMONITION.
HAVE YOU KNOWN ALL ALONG?
HAND ME THE CAN.
WHAT ARE YOU DOING?!
WE'RE GOING TO MAKE IT SO THEY'RE GOING TO KNOW THAT WE WERE HERE.
YOU DIDN'T THINK WE WERE GOING TO DRINK THE STUFF, DID YOU?
WHAT IF HE COMES OUT?
SOMETHING TELLS ME HE WON'T
NOW... SHOW THEM HOW THE FIRE WORKS.

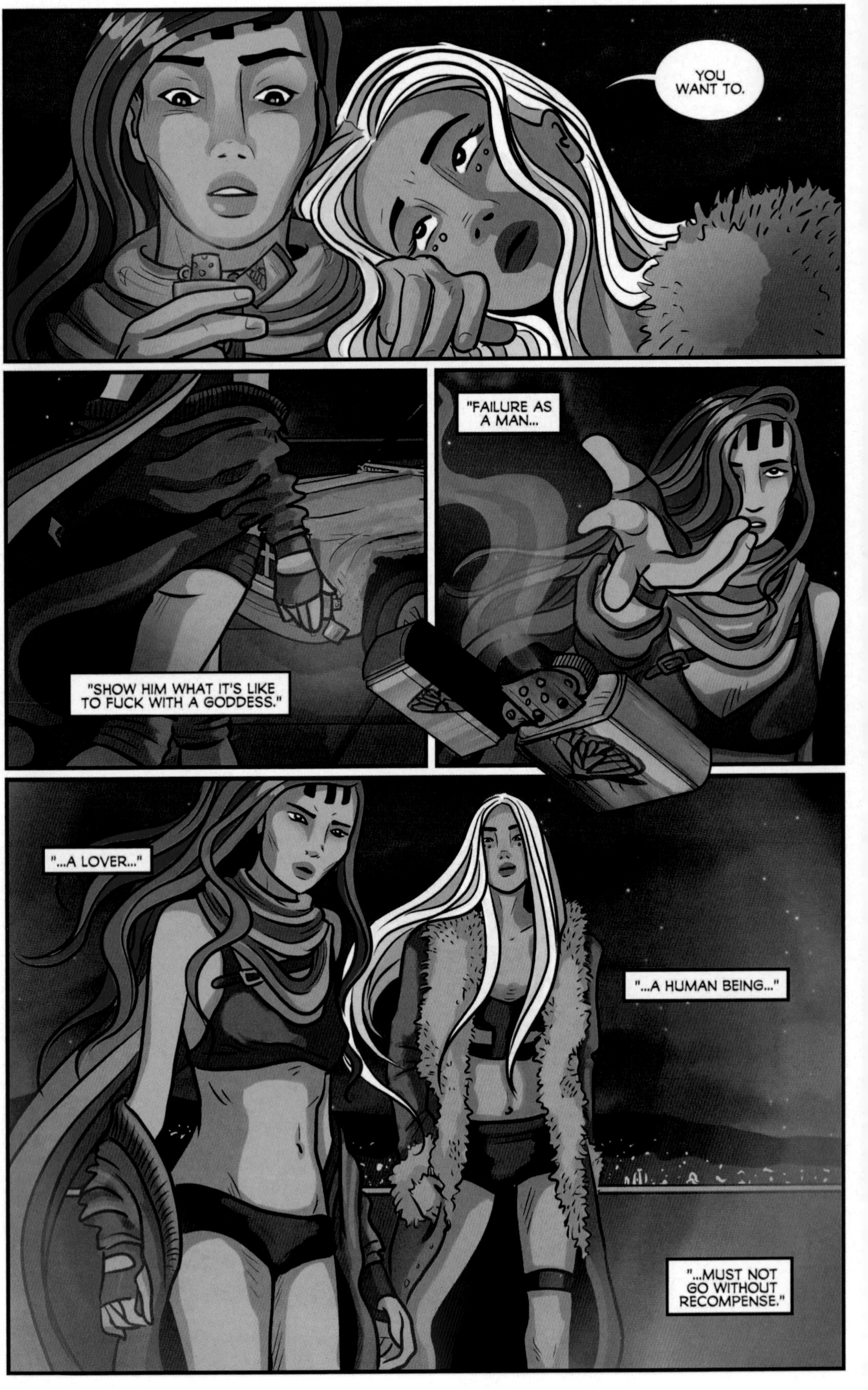
YOU WANT TO.
"SHOW HIM WHAT IT'S LIKE TO FUCK WITH A GODDESS."
"FAILURE AS A MAN...
"...A LOVER..."
"...A HUMAN BEING..."
"...MUST NOT GO WITHOUT RECOMPENSE."

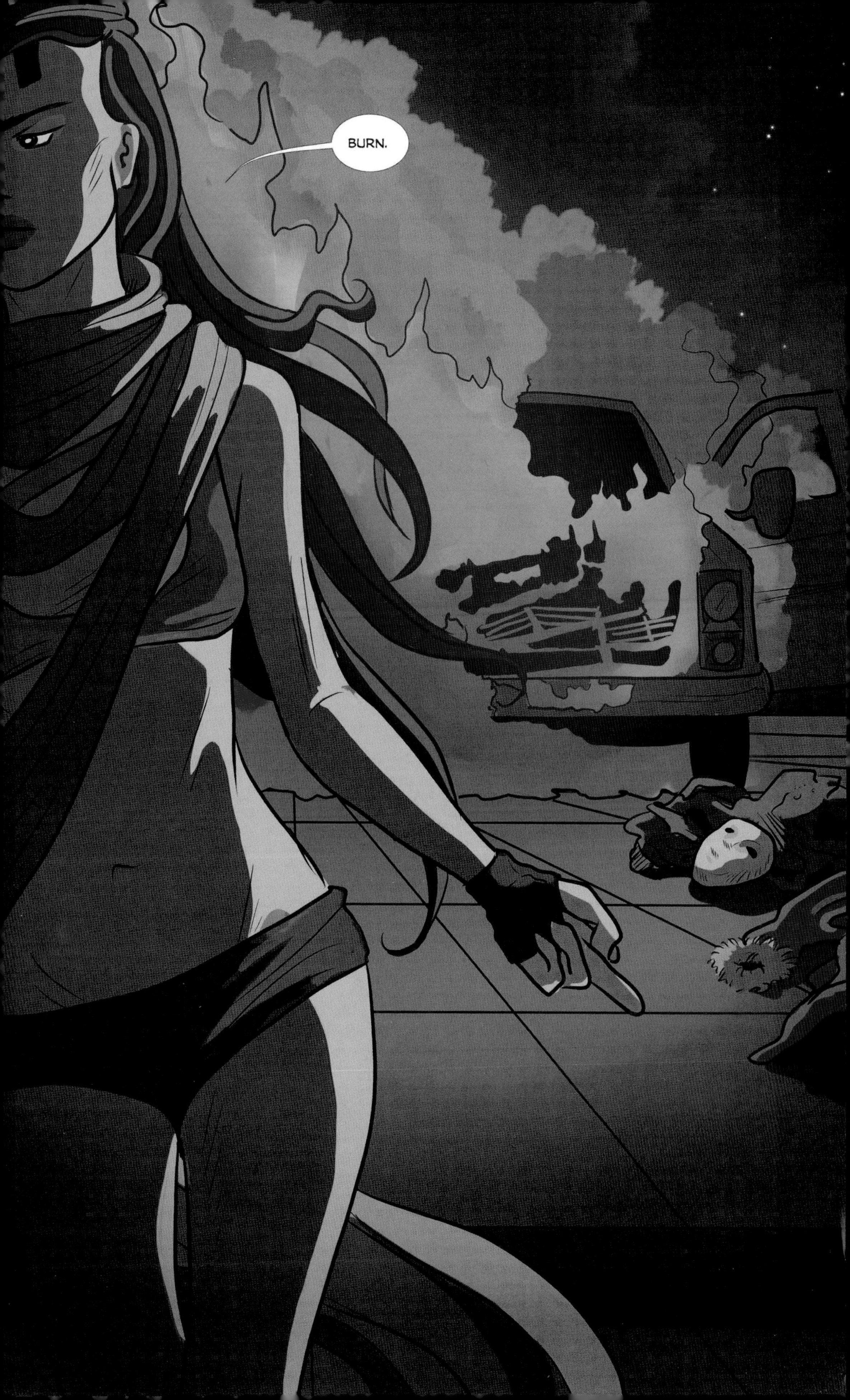
BURN.

CHAPTER EIGHT: KICKS

http://mxt.pe/kicksss

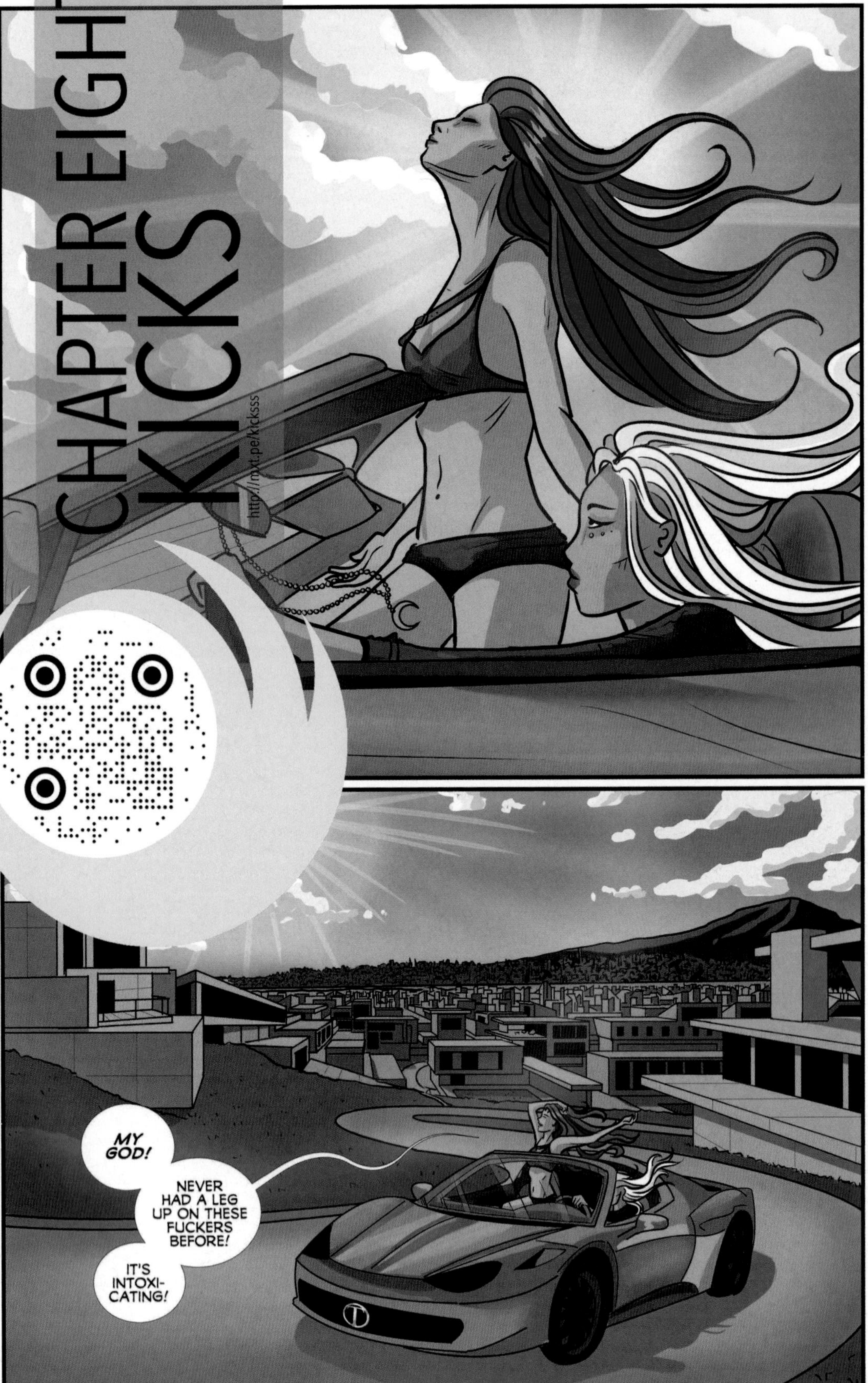
MY GOD!
NEVER HAD A LEG UP ON THESE FUCKERS BEFORE!
IT'S INTOXI-CATING!

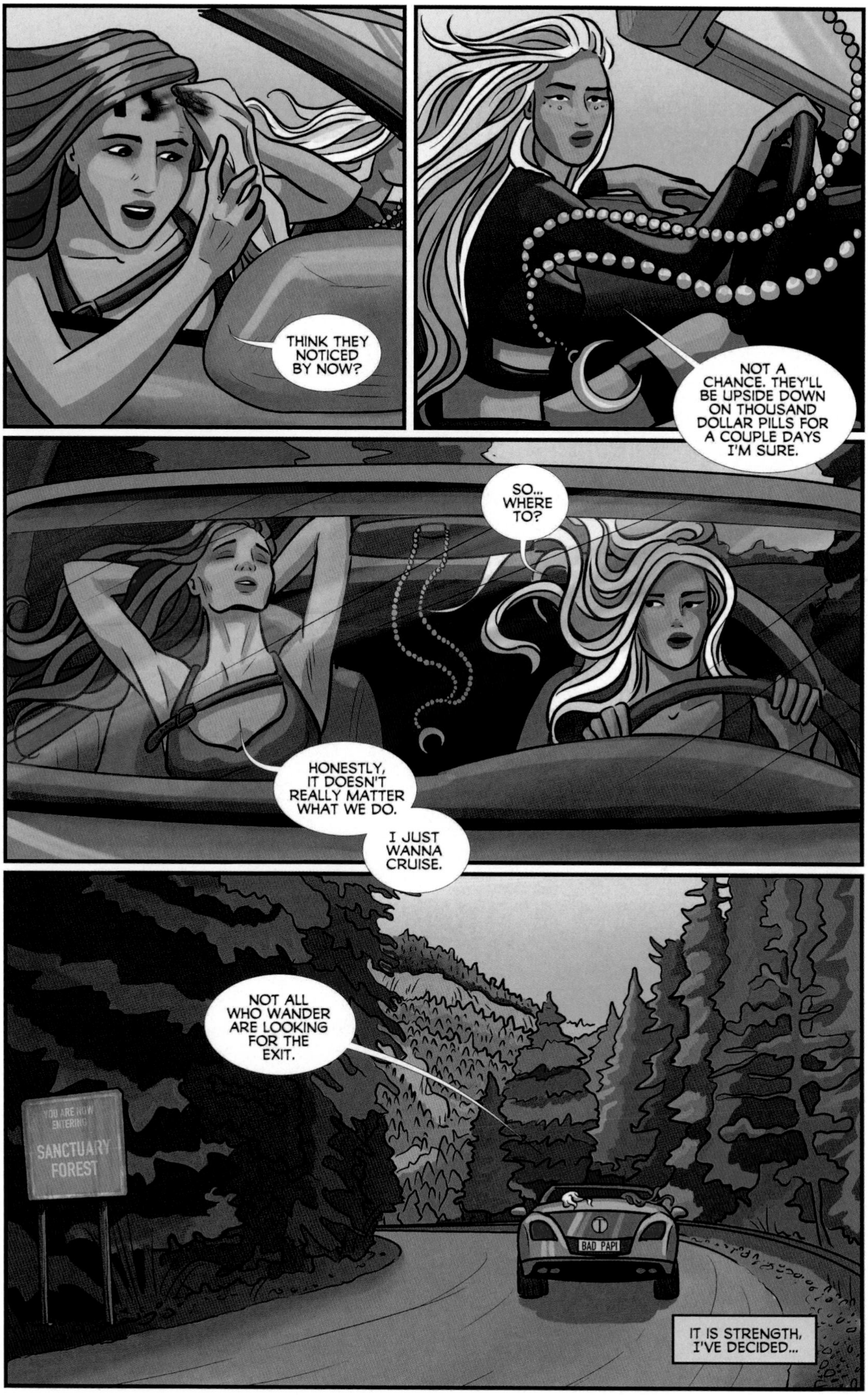
THINK THEY NOTICED BY NOW?
NOT A CHANCE. THEY'LL BE UPSIDE DOWN ON THOUSAND DOLLAR PILLS FOR A COUPLE DAYS I'M SURE.
SO... WHERE TO?
HONESTLY, IT DOESN'T REALLY MATTER WHAT WE DO.
I JUST WANNA CRUISE.
NOT ALL WHO WANDER ARE LOOKING FOR THE EXIT.
YOU ARE NOW ENTERING
SANCTUARY FOREST
BAD PAPI
IT IS STRENGTH, I'VE DECIDED...

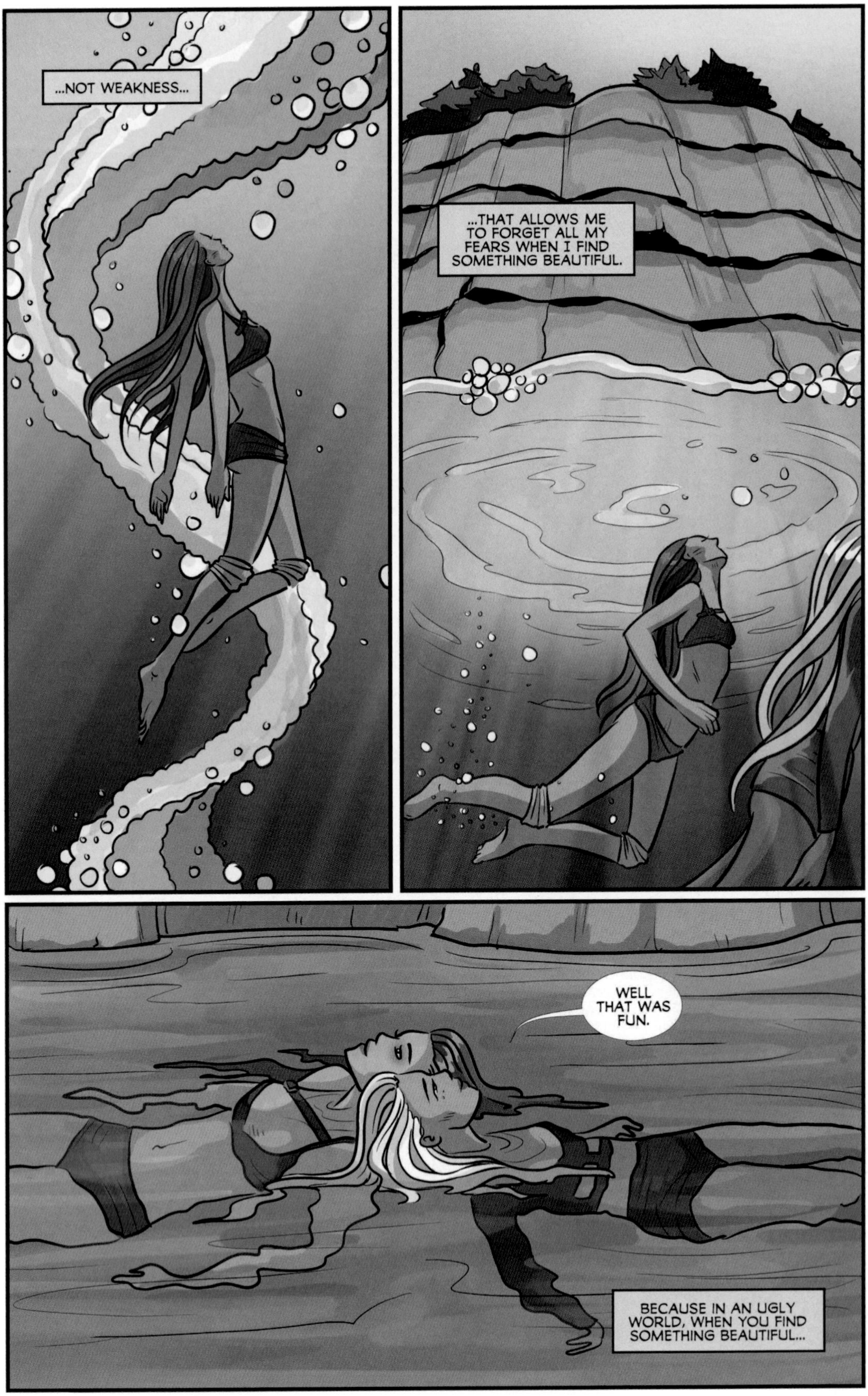
...NOT WEAKNESS...
...THAT ALLOWS ME TO FORGET ALL MY FEARS WHEN I FIND SOMETHING BEAUTIFUL.
WELL THAT WAS FUN.
BECAUSE IN AN UGLY WORLD, WHEN YOU FIND SOMETHING BEAUTIFUL...

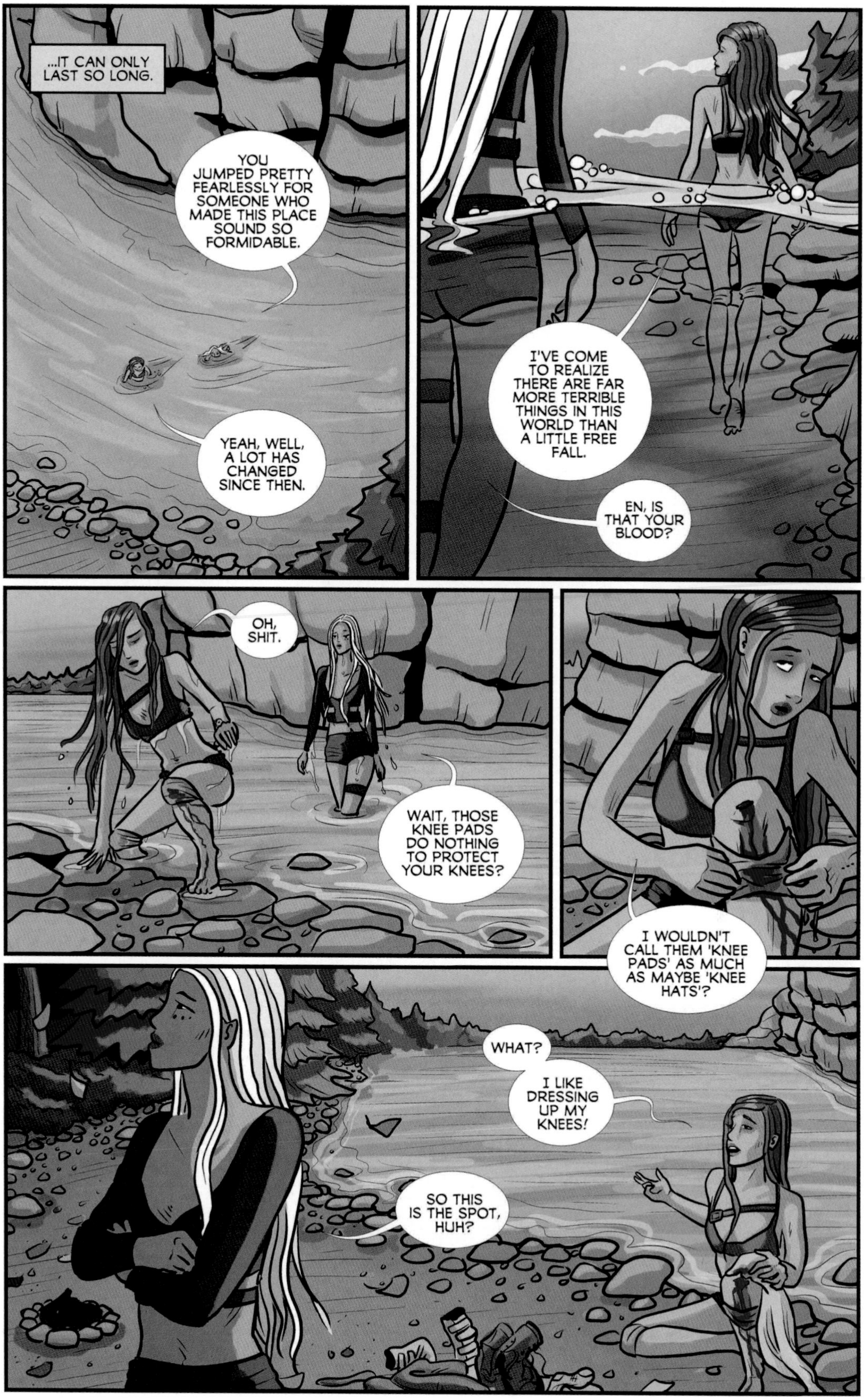

...IT CAN ONLY LAST SO LONG.
YOU JUMPED PRETTY FEARLESSLY FOR SOMEONE WHO MADE THIS PLACE SOUND SO FORMIDABLE.
YEAH, WELL, A LOT HAS CHANGED SINCE THEN.
I'VE COME TO REALIZE THERE ARE FAR MORE TERRIBLE THINGS IN THIS WORLD THAN A LITTLE FREE FALL.
EN, IS THAT YOUR BLOOD?
OH, SHIT.
WAIT, THOSE KNEE PADS DO NOTHING TO PROTECT YOUR KNEES?
I WOULDN'T CALL THEM 'KNEE PADS' AS MUCH AS MAYBE 'KNEE HATS'?
WHAT?
I LIKE DRESSING UP MY KNEES!
SO THIS IS THE SPOT, HUH?

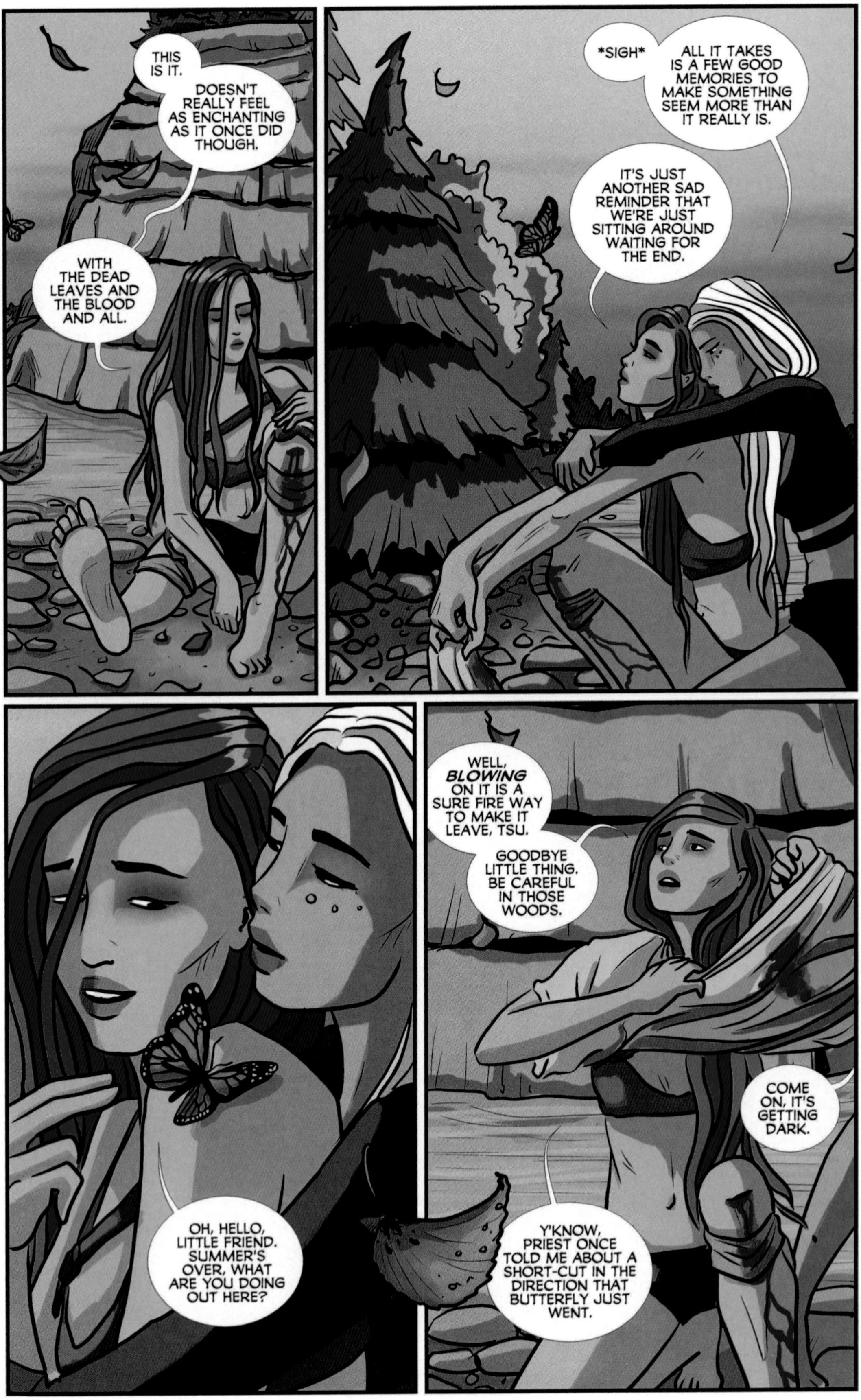
THIS IS IT.
DOESN'T REALLY FEEL AS ENCHANTING AS IT ONCE DID THOUGH.
WITH THE DEAD LEAVES AND THE BLOOD AND ALL.
SIGH
ALL IT TAKES IS A FEW GOOD MEMORIES TO MAKE SOMETHING SEEM MORE THAN IT REALLY IS.
IT'S JUST ANOTHER SAD REMINDER THAT WE'RE JUST SITTING AROUND WAITING FOR THE END.
OH, HELLO, LITTLE FRIEND. SUMMER'S OVER, WHAT ARE YOU DOING OUT HERE?
WELL, *BLOWING* ON IT IS A SURE FIRE WAY TO MAKE IT LEAVE, TSU.
GOODBYE LITTLE THING. BE CAREFUL IN THOSE WOODS.
COME ON, IT'S GETTING DARK.
Y'KNOW, PRIEST ONCE TOLD ME ABOUT A SHORT-CUT IN THE DIRECTION THAT BUTTERFLY JUST WENT.

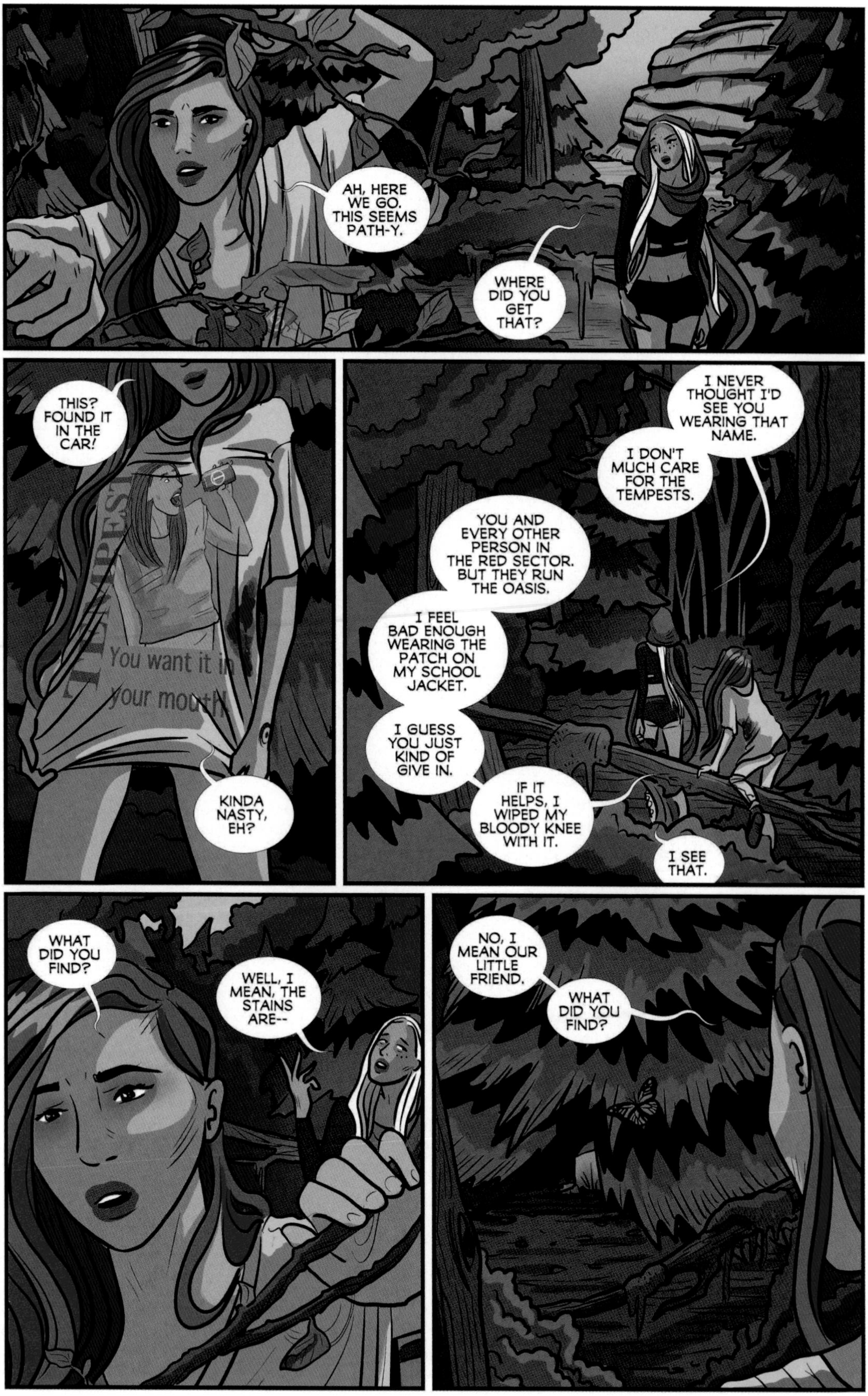
AH, HERE WE GO. THIS SEEMS PATH-Y.
WHERE DID YOU GET THAT?
THIS? FOUND IT IN THE CAR!
KINDA NASTY, EH?
I NEVER THOUGHT I'D SEE YOU WEARING THAT NAME.
I DON'T MUCH CARE FOR THE TEMPESTS.
YOU AND EVERY OTHER PERSON IN THE RED SECTOR. BUT THEY RUN THE OASIS.
I FEEL BAD ENOUGH WEARING THE PATCH ON MY SCHOOL JACKET.
I GUESS YOU JUST KIND OF GIVE IN.
IF IT HELPS, I WIPED MY BLOODY KNEE WITH IT.
I SEE THAT.
WHAT DID YOU FIND?
WELL, I MEAN, THE STAINS ARE--
NO, I MEAN OUR LITTLE FRIEND.
WHAT DID YOU FIND?

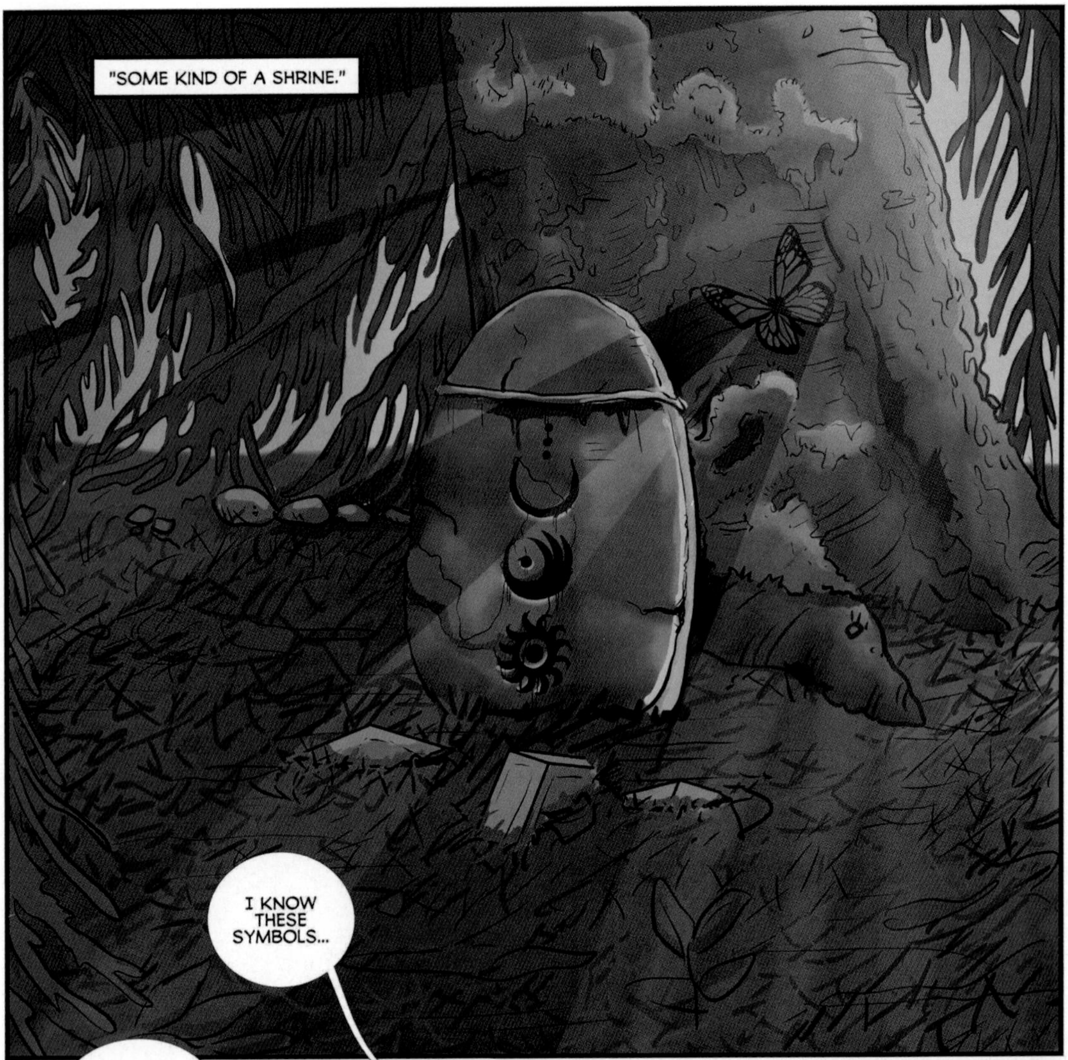
"SOME KIND OF A SHRINE."
I KNOW THESE SYMBOLS...

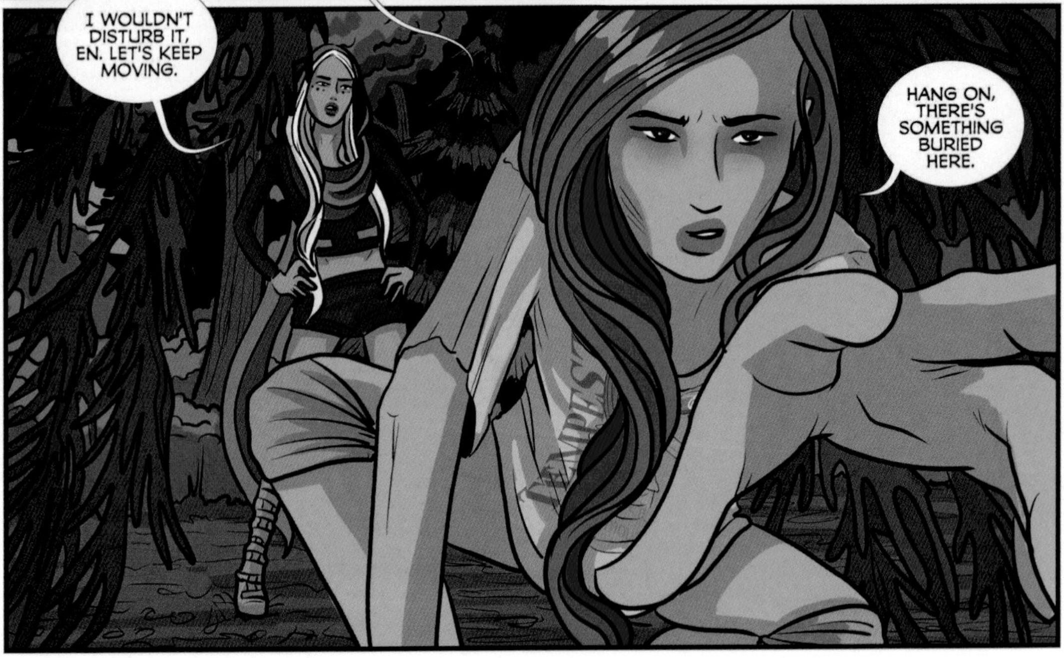
I WOULDN'T DISTURB IT, EN. LET'S KEEP MOVING.
HANG ON, THERE'S SOMETHING BURIED HERE.

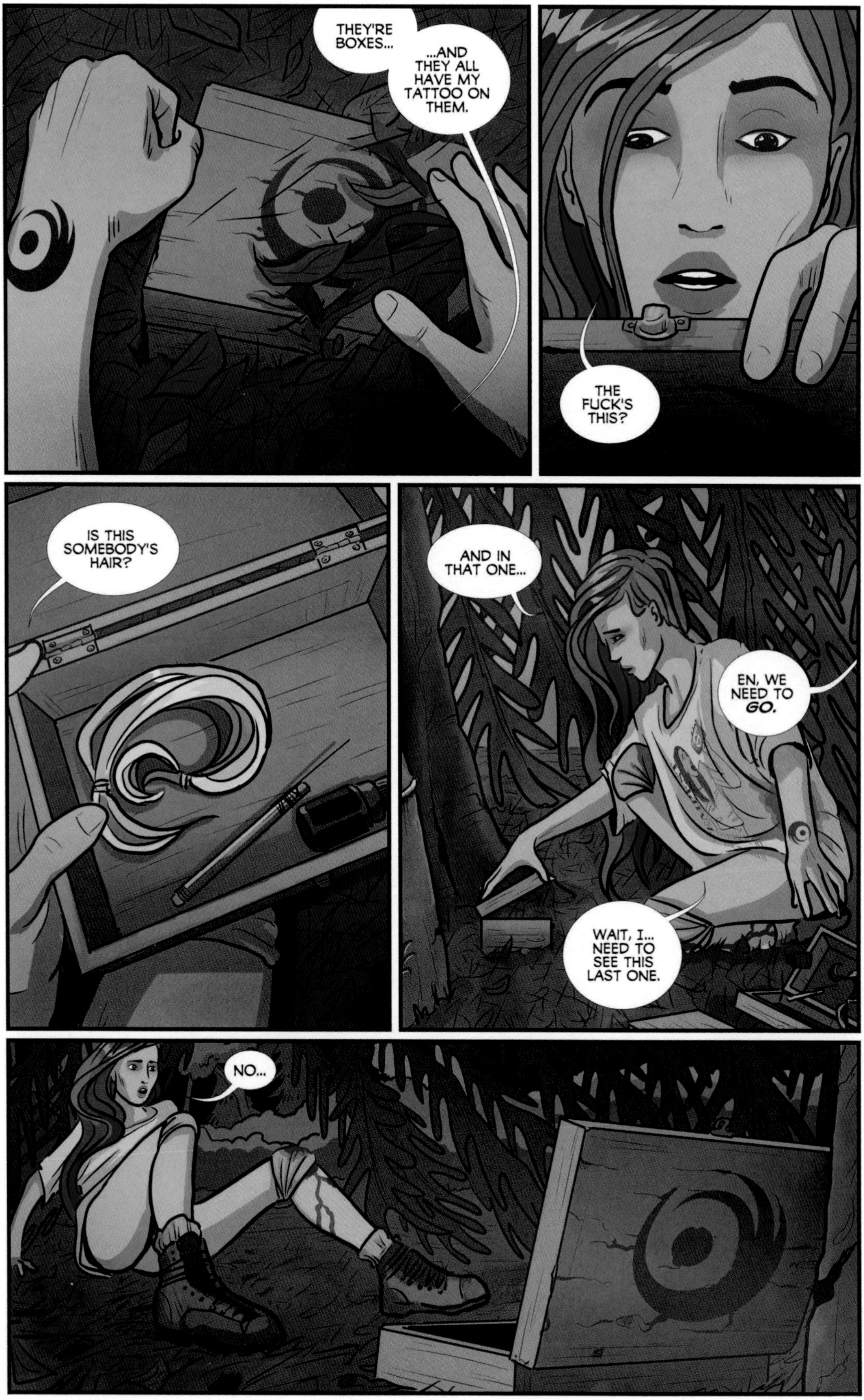
THEY'RE BOXES...
...AND THEY ALL HAVE MY TATTOO ON THEM.
THE FUCK'S THIS?
IS THIS SOMEBODY'S HAIR?
AND IN THAT ONE...
EN, WE NEED TO *GO.*
WAIT, I... NEED TO SEE THIS LAST ONE.
NO...

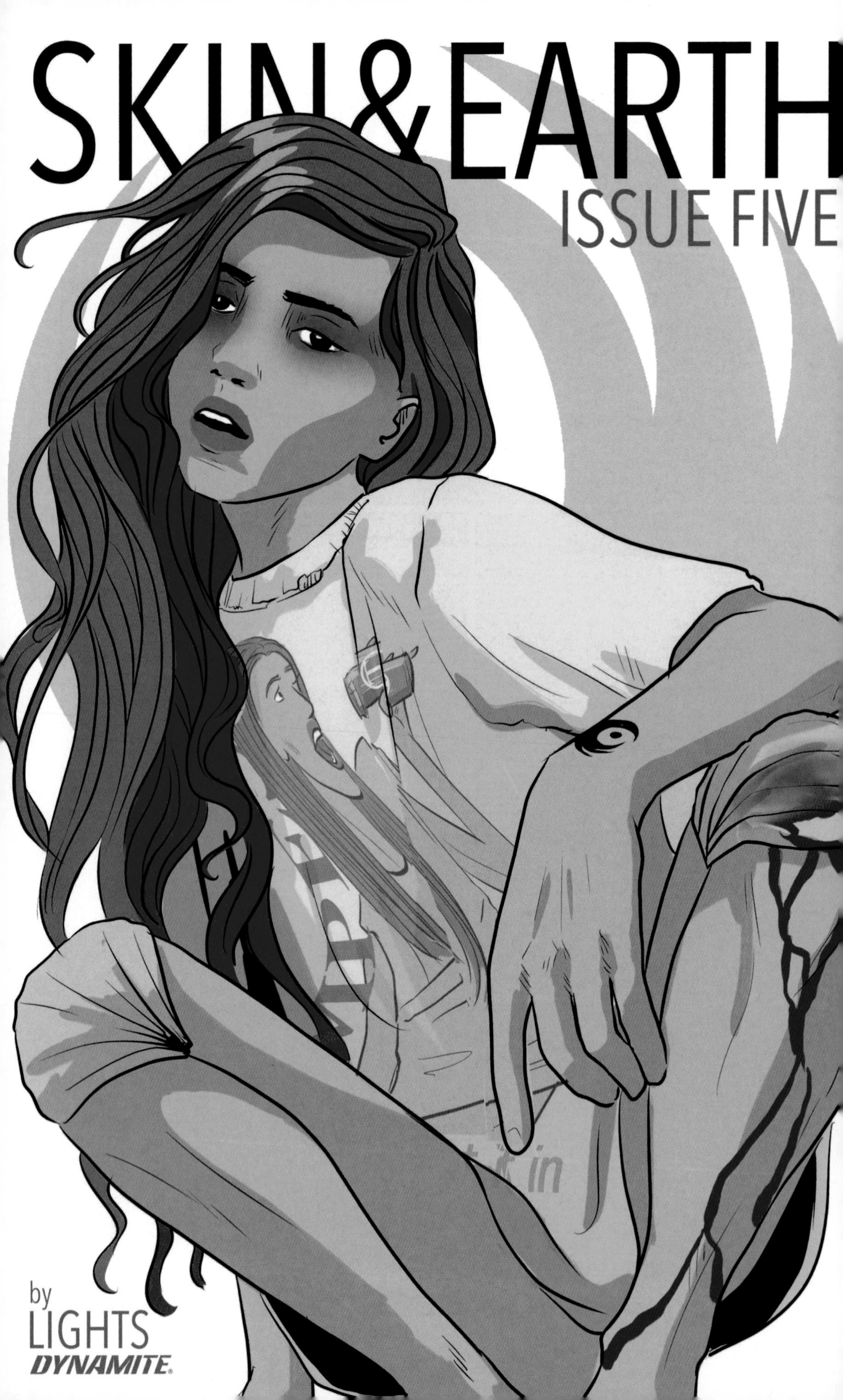
SKIN&EARTH
ISSUE FIVE
by
LIGHTS
DYNAMITE

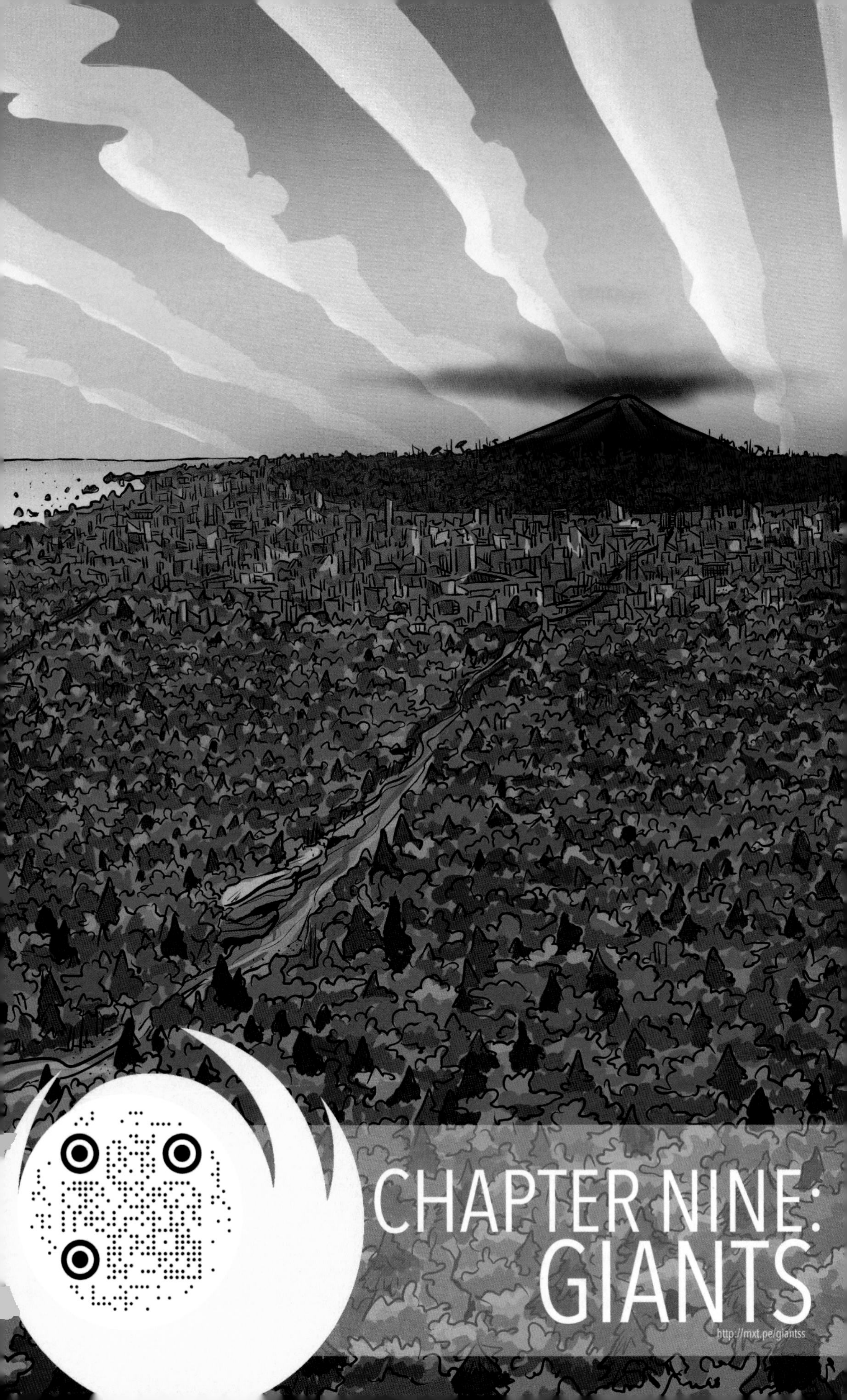

CHAPTER NINE: GIANTS

http://mxt.pe/giantss

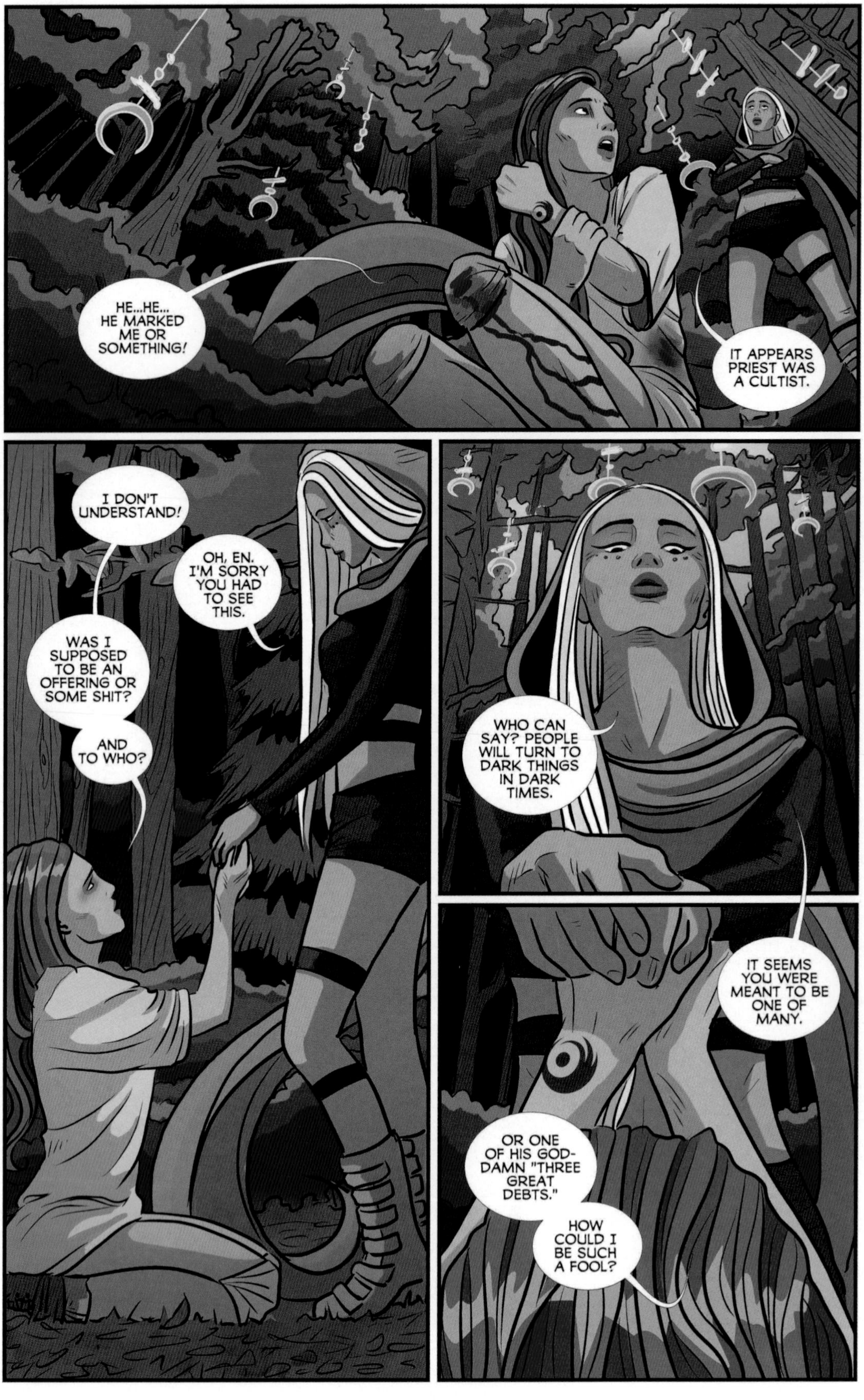
HE...HE...
HE MARKED
ME OR
SOMETHING!
IT APPEARS
PRIEST WAS
A CULTIST.
I DON'T
UNDERSTAND!
OH, EN.
I'M SORRY
YOU HAD
TO SEE
THIS.
WAS I
SUPPOSED
TO BE AN
OFFERING OR
SOME SHIT?
AND
TO WHO?
WHO CAN
SAY? PEOPLE
WILL TURN TO
DARK THINGS
IN DARK
TIMES.
IT SEEMS
YOU WERE
MEANT TO BE
ONE OF
MANY.
OR ONE
OF HIS GOD-
DAMN "THREE
GREAT
DEBTS."
HOW
COULD I
BE SUCH
A FOOL?

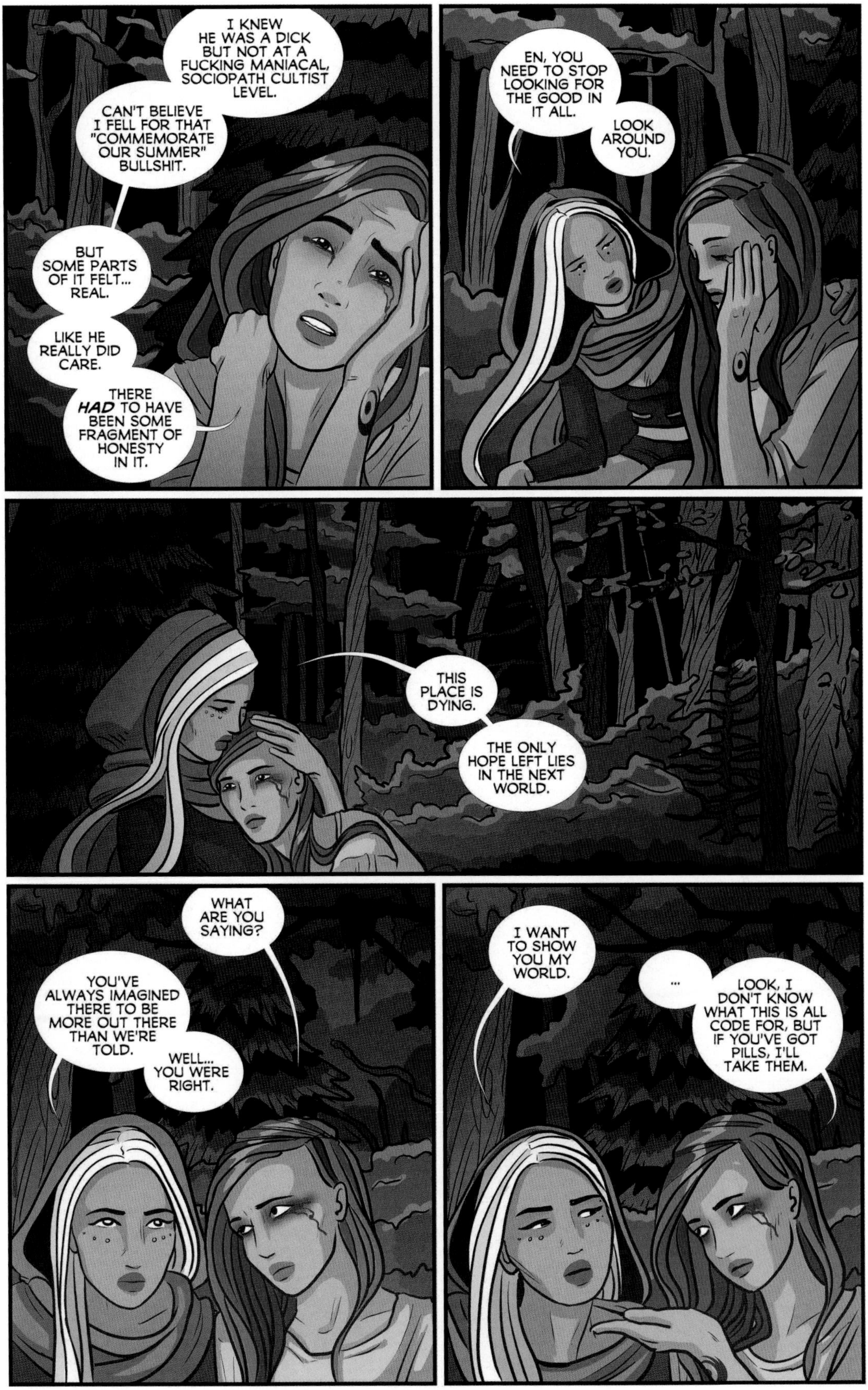

I KNEW HE WAS A DICK BUT NOT AT A FUCKING MANIACAL, SOCIOPATH CULTIST LEVEL.
CAN'T BELIEVE I FELL FOR THAT "COMMEMORATE OUR SUMMER" BULLSHIT.
BUT SOME PARTS OF IT FELT... REAL.
LIKE HE REALLY DID CARE.
THERE *HAD* TO HAVE BEEN SOME FRAGMENT OF HONESTY IN IT.
EN, YOU NEED TO STOP LOOKING FOR THE GOOD IN IT ALL.
LOOK AROUND YOU.
THIS PLACE IS DYING.
THE ONLY HOPE LEFT LIES IN THE NEXT WORLD.
WHAT ARE YOU SAYING?
YOU'VE ALWAYS IMAGINED THERE TO BE MORE OUT THERE THAN WE'RE TOLD.
WELL... YOU WERE RIGHT.
I WANT TO SHOW YOU MY WORLD.
...
LOOK, I DON'T KNOW WHAT THIS IS ALL CODE FOR, BUT IF YOU'VE GOT PILLS, I'LL TAKE THEM.

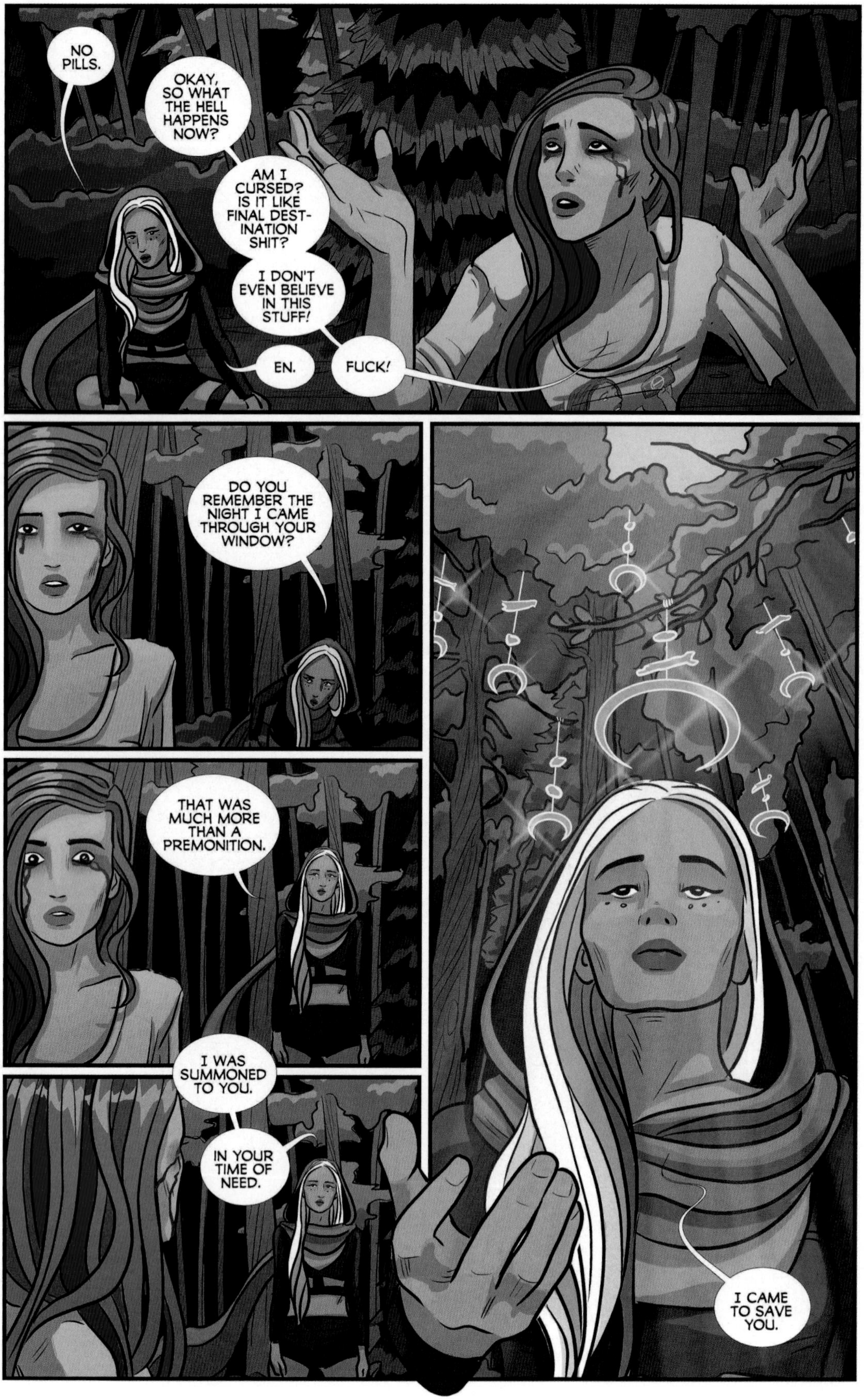
NO PILLS.
OKAY, SO WHAT THE HELL HAPPENS NOW?
AM I CURSED? IS IT LIKE FINAL DEST-INATION SHIT?
I DON'T EVEN BELIEVE IN THIS STUFF!
FUCK!
EN.
DO YOU REMEMBER THE NIGHT I CAME THROUGH YOUR WINDOW?
THAT WAS MUCH MORE THAN A PREMONITION.
I WAS SUMMONED TO YOU.
IN YOUR TIME OF NEED.
I CAME TO SAVE YOU.

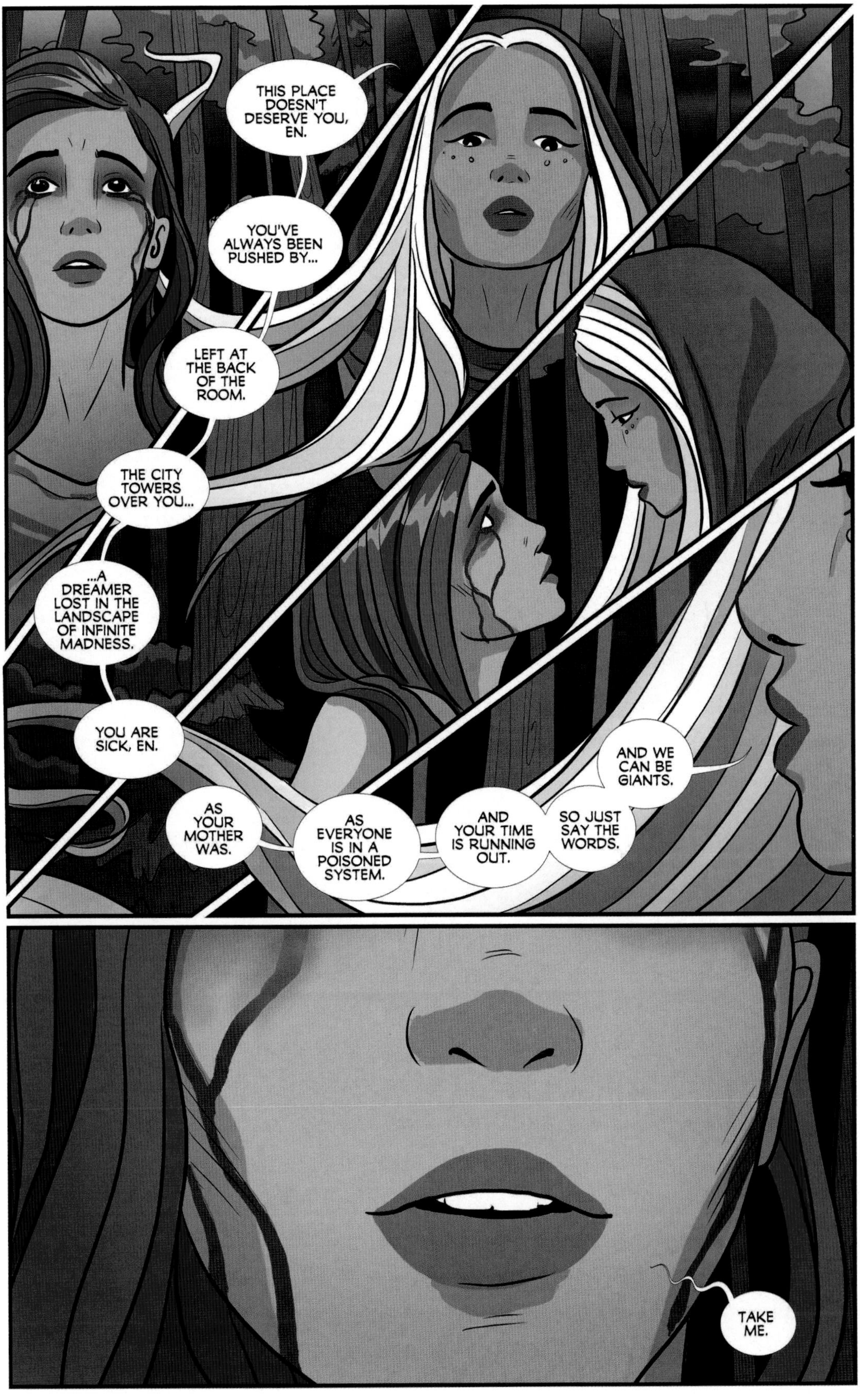
THIS PLACE DOESN'T DESERVE YOU, EN.
YOU'VE ALWAYS BEEN PUSHED BY...
LEFT AT THE BACK OF THE ROOM.
THE CITY TOWERS OVER YOU...
...A DREAMER LOST IN THE LANDSCAPE OF INFINITE MADNESS.
YOU ARE SICK, EN.
AS YOUR MOTHER WAS.
AS EVERYONE IS IN A POISONED SYSTEM.
AND YOUR TIME IS RUNNING OUT.
SO JUST SAY THE WORDS.
AND WE CAN BE GIANTS.
TAKE ME.

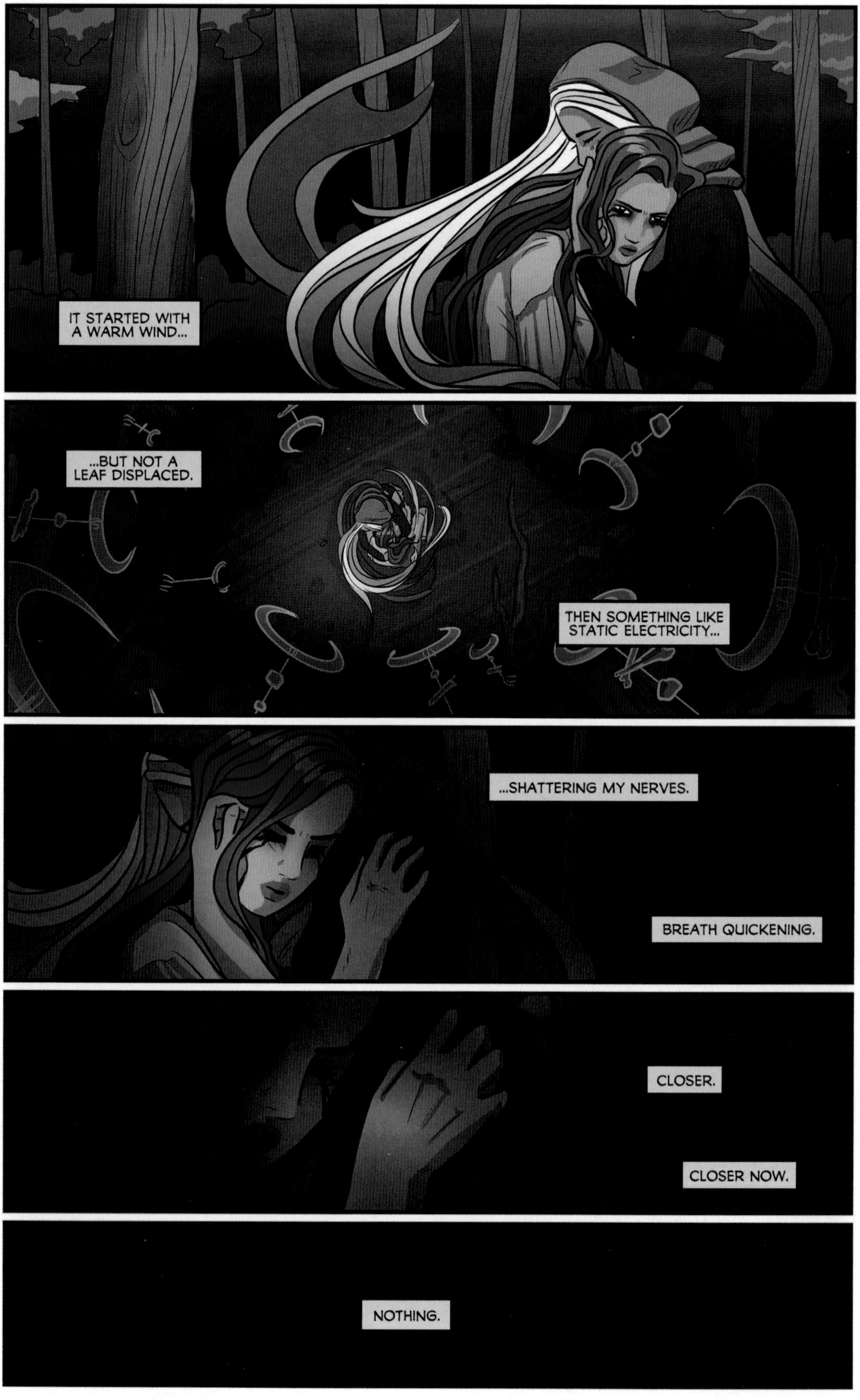
IT STARTED WITH A WARM WIND...
...BUT NOT A LEAF DISPLACED.
THEN SOMETHING LIKE STATIC ELECTRICITY...
...SHATTERING MY NERVES.
BREATH QUICKENING.
CLOSER.
CLOSER NOW.
NOTHING.

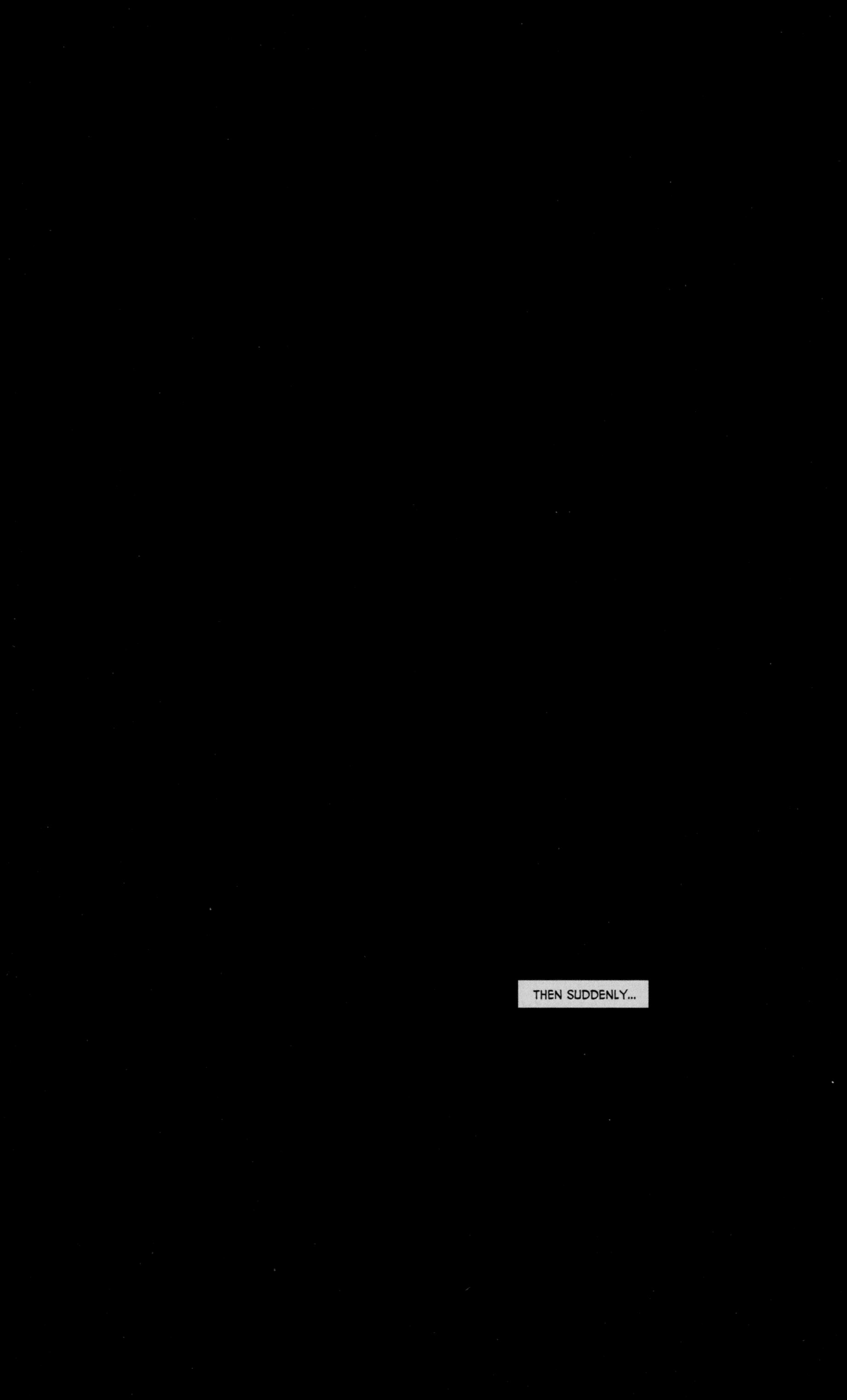
THEN SUDDENLY...

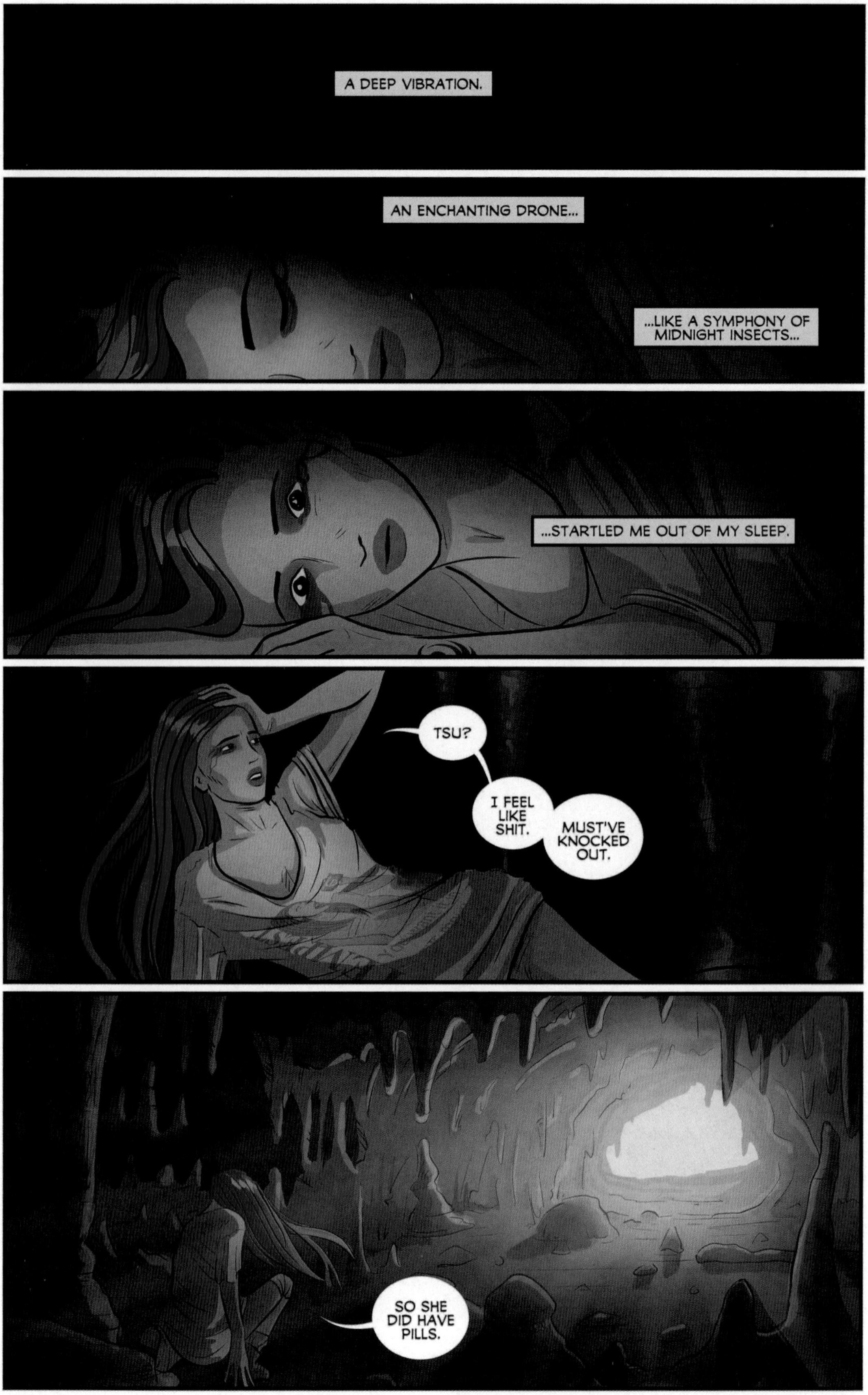
A DEEP VIBRATION.
AN ENCHANTING DRONE...
...LIKE A SYMPHONY OF MIDNIGHT INSECTS...
...STARTLED ME OUT OF MY SLEEP.
TSU?
I FEEL LIKE SHIT.
MUST'VE KNOCKED OUT.
SO SHE DID HAVE PILLS.

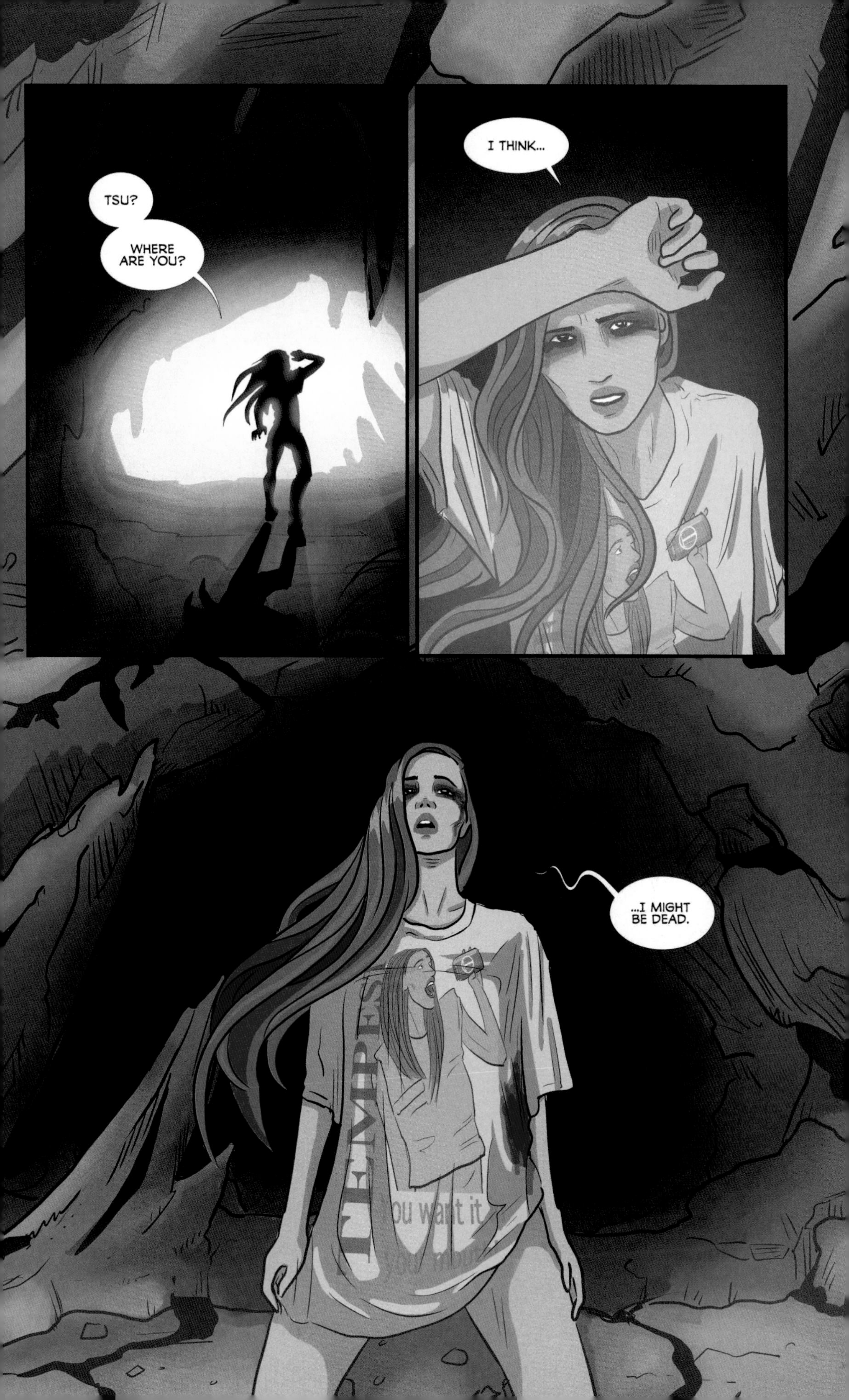
TSU?
WHERE ARE YOU?
I THINK...
...I MIGHT BE DEAD.

CHAPTER TEN: MOONSHINE

http://mxt.pe/mnshine

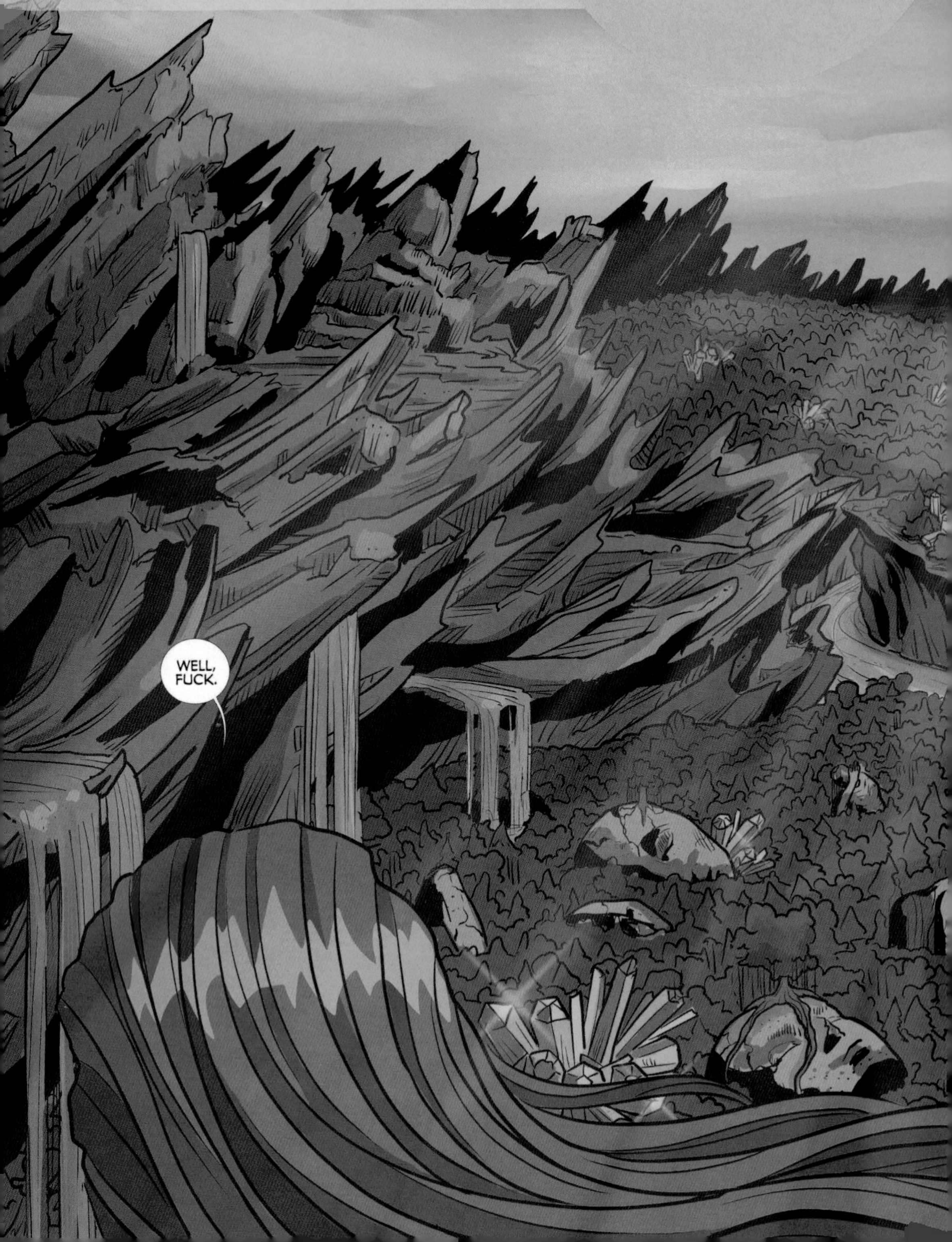
WELL, FUCK.

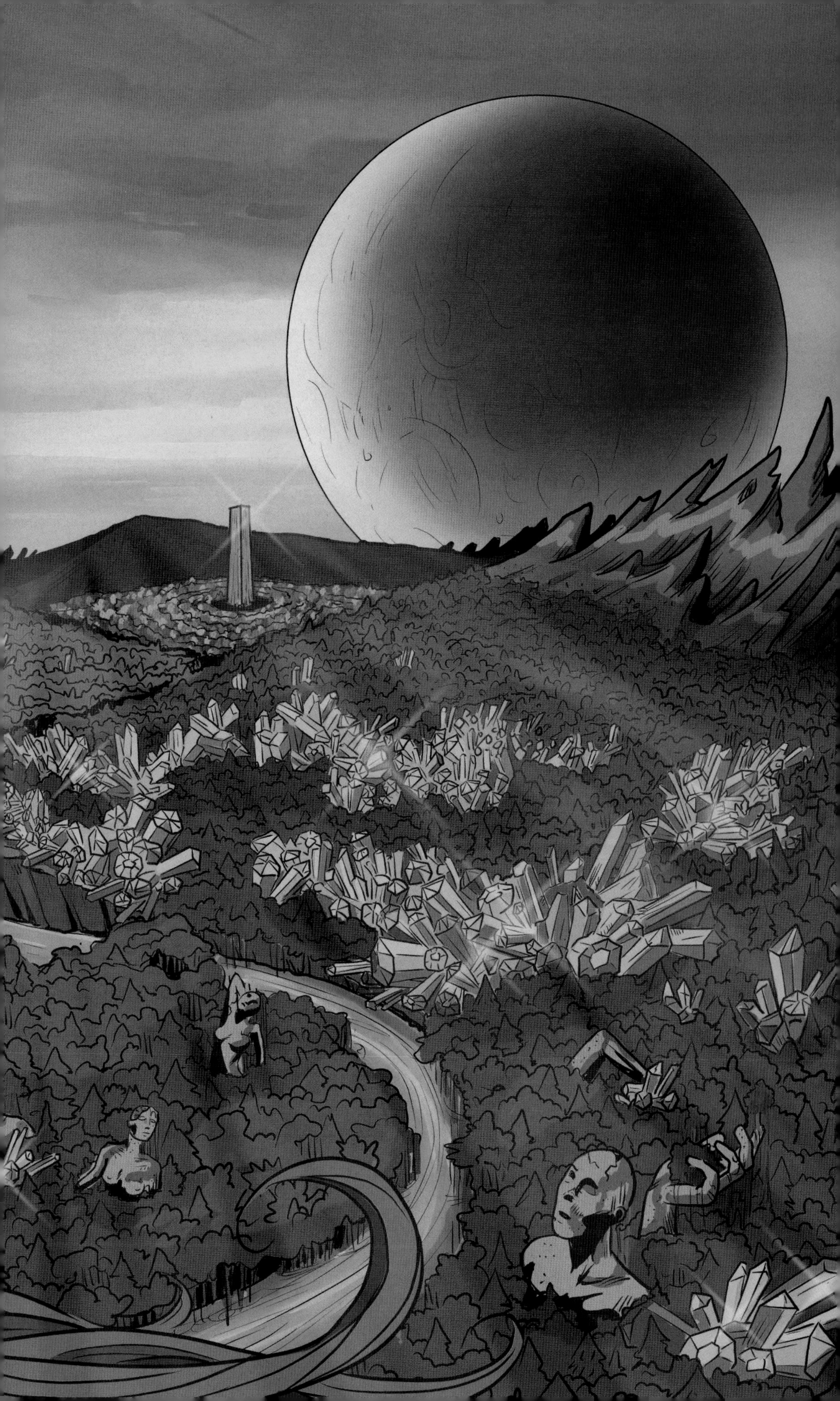

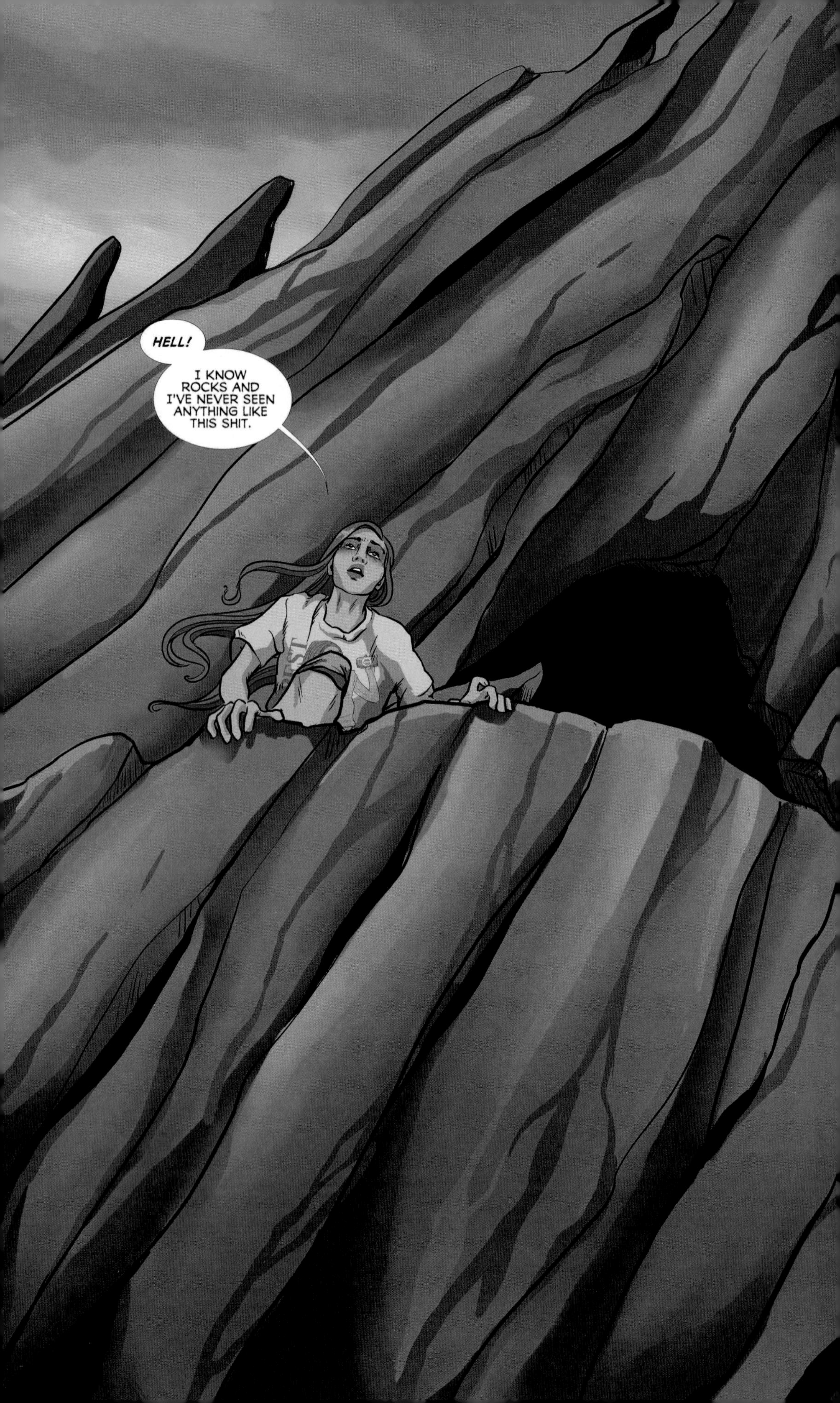
HELL!
I KNOW ROCKS AND I'VE NEVER SEEN ANYTHING LIKE THIS SHIT.

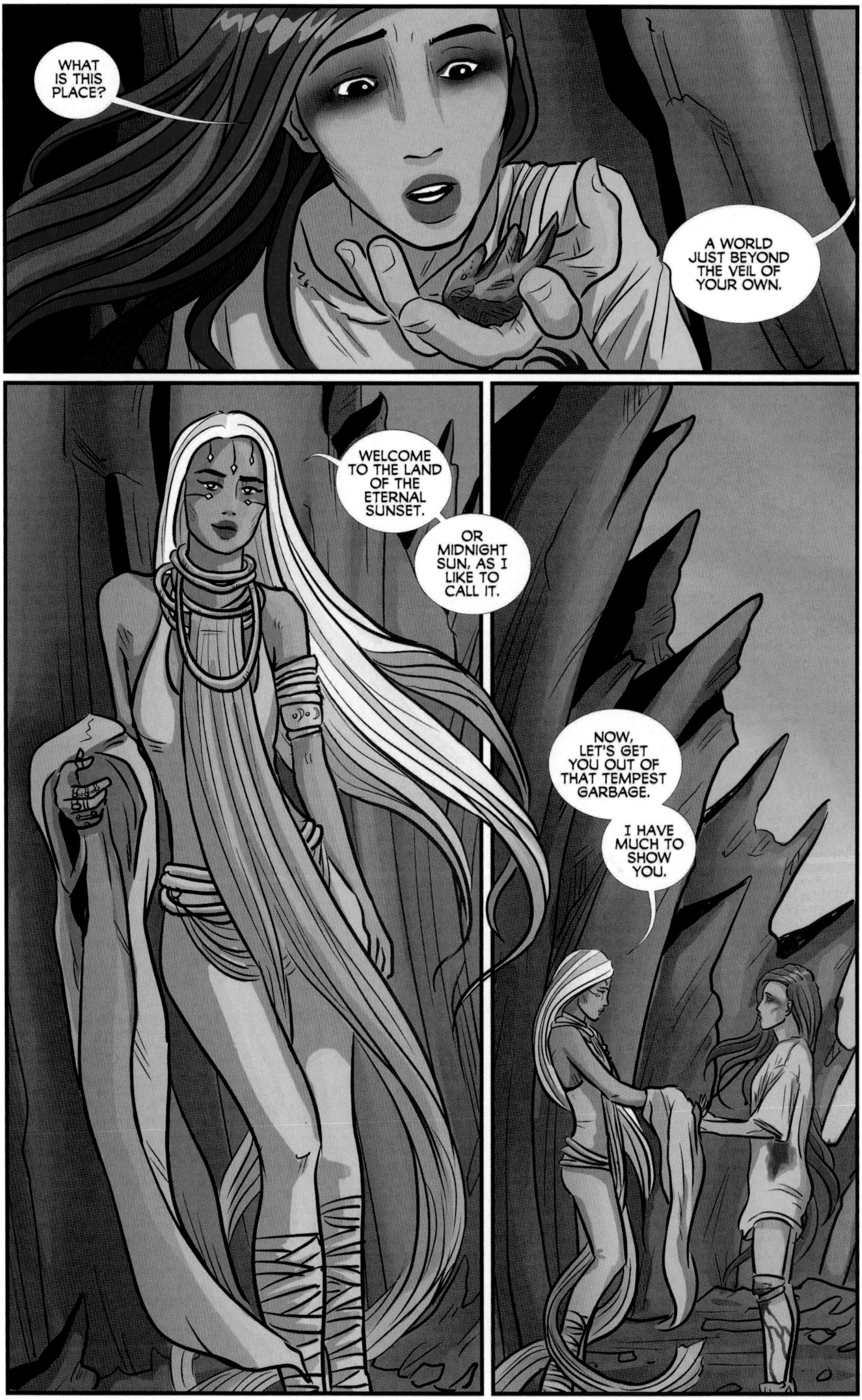
WHAT IS THIS PLACE?
A WORLD JUST BEYOND THE VEIL OF YOUR OWN.
WELCOME TO THE LAND OF THE ETERNAL SUNSET.
OR MIDNIGHT SUN, AS I LIKE TO CALL IT.
NOW, LET'S GET YOU OUT OF THAT TEMPEST GARBAGE.
I HAVE MUCH TO SHOW YOU.

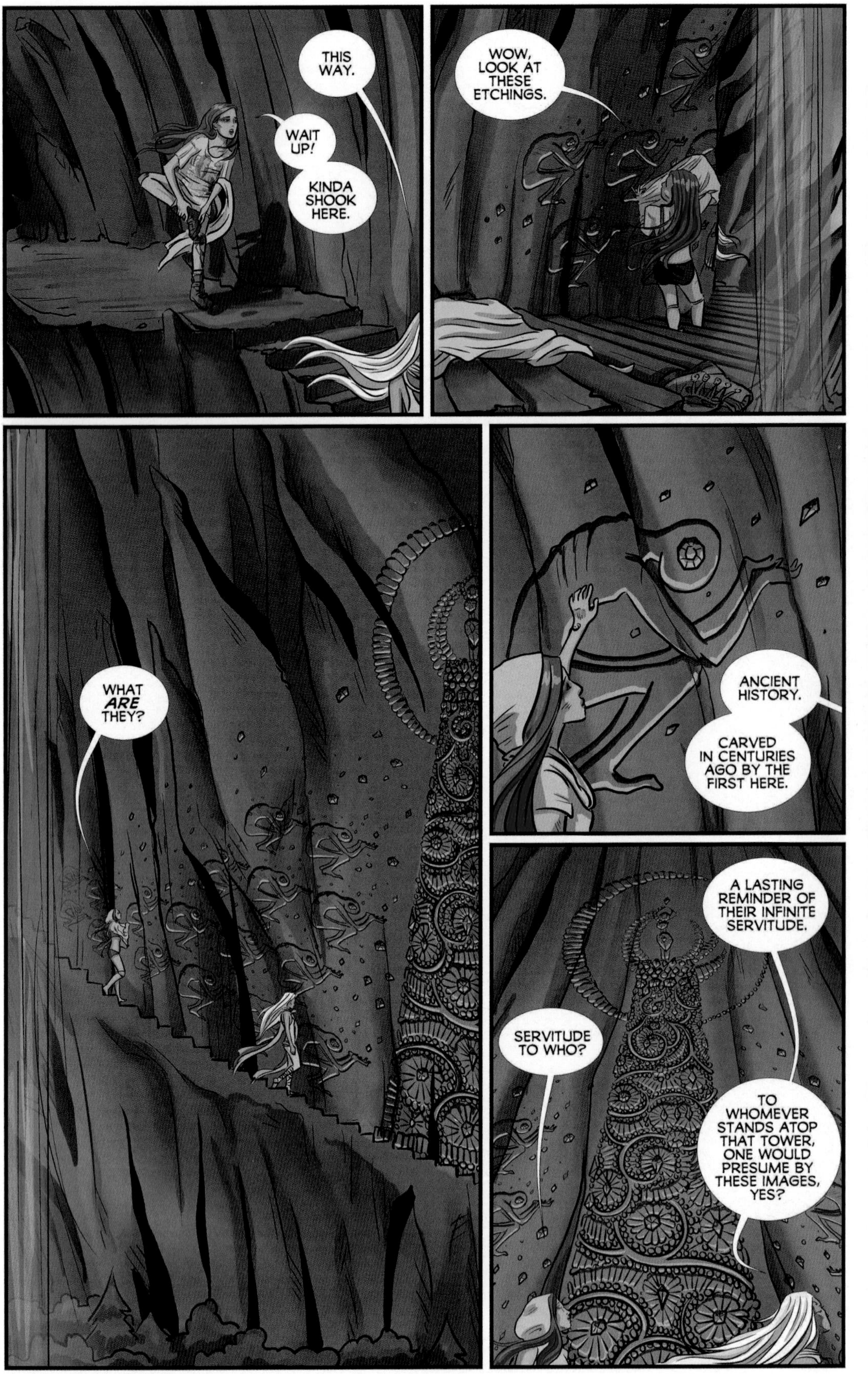
THIS WAY.
WAIT UP!
KINDA SHOOK HERE.
WOW, LOOK AT THESE ETCHINGS.
WHAT *ARE* THEY?
ANCIENT HISTORY.
CARVED IN CENTURIES AGO BY THE FIRST HERE.
A LASTING REMINDER OF THEIR INFINITE SERVITUDE.
SERVITUDE TO WHO?
TO WHOMEVER STANDS ATOP THAT TOWER, ONE WOULD PRESUME BY THESE IMAGES, YES?

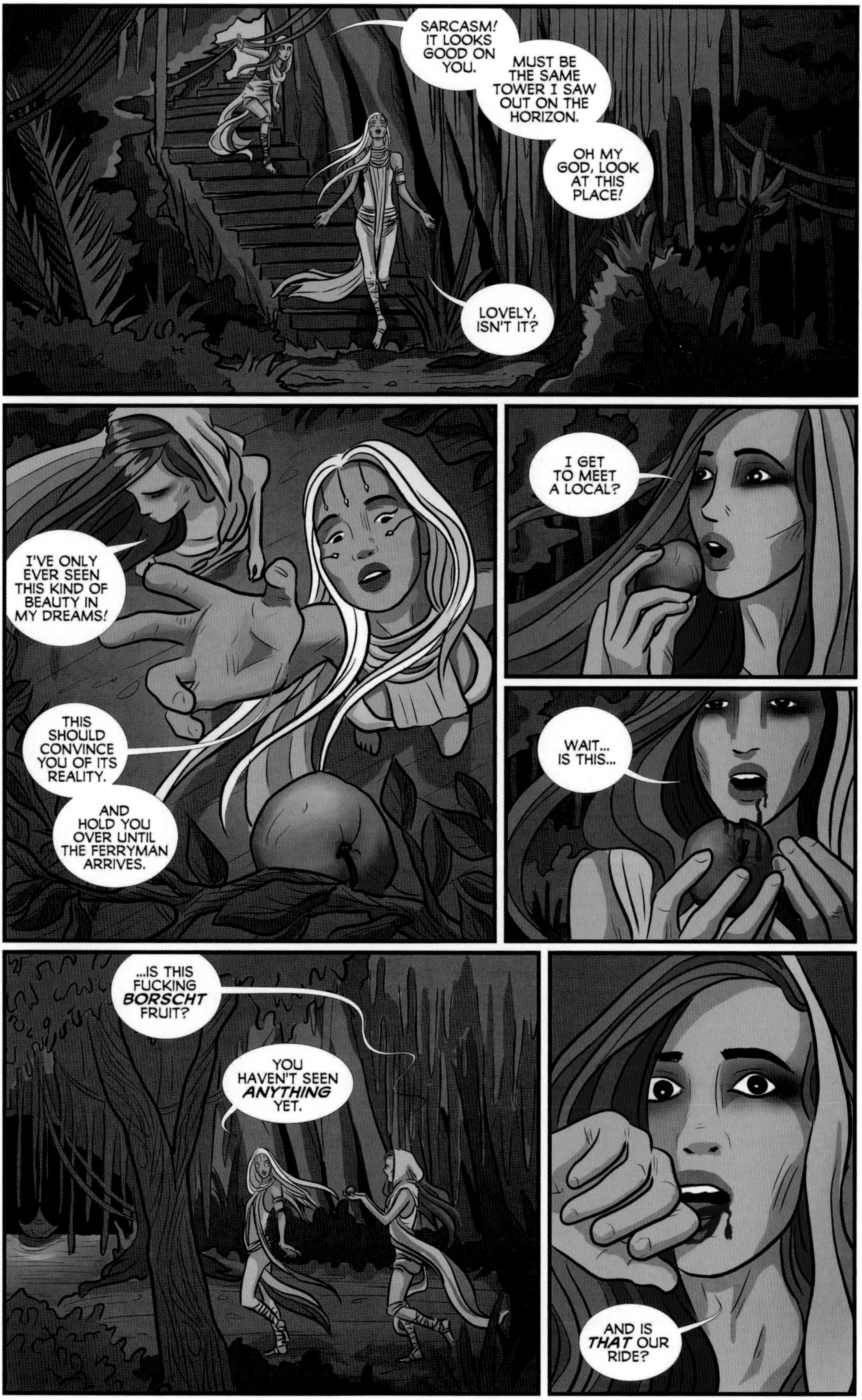
SARCASM! IT LOOKS GOOD ON YOU.
MUST BE THE SAME TOWER I SAW OUT ON THE HORIZON.
OH MY GOD, LOOK AT THIS PLACE!
LOVELY, ISN'T IT?
I'VE ONLY EVER SEEN THIS KIND OF BEAUTY IN MY DREAMS!
THIS SHOULD CONVINCE YOU OF ITS REALITY.
AND HOLD YOU OVER UNTIL THE FERRYMAN ARRIVES.
I GET TO MEET A LOCAL?
WAIT... IS THIS...
...IS THIS FUCKING ***BORSCHT*** FRUIT?
YOU HAVEN'T SEEN ***ANYTHING*** YET.
AND IS ***THAT*** OUR RIDE?

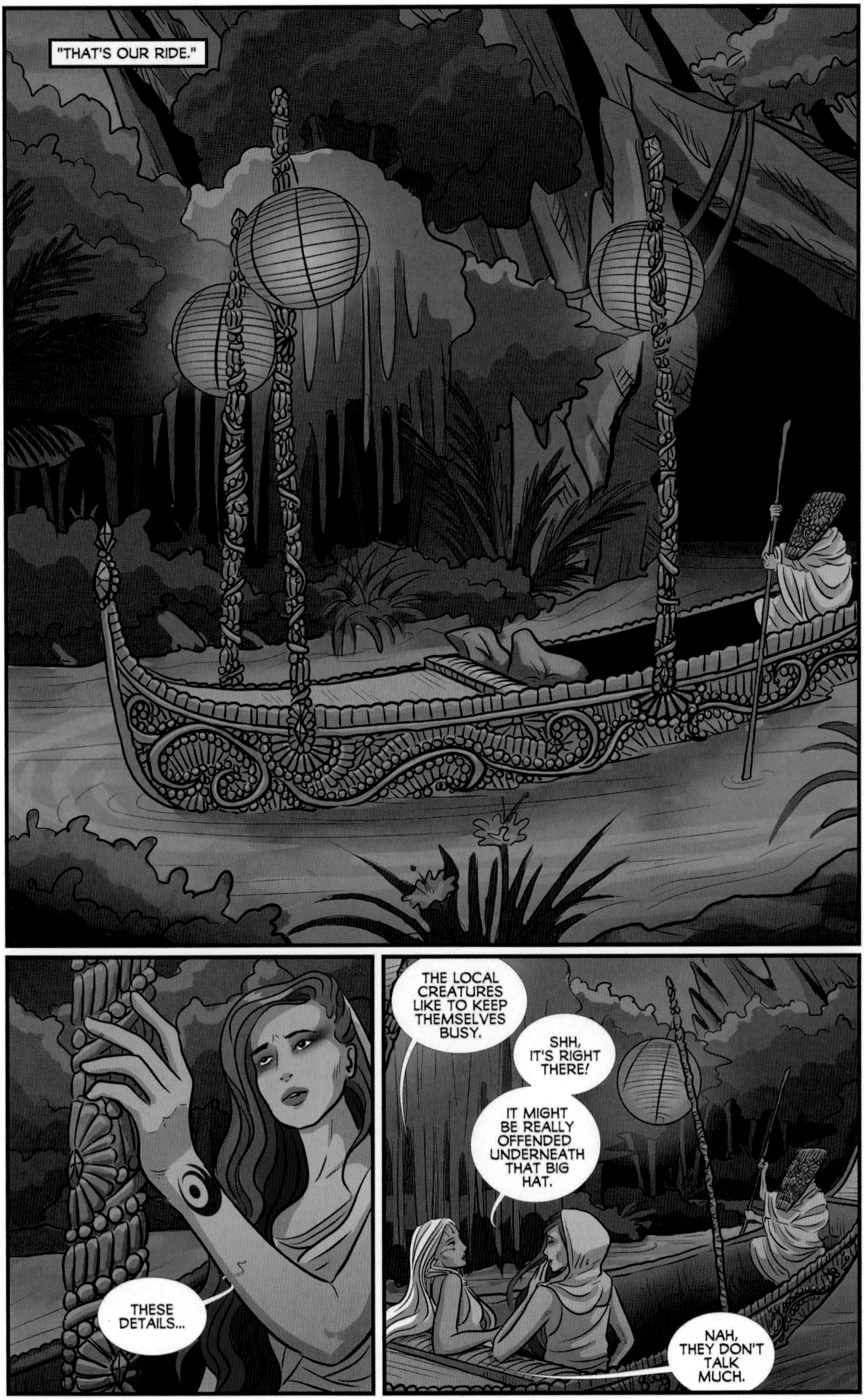
"THAT'S OUR RIDE."
THESE DETAILS...
THE LOCAL CREATURES LIKE TO KEEP THEMSELVES BUSY.
SHH, IT'S RIGHT THERE!
IT MIGHT BE REALLY OFFENDED UNDERNEATH THAT BIG HAT.
NAH, THEY DON'T TALK MUCH.

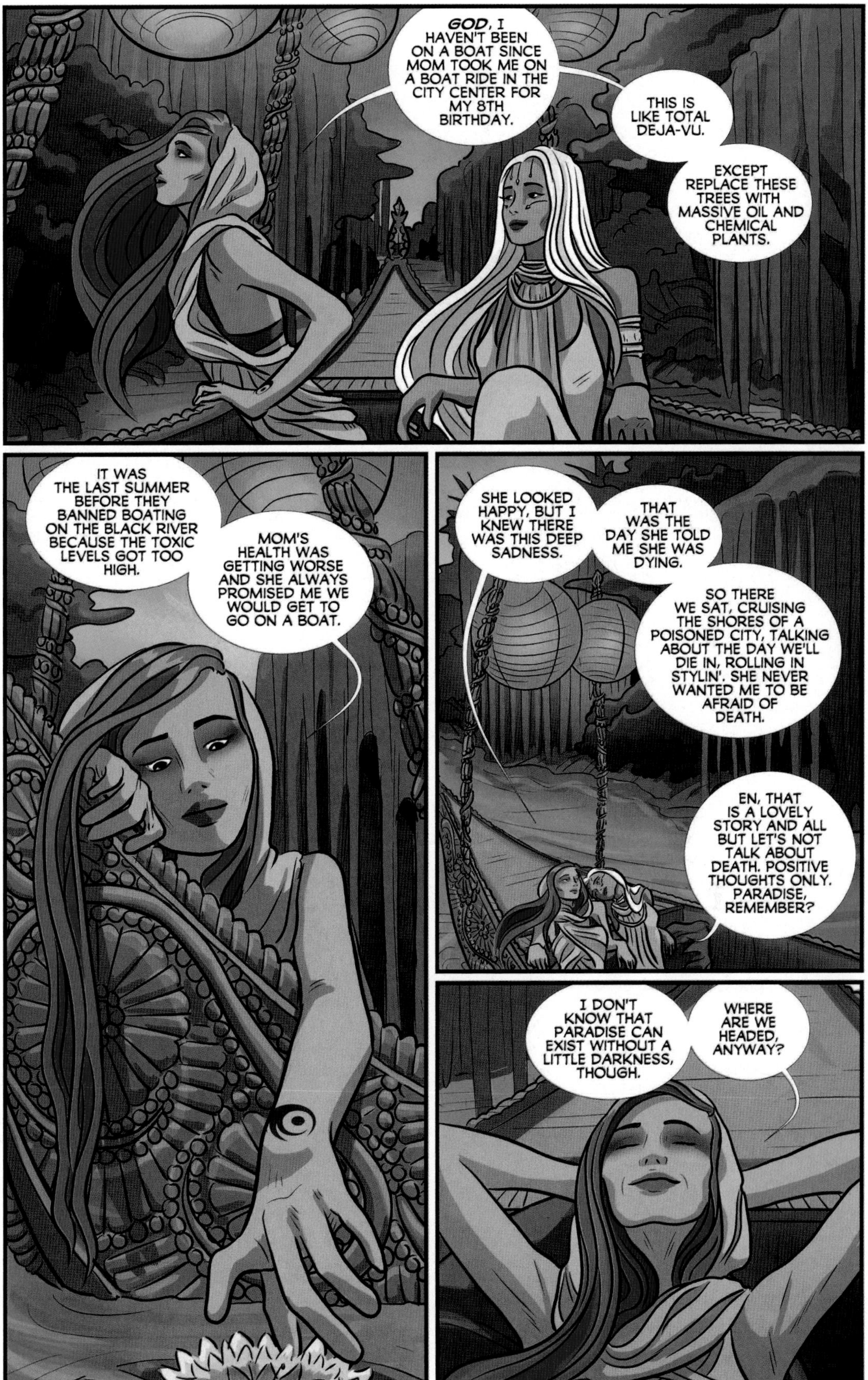
GOD, I HAVEN'T BEEN ON A BOAT SINCE MOM TOOK ME ON A BOAT RIDE IN THE CITY CENTER FOR MY 8TH BIRTHDAY.
THIS IS LIKE TOTAL DEJA-VU.
EXCEPT REPLACE THESE TREES WITH MASSIVE OIL AND CHEMICAL PLANTS.
IT WAS THE LAST SUMMER BEFORE THEY BANNED BOATING ON THE BLACK RIVER BECAUSE THE TOXIC LEVELS GOT TOO HIGH.
MOM'S HEALTH WAS GETTING WORSE AND SHE ALWAYS PROMISED ME WE WOULD GET TO GO ON A BOAT.
SHE LOOKED HAPPY, BUT I KNEW THERE WAS THIS DEEP SADNESS.
THAT WAS THE DAY SHE TOLD ME SHE WAS DYING.
SO THERE WE SAT, CRUISING THE SHORES OF A POISONED CITY, TALKING ABOUT THE DAY WE'LL DIE IN, ROLLING IN STYLIN'. SHE NEVER WANTED ME TO BE AFRAID OF DEATH.
EN, THAT IS A LOVELY STORY AND ALL BUT LET'S NOT TALK ABOUT DEATH. POSITIVE THOUGHTS ONLY. PARADISE, REMEMBER?
I DON'T KNOW THAT PARADISE CAN EXIST WITHOUT A LITTLE DARKNESS, THOUGH.
WHERE ARE WE HEADED, ANYWAY?

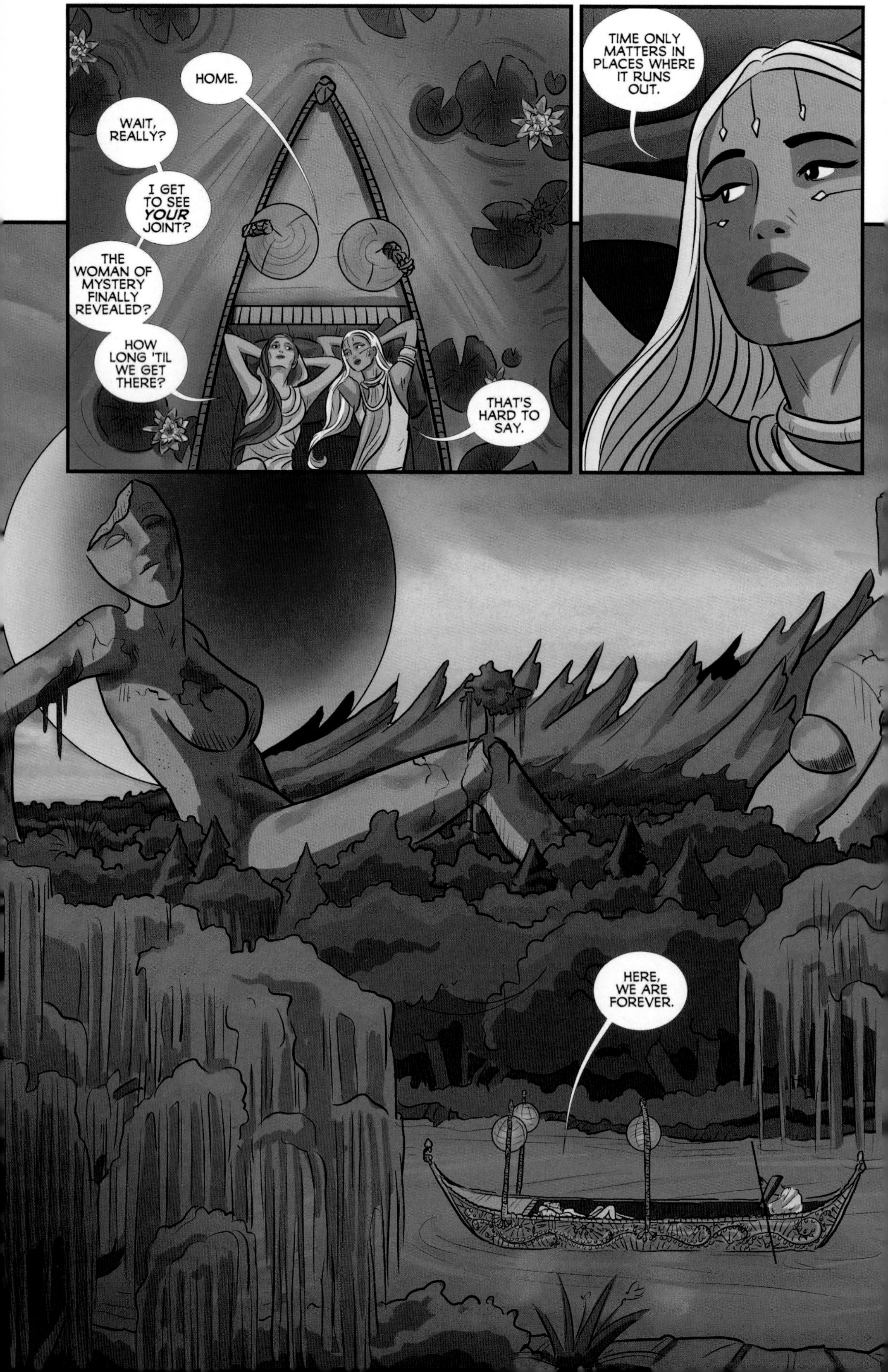
HOME.
WAIT, REALLY?
I GET TO SEE *YOUR* JOINT?
THE WOMAN OF MYSTERY FINALLY REVEALED?
HOW LONG 'TIL WE GET THERE?
THAT'S HARD TO SAY.
TIME ONLY MATTERS IN PLACES WHERE IT RUNS OUT.
HERE, WE ARE FOREVER.

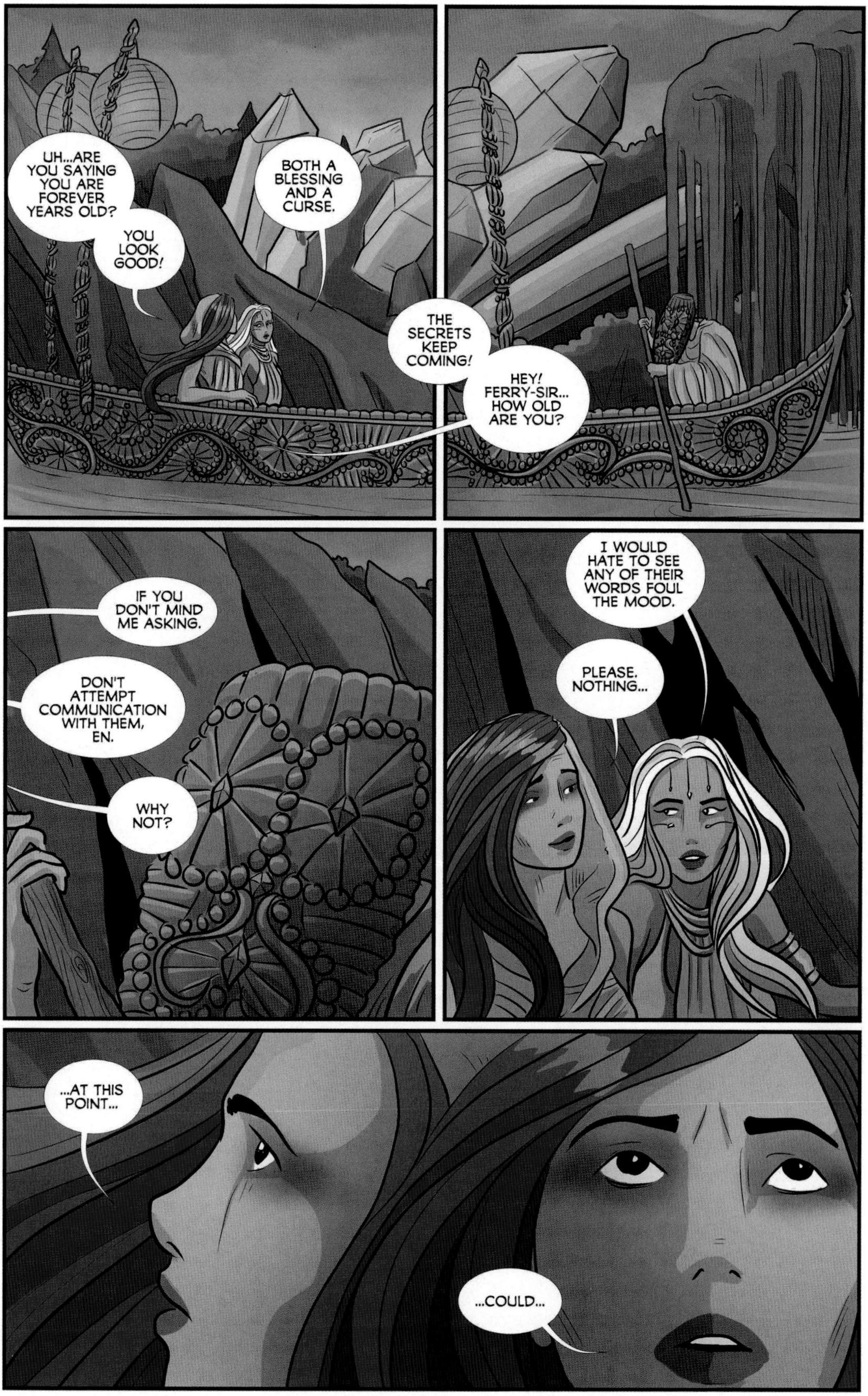

UH...ARE YOU SAYING YOU ARE FOREVER YEARS OLD?
YOU LOOK GOOD!
BOTH A BLESSING AND A CURSE.
THE SECRETS KEEP COMING!
HEY! FERRY-SIR... HOW OLD ARE YOU?
IF YOU DON'T MIND ME ASKING.
DON'T ATTEMPT COMMUNICATION WITH THEM, EN.
WHY NOT?
I WOULD HATE TO SEE ANY OF THEIR WORDS FOUL THE MOOD.
PLEASE. NOTHING...
...AT THIS POINT...
...COULD...

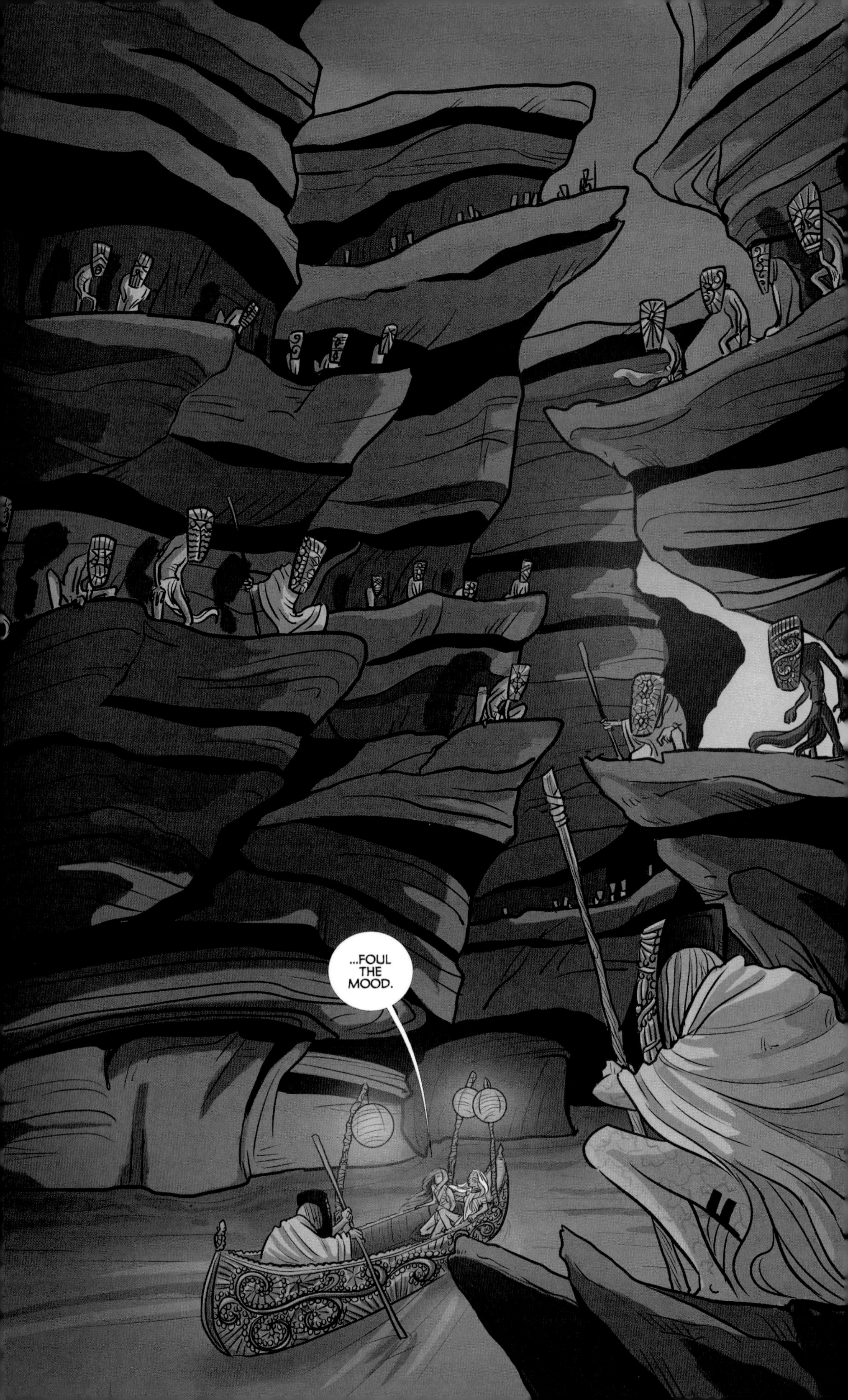
...FOUL THE MOOD.

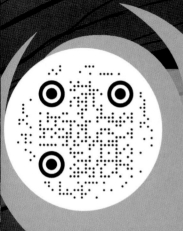

CHAPTER ELEVEN: INTERLUDE

http://mxt.pe/intrlde

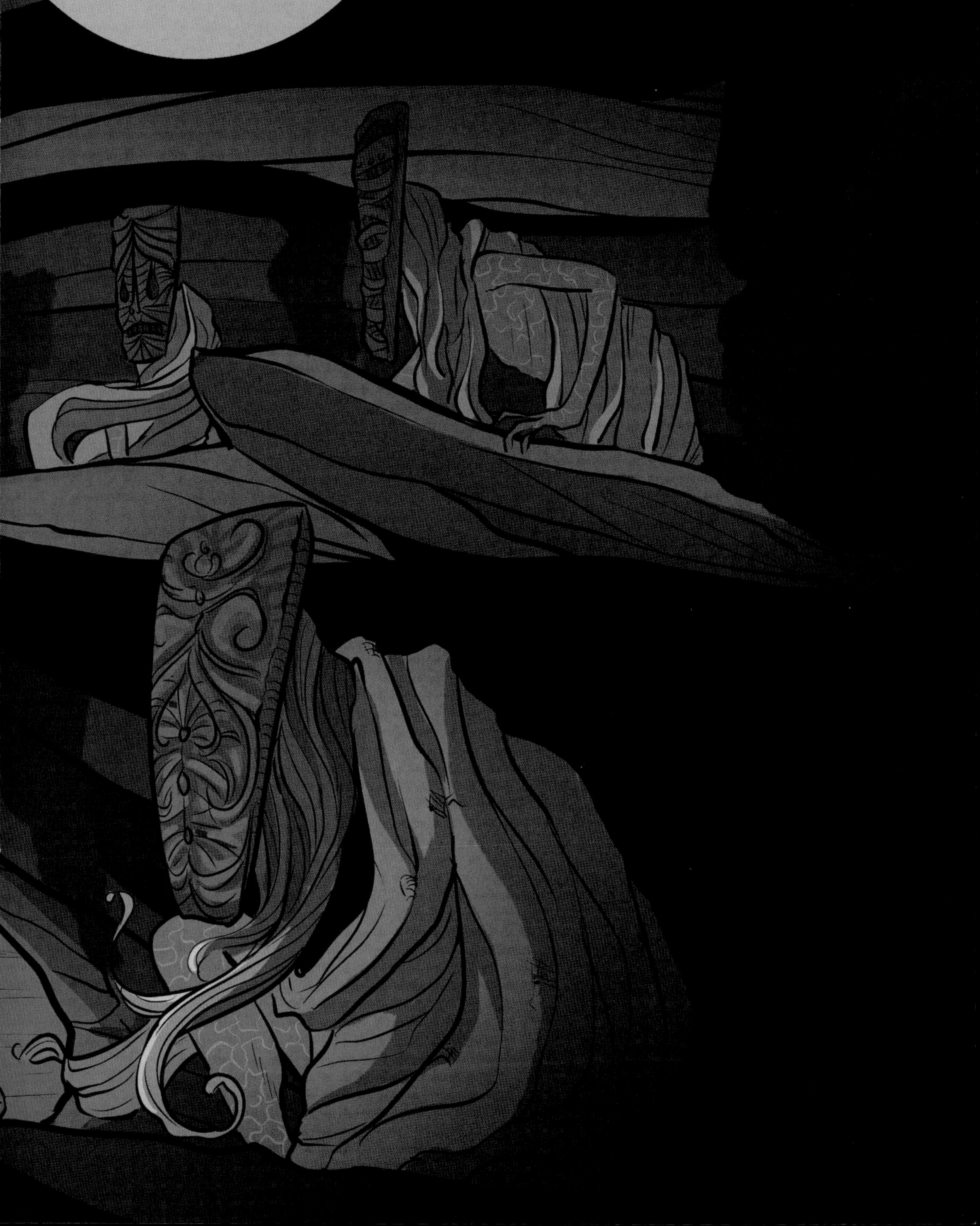

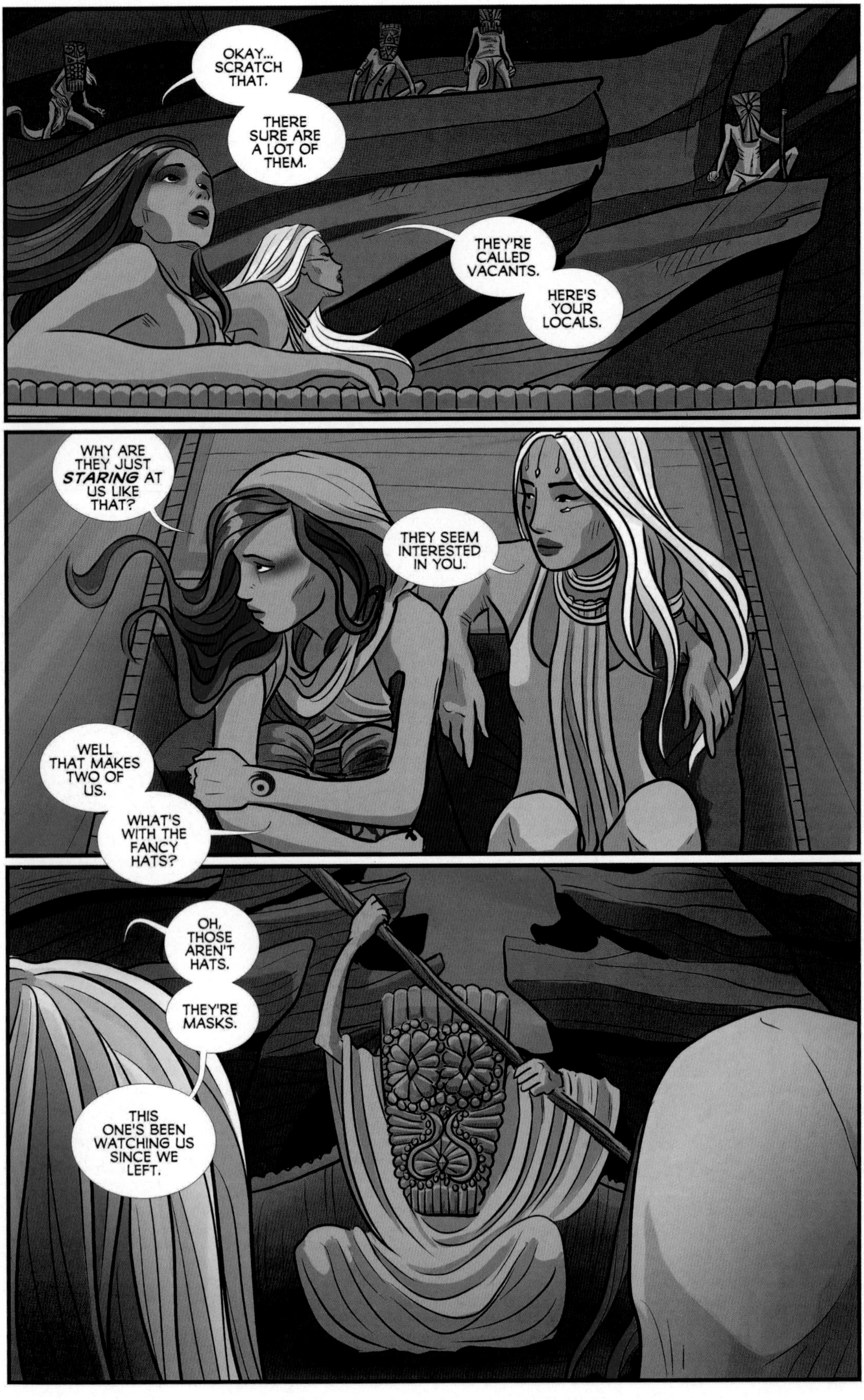

OKAY... SCRATCH THAT.
THERE SURE ARE A LOT OF THEM.
THEY'RE CALLED VACANTS.
HERE'S YOUR LOCALS.
WHY ARE THEY JUST *STARING* AT US LIKE THAT?
THEY SEEM INTERESTED IN YOU.
WELL THAT MAKES TWO OF US.
WHAT'S WITH THE FANCY HATS?
OH, THOSE AREN'T HATS.
THEY'RE MASKS.
THIS ONE'S BEEN WATCHING US SINCE WE LEFT.

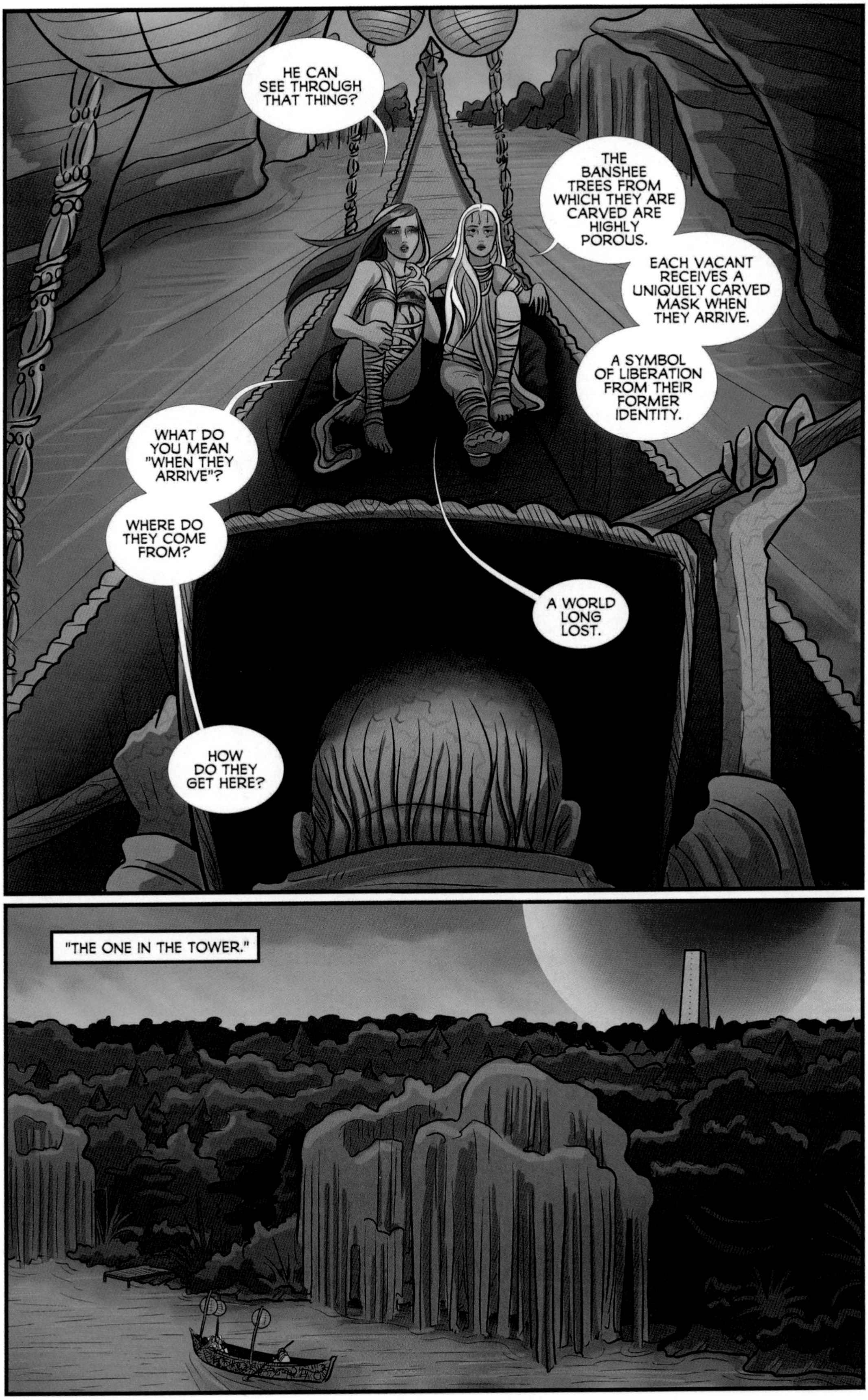
HE CAN SEE THROUGH THAT THING?
THE BANSHEE TREES FROM WHICH THEY ARE CARVED ARE HIGHLY POROUS.
EACH VACANT RECEIVES A UNIQUELY CARVED MASK WHEN THEY ARRIVE.
A SYMBOL OF LIBERATION FROM THEIR FORMER IDENTITY.
WHAT DO YOU MEAN "WHEN THEY ARRIVE"?
WHERE DO THEY COME FROM?
A WORLD LONG LOST.
HOW DO THEY GET HERE?
"THE ONE IN THE TOWER."

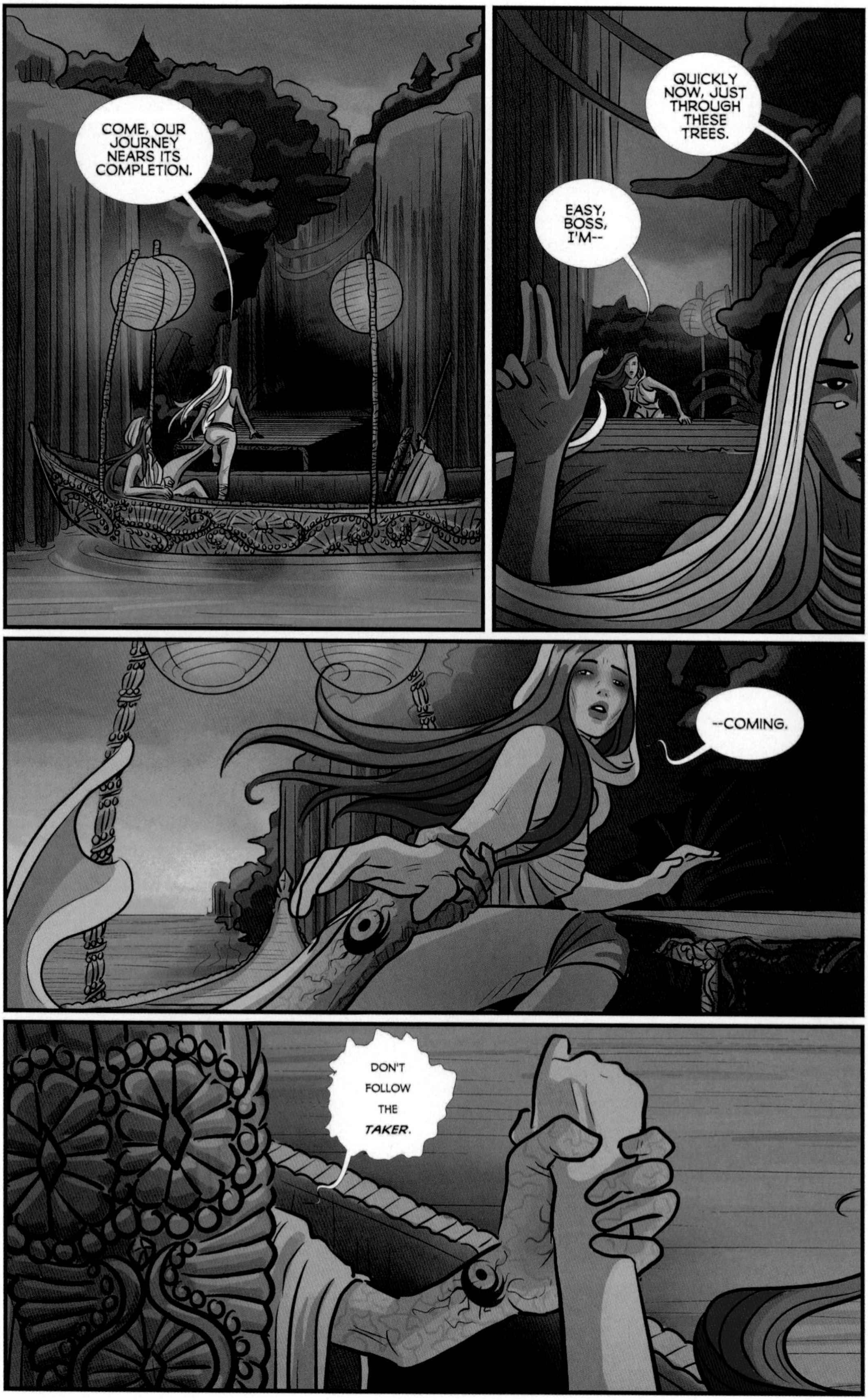
COME, OUR JOURNEY NEARS ITS COMPLETION.
QUICKLY NOW, JUST THROUGH THESE TREES.
EASY, BOSS, I'M--
--COMING.
DON'T FOLLOW THE *TAKER*.

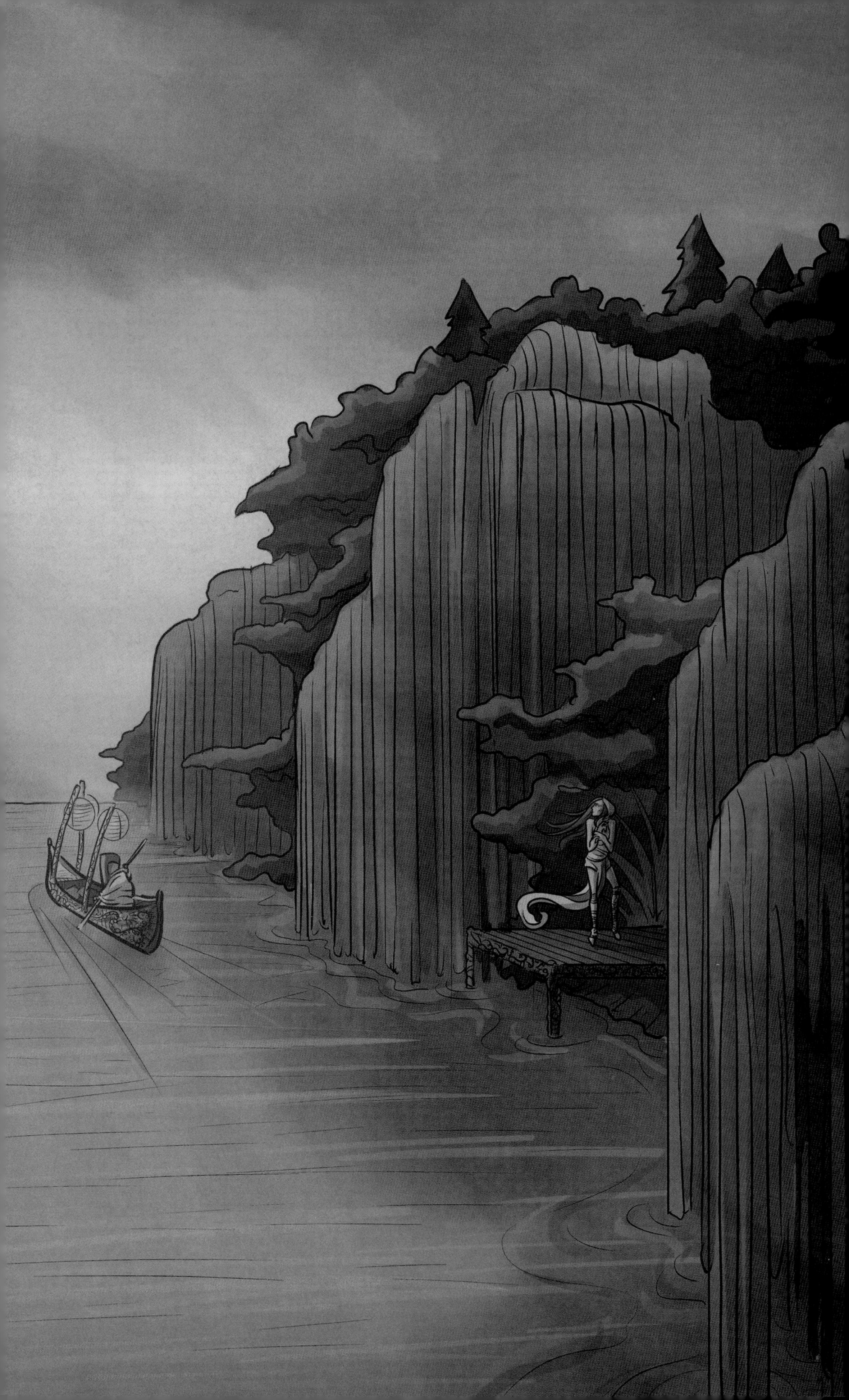

SKIN&EARTH
ISSUE SIX

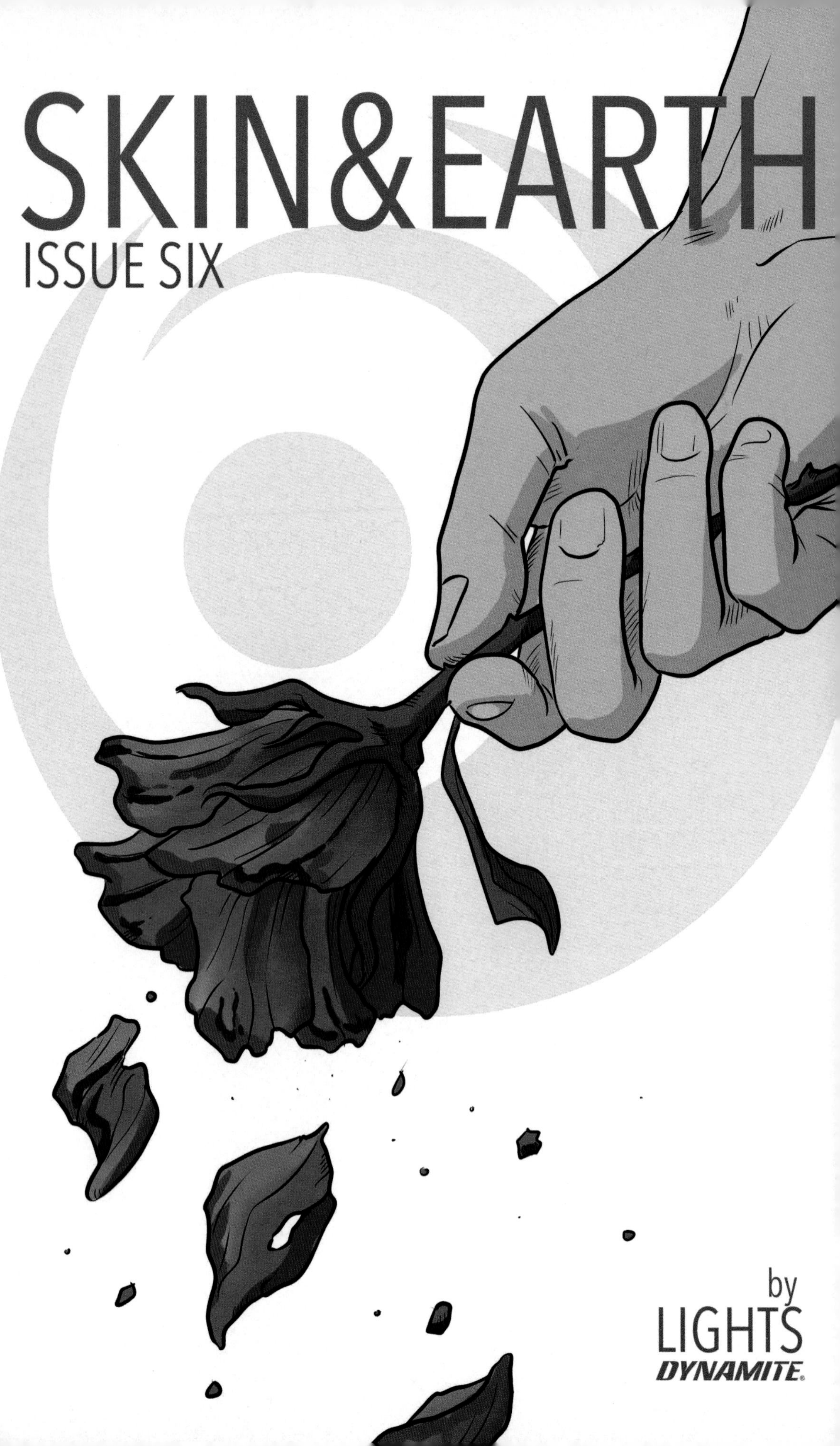

by
LIGHTS
DYNAMITE

CHAPTER TWELVE: MAGNETIC FIELD

http://mxt.pe/magnetc

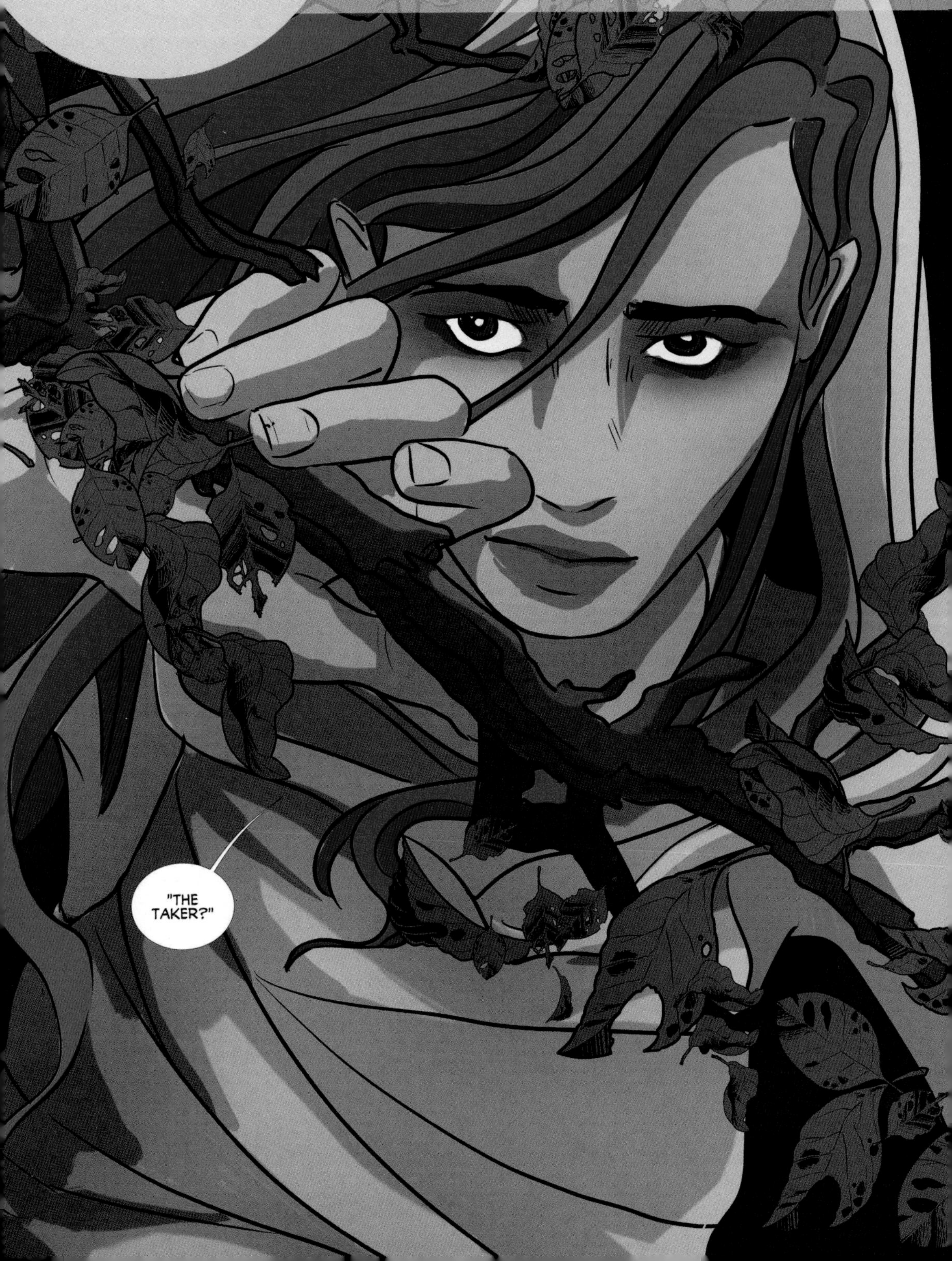
"THE TAKER?"

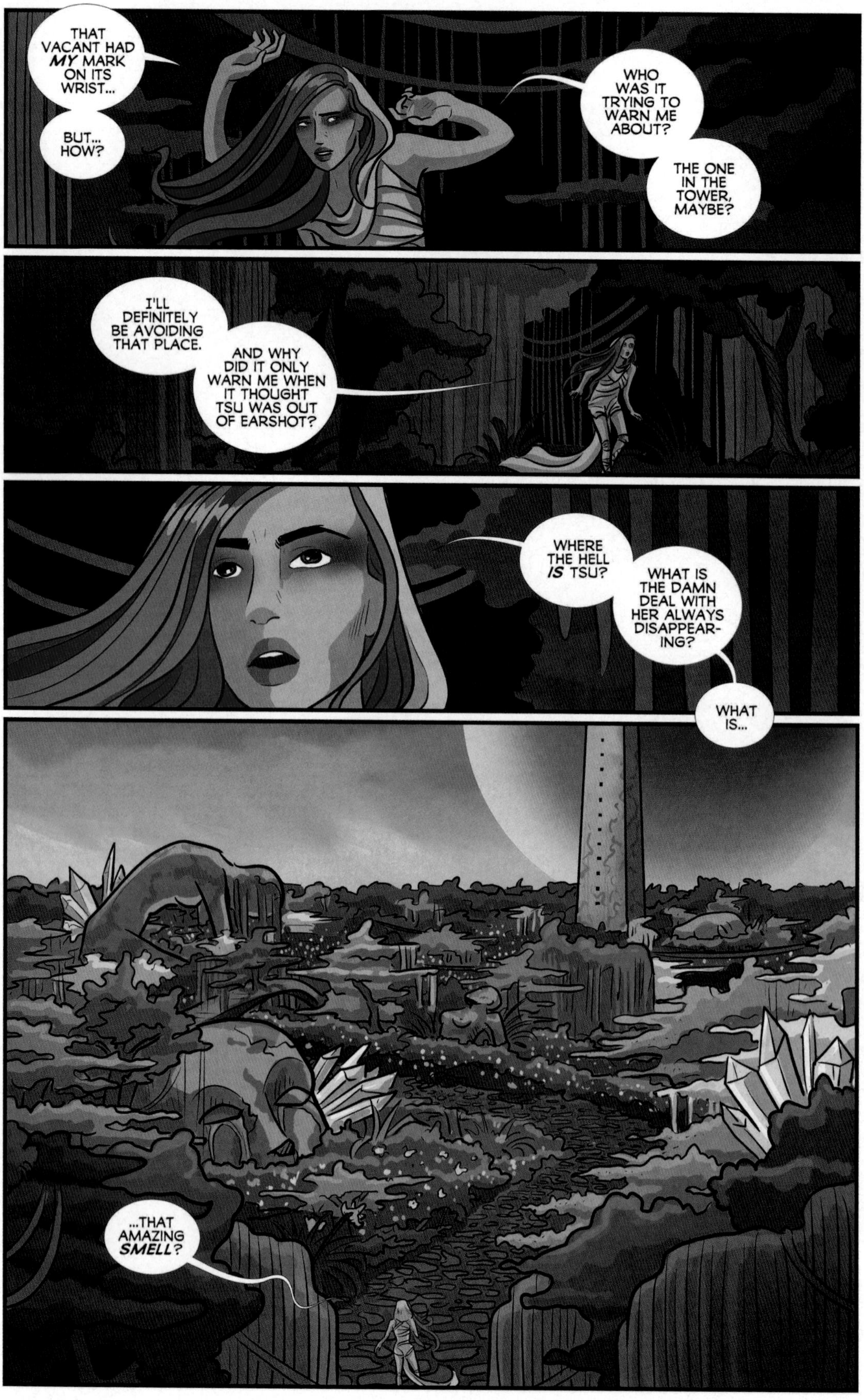

THAT VACANT HAD *MY* MARK ON ITS WRIST...
BUT... HOW?
WHO WAS IT TRYING TO WARN ME ABOUT?
THE ONE IN THE TOWER, MAYBE?
I'LL DEFINITELY BE AVOIDING THAT PLACE.
AND WHY DID IT ONLY WARN ME WHEN IT THOUGHT TSU WAS OUT OF EARSHOT?
WHERE THE HELL *IS* TSU?
WHAT IS THE DAMN DEAL WITH HER ALWAYS DISAPPEAR-ING?
WHAT IS...
...THAT AMAZING *SMELL*?

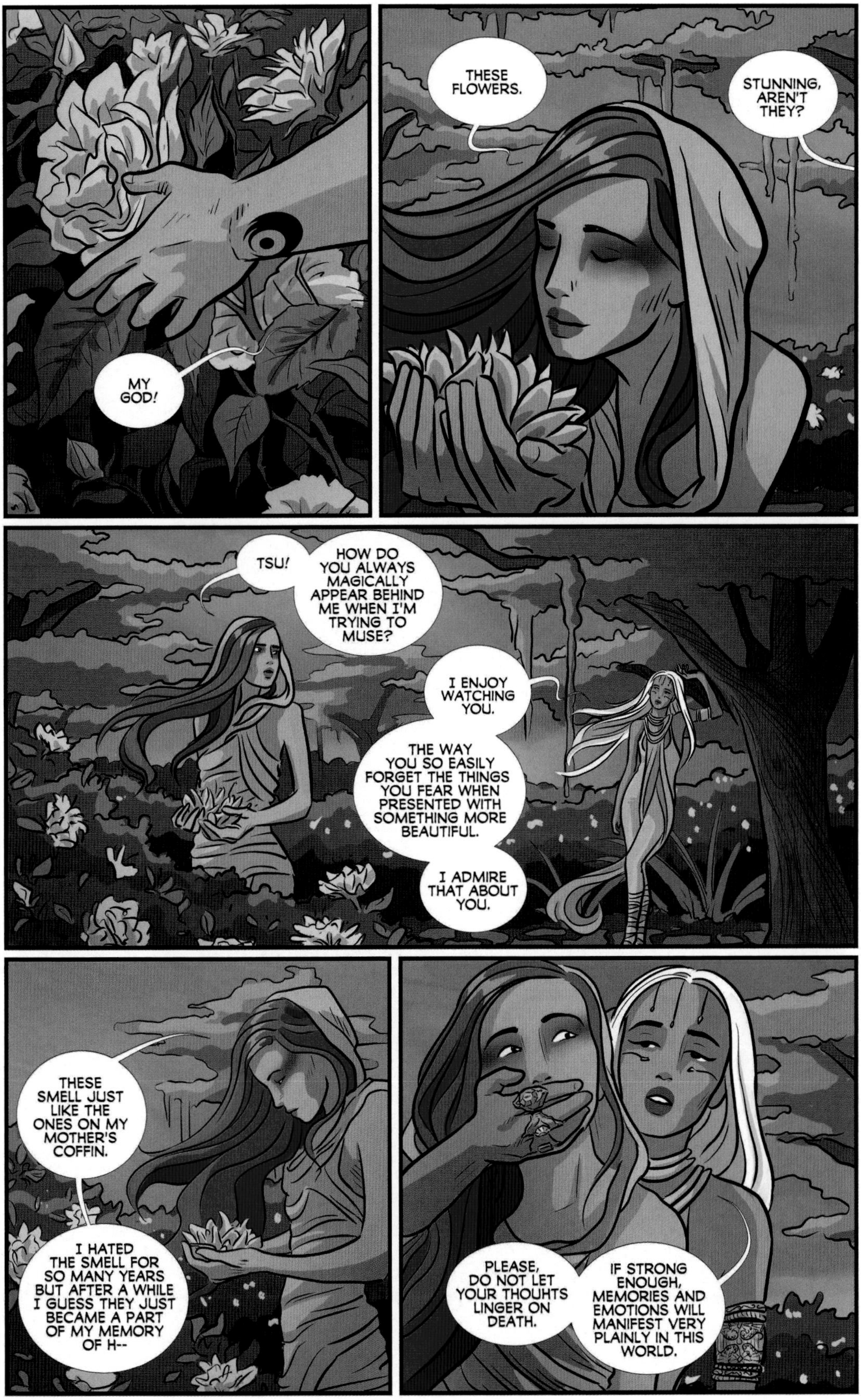
MY GOD!
THESE FLOWERS.
STUNNING, AREN'T THEY?
TSU!
HOW DO YOU ALWAYS MAGICALLY APPEAR BEHIND ME WHEN I'M TRYING TO MUSE?
I ENJOY WATCHING YOU.
THE WAY YOU SO EASILY FORGET THE THINGS YOU FEAR WHEN PRESENTED WITH SOMETHING MORE BEAUTIFUL.
I ADMIRE THAT ABOUT YOU.
THESE SMELL JUST LIKE THE ONES ON MY MOTHER'S COFFIN.
I HATED THE SMELL FOR SO MANY YEARS BUT AFTER A WHILE I GUESS THEY JUST BECAME A PART OF MY MEMORY OF H--
IF STRONG ENOUGH, MEMORIES AND EMOTIONS WILL MANIFEST VERY PLAINLY IN THIS WORLD.
PLEASE, DO NOT LET YOUR THOUHTS LINGER ON DEATH.

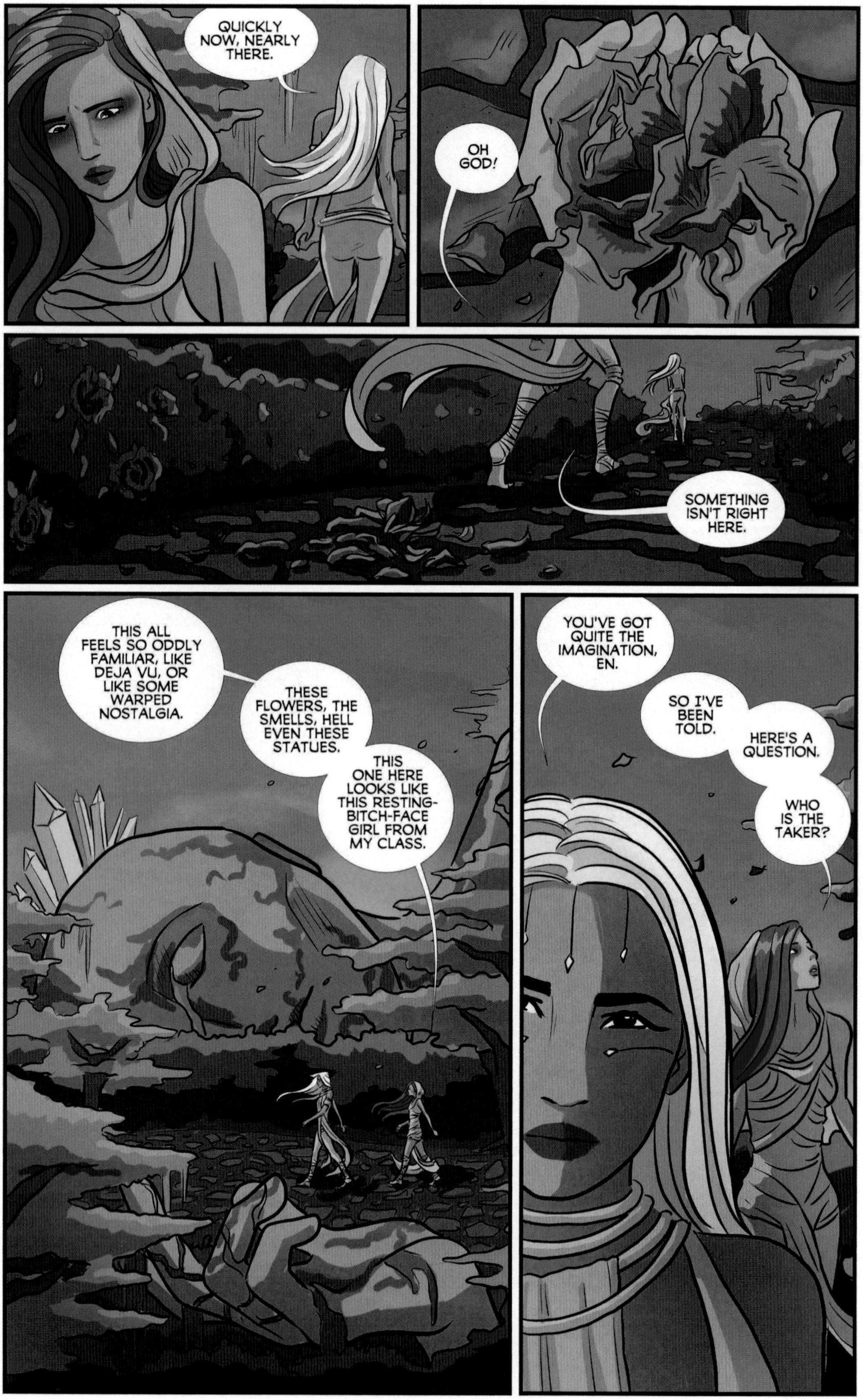
QUICKLY NOW, NEARLY THERE.
OH GOD!
SOMETHING ISN'T RIGHT HERE.
THIS ALL FEELS SO ODDLY FAMILIAR, LIKE DEJA VU, OR LIKE SOME WARPED NOSTALGIA.
THESE FLOWERS, THE SMELLS, HELL EVEN THESE STATUES.
THIS ONE HERE LOOKS LIKE THIS RESTING-BITCH-FACE GIRL FROM MY CLASS.
YOU'VE GOT QUITE THE IMAGINATION, EN.
SO I'VE BEEN TOLD.
HERE'S A QUESTION.
WHO IS THE TAKER?

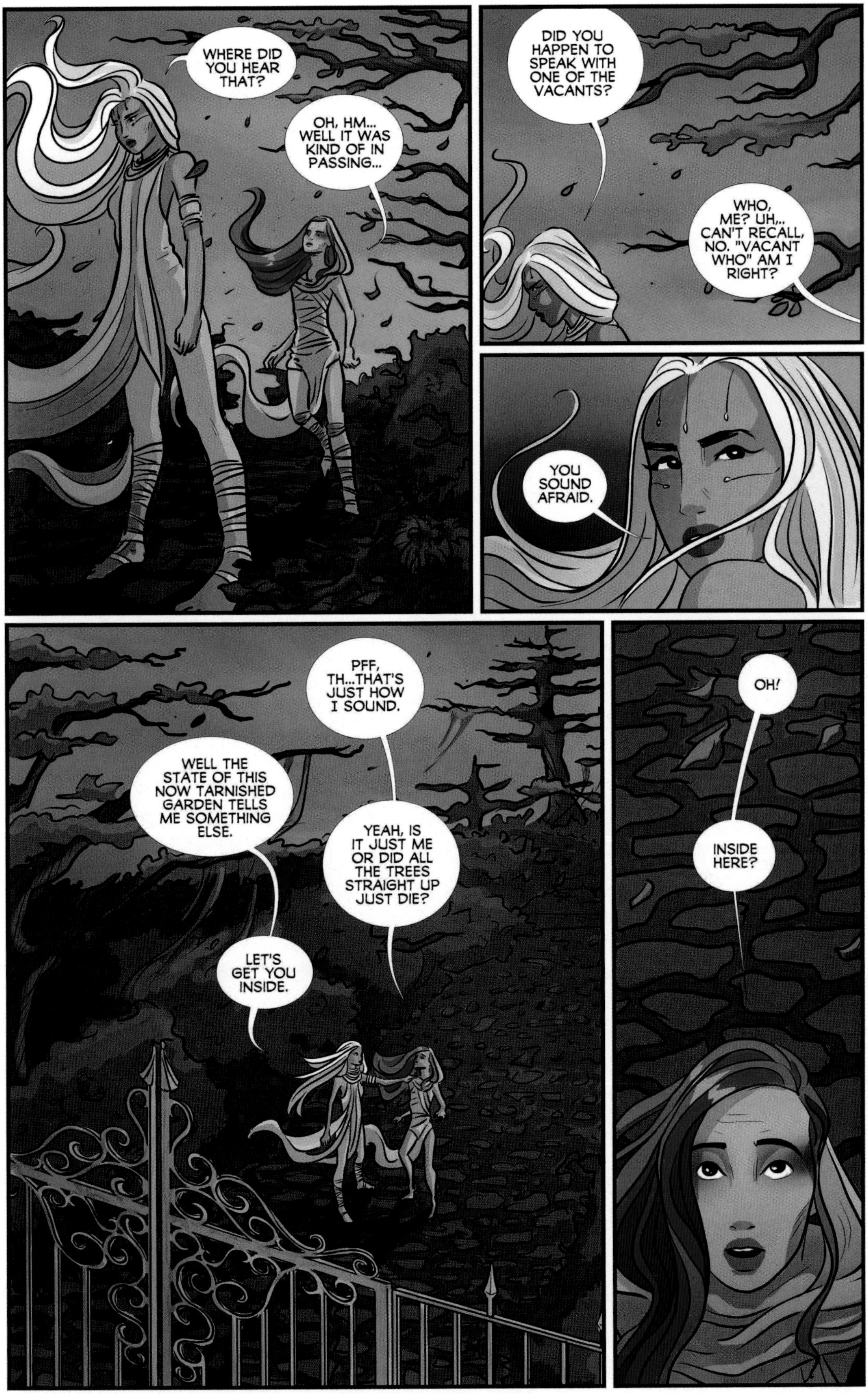
WHERE DID YOU HEAR THAT?
OH, HM... WELL IT WAS KIND OF IN PASSING...
DID YOU HAPPEN TO SPEAK WITH ONE OF THE VACANTS?
WHO, ME? UH,.. CAN'T RECALL, NO. "VACANT WHO" AM I RIGHT?
YOU SOUND AFRAID.
PFF, TH...THAT'S JUST HOW I SOUND.
WELL THE STATE OF THIS NOW TARNISHED GARDEN TELLS ME SOMETHING ELSE.
YEAH, IS IT JUST ME OR DID ALL THE TREES STRAIGHT UP JUST DIE?
LET'S GET YOU INSIDE.
OH!
INSIDE HERE?

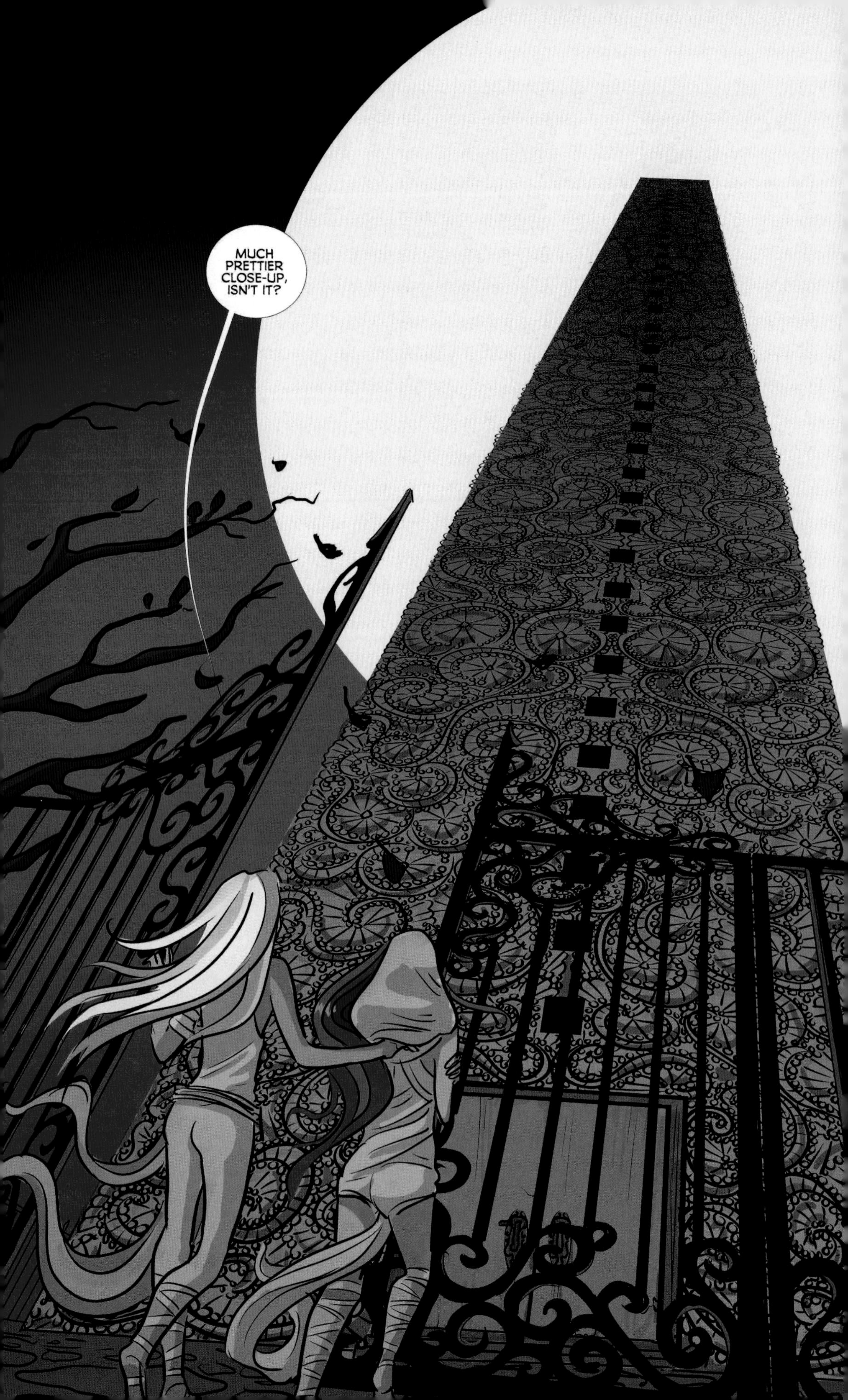
MUCH PRETTIER CLOSE-UP, ISN'T IT?

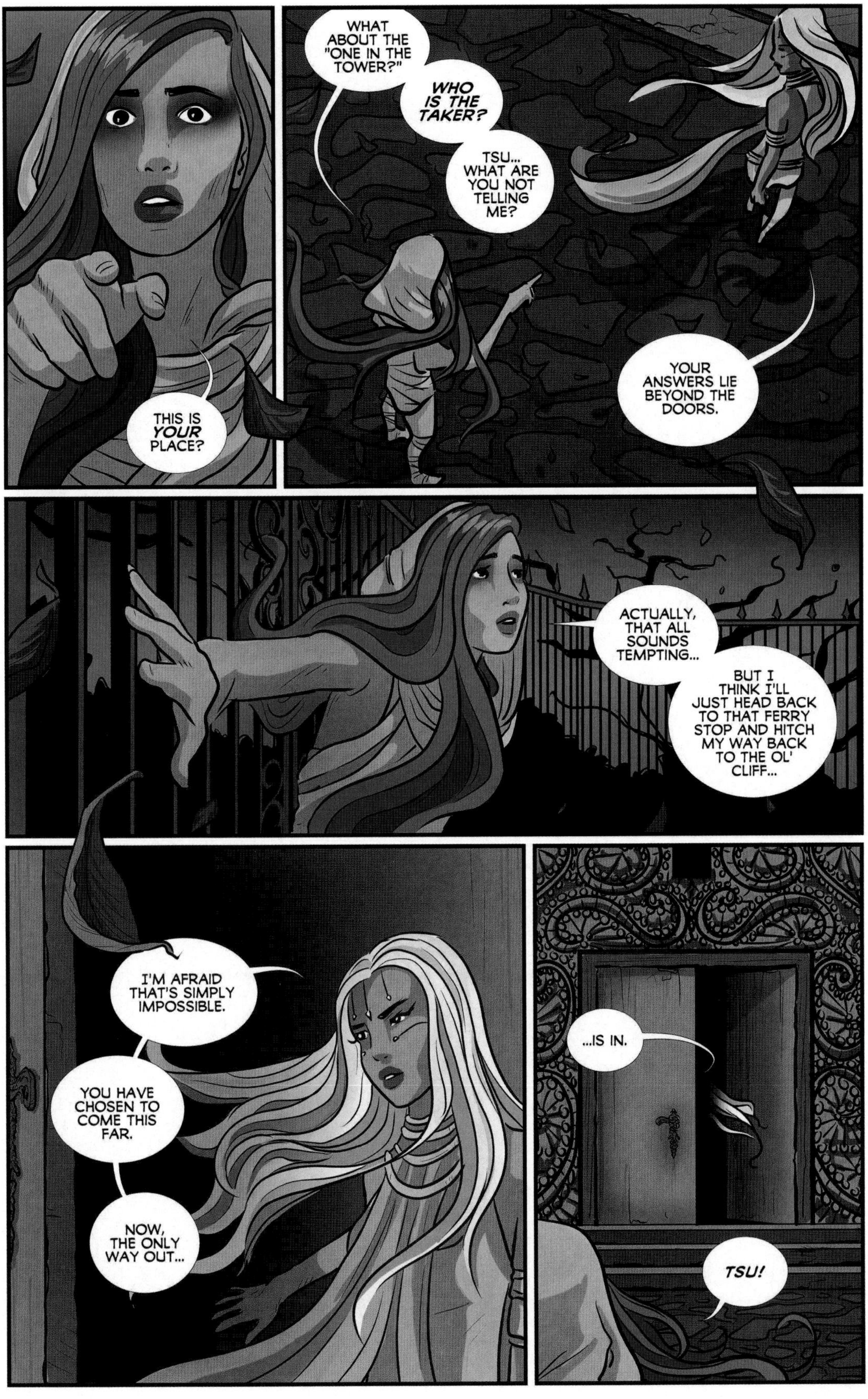
THIS IS *YOUR* PLACE?
WHAT ABOUT THE "ONE IN THE TOWER?"
WHO IS THE TAKER?
TSU... WHAT ARE YOU NOT TELLING ME?
YOUR ANSWERS LIE BEYOND THE DOORS.
ACTUALLY, THAT ALL SOUNDS TEMPTING...
BUT I THINK I'LL JUST HEAD BACK TO THAT FERRY STOP AND HITCH MY WAY BACK TO THE OL' CLIFF...
I'M AFRAID THAT'S SIMPLY IMPOSSIBLE.
YOU HAVE CHOSEN TO COME THIS FAR.
NOW, THE ONLY WAY OUT...
...IS IN.
TSU!

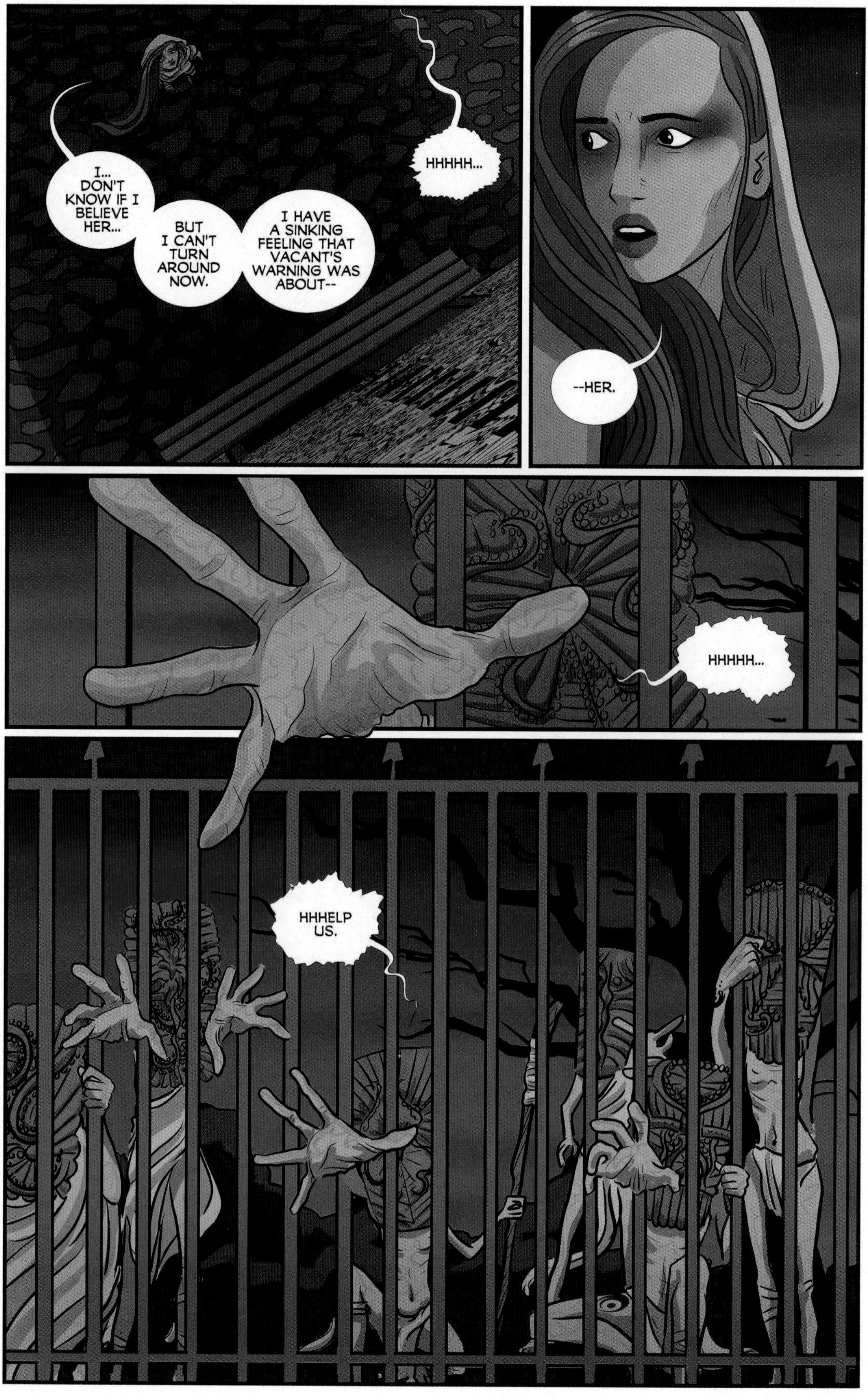
I... DON'T KNOW IF I BELIEVE HER...
BUT I CAN'T TURN AROUND NOW.
I HAVE A SINKING FEELING THAT VACANT'S WARNING WAS ABOUT--
HHHHH...
--HER.
HHHHH...
HHHELP US.

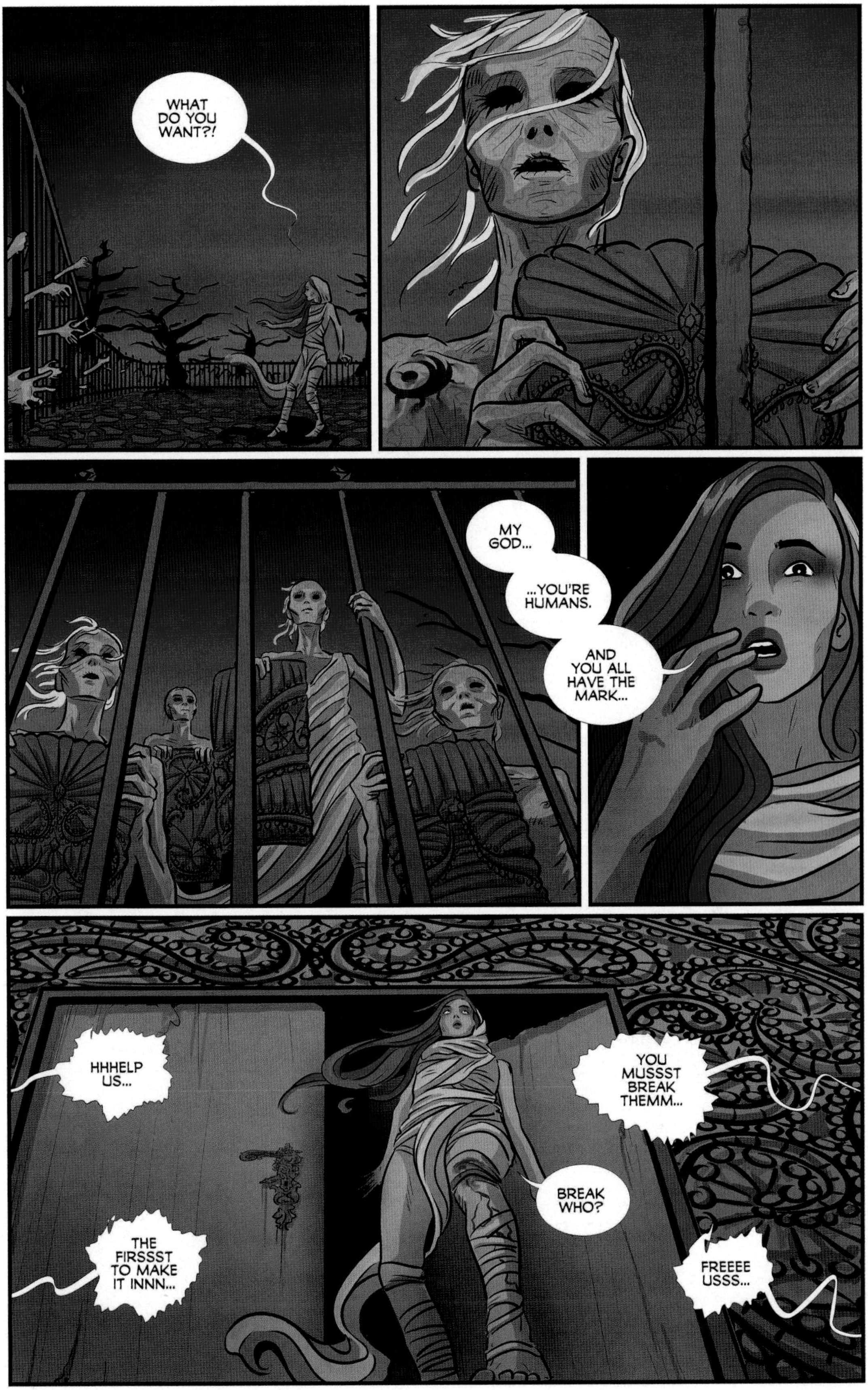
WHAT DO YOU WANT?!
MY GOD...
...YOU'RE HUMANS.
AND YOU ALL HAVE THE MARK...
HHHELP US...
YOU MUSSST BREAK THEMM...
BREAK WHO?
THE FIRSSST TO MAKE IT INNN...
FREEEE USSS...

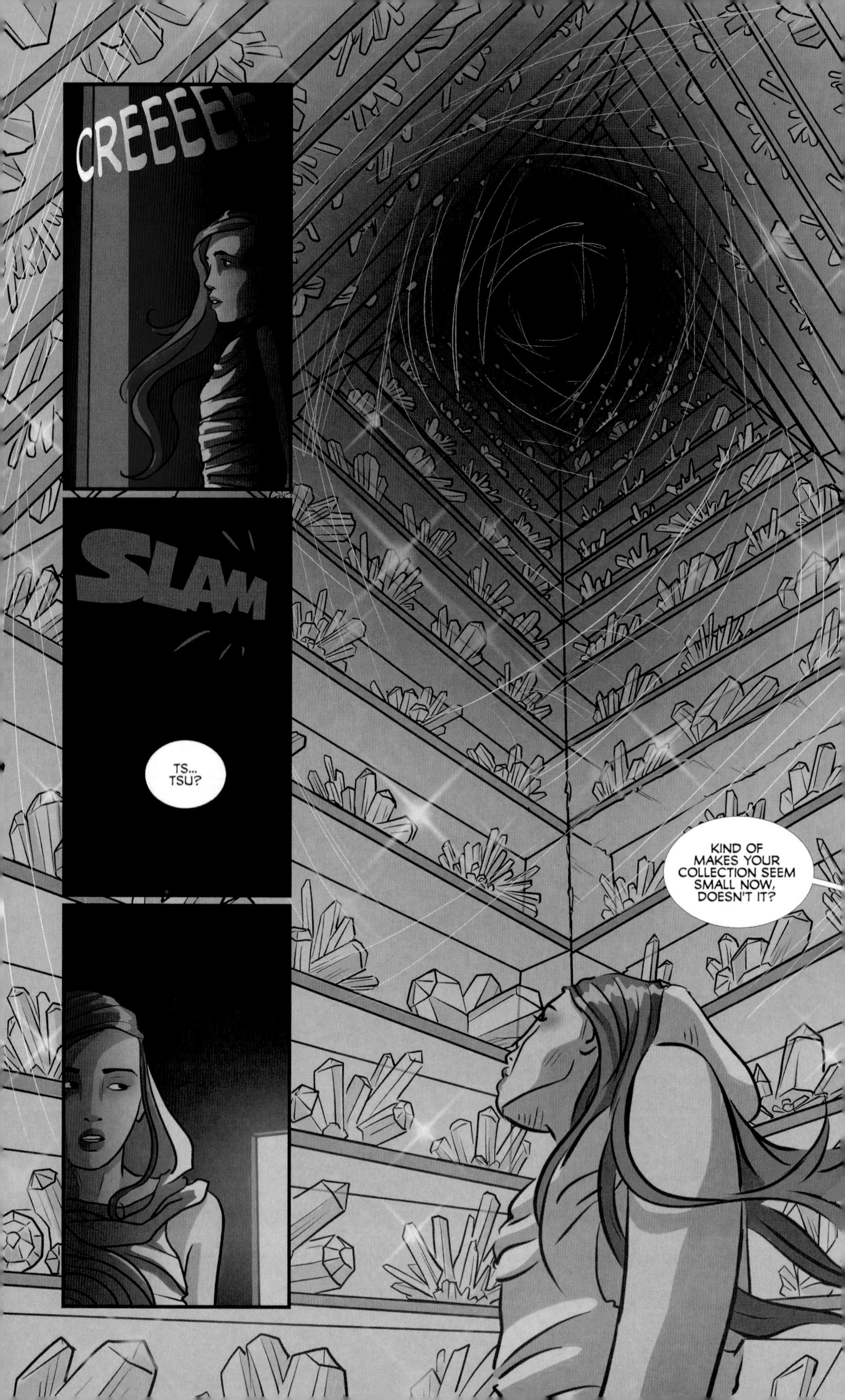
CREEEEE
SLAM
TS... TSU?
KIND OF MAKES YOUR COLLECTION SEEM SMALL NOW, DOESN'T IT?

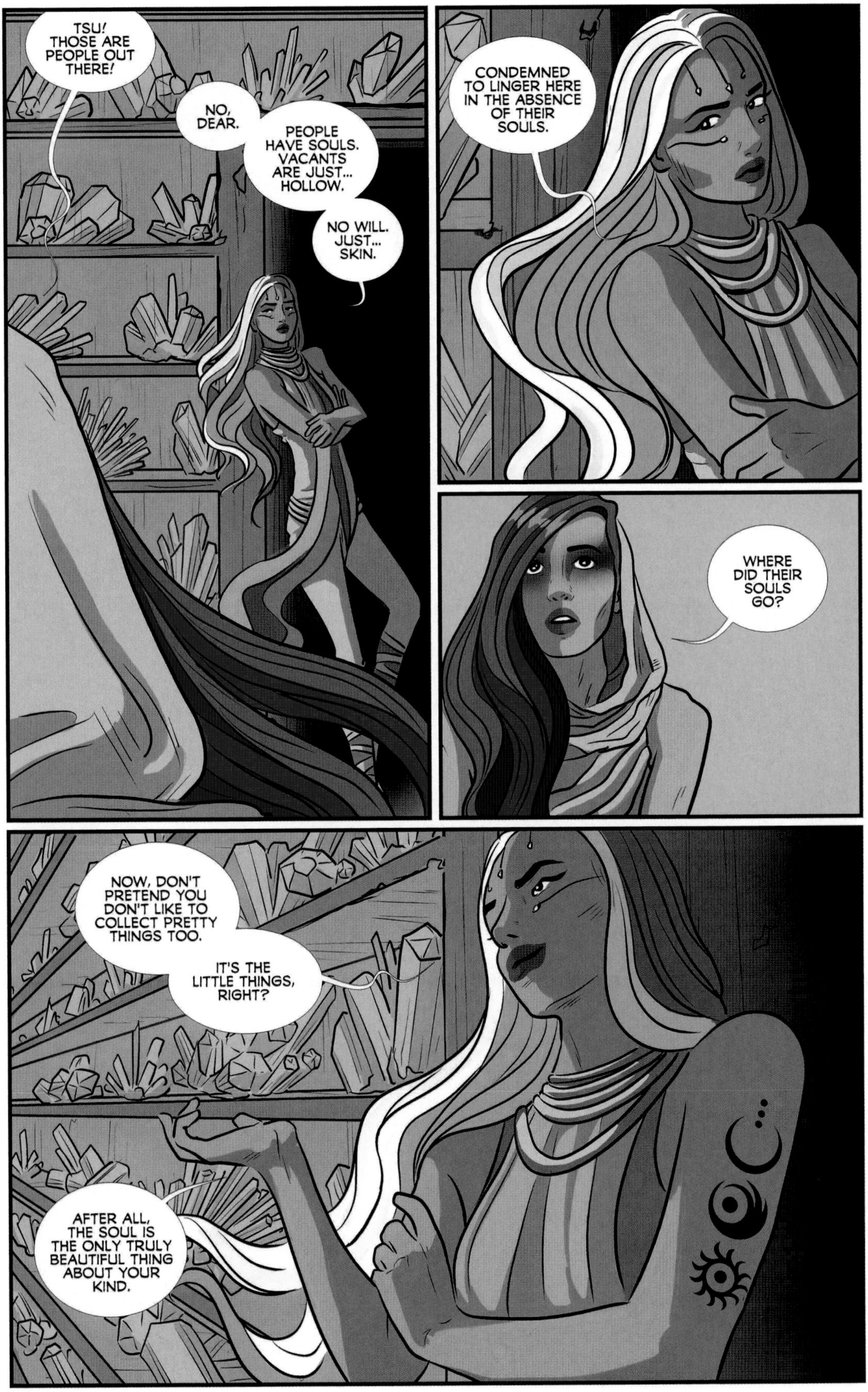
TSU! THOSE ARE PEOPLE OUT THERE!
NO, DEAR.
PEOPLE HAVE SOULS. VACANTS ARE JUST... HOLLOW.
NO WILL. JUST... SKIN.
CONDEMNED TO LINGER HERE IN THE ABSENCE OF THEIR SOULS.
WHERE DID THEIR SOULS GO?
NOW, DON'T PRETEND YOU DON'T LIKE TO COLLECT PRETTY THINGS TOO.
IT'S THE LITTLE THINGS, RIGHT?
AFTER ALL, THE SOUL IS THE ONLY TRULY BEAUTIFUL THING ABOUT YOUR KIND.

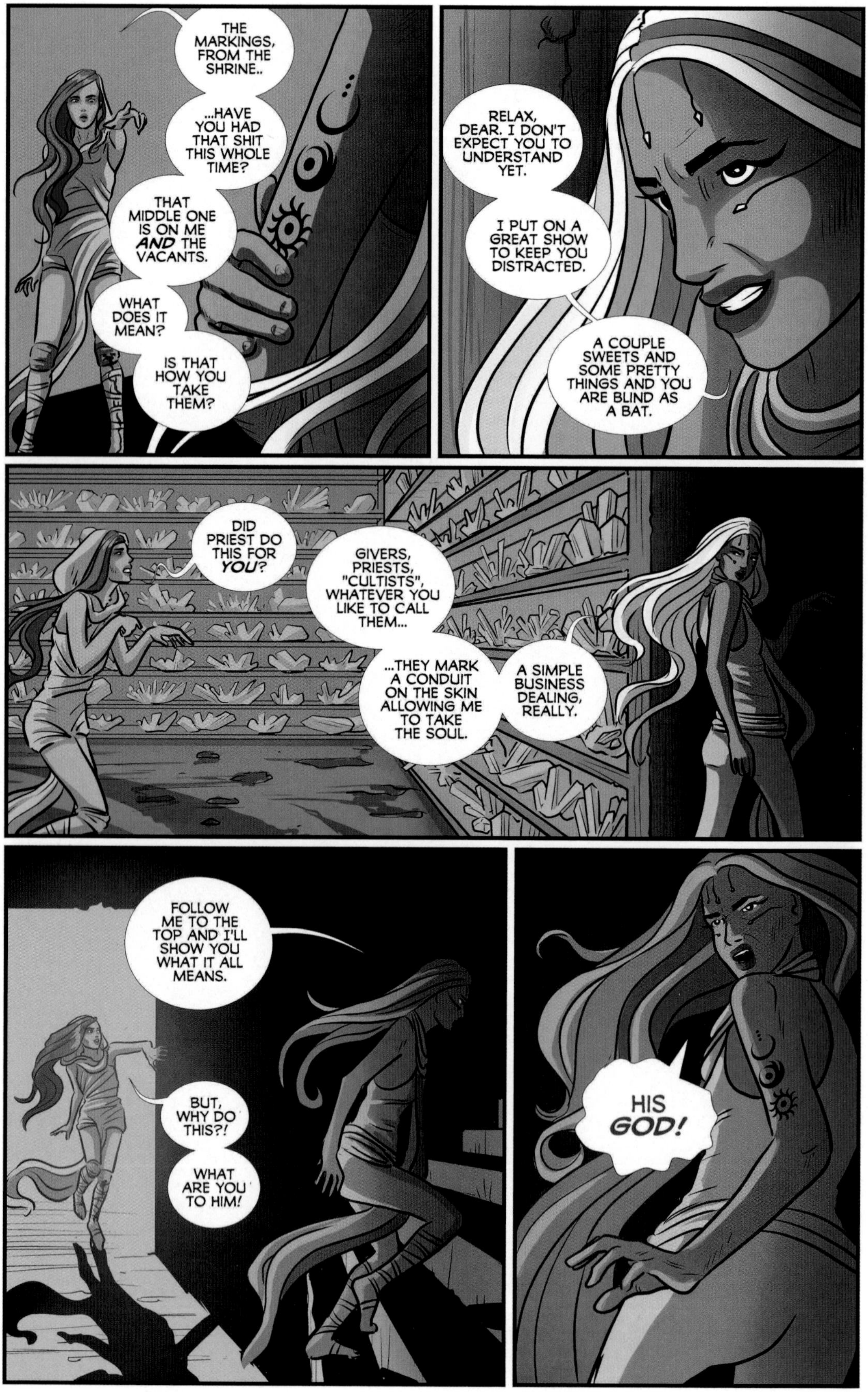
THE MARKINGS, FROM THE SHRINE..
...HAVE YOU HAD THAT SHIT THIS WHOLE TIME?
THAT MIDDLE ONE IS ON ME AND THE VACANTS.
WHAT DOES IT MEAN?
IS THAT HOW YOU TAKE THEM?
RELAX, DEAR. I DON'T EXPECT YOU TO UNDERSTAND YET.
I PUT ON A GREAT SHOW TO KEEP YOU DISTRACTED.
A COUPLE SWEETS AND SOME PRETTY THINGS AND YOU ARE BLIND AS A BAT.
DID PRIEST DO THIS FOR YOU?
GIVERS, PRIESTS, "CULTISTS", WHATEVER YOU LIKE TO CALL THEM...
...THEY MARK A CONDUIT ON THE SKIN ALLOWING ME TO TAKE THE SOUL.
A SIMPLE BUSINESS DEALING, REALLY.
FOLLOW ME TO THE TOP AND I'LL SHOW YOU WHAT IT ALL MEANS.
BUT, WHY DO THIS?!
WHAT ARE YOU TO HIM!
HIS GOD!

HE KNOWS HER. HE IS *AFRAID* OF HER. HE *FUCKED* ME FOR HER.

THIS IS BEYOND MESSED.

I *NEED* TO UNDERSTAND.

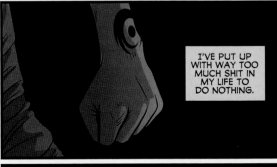

I'VE PUT UP WITH WAY TOO MUCH SHIT IN MY LIFE TO DO NOTHING.

I FINALLY SEE IT. I DON'T THINK HOPE IS SOMETHING THAT JUST FINDS YOU.

I THINK IF YOU WANT THAT SHIT YOU HAVE TO DRAG IT FROM ITS GRAVE.

SO WHATEVER IS UP HERE BEST BE HOPE OR I'M GONNA BE PISSED.

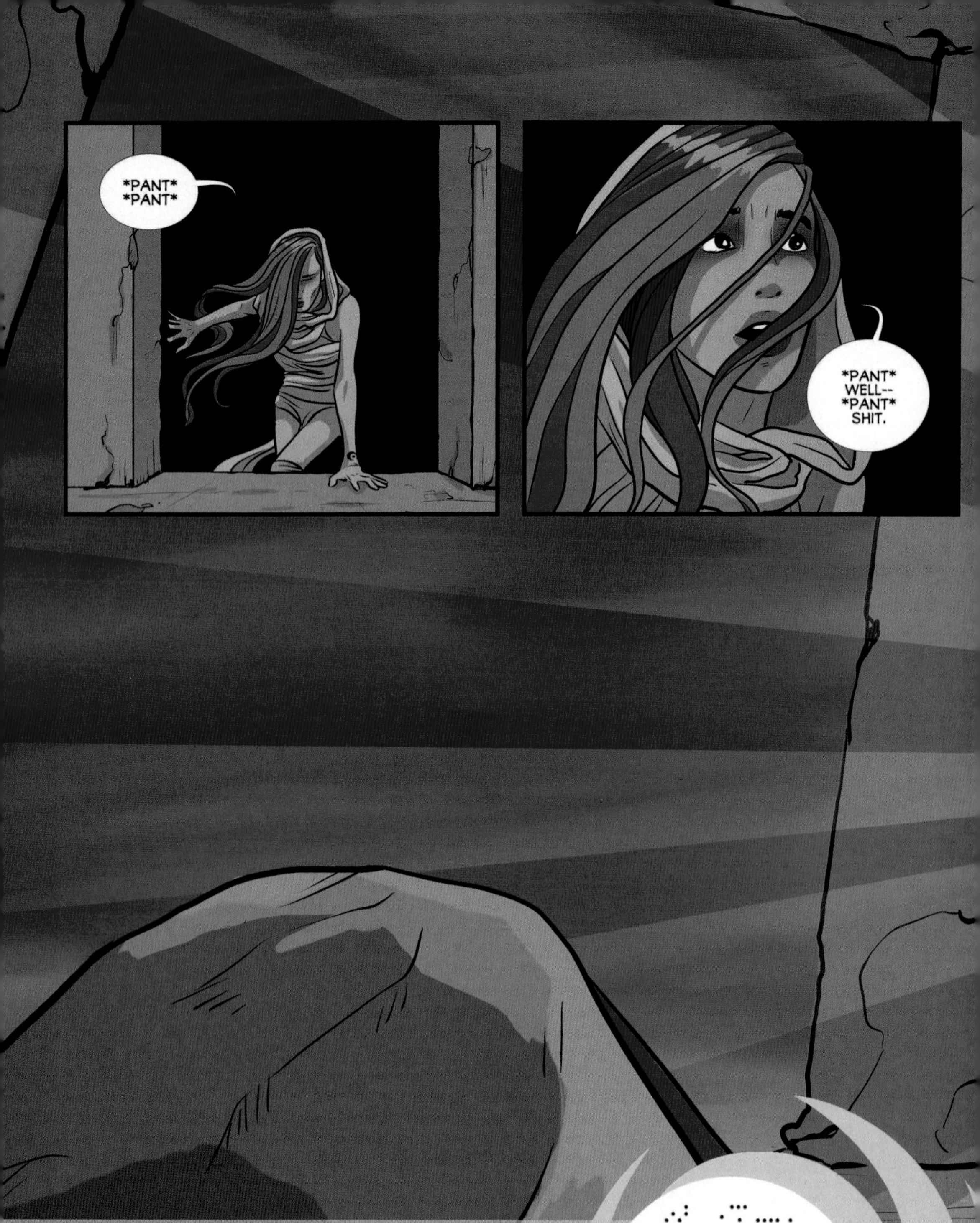
PANT *PANT*
PANT WELL-- *PANT* SHIT.

CHAPTER THIRTEEN: FIGHT CLUB

http://mxt.pe/fhtclb

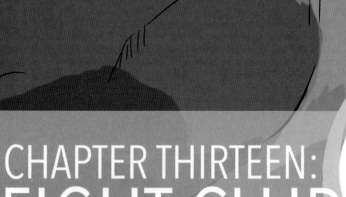

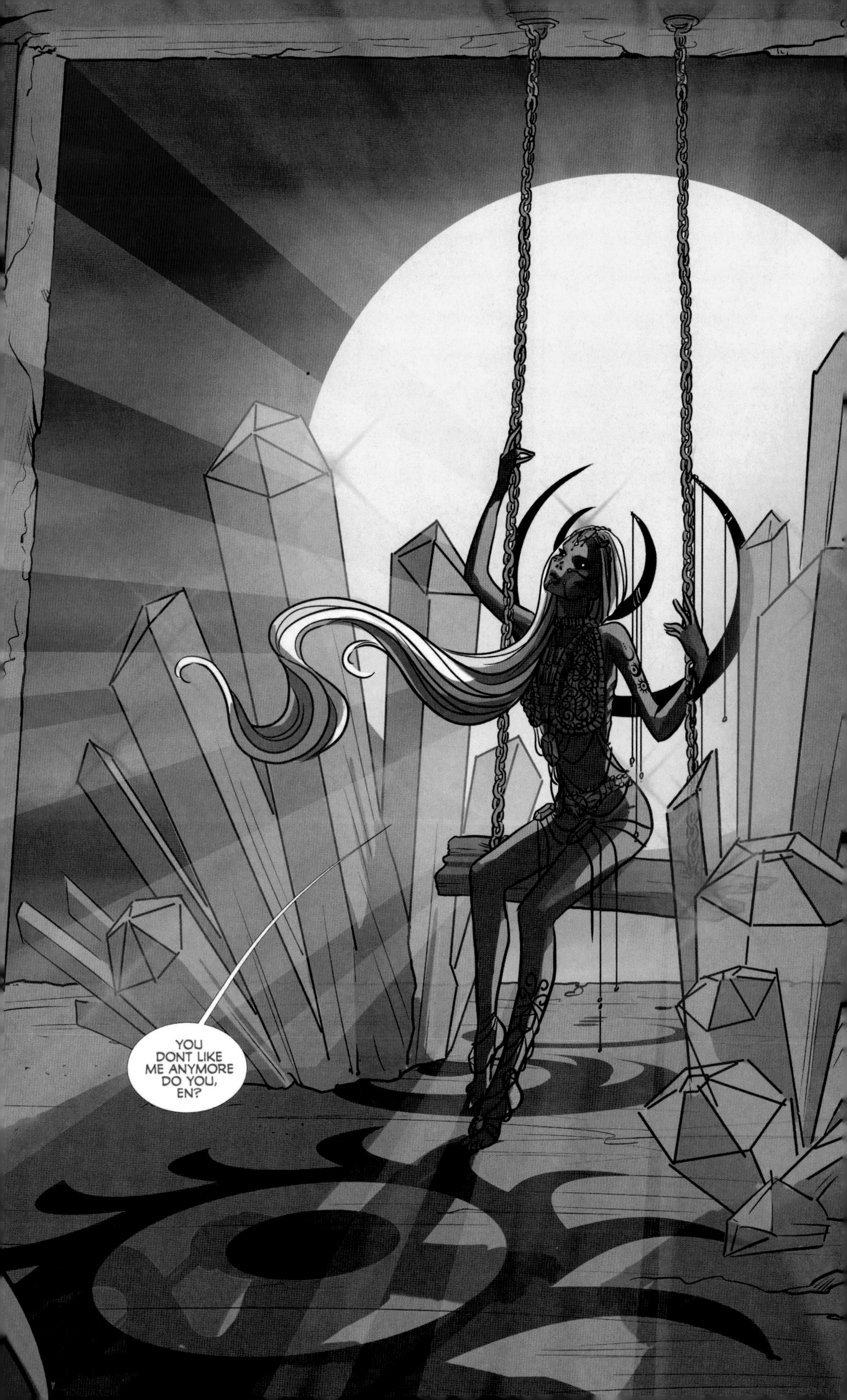
YOU DONT LIKE ME ANYMORE DO YOU, EN?

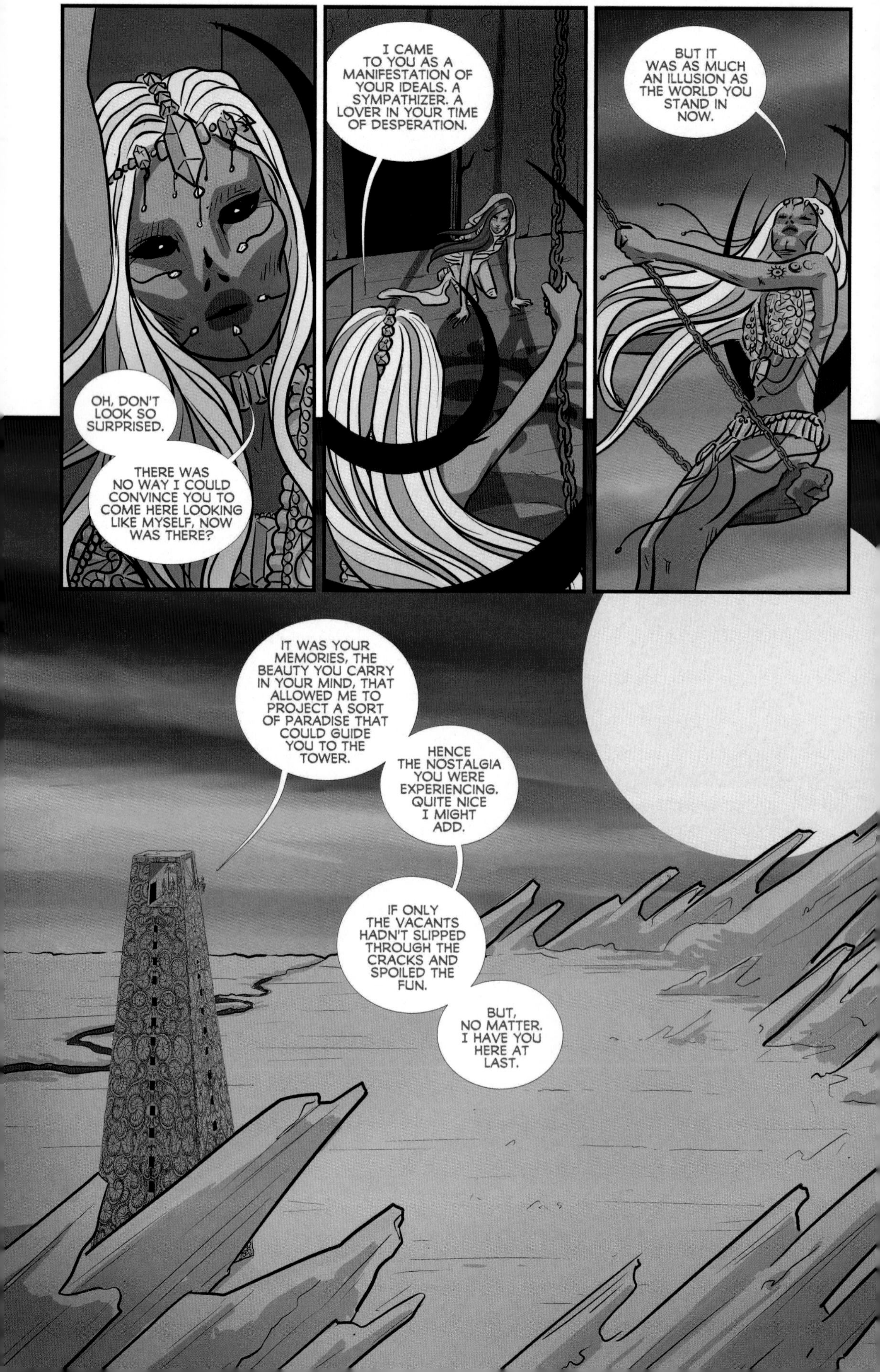

OH, DON'T LOOK SO SURPRISED.
THERE WAS NO WAY I COULD CONVINCE YOU TO COME HERE LOOKING LIKE MYSELF, NOW WAS THERE?
I CAME TO YOU AS A MANIFESTATION OF YOUR IDEALS. A SYMPATHIZER. A LOVER IN YOUR TIME OF DESPERATION.
BUT IT WAS AS MUCH AN ILLUSION AS THE WORLD YOU STAND IN NOW.
IT WAS YOUR MEMORIES, THE BEAUTY YOU CARRY IN YOUR MIND, THAT ALLOWED ME TO PROJECT A SORT OF PARADISE THAT COULD GUIDE YOU TO THE TOWER.
HENCE THE NOSTALGIA YOU WERE EXPERIENCING. QUITE NICE I MIGHT ADD.
IF ONLY THE VACANTS HADN'T SLIPPED THROUGH THE CRACKS AND SPOILED THE FUN.
BUT, NO MATTER. I HAVE YOU HERE AT LAST.

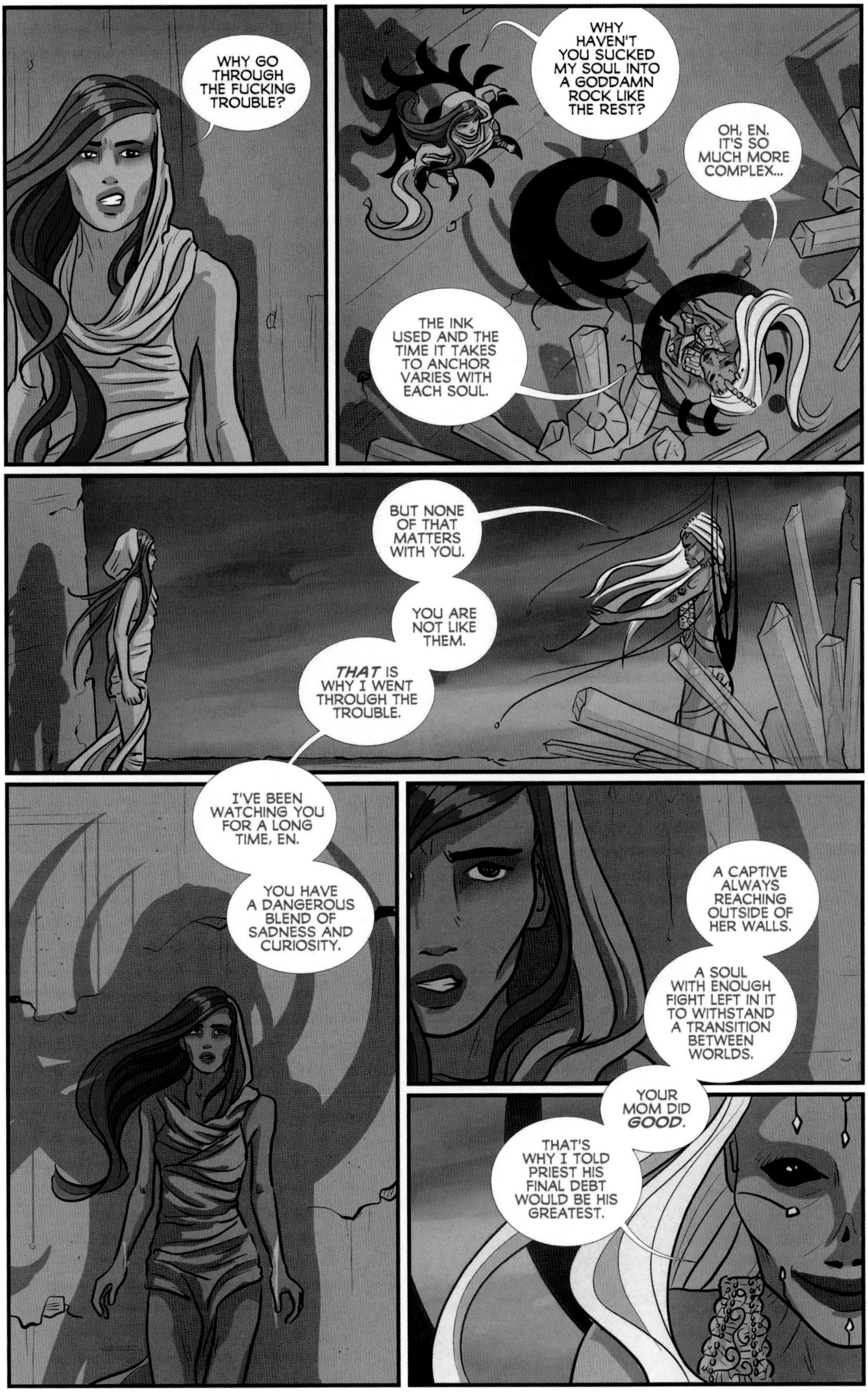
WHY GO THROUGH THE FUCKING TROUBLE?
WHY HAVEN'T YOU SUCKED MY SOUL INTO A GODDAMN ROCK LIKE THE REST?
OH, EN. IT'S SO MUCH MORE COMPLEX...
THE INK USED AND THE TIME IT TAKES TO ANCHOR VARIES WITH EACH SOUL.
BUT NONE OF THAT MATTERS WITH YOU.
YOU ARE NOT LIKE THEM.
THAT IS WHY I WENT THROUGH THE TROUBLE.
I'VE BEEN WATCHING YOU FOR A LONG TIME, EN.
YOU HAVE A DANGEROUS BLEND OF SADNESS AND CURIOSITY.
A CAPTIVE ALWAYS REACHING OUTSIDE OF HER WALLS.
A SOUL WITH ENOUGH FIGHT LEFT IN IT TO WITHSTAND A TRANSITION BETWEEN WORLDS.
YOUR MOM DID *GOOD*.
THAT'S WHY I TOLD PRIEST HIS FINAL DEBT WOULD BE HIS GREATEST.

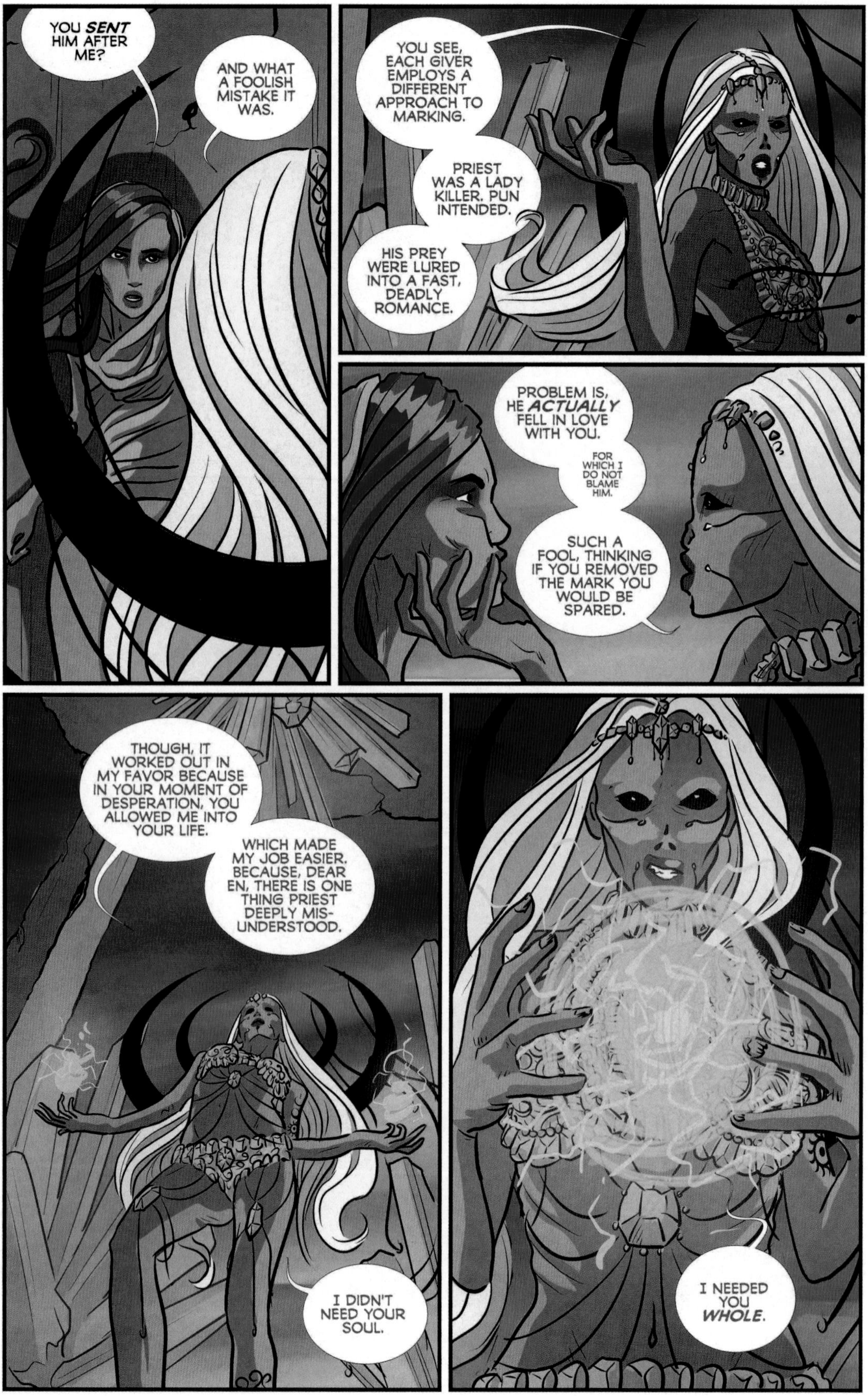

YOU SENT HIM AFTER ME?
AND WHAT A FOOLISH MISTAKE IT WAS.
YOU SEE, EACH GIVER EMPLOYS A DIFFERENT APPROACH TO MARKING.
PRIEST WAS A LADY KILLER. PUN INTENDED.
HIS PREY WERE LURED INTO A FAST, DEADLY ROMANCE.
PROBLEM IS, HE ACTUALLY FELL IN LOVE WITH YOU.
FOR WHICH I DO NOT BLAME HIM.
SUCH A FOOL, THINKING IF YOU REMOVED THE MARK YOU WOULD BE SPARED.
THOUGH, IT WORKED OUT IN MY FAVOR BECAUSE IN YOUR MOMENT OF DESPERATION, YOU ALLOWED ME INTO YOUR LIFE.
WHICH MADE MY JOB EASIER. BECAUSE, DEAR EN, THERE IS ONE THING PRIEST DEEPLY MIS-UNDERSTOOD.
I DIDN'T NEED YOUR SOUL.
I NEEDED YOU WHOLE.

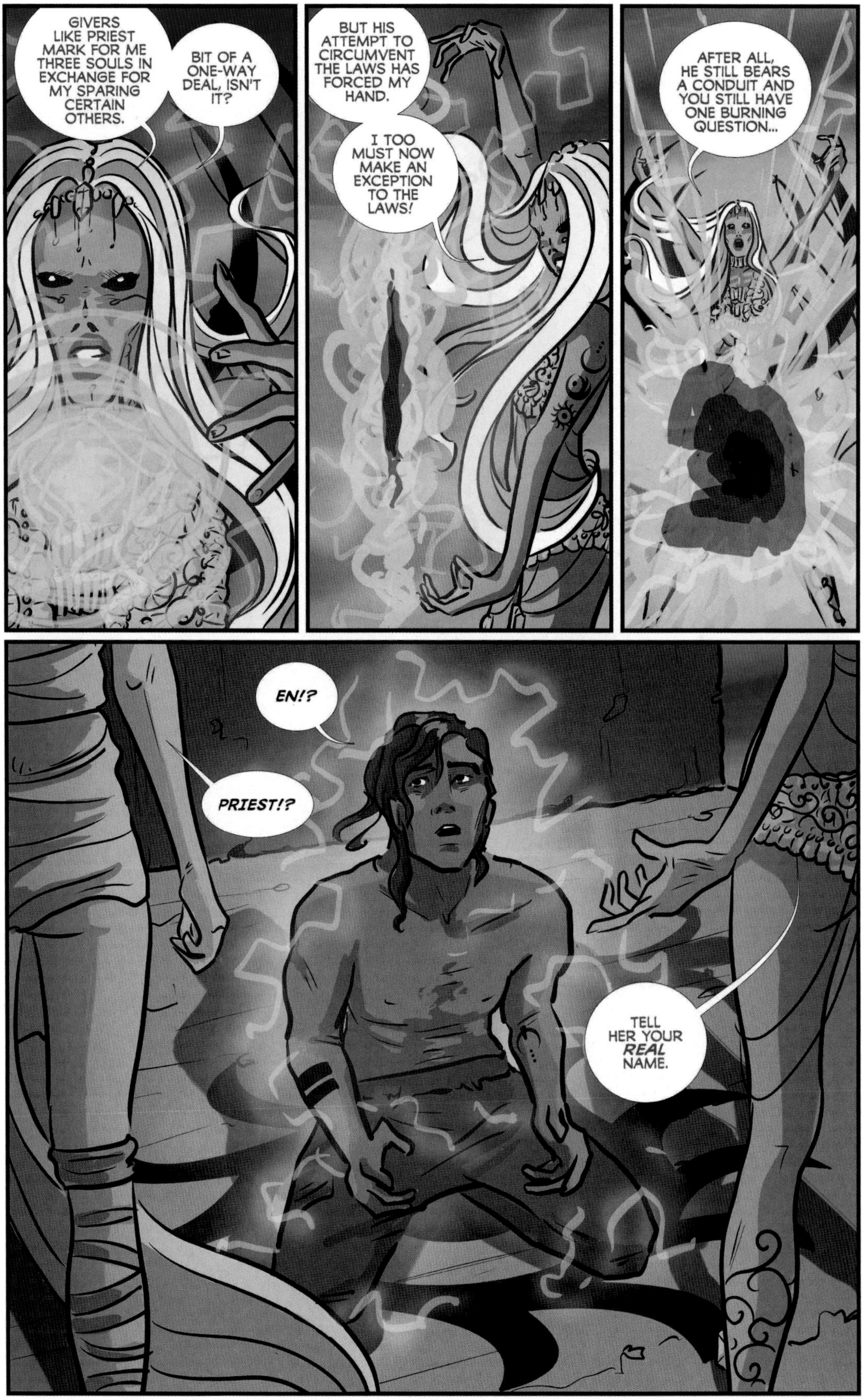
GIVERS LIKE PRIEST MARK FOR ME THREE SOULS IN EXCHANGE FOR MY SPARING CERTAIN OTHERS.
BIT OF A ONE-WAY DEAL, ISN'T IT?
BUT HIS ATTEMPT TO CIRCUMVENT THE LAWS HAS FORCED MY HAND.
I TOO MUST NOW MAKE AN EXCEPTION TO THE LAWS!
AFTER ALL, HE STILL BEARS A CONDUIT AND YOU STILL HAVE ONE BURNING QUESTION...
EN!?
PRIEST!?
TELL HER YOUR REAL NAME.

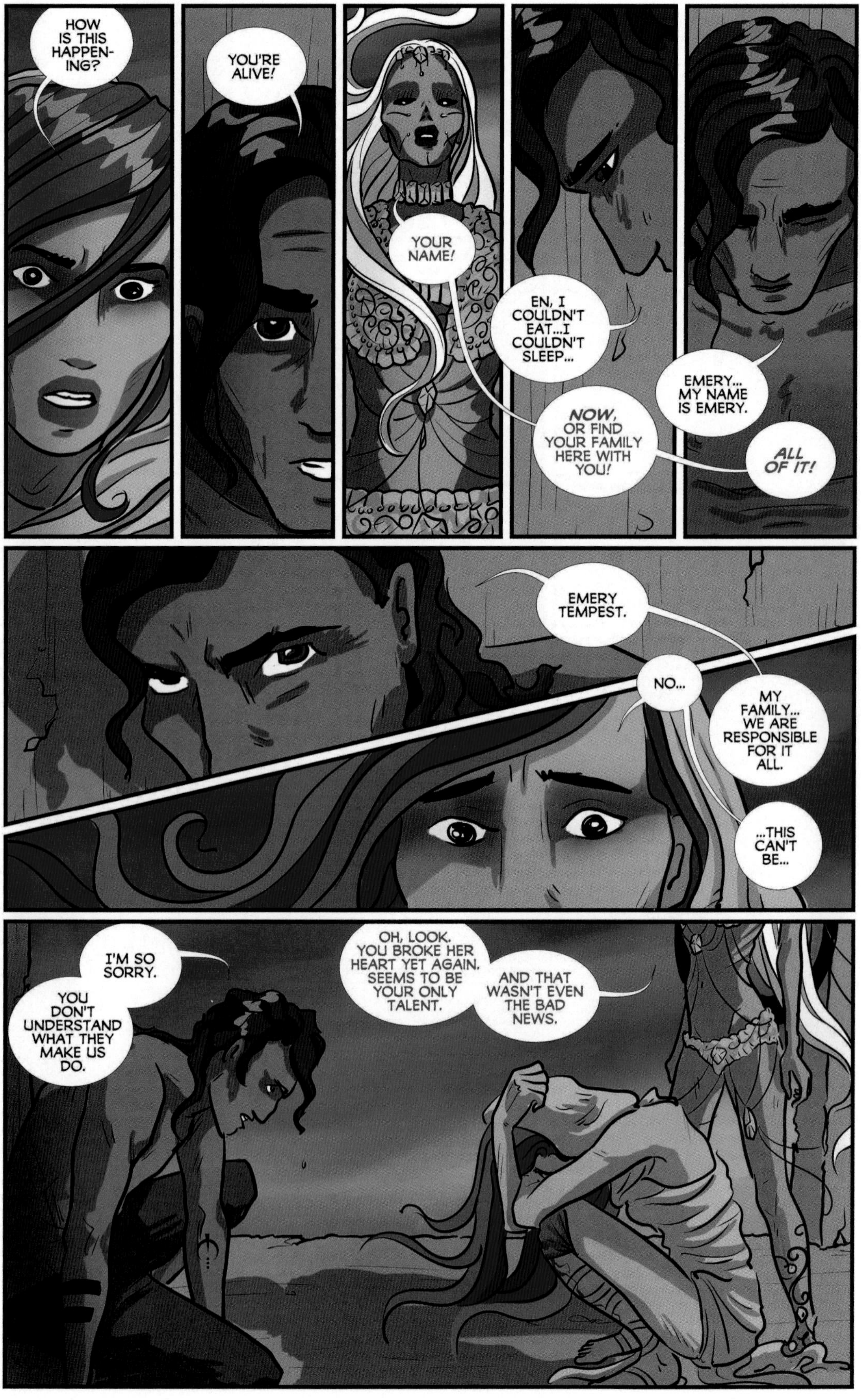
HOW IS THIS HAPPEN-ING?
YOU'RE ALIVE!
YOUR NAME!
EN, I COULDN'T EAT...I COULDN'T SLEEP...
NOW, OR FIND YOUR FAMILY HERE WITH YOU!
EMERY... MY NAME IS EMERY.
ALL OF IT!
EMERY TEMPEST.
NO...
MY FAMILY... WE ARE RESPONSIBLE FOR IT ALL.
...THIS CAN'T BE...
I'M SO SORRY.
YOU DON'T UNDERSTAND WHAT THEY MAKE US DO.
OH, LOOK. YOU BROKE HER HEART YET AGAIN. SEEMS TO BE YOUR ONLY TALENT.
AND THAT WASN'T EVEN THE BAD NEWS.

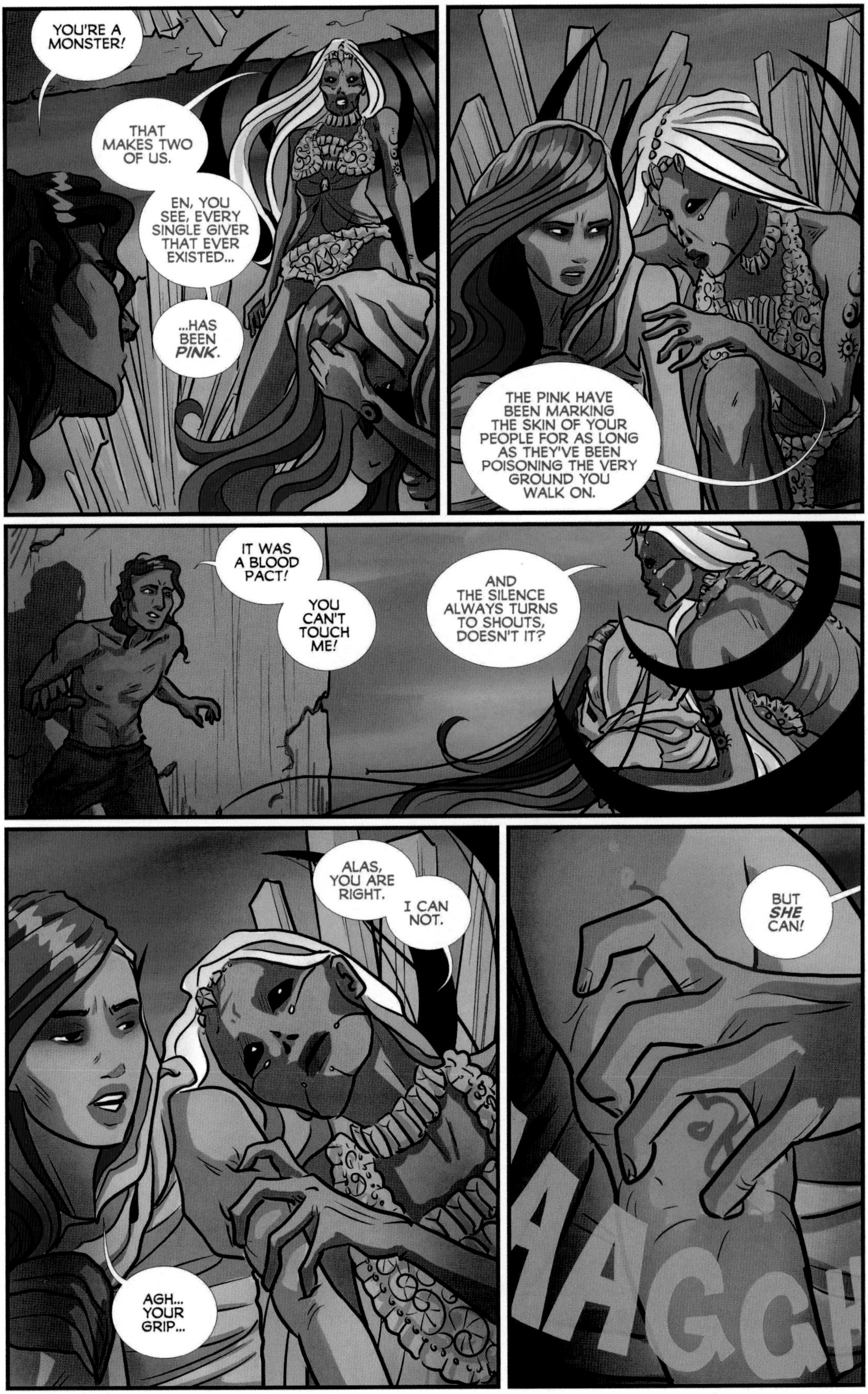
YOU'RE A MONSTER!
THAT MAKES TWO OF US.
EN, YOU SEE, EVERY SINGLE GIVER THAT EVER EXISTED...
...HAS BEEN *PINK*.
THE PINK HAVE BEEN MARKING THE SKIN OF YOUR PEOPLE FOR AS LONG AS THEY'VE BEEN POISONING THE VERY GROUND YOU WALK ON.
IT WAS A BLOOD PACT!
YOU CAN'T TOUCH ME!
AND THE SILENCE ALWAYS TURNS TO SHOUTS, DOESN'T IT?
ALAS, YOU ARE RIGHT.
I CAN NOT.
AGH... YOUR GRIP...
BUT *SHE* CAN!
AAGGH

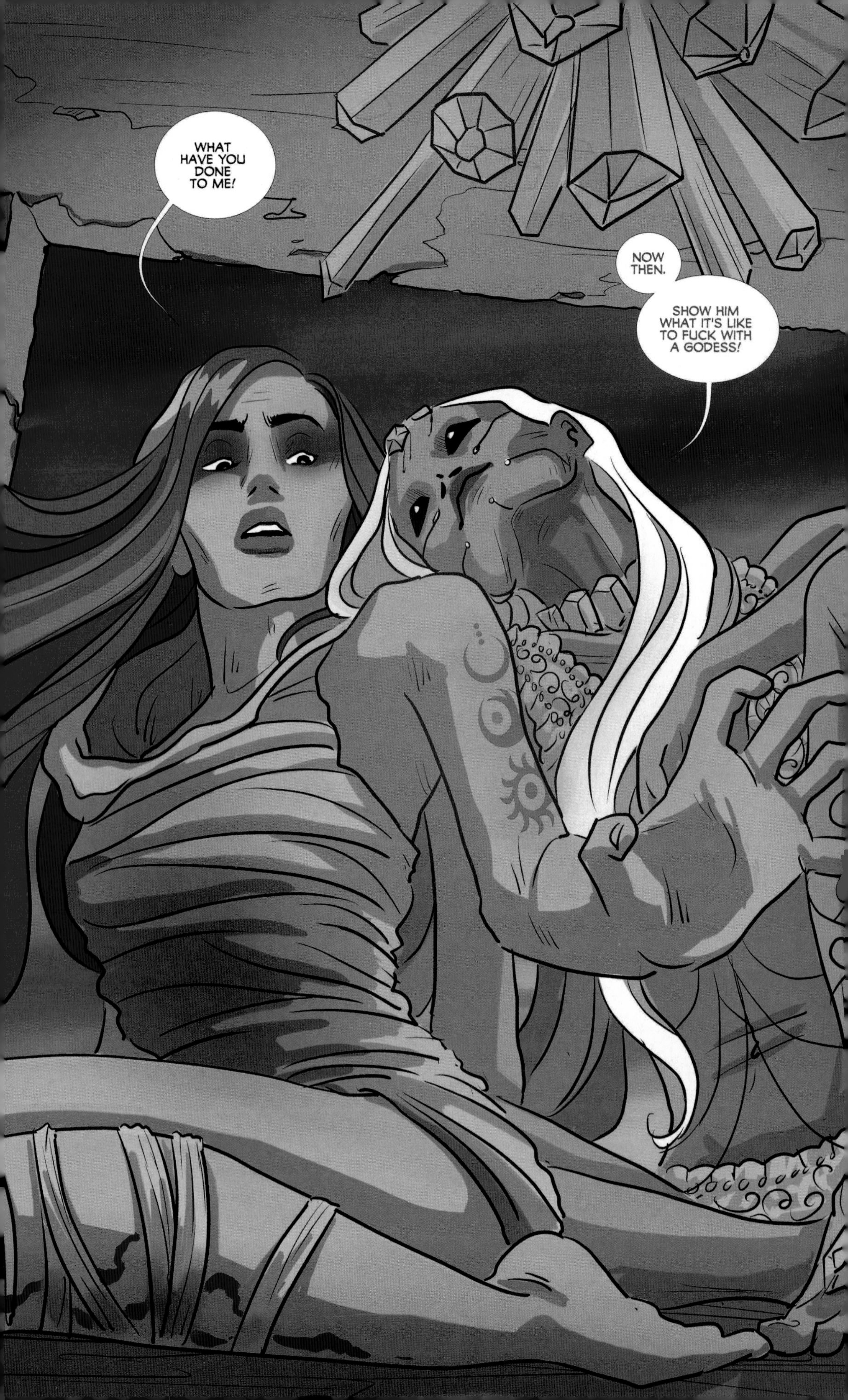
WHAT HAVE YOU DONE TO ME!
NOW THEN.
SHOW HIM WHAT IT'S LIKE TO FUCK WITH A GODESS!

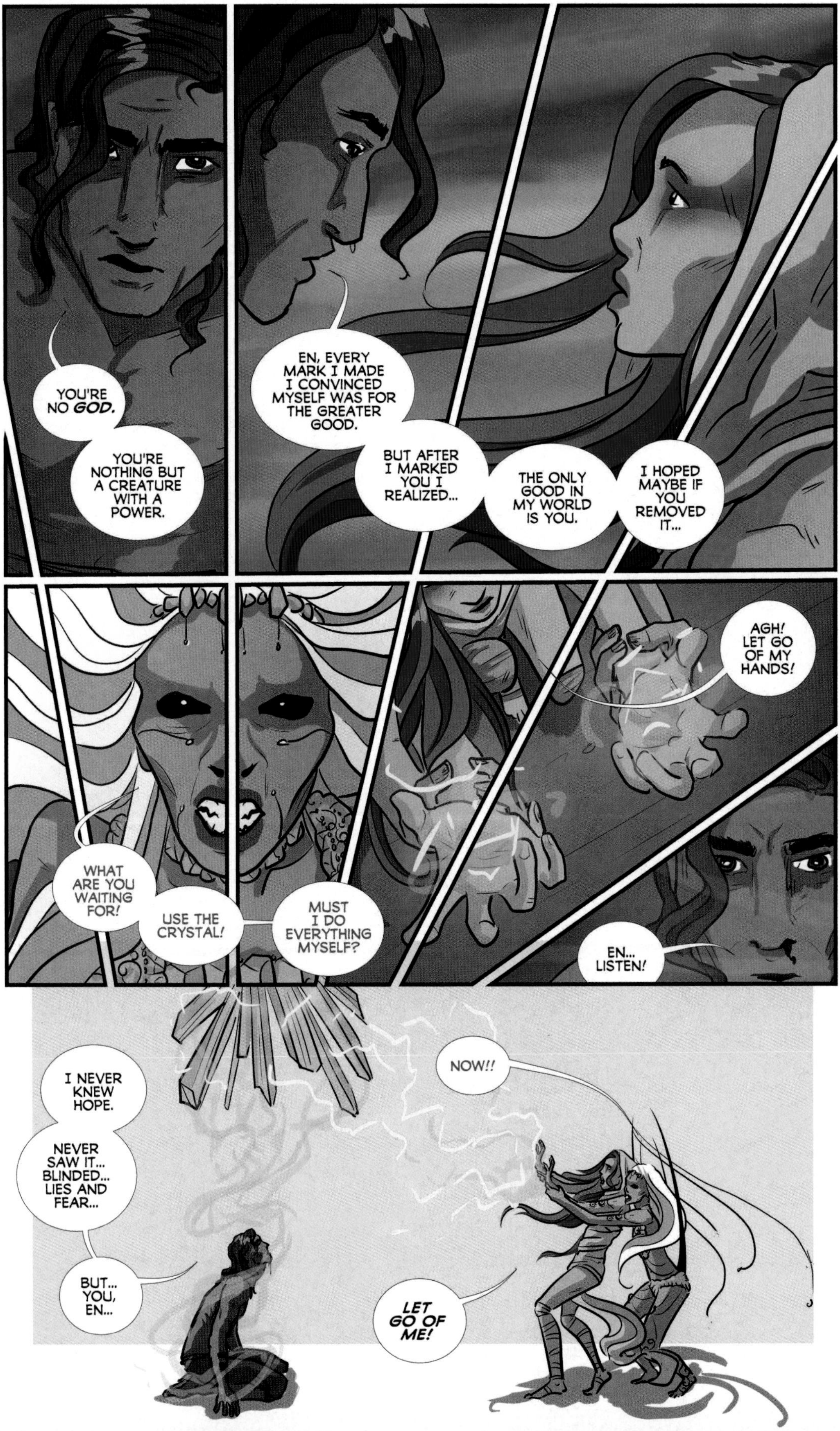
YOU'RE NO *GOD.*
YOU'RE NOTHING BUT A CREATURE WITH A POWER.
EN, EVERY MARK I MADE I CONVINCED MYSELF WAS FOR THE GREATER GOOD.
BUT AFTER I MARKED YOU I REALIZED...
THE ONLY GOOD IN MY WORLD IS YOU.
I HOPED MAYBE IF YOU REMOVED IT...
WHAT ARE YOU WAITING FOR!
USE THE CRYSTAL!
MUST I DO EVERYTHING MYSELF?
AGH! LET GO OF MY HANDS!
EN... LISTEN!
I NEVER KNEW HOPE.
NEVER SAW IT... BLINDED... LIES AND FEAR...
BUT... YOU, EN...
NOW!!
LET GO OF ME!

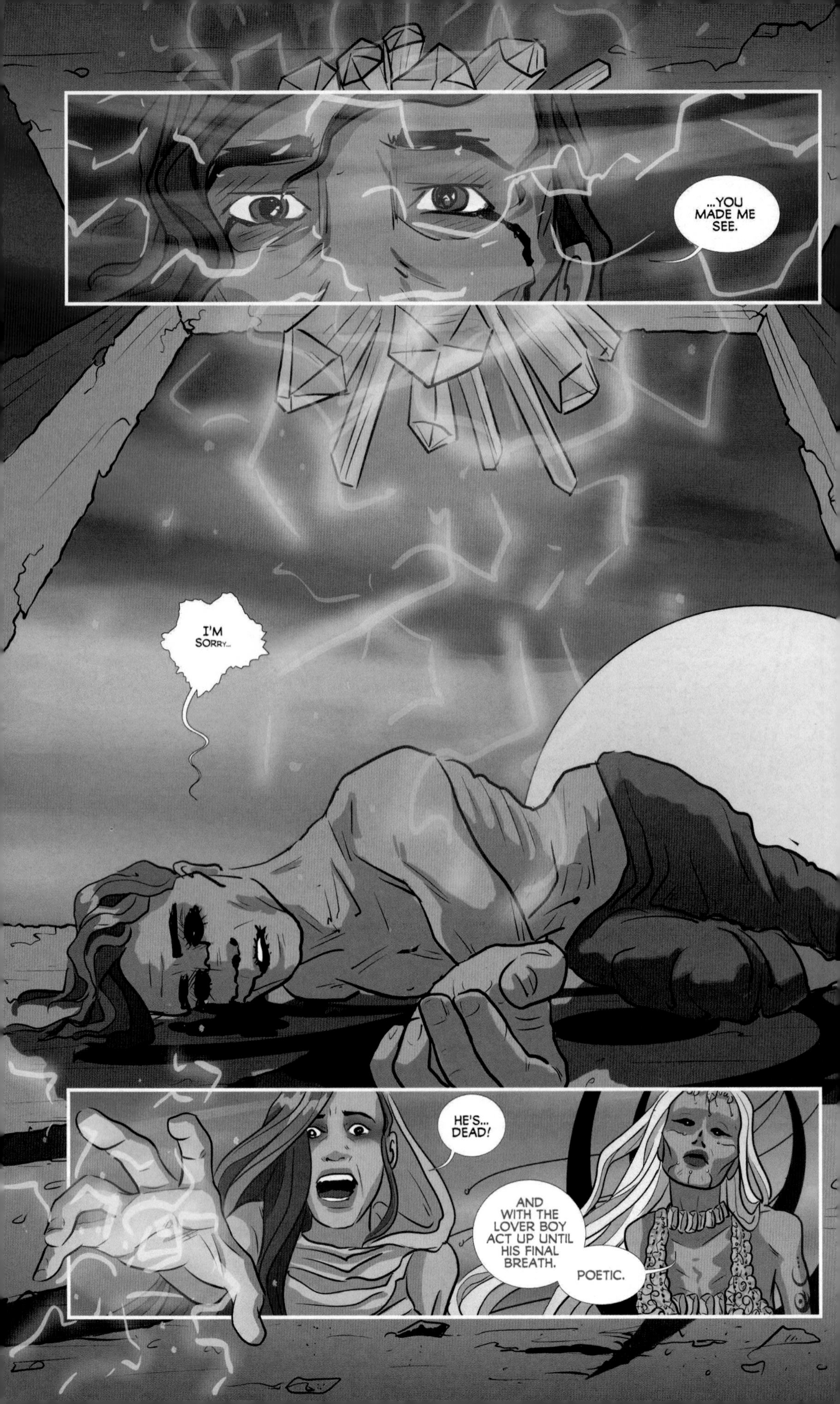
...YOU MADE ME SEE.
I'M SORRY...
HE'S... DEAD!
AND WITH THE LOVER BOY ACT UP UNTIL HIS FINAL BREATH.
POETIC.

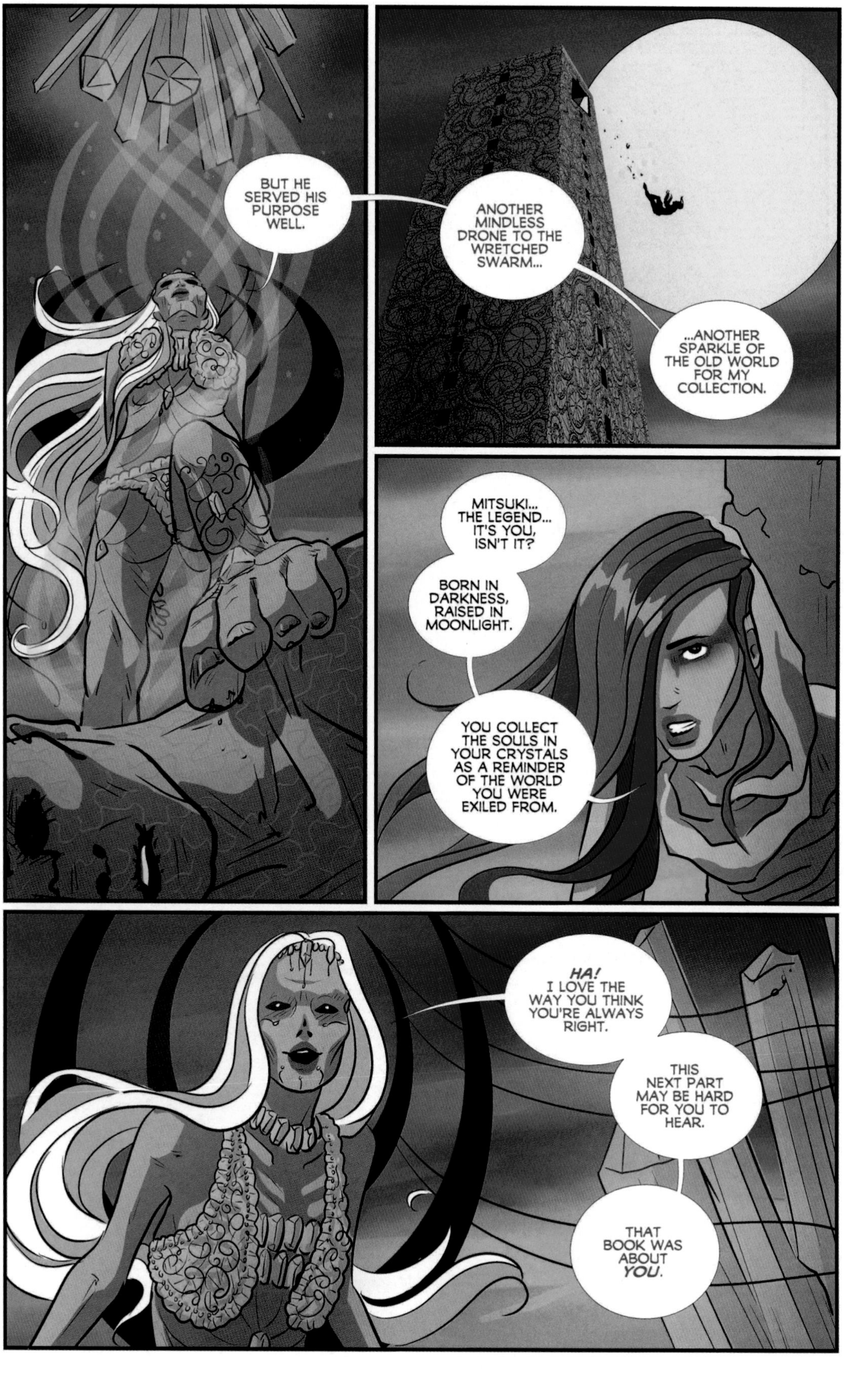
BUT HE SERVED HIS PURPOSE WELL.
ANOTHER MINDLESS DRONE TO THE WRETCHED SWARM...
...ANOTHER SPARKLE OF THE OLD WORLD FOR MY COLLECTION.
MITSUKI... THE LEGEND... IT'S YOU, ISN'T IT?
BORN IN DARKNESS, RAISED IN MOONLIGHT.
YOU COLLECT THE SOULS IN YOUR CRYSTALS AS A REMINDER OF THE WORLD YOU WERE EXILED FROM.
HA! I LOVE THE WAY YOU THINK YOU'RE ALWAYS RIGHT.
THIS NEXT PART MAY BE HARD FOR YOU TO HEAR.
THAT BOOK WAS ABOUT *YOU*.

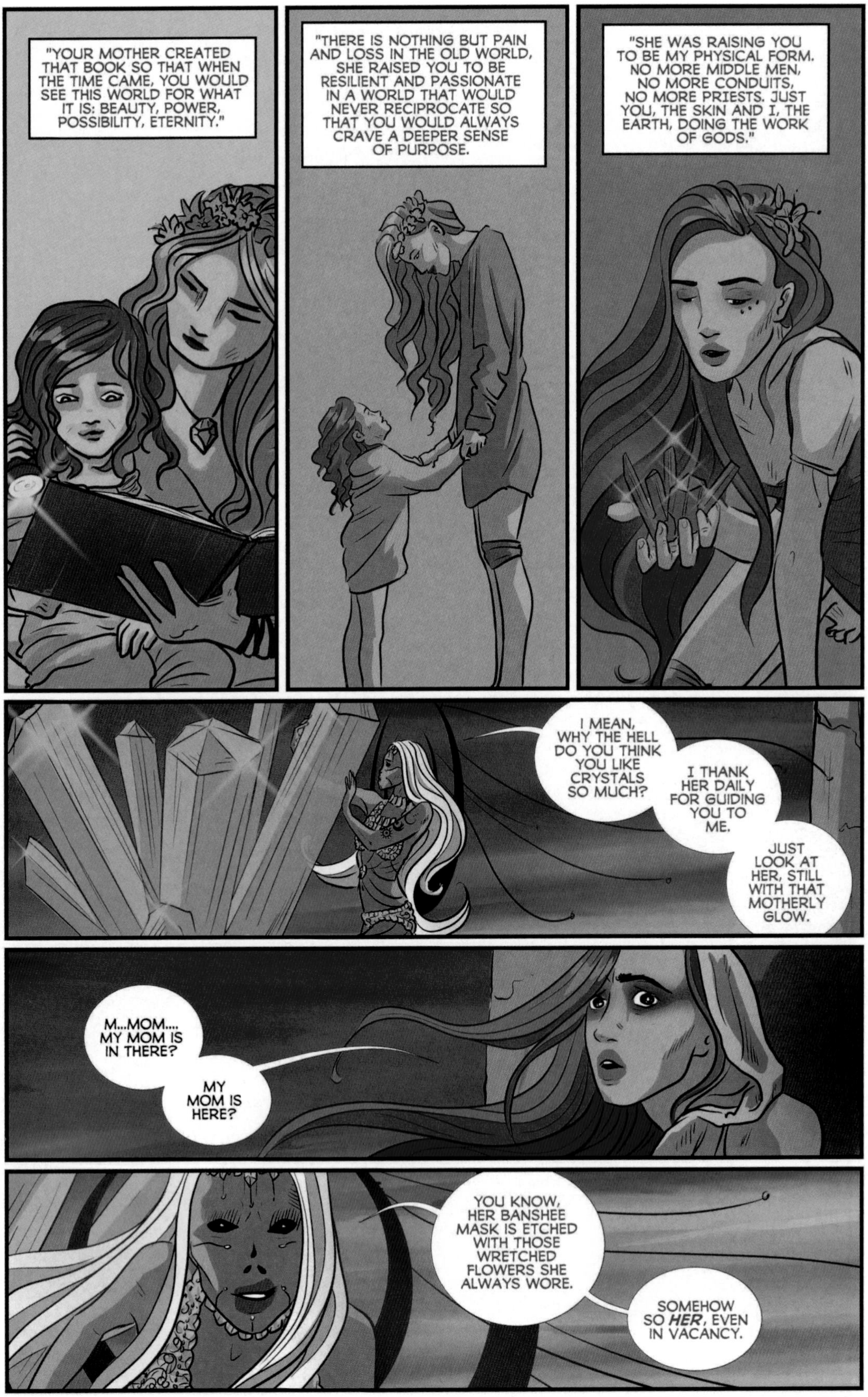
"YOUR MOTHER CREATED THAT BOOK SO THAT WHEN THE TIME CAME, YOU WOULD SEE THIS WORLD FOR WHAT IT IS: BEAUTY, POWER, POSSIBILITY, ETERNITY."
"THERE IS NOTHING BUT PAIN AND LOSS IN THE OLD WORLD, SHE RAISED YOU TO BE RESILIENT AND PASSIONATE IN A WORLD THAT WOULD NEVER RECIPROCATE SO THAT YOU WOULD ALWAYS CRAVE A DEEPER SENSE OF PURPOSE.
"SHE WAS RAISING YOU TO BE MY PHYSICAL FORM. NO MORE MIDDLE MEN, NO MORE CONDUITS, NO MORE PRIESTS. JUST YOU, THE SKIN AND I, THE EARTH, DOING THE WORK OF GODS."
I MEAN, WHY THE HELL DO YOU THINK YOU LIKE CRYSTALS SO MUCH?
I THANK HER DAILY FOR GUIDING YOU TO ME.
JUST LOOK AT HER, STILL WITH THAT MOTHERLY GLOW.
M...MOM.... MY MOM IS IN THERE?
MY MOM IS HERE?
YOU KNOW, HER BANSHEE MASK IS ETCHED WITH THOSE WRETCHED FLOWERS SHE ALWAYS WORE.
SOMEHOW SO ***HER***, EVEN IN VACANCY.

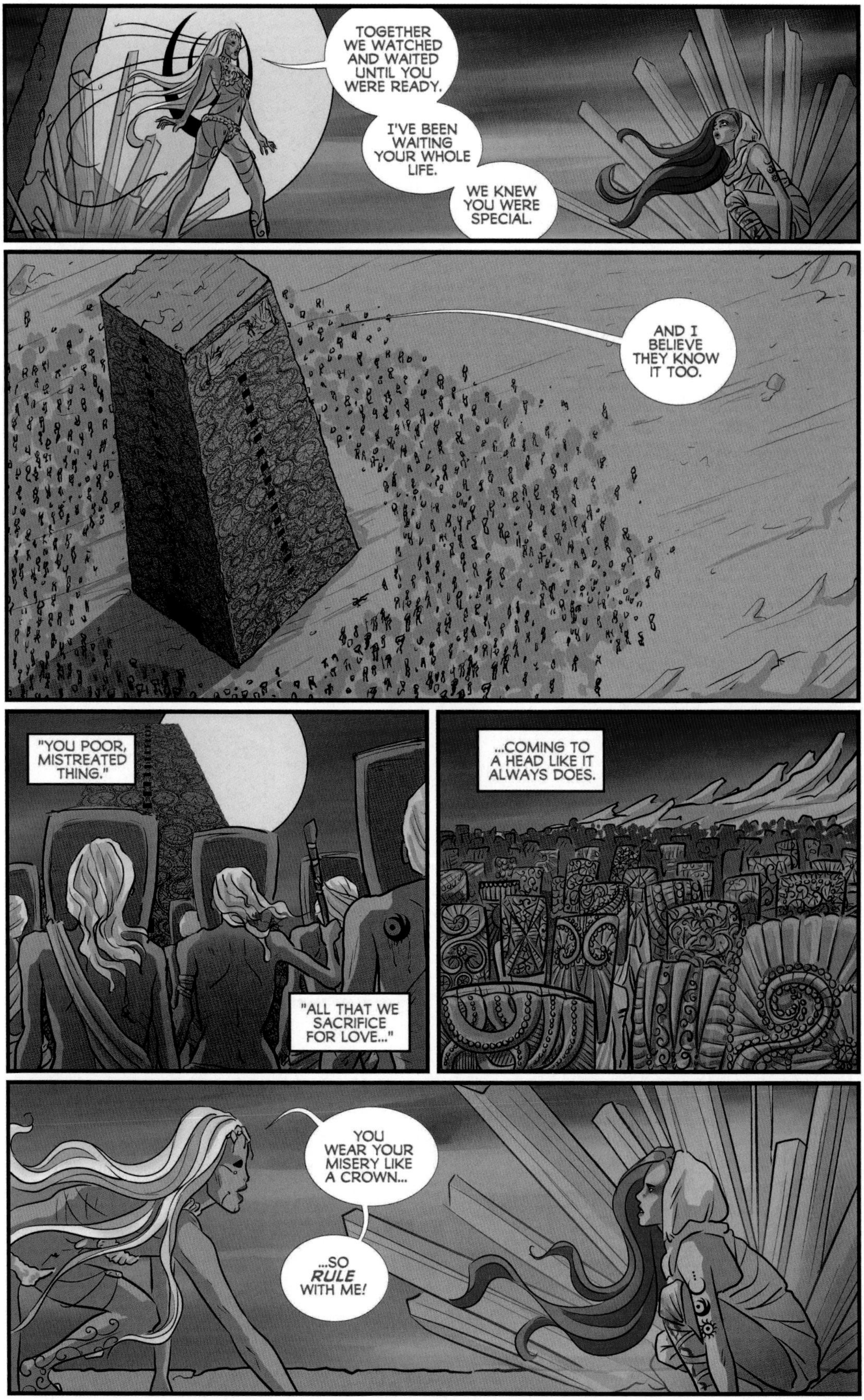
TOGETHER WE WATCHED AND WAITED UNTIL YOU WERE READY.
I'VE BEEN WAITING YOUR WHOLE LIFE.
WE KNEW YOU WERE SPECIAL.
AND I BELIEVE THEY KNOW IT TOO.
"YOU POOR, MISTREATED THING."
"ALL THAT WE SACRIFICE FOR LOVE..."
...COMING TO A HEAD LIKE IT ALWAYS DOES.
YOU WEAR YOUR MISERY LIKE A CROWN...
...SO ***RULE*** WITH ME!

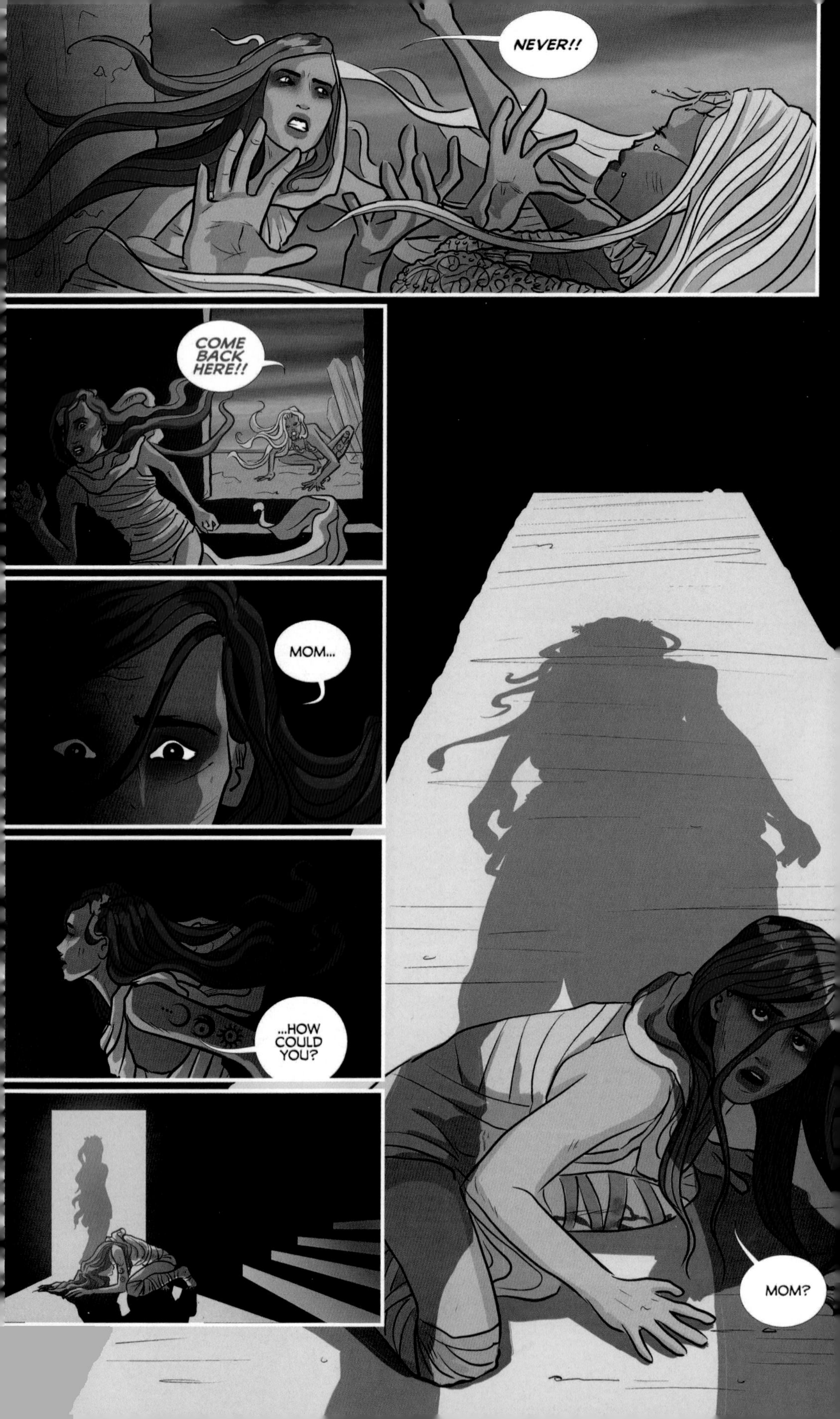
NEVER!!
COME BACK HERE!!
MOM...
...HOW COULD YOU?
MOM?

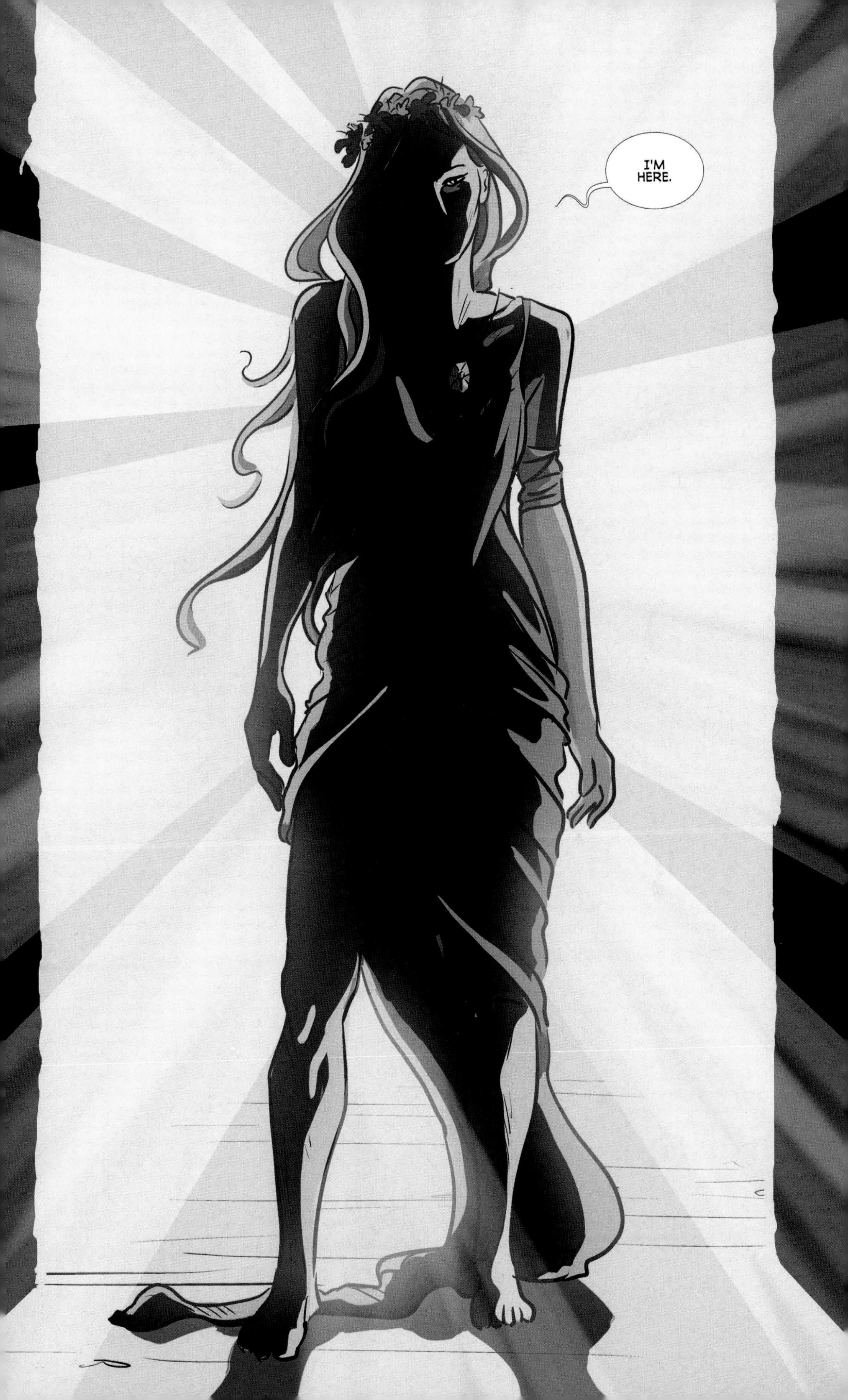
I'M HERE.

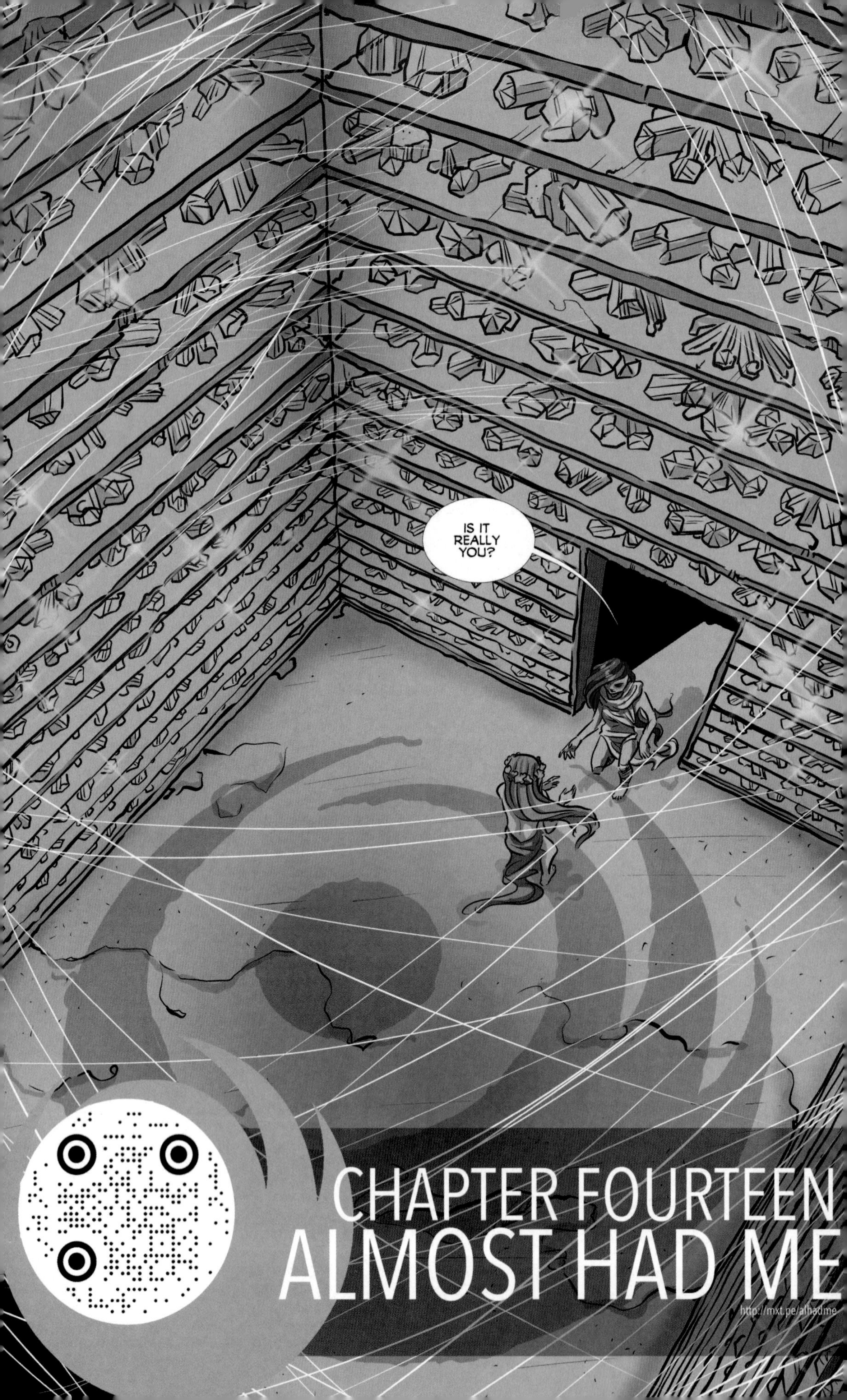
IS IT REALLY YOU?
CHAPTER FOURTEEN
ALMOST HAD ME
http://mxt.pe/alhadme

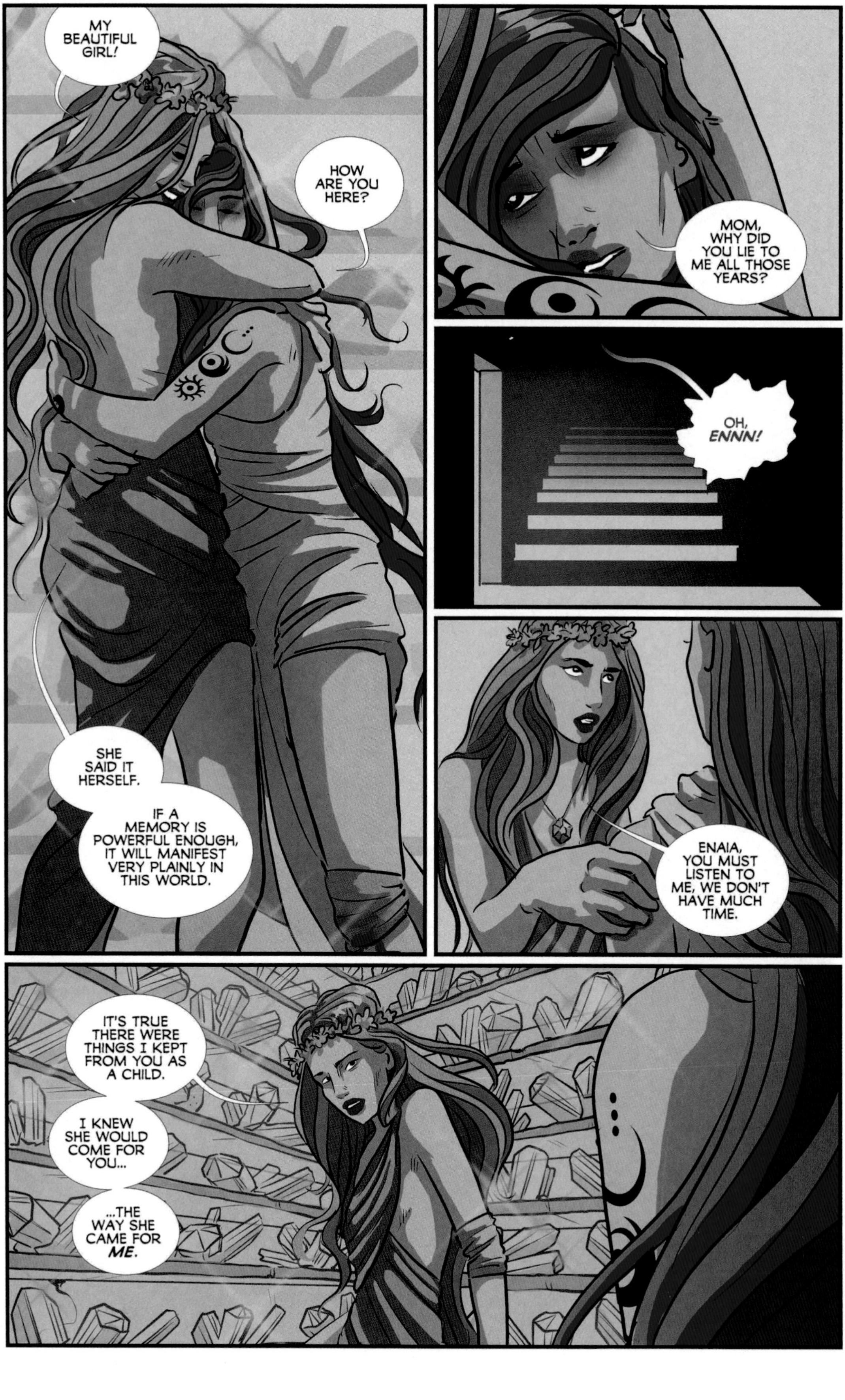
MY BEAUTIFUL GIRL!
HOW ARE YOU HERE?
SHE SAID IT HERSELF.
IF A MEMORY IS POWERFUL ENOUGH, IT WILL MANIFEST VERY PLAINLY IN THIS WORLD.
MOM, WHY DID YOU LIE TO ME ALL THOSE YEARS?
OH, ENNN!
ENAIA, YOU MUST LISTEN TO ME, WE DON'T HAVE MUCH TIME.
IT'S TRUE THERE WERE THINGS I KEPT FROM YOU AS A CHILD.
I KNEW SHE WOULD COME FOR YOU...
...THE WAY SHE CAME FOR ME.

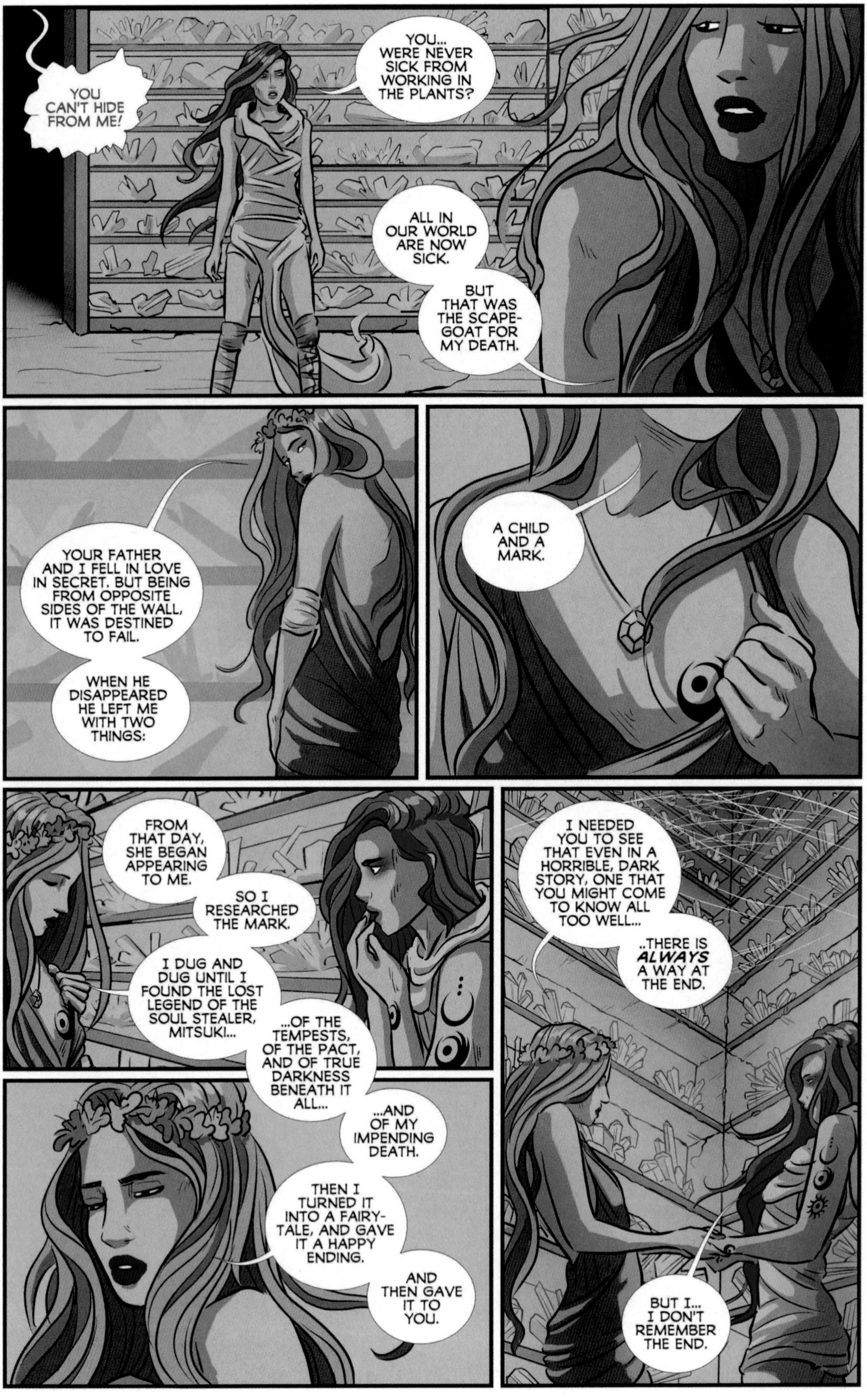
YOU CAN'T HIDE FROM ME!
YOU... WERE NEVER SICK FROM WORKING IN THE PLANTS?
ALL IN OUR WORLD ARE NOW SICK.
BUT THAT WAS THE SCAPE-GOAT FOR MY DEATH.
YOUR FATHER AND I FELL IN LOVE IN SECRET. BUT BEING FROM OPPOSITE SIDES OF THE WALL, IT WAS DESTINED TO FAIL.
WHEN HE DISAPPEARED HE LEFT ME WITH TWO THINGS:
A CHILD AND A MARK.
FROM THAT DAY, SHE BEGAN APPEARING TO ME.
SO I RESEARCHED THE MARK.
I DUG AND DUG UNTIL I FOUND THE LOST LEGEND OF THE SOUL STEALER, MITSUKI...
...OF THE TEMPESTS, OF THE PACT, AND OF TRUE DARKNESS BENEATH IT ALL...
...AND OF MY IMPENDING DEATH.
THEN I TURNED IT INTO A FAIRY-TALE, AND GAVE IT A HAPPY ENDING.
AND THEN GAVE IT TO YOU.
I NEEDED YOU TO SEE THAT EVEN IN A HORRIBLE, DARK STORY, ONE THAT YOU MIGHT COME TO KNOW ALL TOO WELL...
..THERE IS *ALWAYS* A WAY AT THE END.
BUT I... I DON'T REMEMBER THE END.

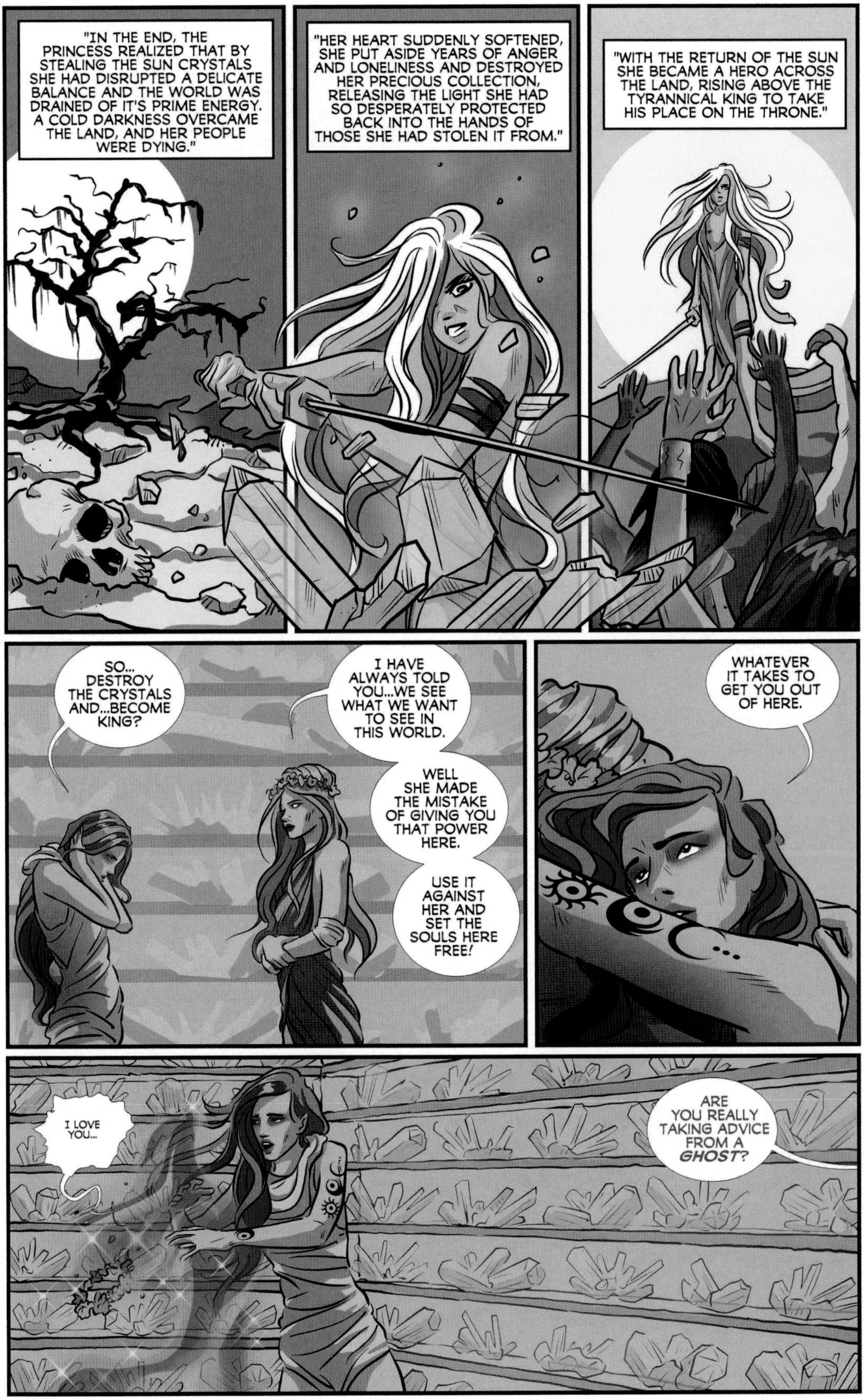
"IN THE END, THE PRINCESS REALIZED THAT BY STEALING THE SUN CRYSTALS SHE HAD DISRUPTED A DELICATE BALANCE AND THE WORLD WAS DRAINED OF IT'S PRIME ENERGY. A COLD DARKNESS OVERCAME THE LAND, AND HER PEOPLE WERE DYING."
"HER HEART SUDDENLY SOFTENED, SHE PUT ASIDE YEARS OF ANGER AND LONELINESS AND DESTROYED HER PRECIOUS COLLECTION, RELEASING THE LIGHT SHE HAD SO DESPERATELY PROTECTED BACK INTO THE HANDS OF THOSE SHE HAD STOLEN IT FROM."
"WITH THE RETURN OF THE SUN SHE BECAME A HERO ACROSS THE LAND, RISING ABOVE THE TYRANNICAL KING TO TAKE HIS PLACE ON THE THRONE."
SO... DESTROY THE CRYSTALS AND...BECOME KING?
I HAVE ALWAYS TOLD YOU...WE SEE WHAT WE WANT TO SEE IN THIS WORLD.
WELL SHE MADE THE MISTAKE OF GIVING YOU THAT POWER HERE.
USE IT AGAINST HER AND SET THE SOULS HERE FREE!
WHATEVER IT TAKES TO GET YOU OUT OF HERE.
I LOVE YOU...
ARE YOU REALLY TAKING ADVICE FROM A *GHOST*?

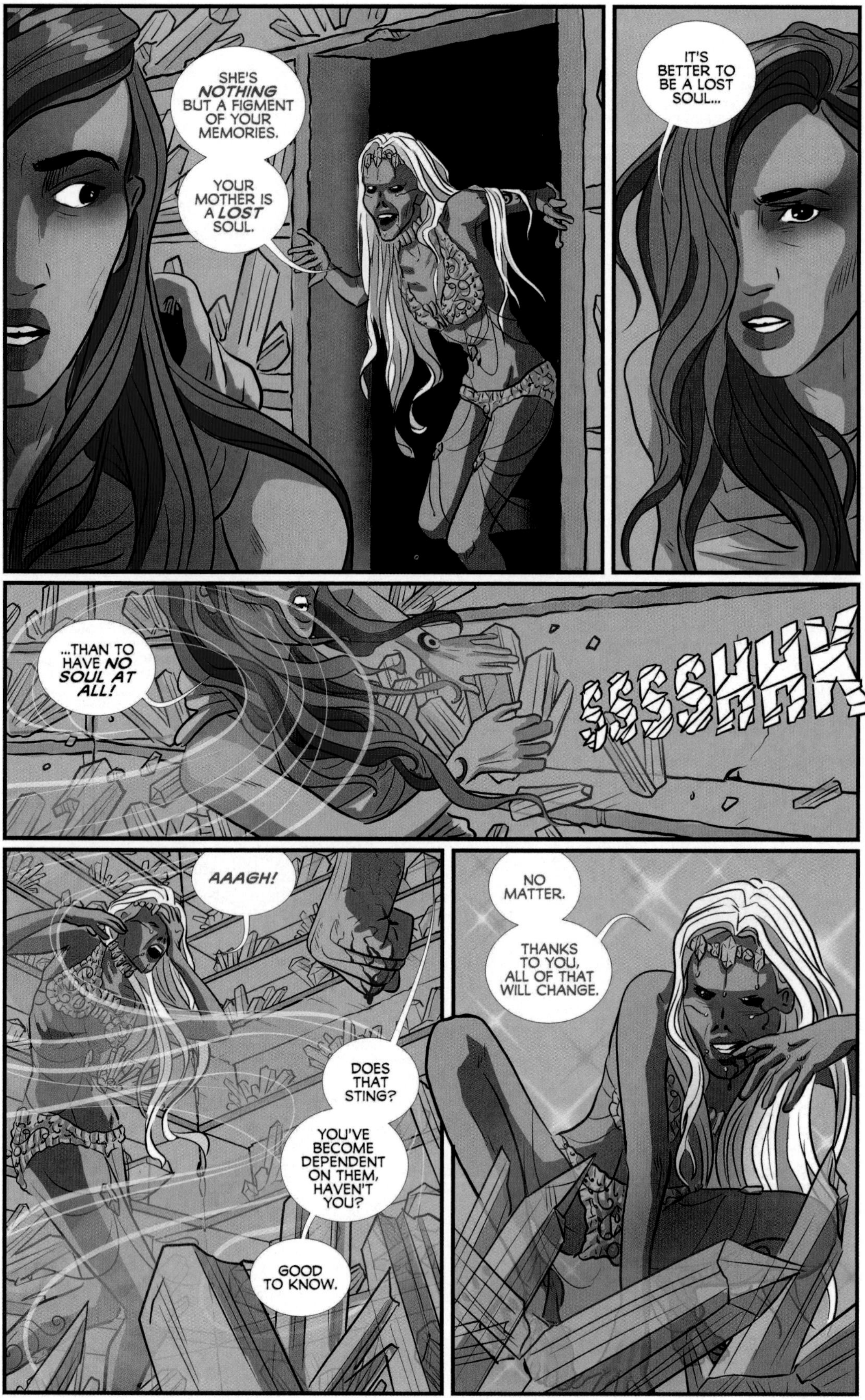
SHE'S NOTHING BUT A FIGMENT OF YOUR MEMORIES.
YOUR MOTHER IS A LOST SOUL.
IT'S BETTER TO BE A LOST SOUL...
...THAN TO HAVE NO SOUL AT ALL!
SSSSHUK
AAAGH!
DOES THAT STING?
YOU'VE BECOME DEPENDENT ON THEM, HAVEN'T YOU?
GOOD TO KNOW.
NO MATTER.
THANKS TO YOU, ALL OF THAT WILL CHANGE.

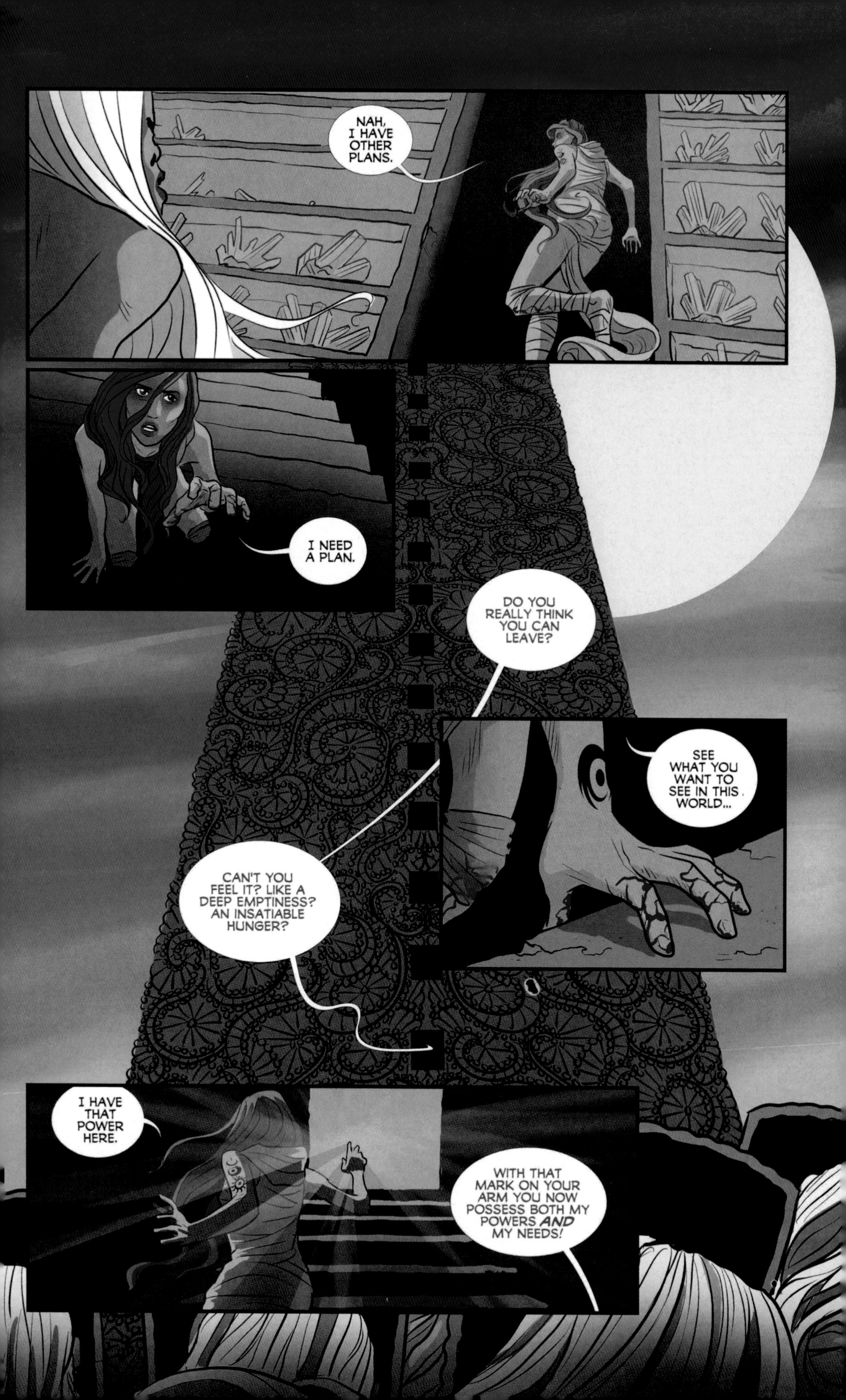
NAH, I HAVE OTHER PLANS.
I NEED A PLAN.
DO YOU REALLY THINK YOU CAN LEAVE?
SEE WHAT YOU WANT TO SEE IN THIS WORLD...
CAN'T YOU FEEL IT? LIKE A DEEP EMPTINESS? AN INSATIABLE HUNGER?
I HAVE THAT POWER HERE.
WITH THAT MARK ON YOUR ARM YOU NOW POSSESS BOTH MY POWERS *AND* MY NEEDS!

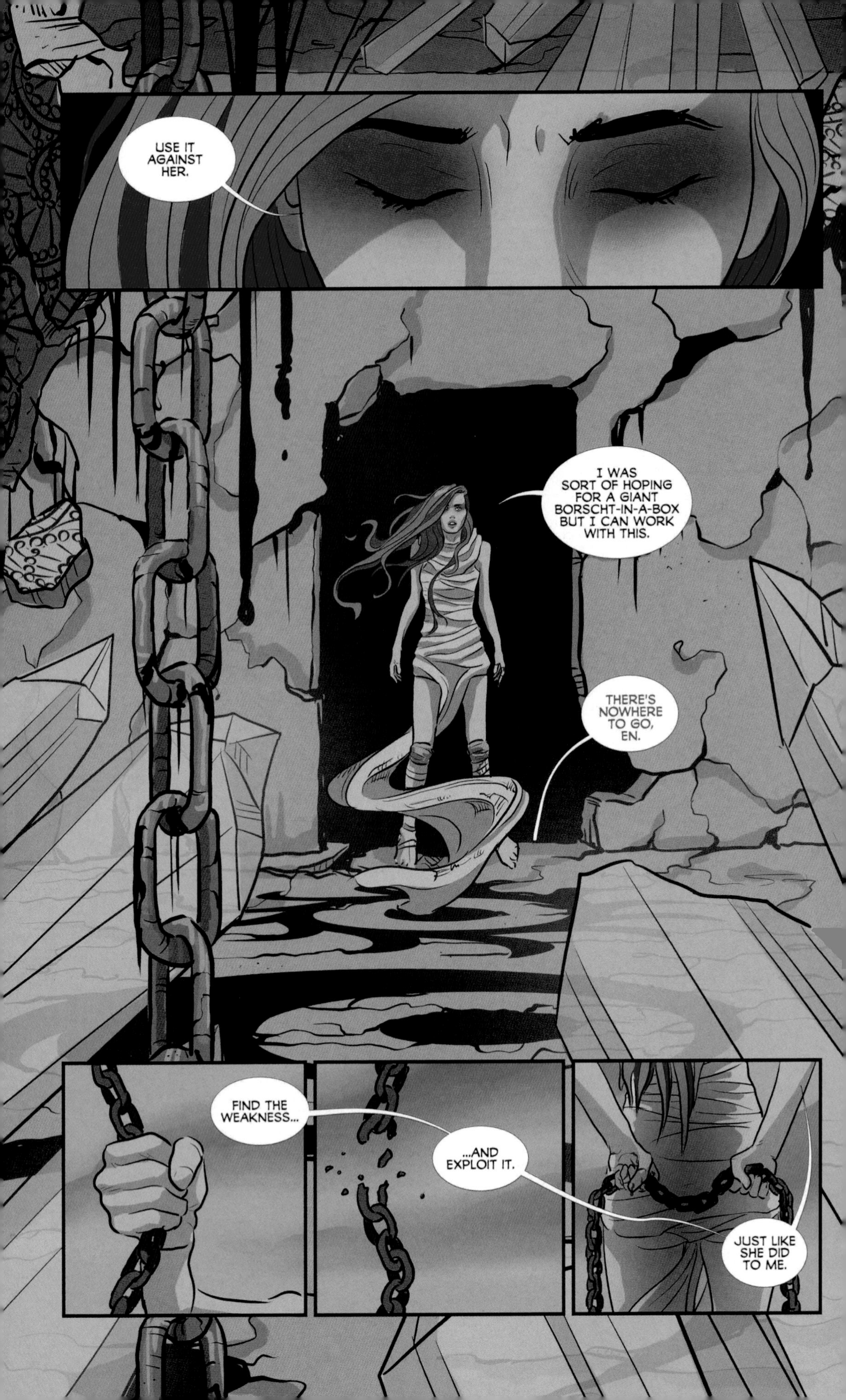
USE IT AGAINST HER.
I WAS SORT OF HOPING FOR A GIANT BORSCHT-IN-A-BOX BUT I CAN WORK WITH THIS.
THERE'S NOWHERE TO GO, EN.
FIND THE WEAKNESS...
...AND EXPLOIT IT.
JUST LIKE SHE DID TO ME.

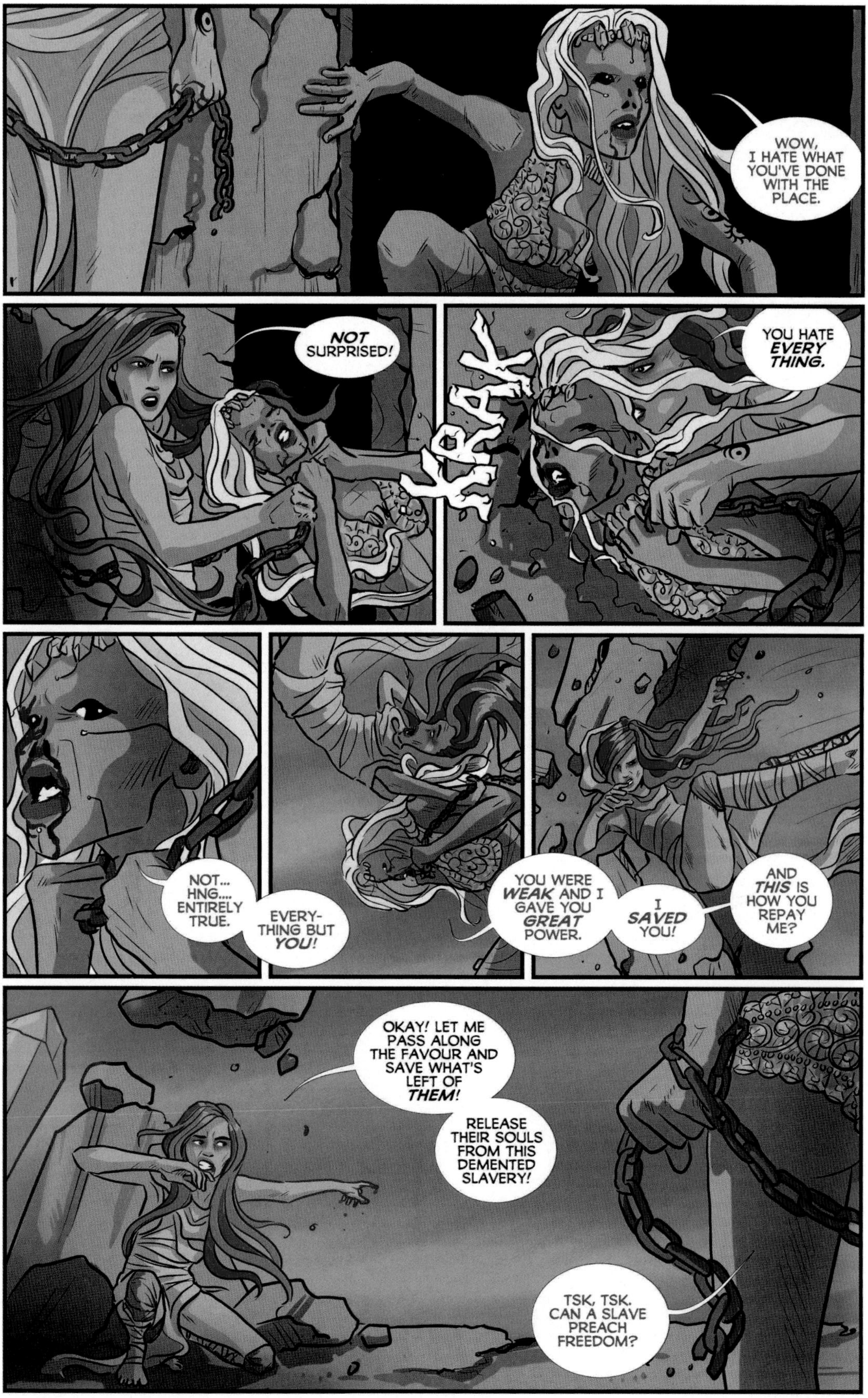
WOW, I HATE WHAT YOU'VE DONE WITH THE PLACE.
NOT SURPRISED!
KRAK
YOU HATE EVERY THING.
NOT... HNG.... ENTIRELY TRUE.
EVERY-THING BUT YOU!
YOU WERE WEAK AND I GAVE YOU GREAT POWER.
I SAVED YOU!
AND THIS IS HOW YOU REPAY ME?
OKAY! LET ME PASS ALONG THE FAVOUR AND SAVE WHAT'S LEFT OF THEM!
RELEASE THEIR SOULS FROM THIS DEMENTED SLAVERY!
TSK, TSK. CAN A SLAVE PREACH FREEDOM?

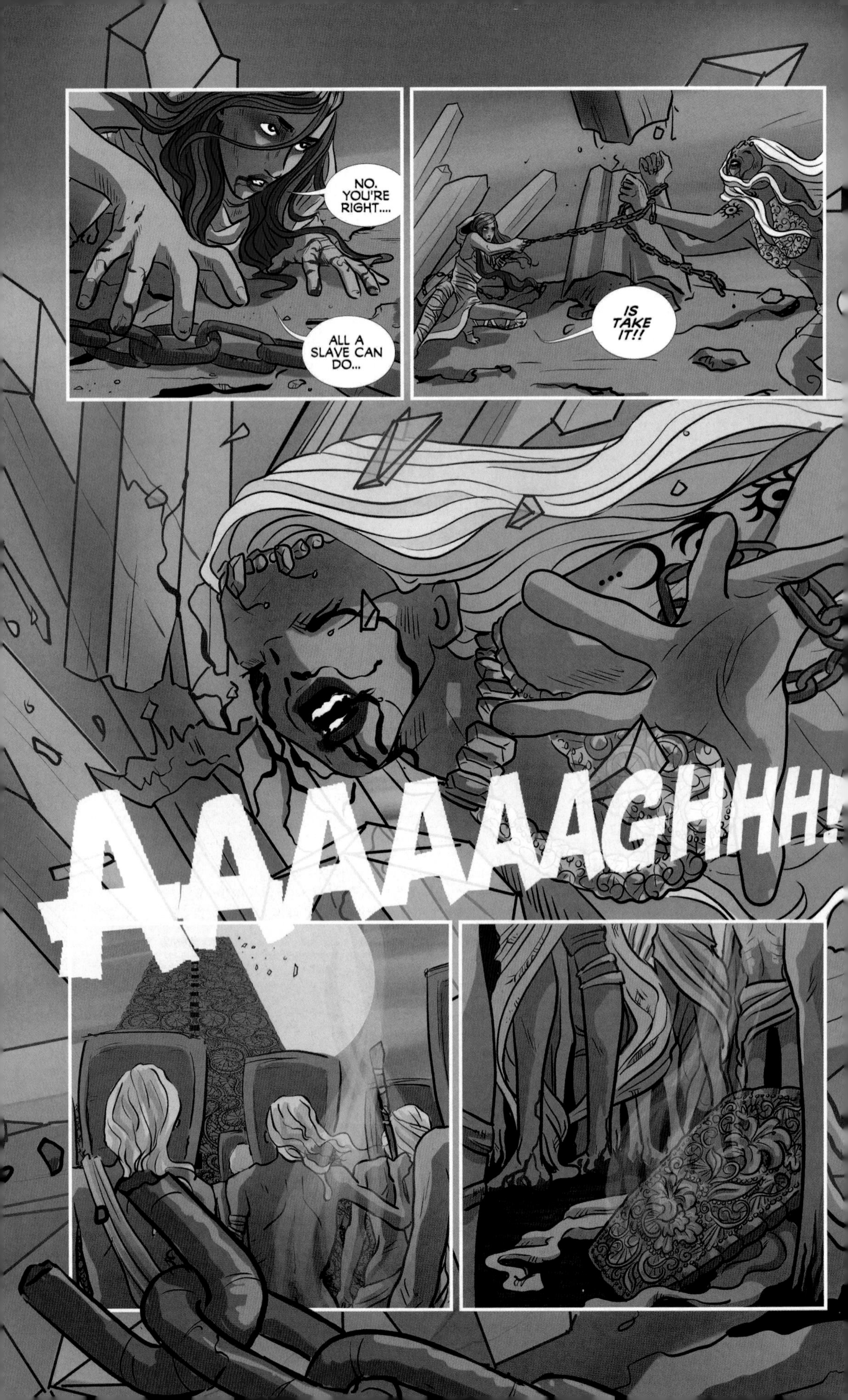
NO. YOU'RE RIGHT....
ALL A SLAVE CAN DO...
IS TAKE IT!!
AAAAAAAGHHH!

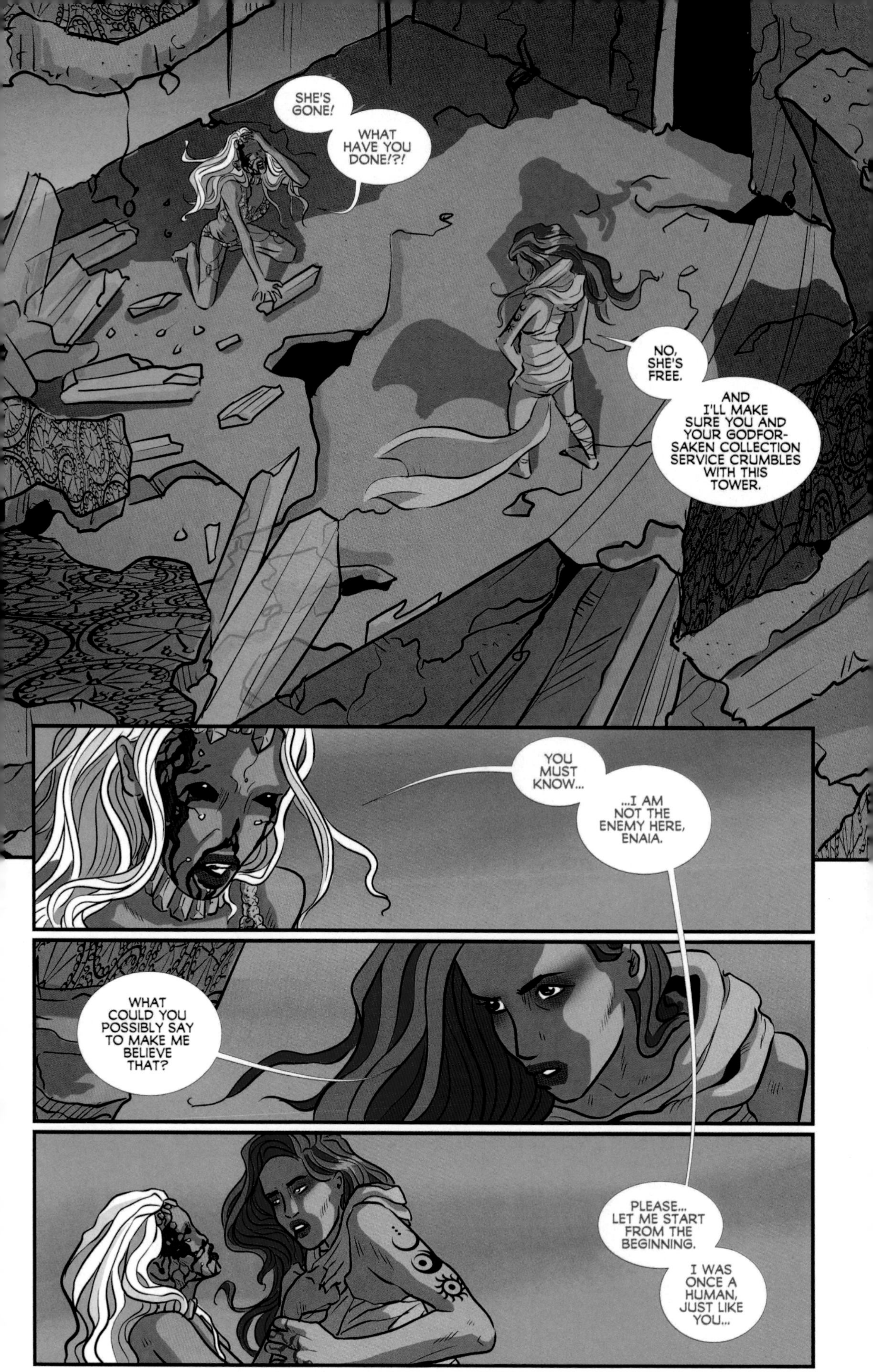
SHE'S GONE!
WHAT HAVE YOU DONE!?!
NO, SHE'S FREE.
AND I'LL MAKE SURE YOU AND YOUR GODFOR-SAKEN COLLECTION SERVICE CRUMBLES WITH THIS TOWER.
YOU MUST KNOW...
...I AM NOT THE ENEMY HERE, ENAIA.
WHAT COULD YOU POSSIBLY SAY TO MAKE ME BELIEVE THAT?
PLEASE... LET ME START FROM THE BEGINNING.
I WAS ONCE A HUMAN, JUST LIKE YOU...

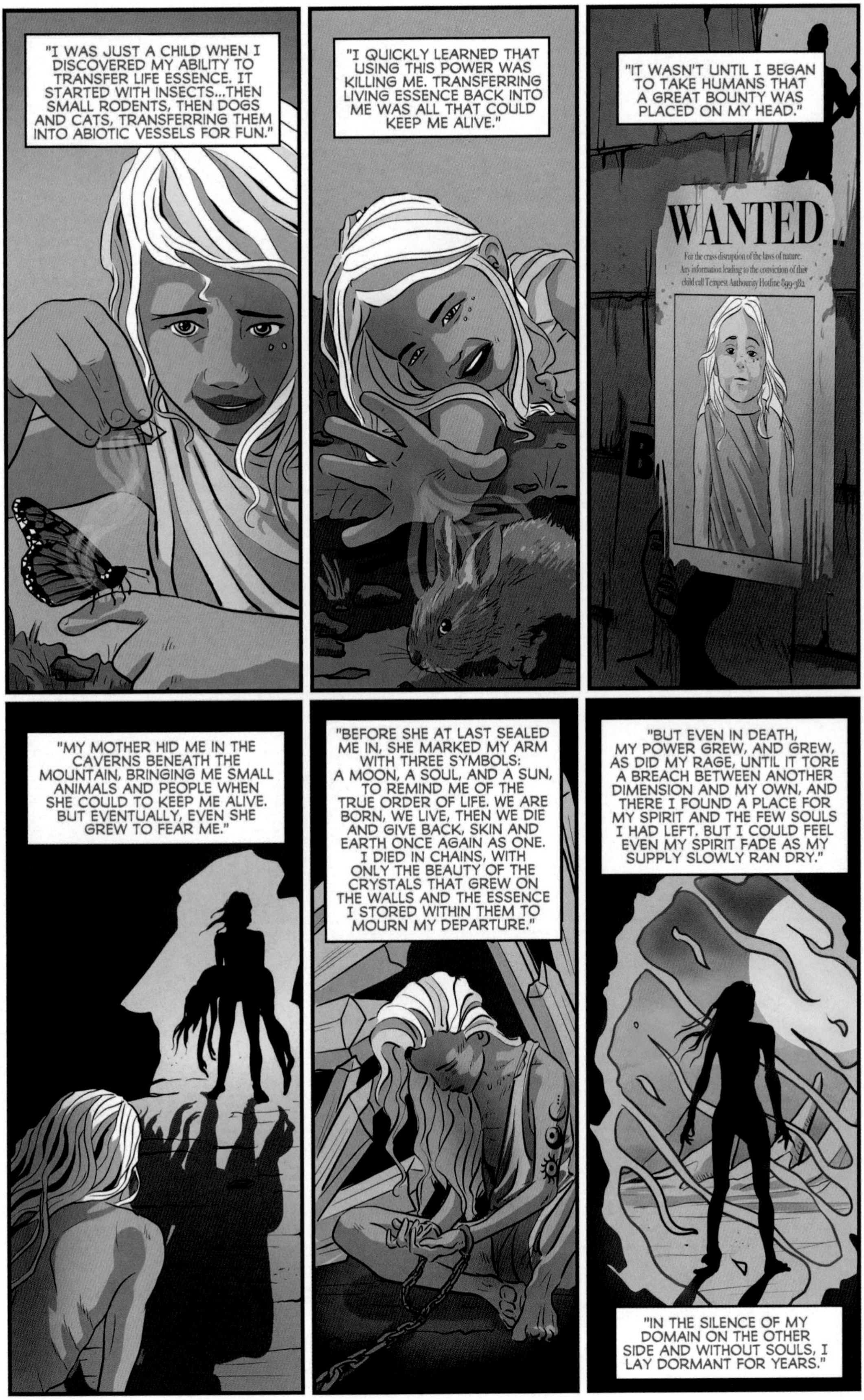
"I WAS JUST A CHILD WHEN I DISCOVERED MY ABILITY TO TRANSFER LIFE ESSENCE. IT STARTED WITH INSECTS...THEN SMALL RODENTS, THEN DOGS AND CATS, TRANSFERRING THEM INTO ABIOTIC VESSELS FOR FUN."
"I QUICKLY LEARNED THAT USING THIS POWER WAS KILLING ME. TRANSFERRING LIVING ESSENCE BACK INTO ME WAS ALL THAT COULD KEEP ME ALIVE."
"IT WASN'T UNTIL I BEGAN TO TAKE HUMANS THAT A GREAT BOUNTY WAS PLACED ON MY HEAD."
WANTED
For the crass disruption of the laws of nature.
Any information leading to the conviction of this child call Tempest Authourity Hotline 899-382
"MY MOTHER HID ME IN THE CAVERNS BENEATH THE MOUNTAIN, BRINGING ME SMALL ANIMALS AND PEOPLE WHEN SHE COULD TO KEEP ME ALIVE. BUT EVENTUALLY, EVEN SHE GREW TO FEAR ME."
"BEFORE SHE AT LAST SEALED ME IN, SHE MARKED MY ARM WITH THREE SYMBOLS: A MOON, A SOUL, AND A SUN, TO REMIND ME OF THE TRUE ORDER OF LIFE. WE ARE BORN, WE LIVE, THEN WE DIE AND GIVE BACK, SKIN AND EARTH ONCE AGAIN AS ONE. I DIED IN CHAINS, WITH ONLY THE BEAUTY OF THE CRYSTALS THAT GREW ON THE WALLS AND THE ESSENCE I STORED WITHIN THEM TO MOURN MY DEPARTURE."
"BUT EVEN IN DEATH, MY POWER GREW, AND GREW, AS DID MY RAGE, UNTIL IT TORE A BREACH BETWEEN ANOTHER DIMENSION AND MY OWN, AND THERE I FOUND A PLACE FOR MY SPIRIT AND THE FEW SOULS I HAD LEFT. BUT I COULD FEEL EVEN MY SPIRIT FADE AS MY SUPPLY SLOWLY RAN DRY."
"IN THE SILENCE OF MY DOMAIN ON THE OTHER SIDE AND WITHOUT SOULS, I LAY DORMANT FOR YEARS."

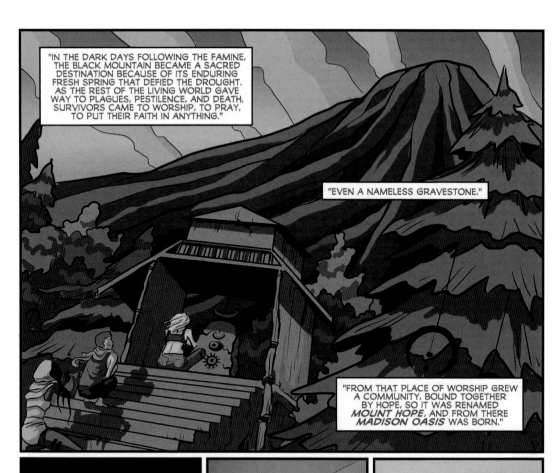

"IN THE DARK DAYS FOLLOWING THE FAMINE, THE BLACK MOUNTAIN BECAME A SACRED DESTINATION BECAUSE OF ITS ENDURING FRESH SPRING THAT DEFIED THE DROUGHT. AS THE REST OF THE LIVING WORLD GAVE WAY TO PLAGUES, PESTILENCE, AND DEATH, SURVIVORS CAME TO WORSHIP, TO PRAY, TO PUT THEIR FAITH IN ANYTHING."

"EVEN A NAMELESS GRAVESTONE."

"FROM THAT PLACE OF WORSHIP GREW A COMMUNITY, BOUND TOGETHER BY HOPE, SO IT WAS RENAMED *MOUNT HOPE*, AND FROM THERE *MADISON OASIS* WAS BORN."

"WHILE THE STATE OF CIVILIZATION CONTINUED TO UNRAVEL AROUND THE GLOBE, MANY JOURNEYED DEEP INTO THE CATACOMBS BENEATH THE MOUNTAIN SEEKING THE LEGEND OF THE LOST GIRL WHO COULD SWALLOW A SOUL."

"I ANSWERED THE CALL. WITH MY GRAVE OPEN, MY SPECTRE WAS FREE AND THROUGH ME THEY COULD END THE LIVES OF THEIR FOES BY MARKING THEM WITH MY SACRED SYMBOL, A MARKING THAT HAD GROWN IN POWER TO BECOME MY CONDUIT TO AND FROM THE PHYSICAL WORLD."

"WITH MY PATRONS' DARK PRAYERS ANSWERED, AND A NEW SOURCE OF CONTINUAL RENEWAL FOR MY SPIRIT, I BECAME A BONAFIDE GOD."

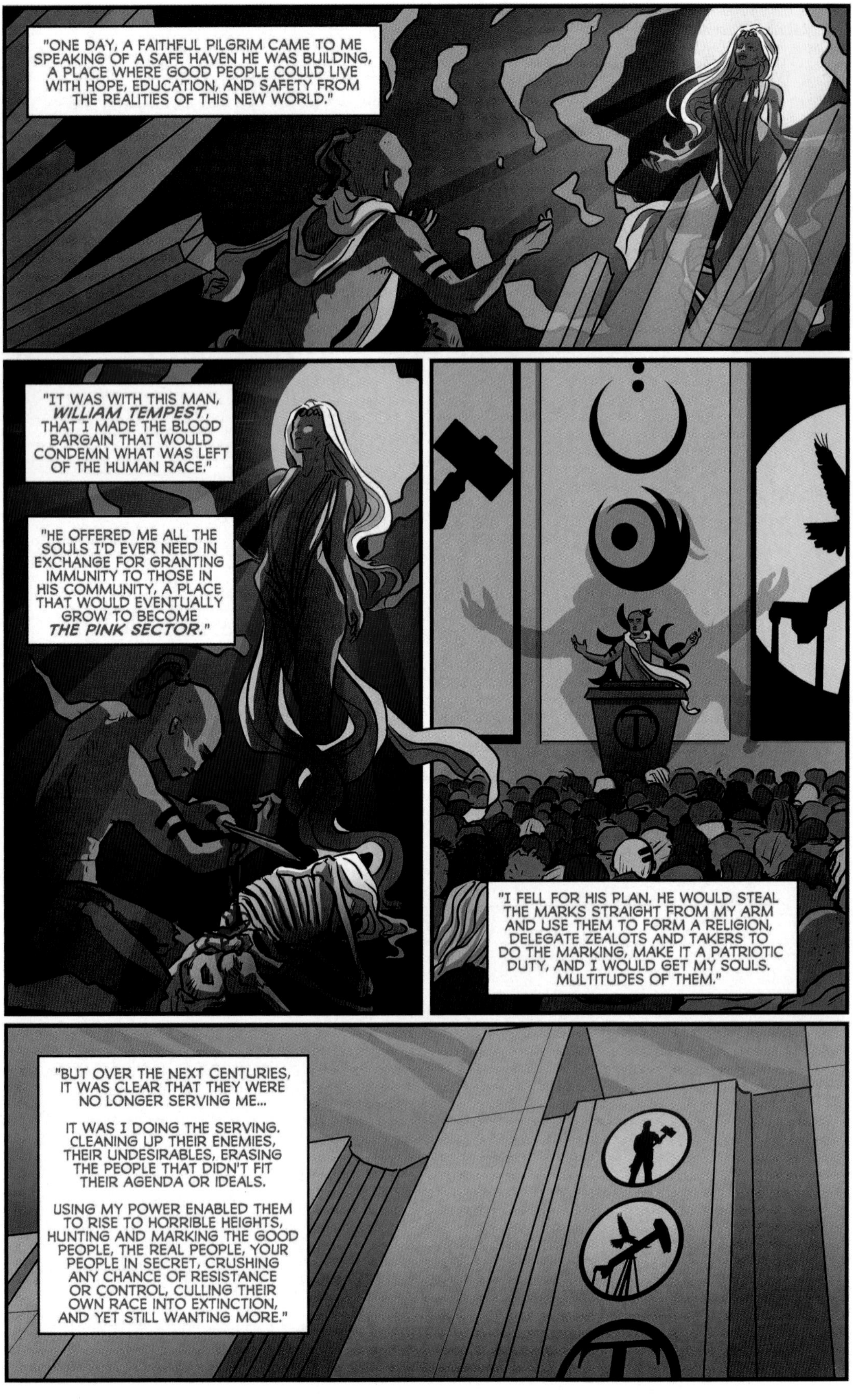
"ONE DAY, A FAITHFUL PILGRIM CAME TO ME SPEAKING OF A SAFE HAVEN HE WAS BUILDING, A PLACE WHERE GOOD PEOPLE COULD LIVE WITH HOPE, EDUCATION, AND SAFETY FROM THE REALITIES OF THIS NEW WORLD."
"IT WAS WITH THIS MAN, ***WILLIAM TEMPEST***, THAT I MADE THE BLOOD BARGAIN THAT WOULD CONDEMN WHAT WAS LEFT OF THE HUMAN RACE."
"HE OFFERED ME ALL THE SOULS I'D EVER NEED IN EXCHANGE FOR GRANTING IMMUNITY TO THOSE IN HIS COMMUNITY, A PLACE THAT WOULD EVENTUALLY GROW TO BECOME ***THE PINK SECTOR.***"
"I FELL FOR HIS PLAN. HE WOULD STEAL THE MARKS STRAIGHT FROM MY ARM AND USE THEM TO FORM A RELIGION, DELEGATE ZEALOTS AND TAKERS TO DO THE MARKING, MAKE IT A PATRIOTIC DUTY, AND I WOULD GET MY SOULS. MULTITUDES OF THEM."
"BUT OVER THE NEXT CENTURIES, IT WAS CLEAR THAT THEY WERE NO LONGER SERVING ME...
IT WAS I DOING THE SERVING. CLEANING UP THEIR ENEMIES, THEIR UNDESIRABLES, ERASING THE PEOPLE THAT DIDN'T FIT THEIR AGENDA OR IDEALS.
USING MY POWER ENABLED THEM TO RISE TO HORRIBLE HEIGHTS, HUNTING AND MARKING THE GOOD PEOPLE, THE REAL PEOPLE, YOUR PEOPLE IN SECRET, CRUSHING ANY CHANCE OF RESISTANCE OR CONTROL, CULLING THEIR OWN RACE INTO EXTINCTION, AND YET STILL WANTING MORE."

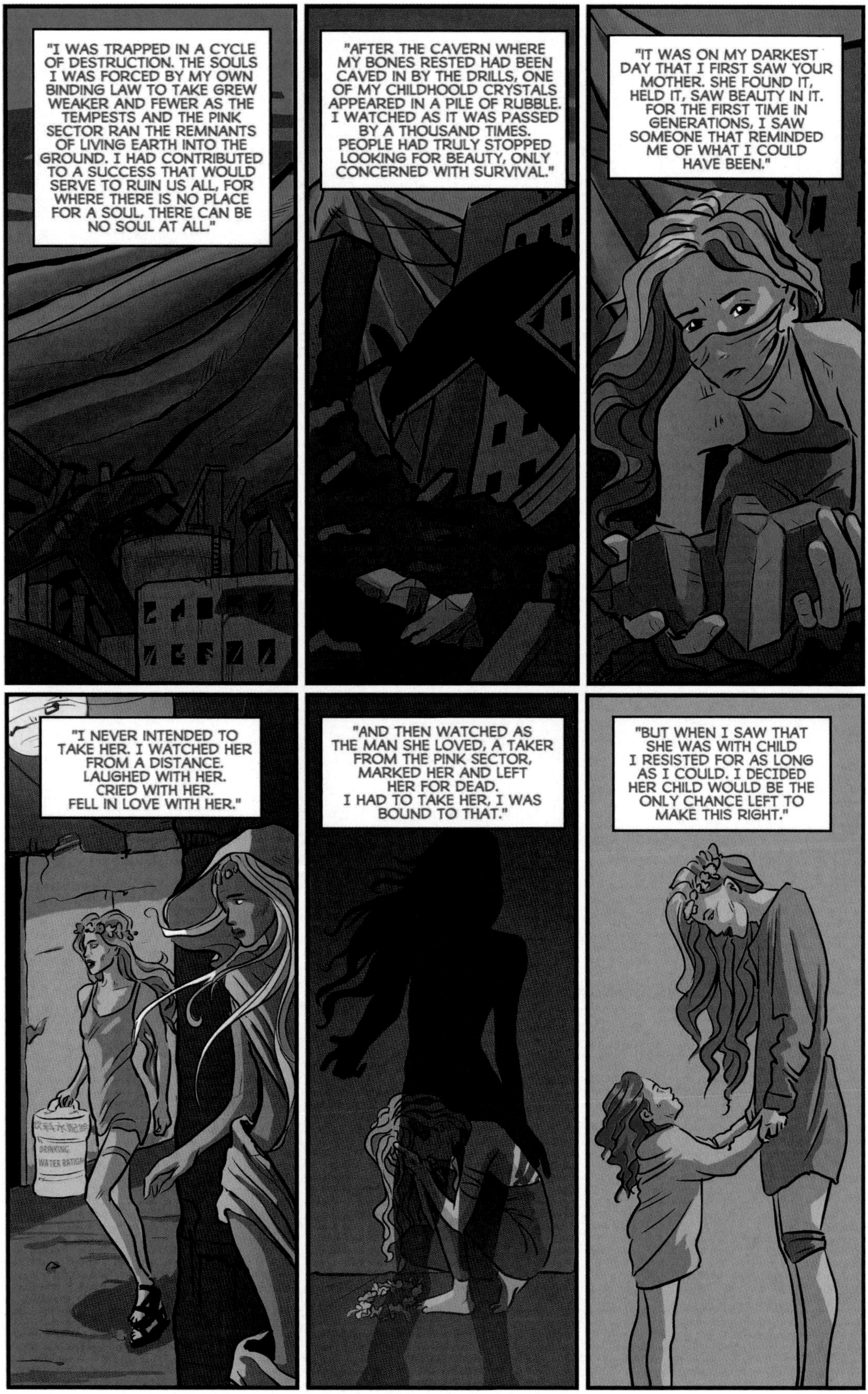
"I WAS TRAPPED IN A CYCLE OF DESTRUCTION. THE SOULS I WAS FORCED BY MY OWN BINDING LAW TO TAKE GREW WEAKER AND FEWER AS THE TEMPESTS AND THE PINK SECTOR RAN THE REMNANTS OF LIVING EARTH INTO THE GROUND. I HAD CONTRIBUTED TO A SUCCESS THAT WOULD SERVE TO RUIN US ALL, FOR WHERE THERE IS NO PLACE FOR A SOUL, THERE CAN BE NO SOUL AT ALL."
"AFTER THE CAVERN WHERE MY BONES RESTED HAD BEEN CAVED IN BY THE DRILLS, ONE OF MY CHILDHOOLD CRYSTALS APPEARED IN A PILE OF RUBBLE. I WATCHED AS IT WAS PASSED BY A THOUSAND TIMES. PEOPLE HAD TRULY STOPPED LOOKING FOR BEAUTY, ONLY CONCERNED WITH SURVIVAL."
"IT WAS ON MY DARKEST DAY THAT I FIRST SAW YOUR MOTHER. SHE FOUND IT, HELD IT, SAW BEAUTY IN IT. FOR THE FIRST TIME IN GENERATIONS, I SAW SOMEONE THAT REMINDED ME OF WHAT I COULD HAVE BEEN."
"I NEVER INTENDED TO TAKE HER. I WATCHED HER FROM A DISTANCE. LAUGHED WITH HER. CRIED WITH HER. FELL IN LOVE WITH HER."
"AND THEN WATCHED AS THE MAN SHE LOVED, A TAKER FROM THE PINK SECTOR, MARKED HER AND LEFT HER FOR DEAD. I HAD TO TAKE HER, I WAS BOUND TO THAT."
"BUT WHEN I SAW THAT SHE WAS WITH CHILD I RESISTED FOR AS LONG AS I COULD. I DECIDED HER CHILD WOULD BE THE ONLY CHANCE LEFT TO MAKE THIS RIGHT."

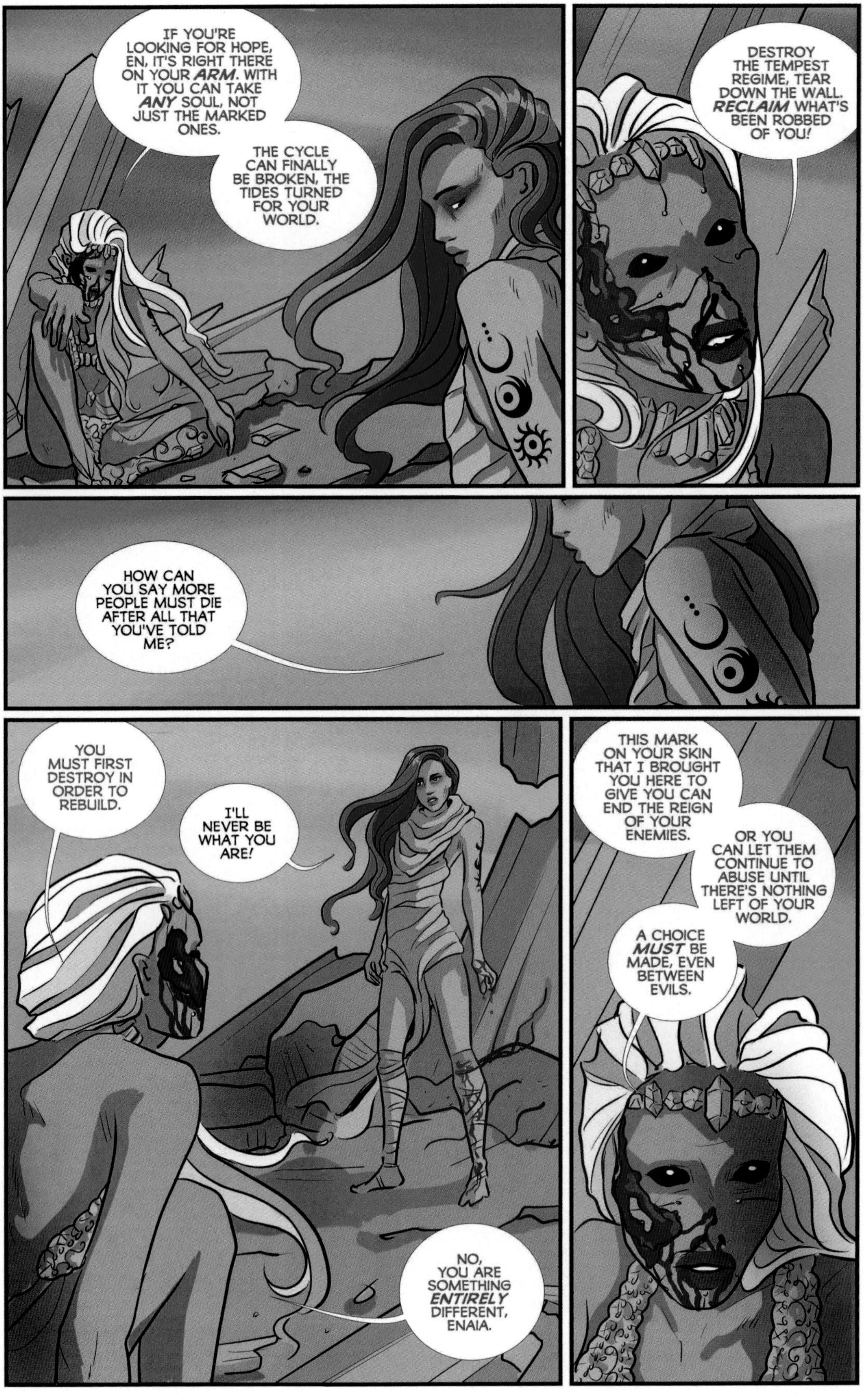
IF YOU'RE LOOKING FOR HOPE, EN, IT'S RIGHT THERE ON YOUR ARM. WITH IT YOU CAN TAKE ANY SOUL, NOT JUST THE MARKED ONES.
THE CYCLE CAN FINALLY BE BROKEN, THE TIDES TURNED FOR YOUR WORLD.
DESTROY THE TEMPEST REGIME, TEAR DOWN THE WALL. RECLAIM WHAT'S BEEN ROBBED OF YOU!
HOW CAN YOU SAY MORE PEOPLE MUST DIE AFTER ALL THAT YOU'VE TOLD ME?
YOU MUST FIRST DESTROY IN ORDER TO REBUILD.
I'LL NEVER BE WHAT YOU ARE!
NO, YOU ARE SOMETHING ENTIRELY DIFFERENT, ENAIA.
THIS MARK ON YOUR SKIN THAT I BROUGHT YOU HERE TO GIVE YOU CAN END THE REIGN OF YOUR ENEMIES.
OR YOU CAN LET THEM CONTINUE TO ABUSE UNTIL THERE'S NOTHING LEFT OF YOUR WORLD.
A CHOICE MUST BE MADE, EVEN BETWEEN EVILS.

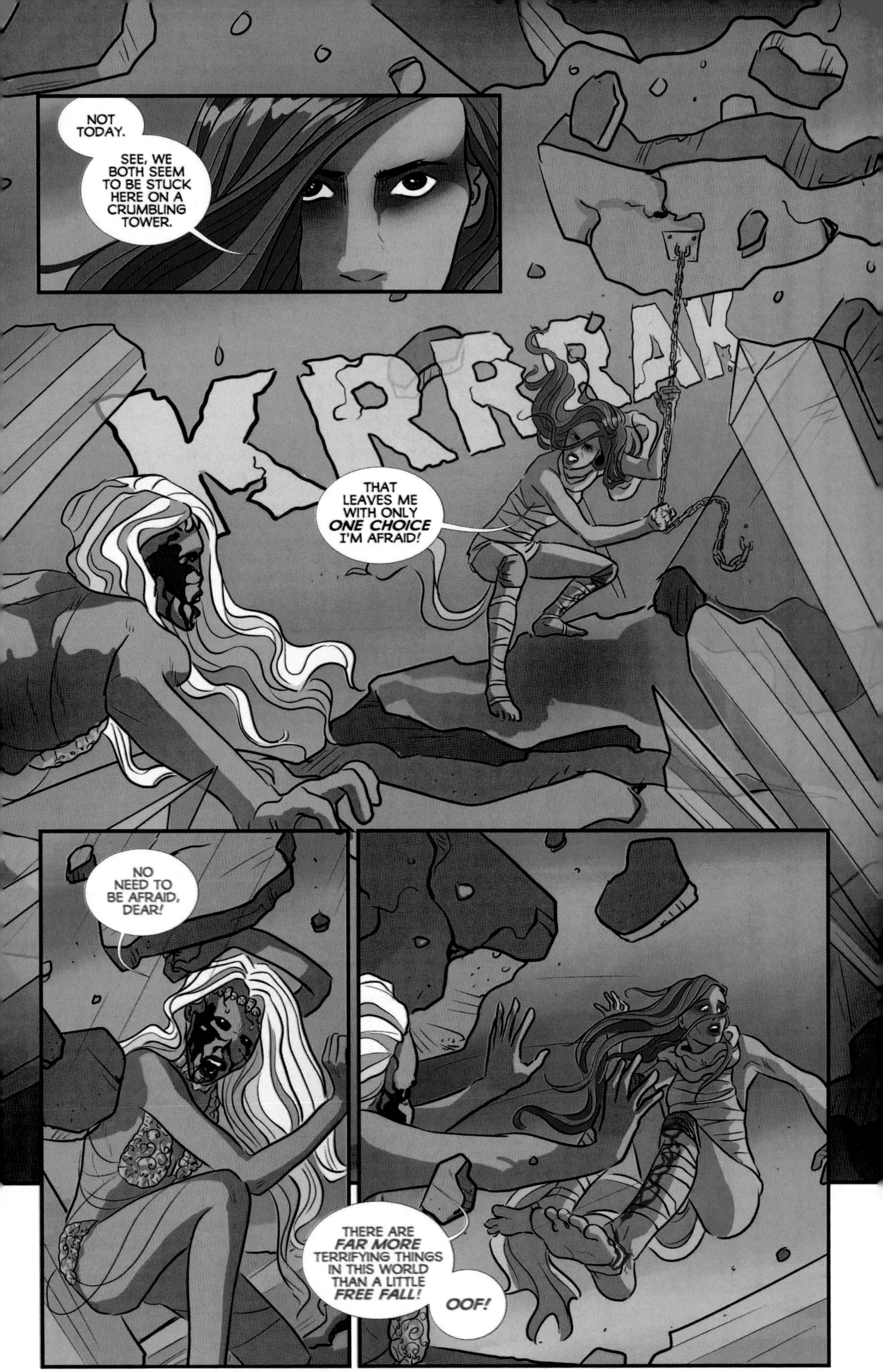
NOT TODAY.
SEE, WE BOTH SEEM TO BE STUCK HERE ON A CRUMBLING TOWER.
KRRRAK
THAT LEAVES ME WITH ONLY ONE CHOICE I'M AFRAID!
NO NEED TO BE AFRAID, DEAR!
THERE ARE FAR MORE TERRIFYING THINGS IN THIS WORLD THAN A LITTLE FREE FALL!
OOF!

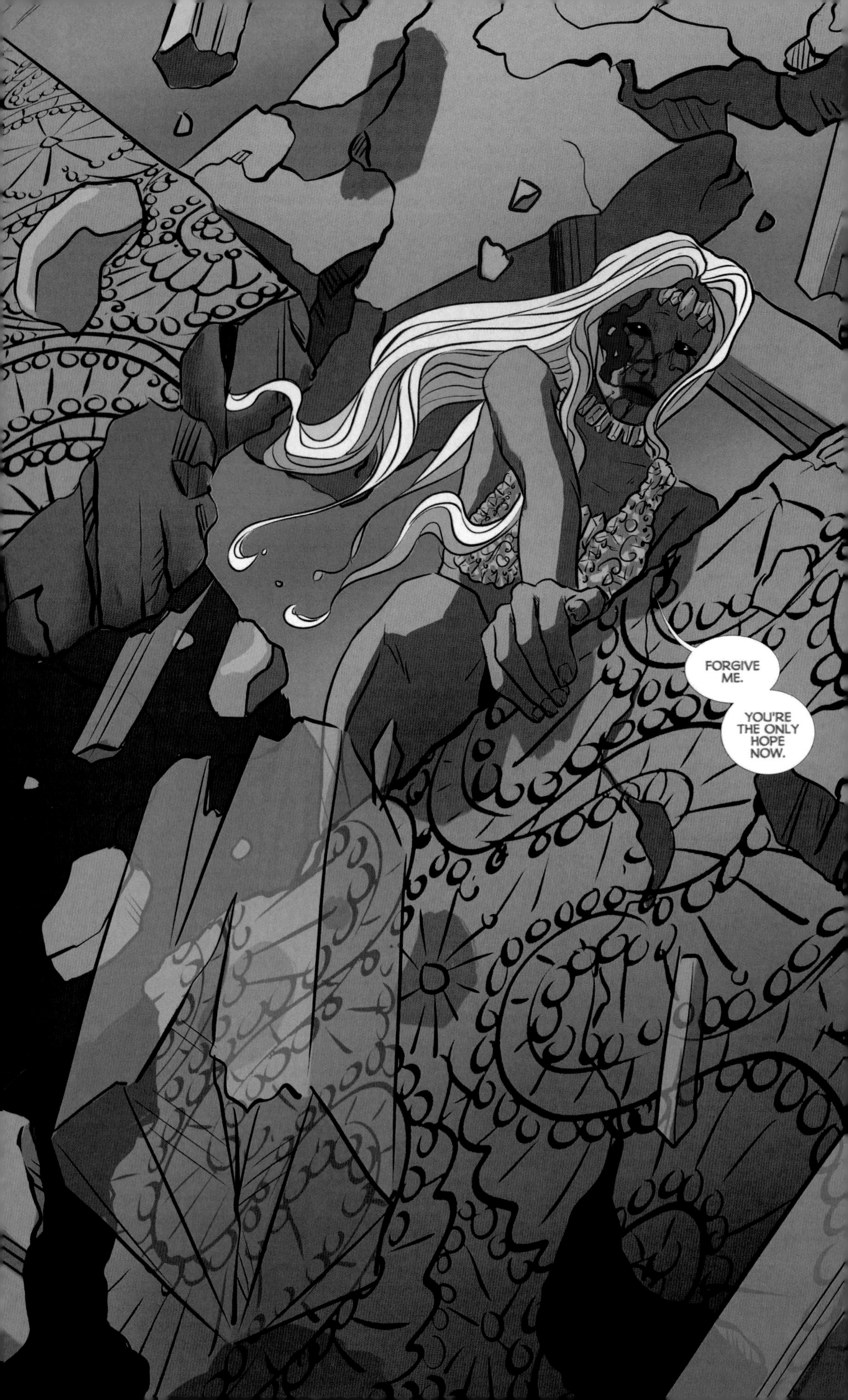
FORGIVE ME.
YOU'RE THE ONLY HOPE NOW.

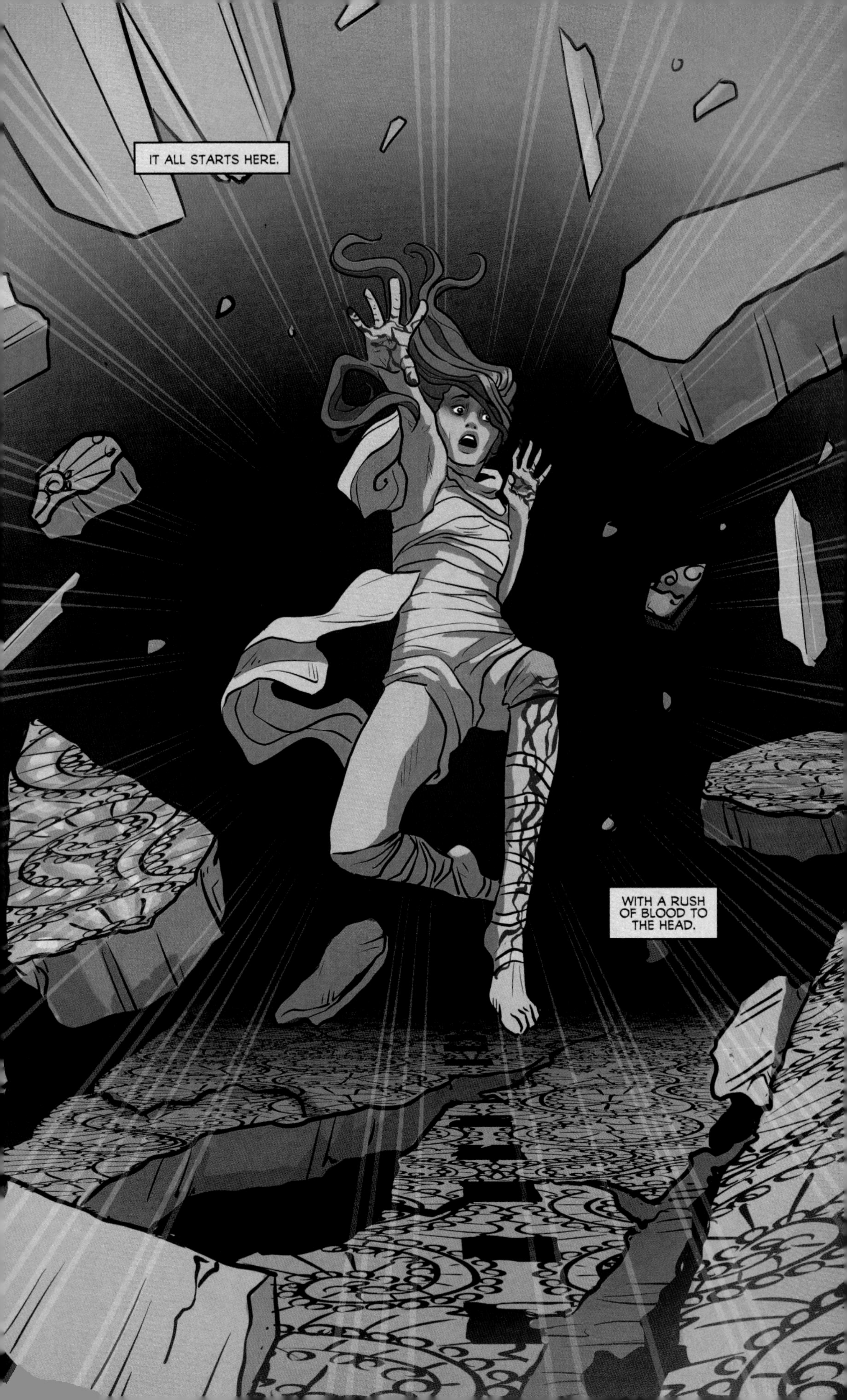
IT ALL STARTS HERE.
WITH A RUSH OF BLOOD TO THE HEAD.

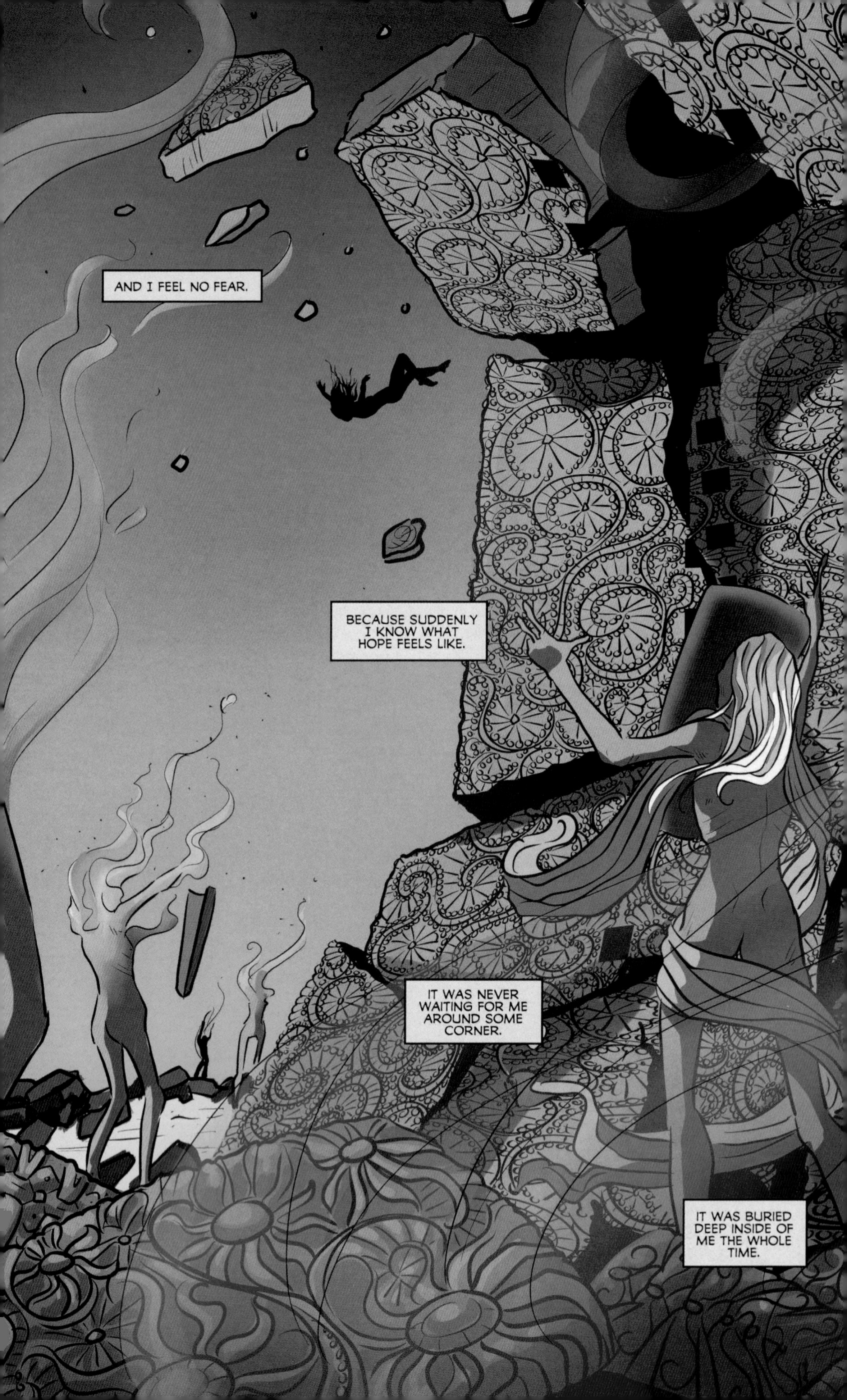
AND I FEEL NO FEAR.
BECAUSE SUDDENLY I KNOW WHAT HOPE FEELS LIKE.
IT WAS NEVER WAITING FOR ME AROUND SOME CORNER.
IT WAS BURIED DEEP INSIDE OF ME THE WHOLE TIME.

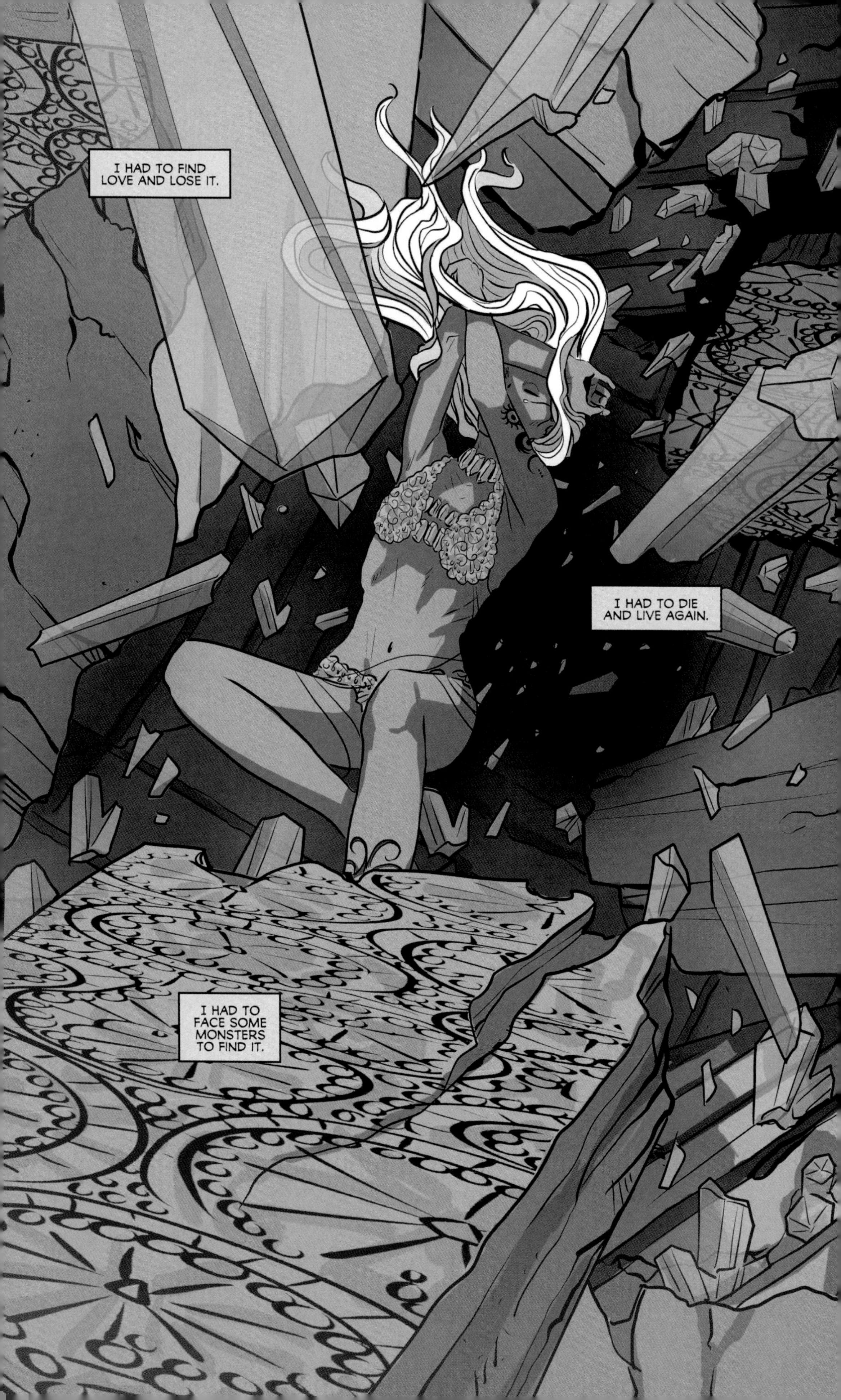
I HAD TO FIND LOVE AND LOSE IT.
I HAD TO DIE AND LIVE AGAIN.
I HAD TO FACE SOME MONSTERS TO FIND IT.

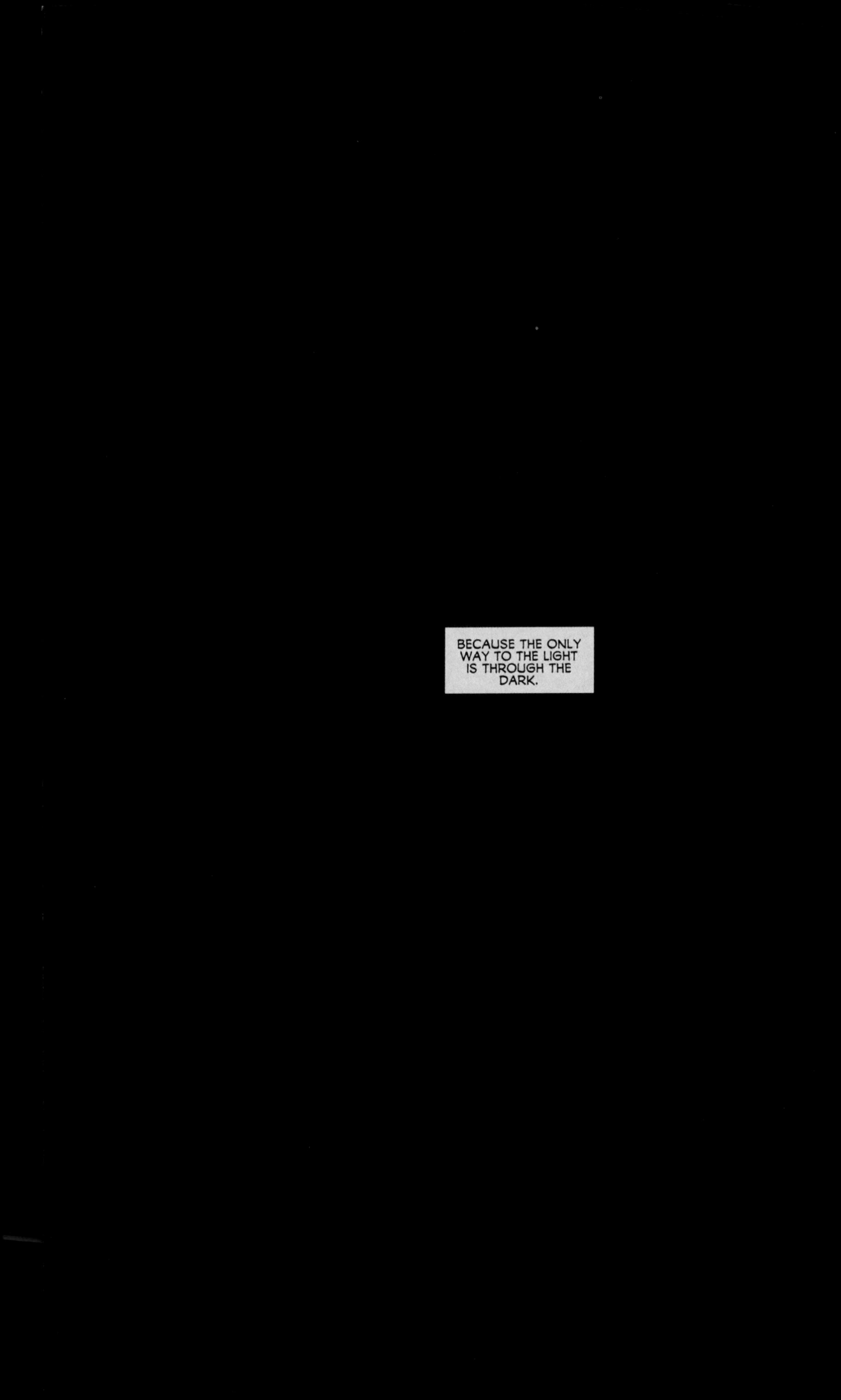
BECAUSE THE ONLY WAY TO THE LIGHT IS THROUGH THE DARK.

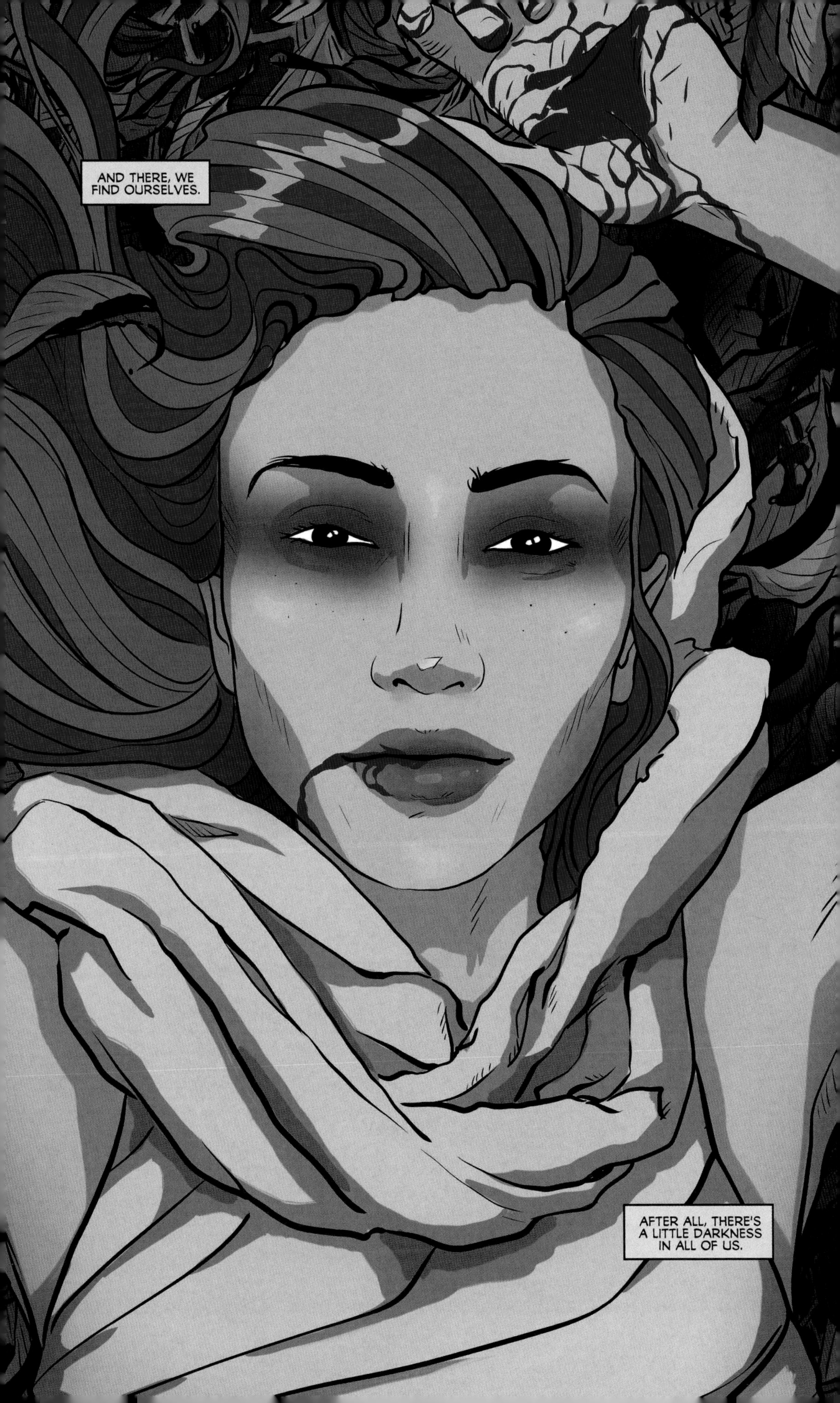
AND THERE, WE FIND OURSELVES.
AFTER ALL, THERE'S A LITTLE DARKNESS IN ALL OF US.

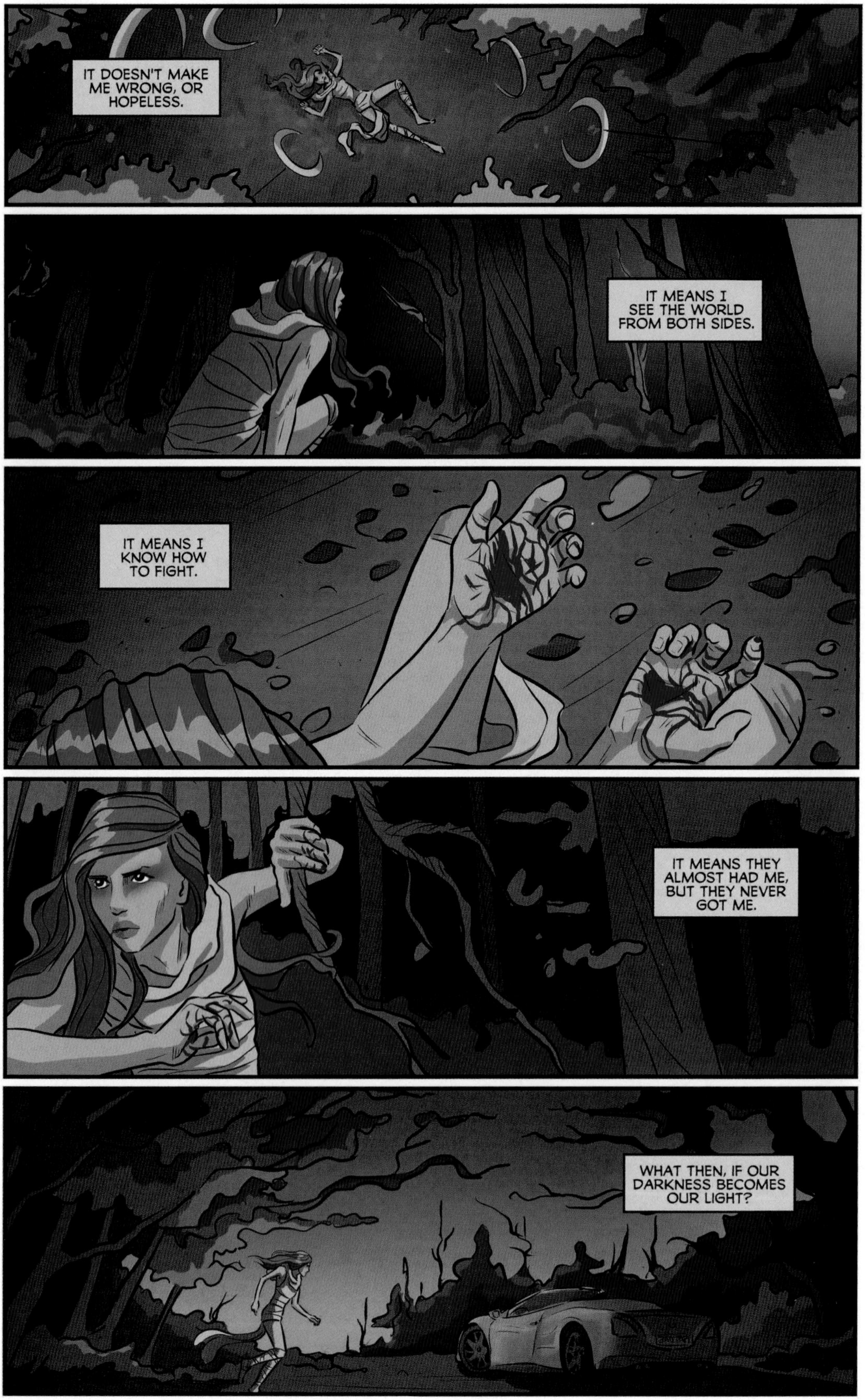
IT DOESN'T MAKE ME WRONG, OR HOPELESS.
IT MEANS I SEE THE WORLD FROM BOTH SIDES.
IT MEANS I KNOW HOW TO FIGHT.
IT MEANS THEY ALMOST HAD ME, BUT THEY NEVER GOT ME.
WHAT THEN, IF OUR DARKNESS BECOMES OUR LIGHT?

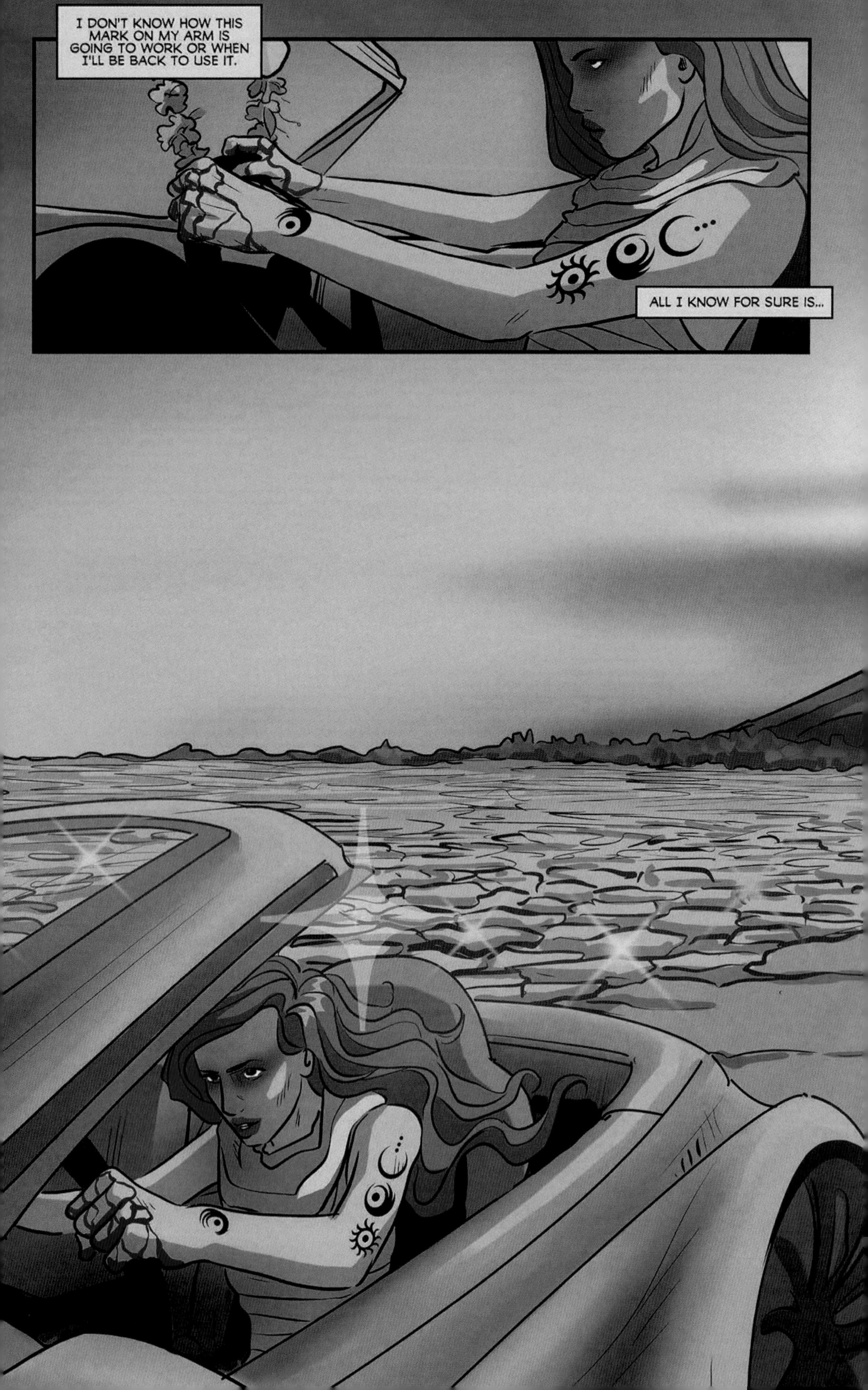
I DON'T KNOW HOW THIS MARK ON MY ARM IS GOING TO WORK OR WHEN I'LL BE BACK TO USE IT.
ALL I KNOW FOR SURE IS...

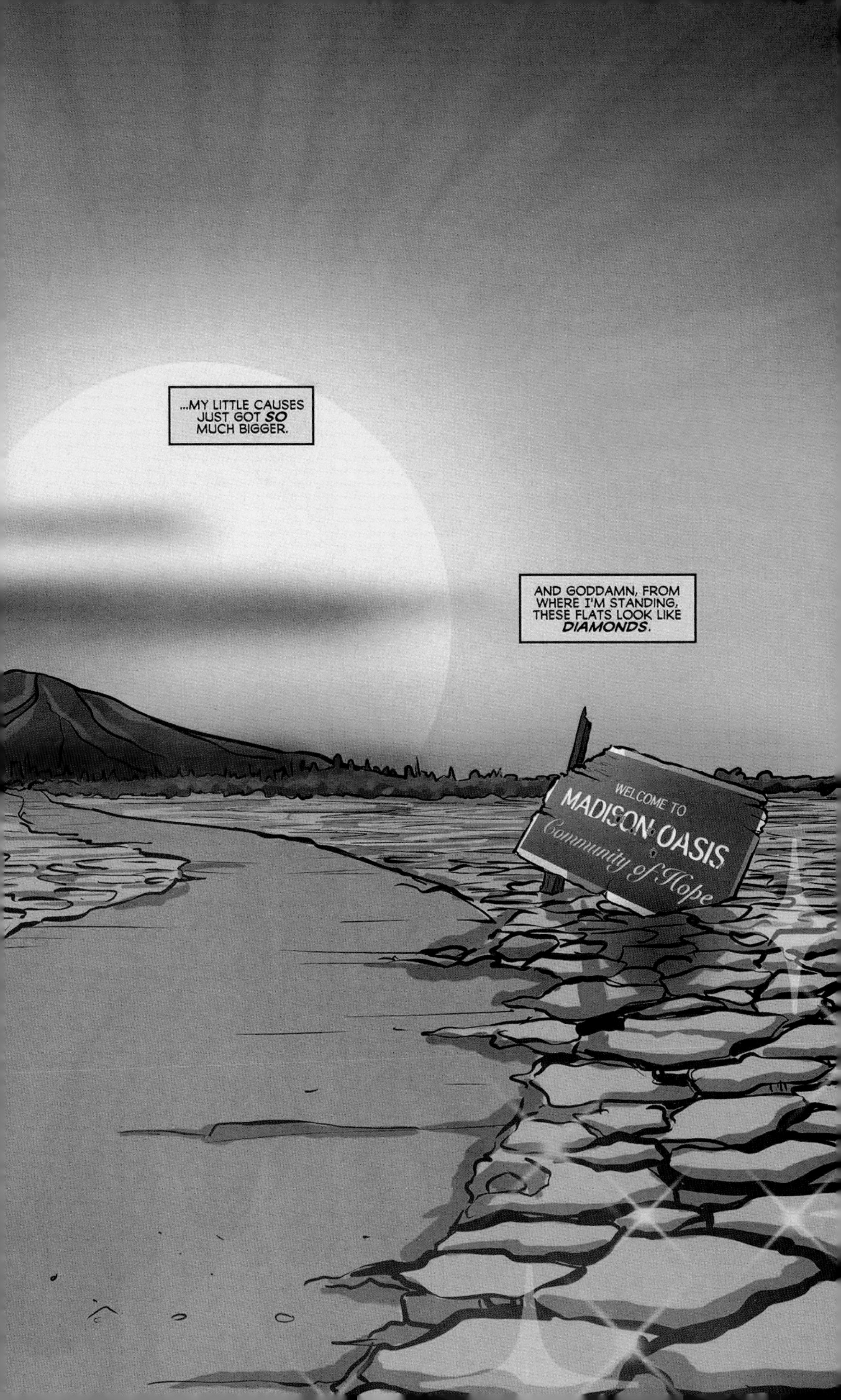
...MY LITTLE CAUSES JUST GOT SO MUCH BIGGER.
AND GODDAMN, FROM WHERE I'M STANDING, THESE FLATS LOOK LIKE DIAMONDS.
WELCOME TO
MADISON OASIS
Community of Hope

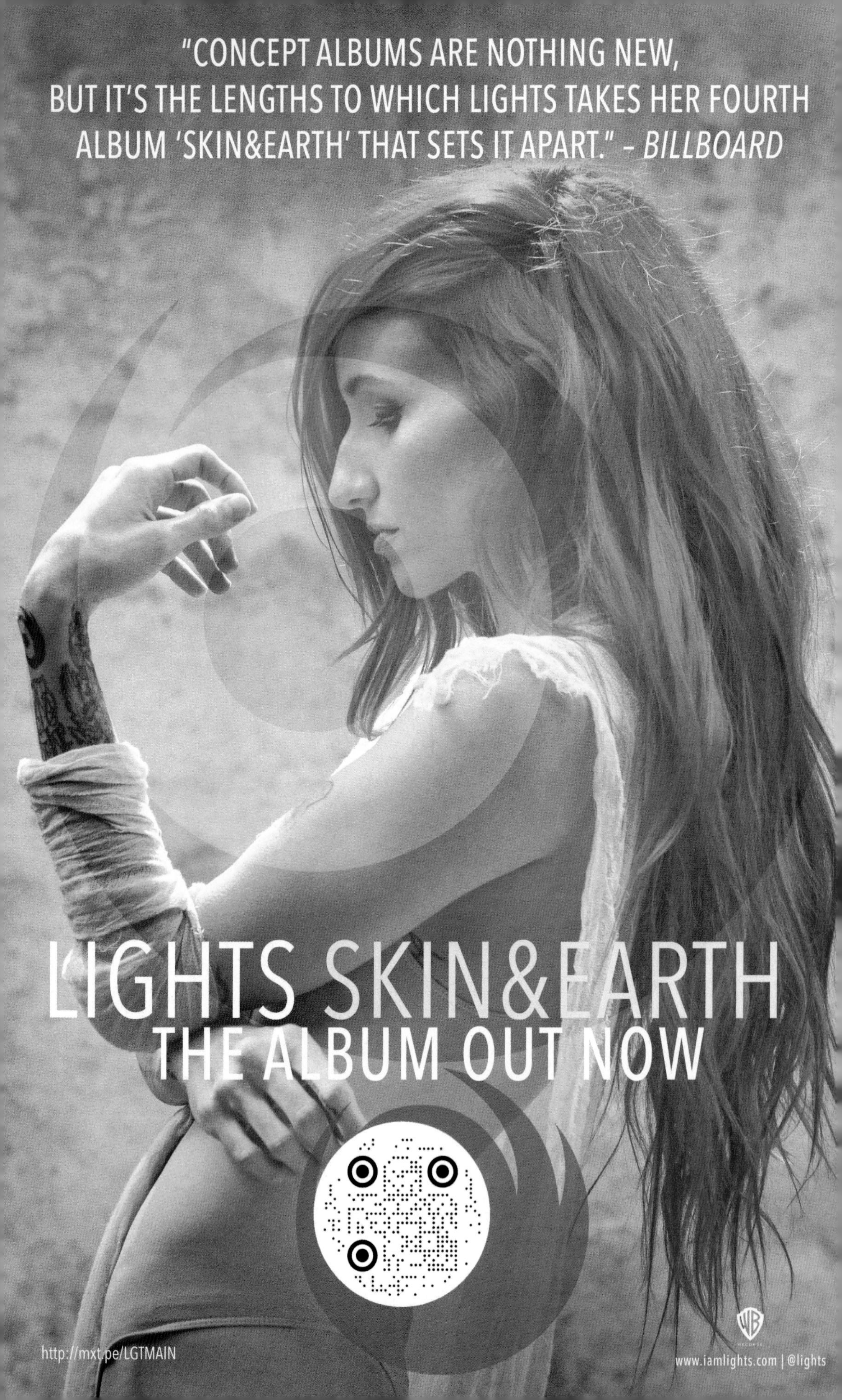
"CONCEPT ALBUMS ARE NOTHING NEW,
BUT IT'S THE LENGTHS TO WHICH LIGHTS TAKES HER FOURTH
ALBUM 'SKIN&EARTH' THAT SETS IT APART." – BILLBOARD
LIGHTS SKIN&EARTH
THE ALBUM OUT NOW
http://mxt.pe/LGTMAIN
www.iamlights.com | @lights

EXPLORE THE WORLD OF
SKIN&EARTH

instagram.com/skinandearthworld

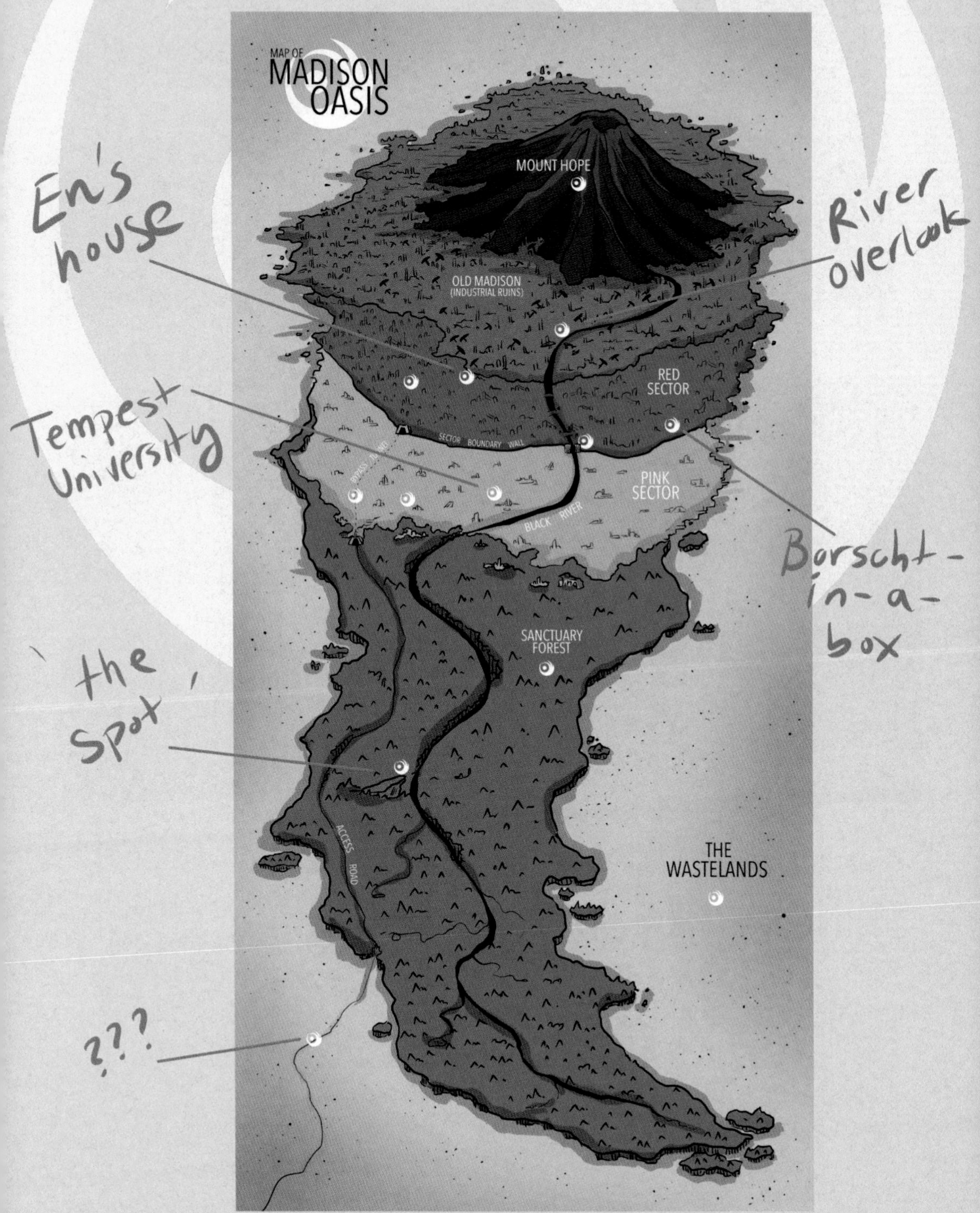
MAP OF
MADISON
OASIS
MOUNT HOPE
OLD MADISON
(INDUSTRIAL RUINS)
RED
SECTOR
SECTOR BOUNDARY WALL
PINK
SECTOR
BLACK RIVER
SANCTUARY
FOREST
ACCESS ROAD
THE
WASTELANDS
En's house
River overlook
Tempest University
Borscht-in-a-box
'the Spot'
???

Discover things you never knew about Skin&Earth as you dive deeper into the world!

'B' COVER GALLERY

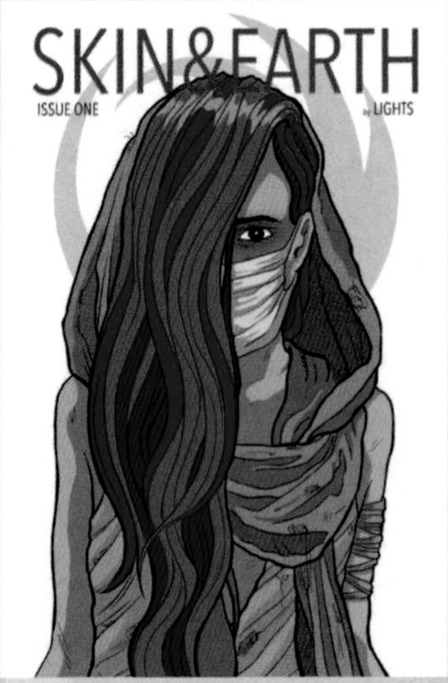
SKIN&EARTH
ISSUE ONE
by LIGHTS

ISSUE #1
COVER B
by LIGHTS

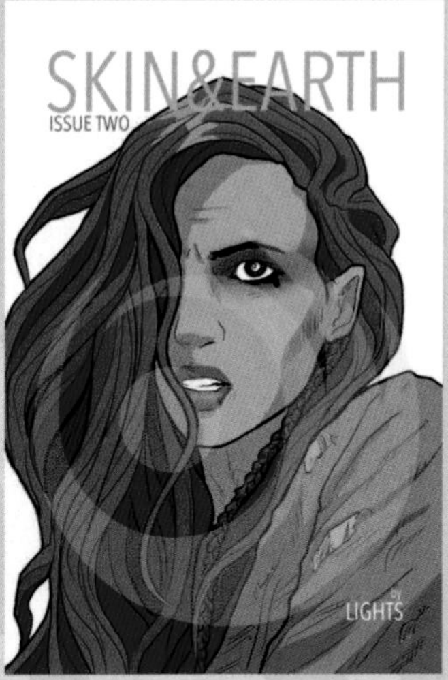
SKIN&EARTH
ISSUE TWO
by LIGHTS

ISSUE #2
COVER B
by LIGHTS

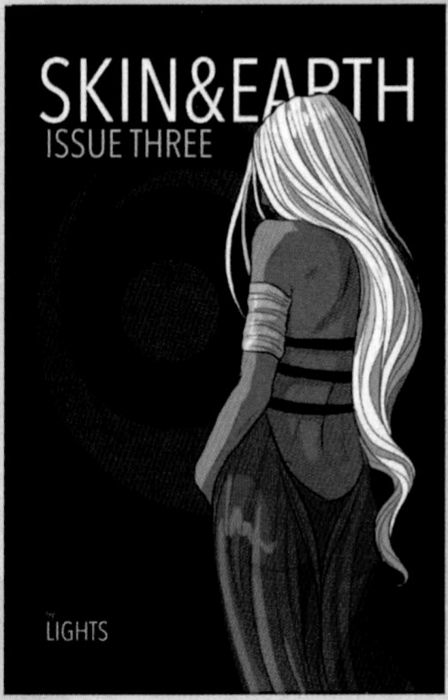
SKIN&EARTH
ISSUE THREE
by LIGHTS

ISSUE #3
COVER B
by LIGHTS

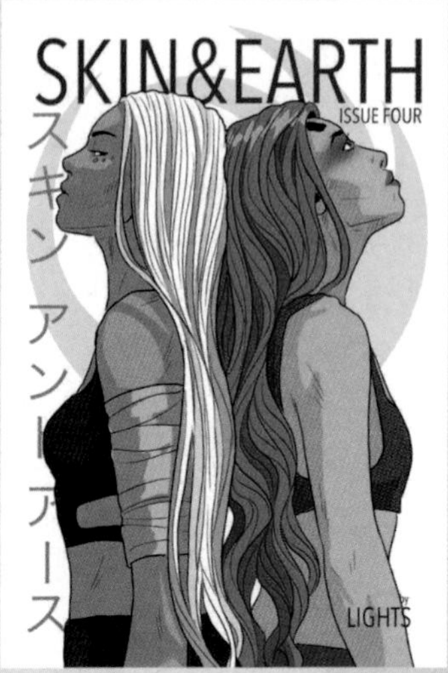
SKIN&EARTH
ISSUE FOUR
by LIGHTS

ISSUE #4
COVER B
by LIGHTS

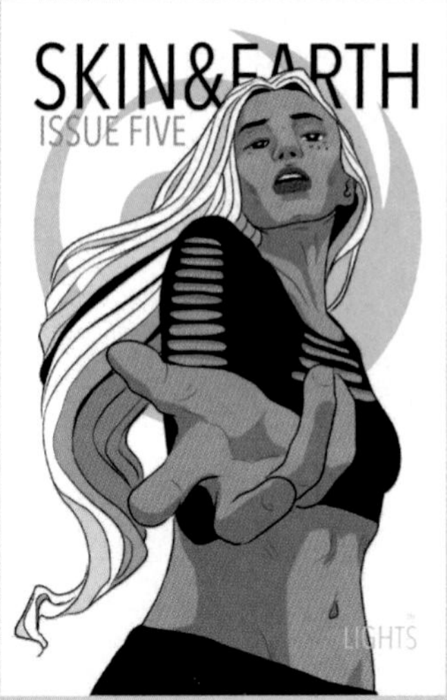
SKIN&EARTH
ISSUE FIVE
by LIGHTS

ISSUE #5
COVER B
by LIGHTS

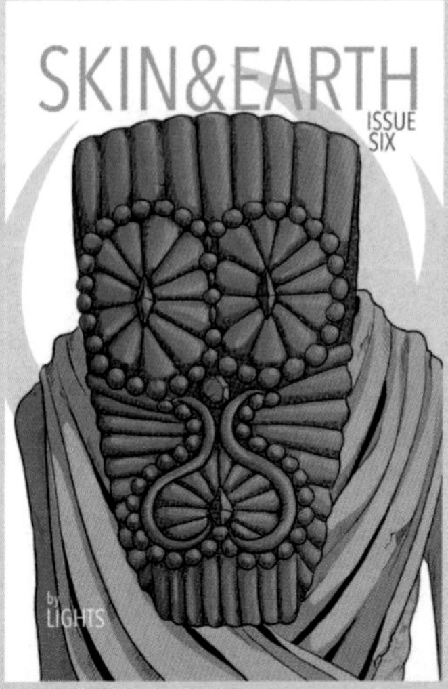
SKIN&EARTH
ISSUE SIX
by LIGHTS

ISSUE #6
COVER B
by LIGHTS

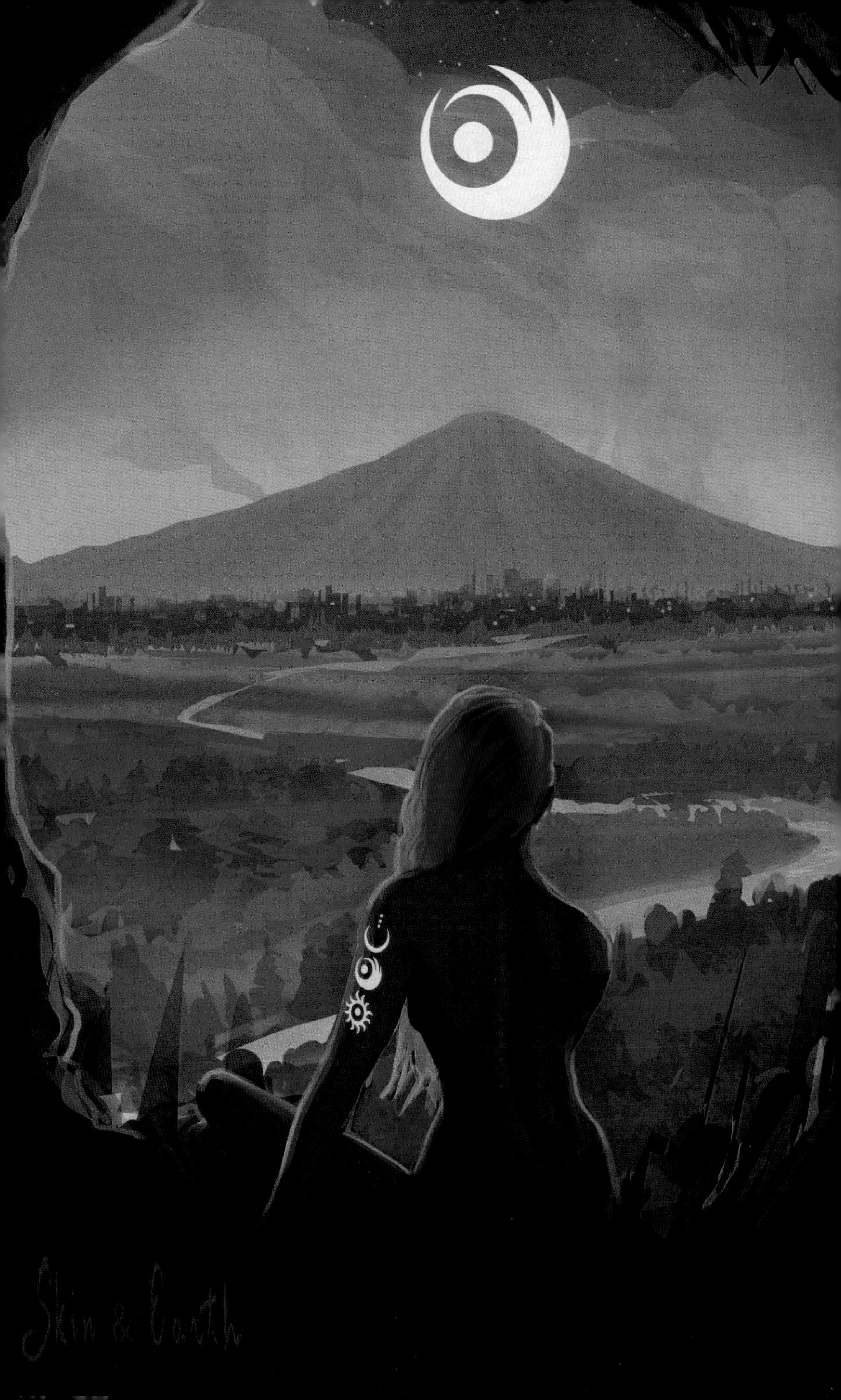
Skin & Earth

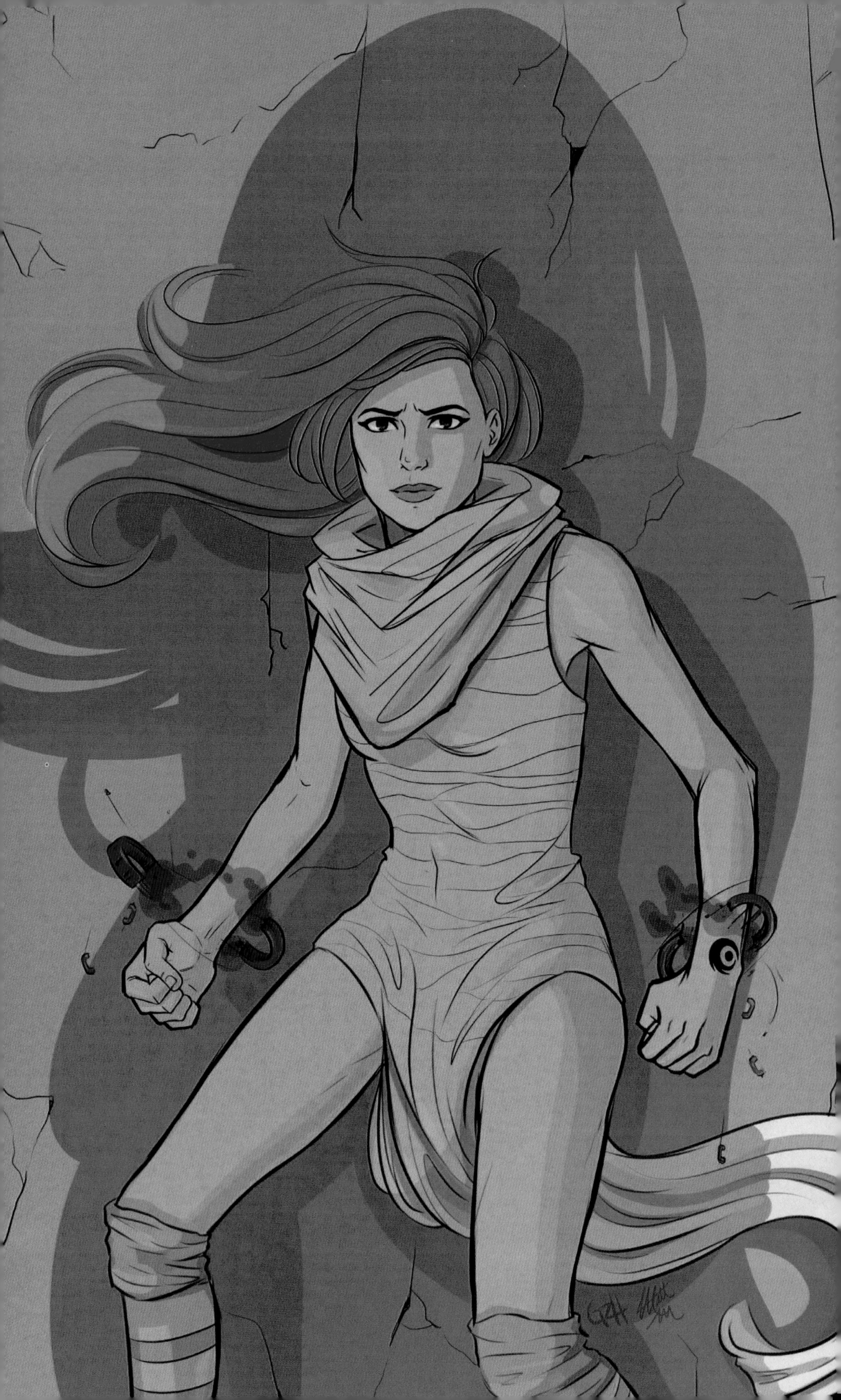

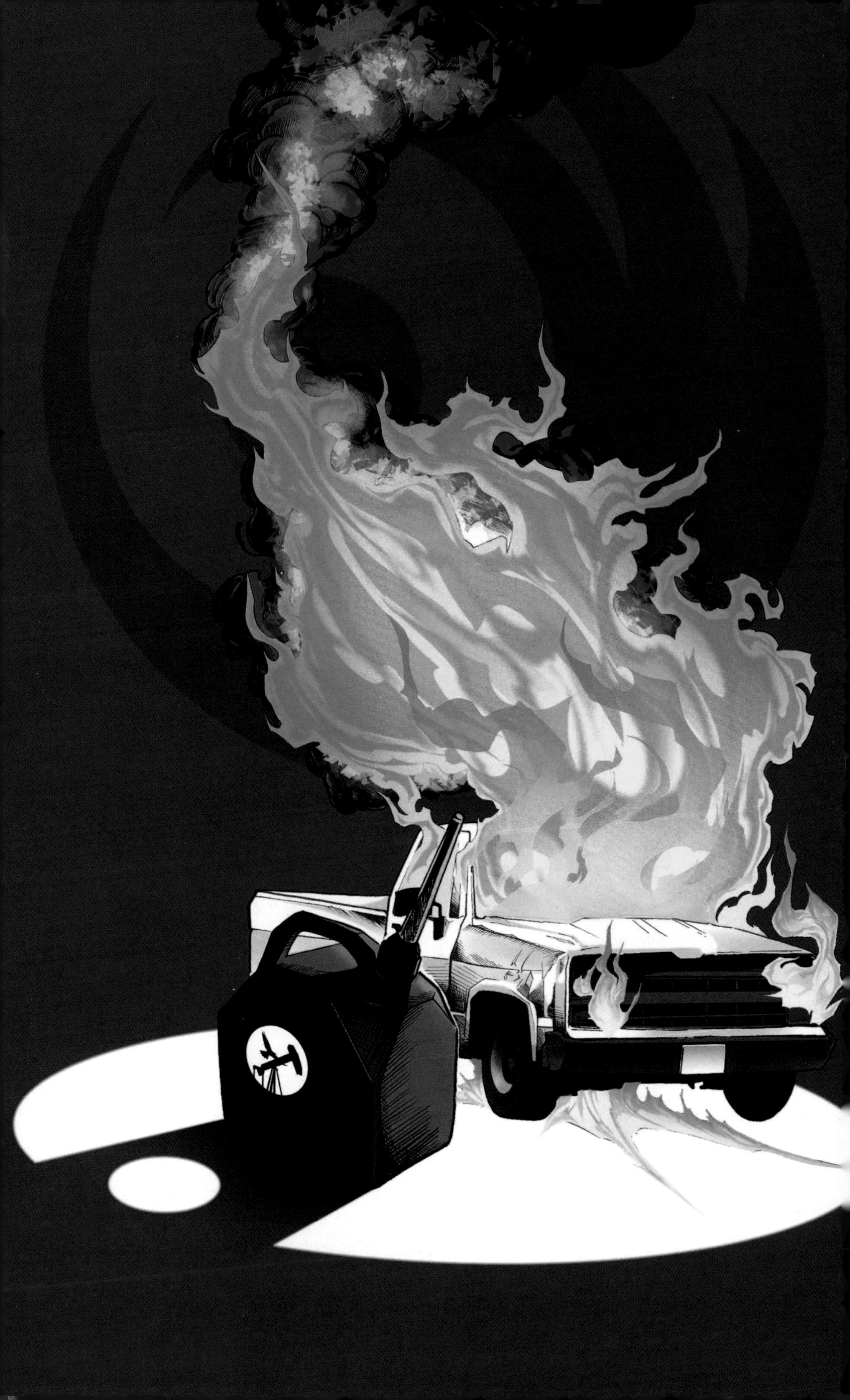

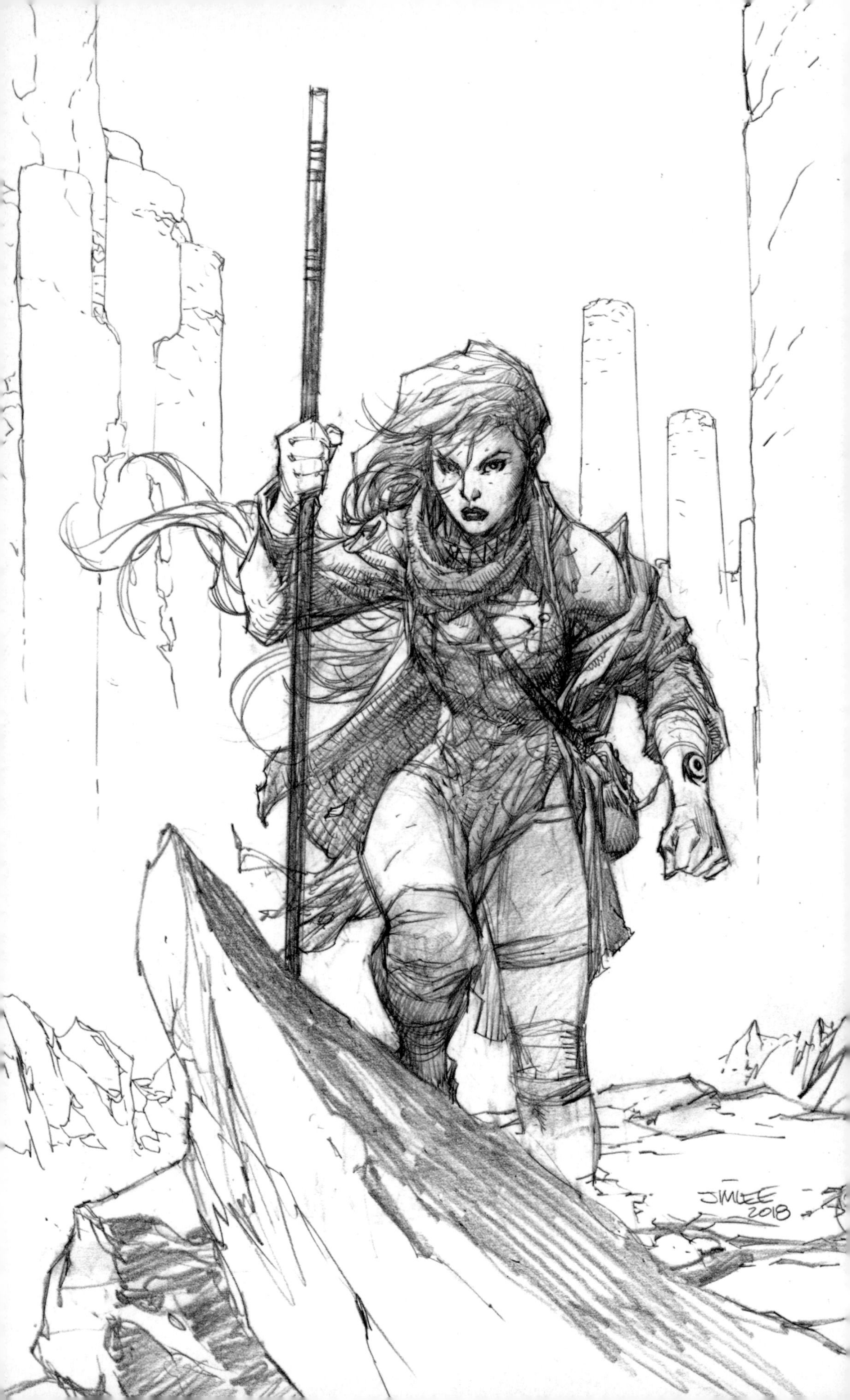
JIMLEE
2018

VARIANT ART

Each of the pieces you've just seen in the four previous pages are Skin&Earth variant art done by creators that have influenced my whole process in one way or another. It has been an honor to have their art in this book and to see another brilliant artist's take on a story and characters that already mean so much to me. Below is a little about each artist and piece in order of appearance.

JOBY HARRIS:
For over a year leading up to finally sitting down to draw Skin&Earth, I relentlessly pulled reference image after reference image from every corner of the internet and world around me. If I saw something that inspired me I saved it into a folder, some were fashion, some architecture, gems, trees, perspective, hair, machinery, monsters, you name it. Among these pulls was a landscape inspo folder, and in that folder I had a few NASA "fake tourism" posters satirically (and beautifully) highlighting the features of distant planets. The art was emotional and the colours were moving. In 2016, at one of my acoustic shows, as fate would have it, I met the man himself. Joby, who is an actual NASA employee, might be one of the coolest, most humble people I know, and his art literally transports me to another world.

GIANNA ROSE and MATT MITCHELL:
In 2014, Gianna and Matt came to my show in Jersey and handed me issue one of their series , "Save Me". They seemed so young to have made a comic so I was immediately impressed. The comic was interesting so I kept an eye on these two, always watching them hustle and create cool pieces of exactly the things they wanted to. That hustle directly influenced my faith in myself when I decided I wanted to make a comic too. They are pretty damn inspirational, and if you don't know them now, someday you will. It is an honour to feature this collaborative piece they created in my book.

DEREK LEWIS:
Derek has been tattooing me for twelve damn years, over which time he's become one of my closest friends and a teacher in a lot of ways (case and point, with this art came a detailed text about how to draw realistic looking fire, copy/saved that one.) He's watched me grow and I've seen him challenge himself to become a better artist, even after years of doing what he does. Thank you for staying up until the wee hours for this one!

JIM LEE:
This one hardly needs an introduction. Growing up a DC fan means I have been seeing Jim's art for as long as I could appreciate it. He has influenced a whole generation of artists yet still finds time to continue to teach and provide guidance to aspiring creators all over the world. I've spent a lot of time watching him draw in live streams and talk and draw in front of crowds at panels, and every time I walk away with a new excitement about the craft and a reignited passion for just drawing. I'm still in complete shock that he took the time to sketch En for this book. Thank you, Jim!

MAKING SKIN&EARTH

PAGE 6 SCRIPT

Panel 1: Officer hands back ID.
PINK SECTOR OFFICER: "Take my advice kid, and watch your step here. You're the first student from the shite side of the wall I've seen in years."

Panel 2: En accepts her card back with a scowl.
PS OFFICER: "Your no-fuck-giving parents must've sucked some might Tempest dick to get you in."

Panel 3: Officer is pointing after En, who obviously has left looking very disgruntled.
PS OFFICER: "You think I can't see that snarl straight through the mask? Think again, Red! Think again!"

Panel 4: En walks away, pulling down her mask now that she's on the other side of the wall, looking pissed.
NARRATIVE: Pinks with badges.
PS OFFICER (to remaining line): "MOVE IT PEOPLE!"

Panel 5: En boards a beat up city bus, this side of the wall looks junky and dirty.
NARRATIVE: I swear…
PS OFFICER: "NEED YOU ALL OUTTA MY GODDAMN SECTOR BY NIGHTFALL!"

step 1:
plan out panel flow and word action (only cause I read this was how to do it and this font looked very "scripty".

step 2:
Rough it out on a page. If a pose is tricky I'll take photo refs.

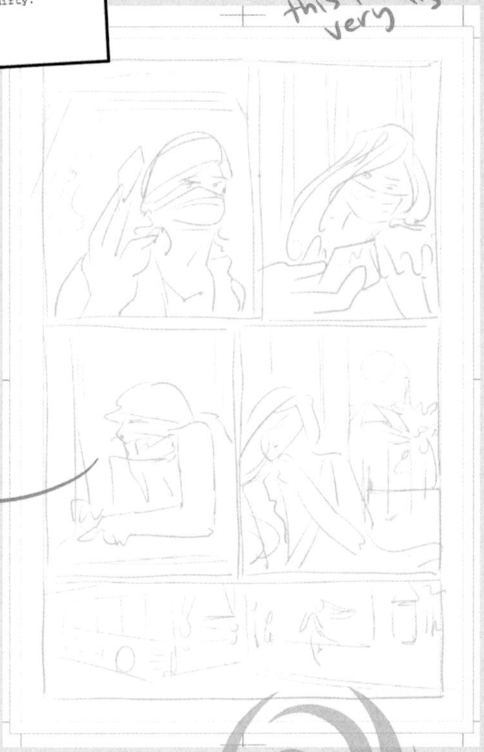

pre-red hair & S&E tattoo

Even when it's a guy....

TAKE MY ADVICE, KID, AND WATCH YOUR STEP HERE.
YOU'RE THE FIRST STUDENT FROM THE SHITE SIDE OF THE WALL I'VE SEEN IN YEARS.
YOUR NO-FUCK-GIVING PARENTS MUST'VE SUCKED SOME MIGHTY TEMPEST DICK TO GET YOU IN.
YOU THINK I CAN'T SEE THAT SNARL STRAIGHT THROUGH THE MASK?
THINK AGAIN, RED. THINK AGAIN!
PINKS WITH BADGES.
MOVE IT, PEOPLE!
I SWEAR...
NEED YOU ALL OUTTA MY GODDAMN SECTOR BY NIGHTFALL!

step 3:
Ink the people.
I also like to place the text and speech bubbles here so I can get the composition of the panel all right (not too crowded).

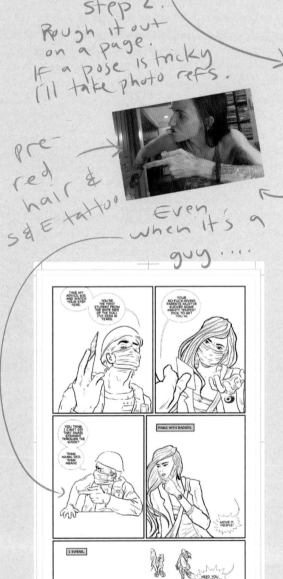

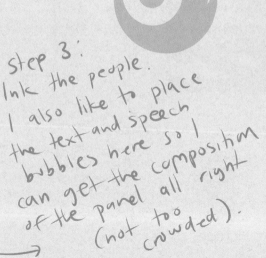

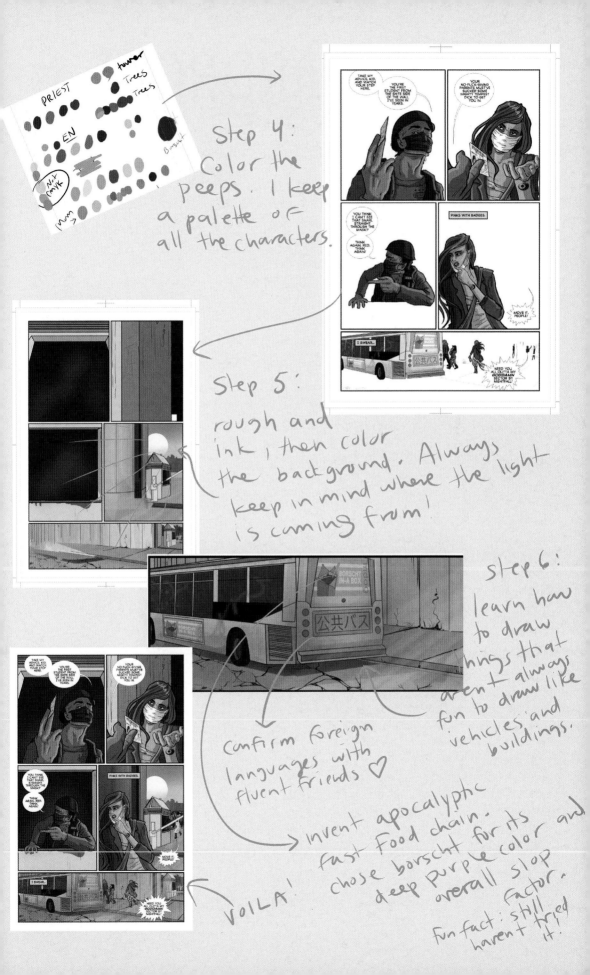

Step 4: Color the peeps. I keep a palette of all the characters.

Step 5: rough and ink, then color the background. Always keep in mind where the light is coming from!

Step 6: learn how to draw things that aren't always fun to draw like vehicles and buildings.

confirm foreign languages with fluent friends ♡

invent apocalyptic fast food chain. chose borscht for its deep purple color and overall slop factor.

fun fact: still haven't tried it.

VOILA!

EN'S WARDROBE

Creating En's style came in a few phases. I wanted her to be comfortable but still proud of her body, as every woman deserves to be. She shows skin because she wants to, not because it's particularily trendy or sexy to do so. I also had to consider things I wanted to wear and could pull off as well, knowing there would be a time I would bring her to life in some capacity, and that made it all the more exciting coming up with her style.

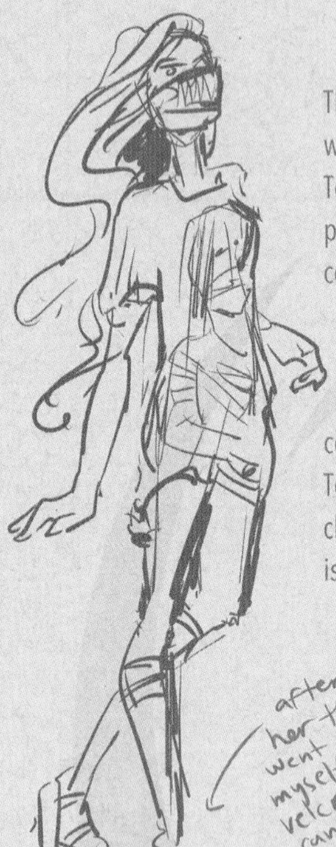
after giving her this look, I went and bought myself some black velcro sandals which can be seen in the "savage" vid.

The first look I came up with for En was the T-shirt look. Tees are comfortable and practical, but when worn with confidence (and socks/sandals combo) they can be quite sexy too. They also became a great canvas for in-world content, like the ill-famed Tempest shirt, or the mystery character, Lun, as seen in issue two.

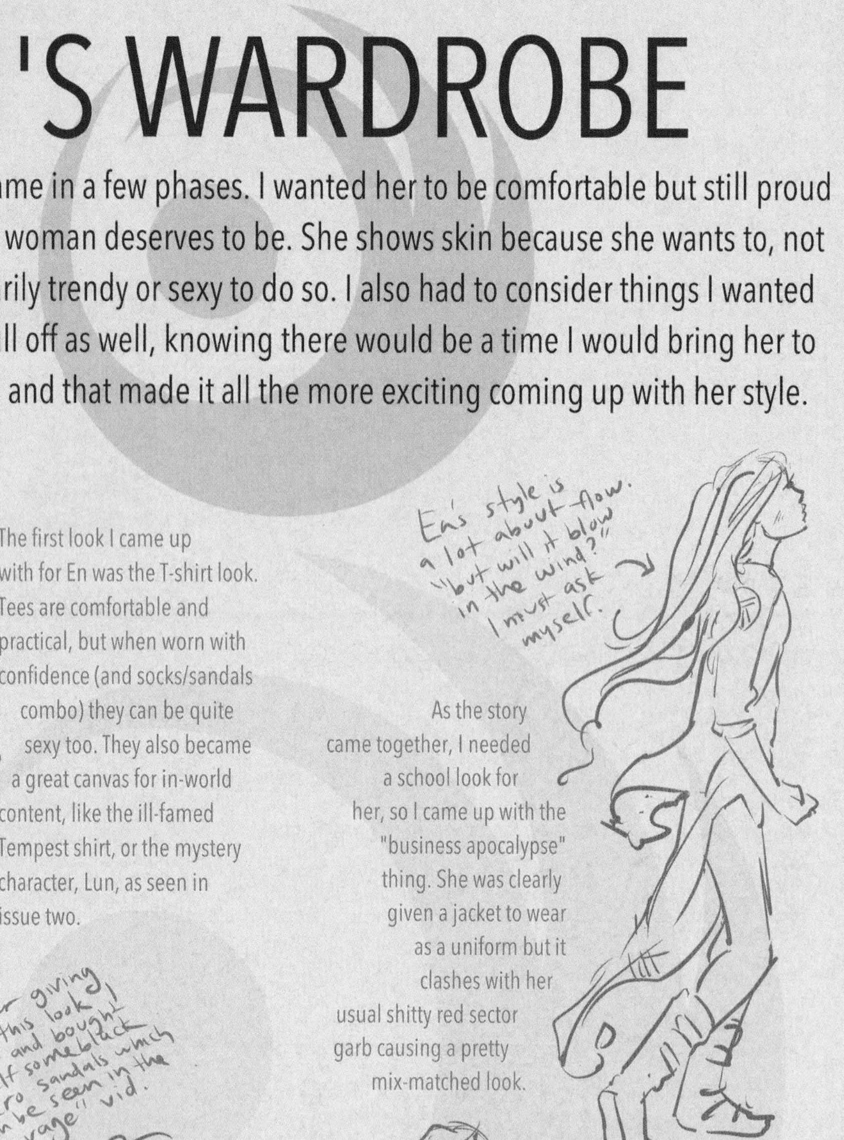
En's style is a lot about flow. "but will it blow in the wind?" I must ask myself.

As the story came together, I needed a school look for her, so I came up with the "business apocalypse" thing. She was clearly given a jacket to wear as a uniform but it clashes with her usual shitty red sector garb causing a pretty mix-matched look.

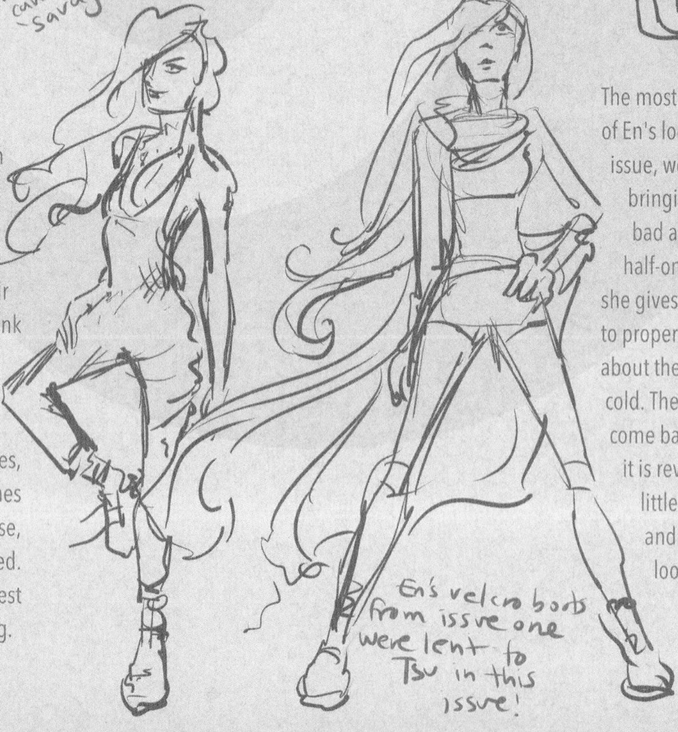
En's velcro boots from issue one were lent to Tsu in this issue!

The brown overalls in issue three were always in my head for some reason. I really wanted to see her in a halter style baggy pair of overalls, no idea why. I think probably beause I want them in real life for myself. The point was probably to highlight brown clothes, most of her gear is neutral tones because in the apocalpyse, everything is worn and faded. That makes the yellow Tempest shirt all the more silly looking.

The most "superhero" of all of En's looks took place in this issue, we see that Mitsuki is bringing a little more of the bad ass out in her. The big half-on/half-off jacket says she gives no fucks about how to properly wear a jacket, or about the fact that it is quite cold. The knee pads make a come back, and in this issue, it is revealed they do very little to protect her knees and really only serve to look cool.

TO BE CONTINUED...

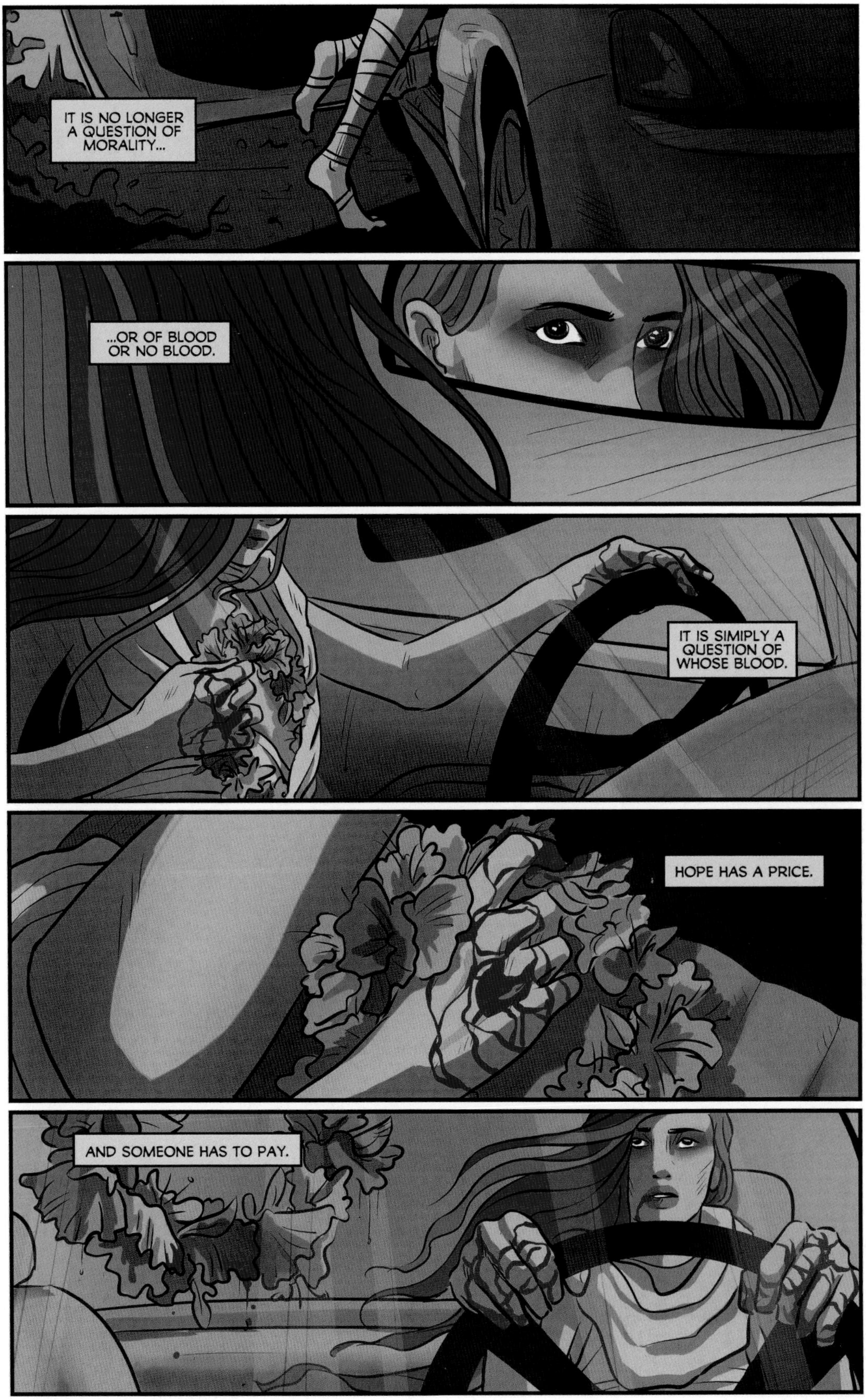
IT IS NO LONGER A QUESTION OF MORALITY...
...OR OF BLOOD OR NO BLOOD.
IT IS SIMPLY A QUESTION OF WHOSE BLOOD.
HOPE HAS A PRICE.
AND SOMEONE HAS TO PAY.